Scholarly Communications

A History from Content as King to Content as Kingmaker

John J. Regazzi

ROWMAN & LITTLEFIELD
Lanham • Boulder • New York • London

1007473510

Published by Rowman & Littlefield
A wholly owned subsidiary of The Rowman & Littlefield Publishing Group, Inc.
4501 Forbes Boulevard, Suite 200, Lanham, Maryland 20706
www.rowman.com

Unit A, Whitacre Mews, 26-34 Stannary Street, London SE11 4AB

British Library Cataloguing in Publication Information Available

Library of Congress Cataloging-in-Publication Data

Regazzi, John J., 1948–
Scholarly communications : a history from content as king to content as kingmaker / John J. Regazzi.
pages cm
Includes bibliographical references and index.
ISBN 978-0-8108-9087-9 (cloth : alk. paper) – ISBN 978-0-8108-9088-6 (ebook)
1. Scholarly publishing. 2. Scholarly publishing–Economic aspects. 3. Scholarly electronic publishing. 4. Scholarly periodicals–Publishing. 5. Communication in learning and scholarship. 6. Communication in learning and scholarship–Technological innovations. 7. Communication in science. 8. Open access publishing. 9. Science publishing. 10. Information services industry. I. Title.
Z286.S37R44 2015
070.5–dc23
2014040648

∞™ The paper used in this publication meets the minimum requirements of American National Standard for Information Sciences Permanence of Paper for Printed Library Materials, ANSI/NISO Z39.48-1992.

Printed in the United States of America

For my sons—John, Tom, and Mike—my treasured past, extraordinary present, and boundless future

Contents

List of Figures

Preface

Consider the kingmakers in our society and throughout history.

They have been long admired, or reviled, for their power and ability to influence political elections, coronations, or propelling someone to a formidable position, as they remain unrealizable candidates for assuming any of these powers or authorities. Prized for their political, social, and strategic skills, kingmakers have been used for thousands of years and throughout the history of humankind.

The term is perhaps most associated with Richard Neville, the 16th Earl of Warwick, who was known as "Warwick the Kingmaker," during the War of the Roses. Through various circumstances of his birth, linage, inheritance, and marriage, Warwick in 1450 emerged in the center of English politics and over a period of about ten years was responsible for the coronation of not one but two kings of England—Edward IV and Henry VI. These efforts earned him the moniker "kingmaker" for later generations and today.

The world has had many such "kingmakers," however, even if they were not called such in their lifetimes. India had Chanakya, and legend has it that as a young economics professor at the ancient Takshashila University in 300 BC, the then leader of the Nanda Empire, King Dhana Nanda, insulted him, and as a result, Chanakya swore to dethrone this king and destroy his empire. Chanakya befriends what he believes to be a successor to Nanda in the person of Chandragupta Maurya. With the help of only a small group, they bring down King Nanda and the entire empire, using their skills of manipulation, surreptitiousness, and intimidation. Maurya becomes king, and Chanakya serves as his key adviser until his death.

King making takes a variety of forms as well. From 456 until his death in 472, Flavius Ricimer is said to have ruled the entire Western Roman Empire through a series of handpicked puppet emperors. Ricimer was able to maintain his power through his control of the military as well as his elaborate though often secretive social network of Roman senators. King making and kingmakers are without question forces to be reckoned with and noted. A kingmaker, in game theory for example, is a player without adequate or required resources to win the game but possesses enough resources to decide which player will win. Game theorists often see the kingmaker as far more formidable and more powerful than any other player, even the eventual game winner.

The story of kingmakers is a story of control, power, partnership, and value creation. But their story more likely operates only behind the scenes and always with at least one other party. Kingmakers are never kings themselves, as they always lack some basis for their own coronation. Their central value lies in the partnerships to power that they create and sustain. Their partners, themselves, also lack the credentials or resources for power on their own, and only together does the king and kingmaker create sustainable power and value.

Has scholarly communications and scholarly information become the kingmaker of today, or is it still king? That is the central question of this book. *Scholarly Communications: A History from Content as King to Content as Kingmaker* is aimed at those professionals who manage scholarly communications services and valuable content and who are continuing to try to make these services sustainable and viable.

To be sure, scholarly communications is in transition, both in its form and format as well as in economic terms, both as raw data and structured content as well as when it is embedded in the electronic processes and services that are continuing to grow and expand in size, form, and function.

These transformations also drive many of the changes seen in the pricing and selling of scholarly content and services, which will be discussed throughout the work: from electronic journals to open access business models to professional work flow services. Scholarly content is being paired with greater and greater digital functionality, and this bundling is creating exciting and innovative scholarly services. However, bundling is effective only if it does not cost too much, that is, having too high a price for extra items in a bundle that are unwanted—and these innovations and their costs are also discussed throughout the work.

There was a time, without question, when scholarly communication was king and generating that content could itself lead to fame and fortune for a variety of players in the scholarly information supply chain. Are we still living in an age where scholarly content is king, or does scholarly communications now play the role of kingmaker—able to create great value but not alone and only in partnership with other resources? The scholarly communications of 100 years ago are certainly different from the scholarly communications of today, but perhaps even more important, the scholarly processes of today are markedly different from even 10 years ago. Without question, the form and value of scholarly content is in a great state of flux. How the scholarly communications industry can create and derive value in this new phase is becoming less clear as the rules of the market shift.

The Internet and the changes in the distribution of human knowledge have vastly altered the value of information, as Chris Anderson notes in his book *Free*:

> There is only one way to have unlimited shelf space: if that shelf space costs nothing. The near-zero "marginal costs" of digital distribution . . . allow us to be indiscriminate in what we use it for—no gatekeepers are required to decide if something deserves global reach or not. And out of that free-for-all came the miracle of today's Web, the greatest accumulation of human knowledge, experience, and expression the world has ever seen. (Anderson, 2009: 3)

As we look at the changing landscape of scholarly communications, a compelling challenge emerges: while the new digital channels of information distribution have reduced information users' costs to zero or near zero, these same channels have increased the corresponding benefits significantly. *Scholarly Communications: A History from Content as King to Content as Kingmaker* examines how the fundamental value propositions of scholarly content have changed, how businesses that are generating and distributing scholarly content need to think differently about creating value and profits in the new digital age, and how researchers will derive increased value from the new forms of scholarly content, communications, and enterprise.

REFERENCE

Anderson, Chris. 2009. *Free—The Future of a Radical Price*. New York: Hyperion.

Acknowledgments

This book brings together strands from a lifelong career in the information services industry, many of them people I've worked with and have helped me in this journey. Their insights have enriched my understanding here. They are too many to name, but there are few who played important roles in changing the industry and my work in it: Thomas Buckman (The Foundation Center), Leo Weins (The HW Wilson Company), William A. Ziegler (Sullivan & Cromwell), Derk Haank (Elsevier Science), and my colleagues at these companies, particularly Eric Johnson, Barbara Cooperman, David Marques, and so many others.

I also want to thank my colleagues at the Ei Foundation—Hans Rutimann, Julie Shimer, Eisen Jo Casaclang, and Ruth Miller—who are challenged, as I am, to find new programs supporting the dissemination of engineering information throughout the world. And my colleagues at Akoya Capital—Max DeZera, Jim Appleton, Jason Apple, Lori Cunningham, Lukasz Wrona, Pat Reilly, Liz Dominic, and Karen Scalise—who are trying to determine the opportunities for investment in this area.

I have also had the encouragement of several academic institutions to pursue the understanding of scholarly communications development, including the library and information science faculty of Long Island University and New York University as well as the faculties of Stuttgart University (Germany), Hacettepe University (Turkey), and Polytechnic University of Valencia (Spain), particularly two colleagues there, Dr. Nuria Lloret Romero and Dr. Enrique Ordona.

When I began this manuscript, I had no idea of the journey that I was to go on. I would not have been able to complete this process were it not for the constant encouragement and good guidance from my editor Charles Harmon, and to him I am deeply indebted. The final manuscript was genuinely put through an exacting and precise review by Sandy Wood, and she found inconsistencies in the manuscript that needed to be changed, and without question the book is exceedingly better from her efforts.

Finally, I would like to thank my wife, Marie, for all her understanding and patience, particularly for excessive work hours that can carve into our time together as well as for her support throughout our lives. She has been an endless source of inspiration, insight, and love.

Chapter One

Scholarly Communications

The Intersection of Research and Commerce

Scholarly communication, as both an industry and a flow of scholarship, is at an inflection point. Some might say it is in turmoil. As an industry, it is not clear how scholarly publishers will address the changes confronting them or if journals will even survive. And the current processes of scholars exchanging information are changing significantly as modern information technologies drive the form and distribution channels of scholarly communication to new and different electronic modes. The scholarly communications industry is being confronted by a variety of issues that could profoundly influence its business models and overall structure, including open access, institutional repositories, copyright issues, archiving, and preserving the scholarship of science. As newer communication tools speed up communication and offer the possibility of bypassing journals, authors are equally confronted with new trends and choices in such fundamental areas as peer review, multiple versions of articles, blogs, websites, and podcasts. In this environment, publishers may be transformed, scholars may communicate in new ways, and journals may have a different role than in the past, but documents of record are still essential to the business.

The industry is changing not only from the trends driven by technology and new business models but also through increasing government regulation around the globe. Governments and not-for-profit granting agencies are increasingly directing that research published under their research grant programs be deposited and made freely available after some embargo period, usually six months to one year. These deposits can be made in open access journals, institutional repositories, as well as the author's own website, among others. The length of embargo periods is a critical element in a buyer's decision to initiate, continue, or cancel a journal subscription. However, in order to meet the need for new journals and the increasing demands of scholars as well as readers, scholarly content providers, be they be commercial, societies, or other not-for-profit institutions, will have to generate a surplus for future investment. Investing in such innovations usually requires capital generated from reinvesting profits from publishing operations. As the standard industry business models shift, the sources of investment will need to change and the level of investment recalibrated.

As we will discuss in this chapter and throughout this book, scholarly communications, though it has a long history beginning 400 years ago with the Royal Society of London publishing its *Philosophical Transactions*, has an uncertain future. Some of its industry players, particularly content providers, perceive clear threats—from institutional repositories, open access, and services facilitated by the Internet—while others see huge opportunities. There is clearly now some turmoil and turbulence, which need to be better understood if scholarship and scholarly communications are to prosper and have a meaningful role in the lives of citizens and the fabric of modern society.

THE SCHOLARLY COMMUNICATIONS PROCESS

Scholarly communication has been defined in several ways over the years. One of the broadest and most oft-quoted definitions is that by C. L. Borgman, which describes scholarly communication as

> the study of how scholars in any field (e.g. physical, biology, social, and behavioural sciences, humanities, technology) use and disseminate information through formal and informal channels. The study of scholarly communication includes the growth of scholarly information, the relationships among research areas and disciplines, the information needs and uses of individual user groups, and the relationships among formal and informal methods of communication. (Borgman, 2000: 413)

The Association of College and Research Libraries (ACRL) has spent considerable time studying the state of scholarly communication and how it is changing the roles of both publishers and libraries. ACRL identifies four central elements of scholarly communication as

> the system through which research and other scholarly writings are created, evaluated for quality, disseminated to the scholarly community, and preserved for future use. The system includes both formal means of communication, such as publication in peer-reviewed journals, and informal channels, such as electronic listservs. (ACRL, 2003)

These key elements represent a research process that has evolved over hundreds of years and leads ultimately to a publication that represents the scientific thinking and scholarship at that moment in time and to be preserved for all time. This process is summarized as the research cycle (figure 1.1).

Each article—each piece of scholarship and research, as represented by the peer-review process—may be seen as a piece of evidence in a court of law or as a recorded note in fiduciary meetings, much like the minutes of the court case or board meeting. Scholarly communication following the four steps noted by the ACRL constitutes the minutes of science and as such holds the recording of scientific human knowledge for all time.

Although scholarly communication can be seen as a stepwise cycle, the process leading to a final output is a highly interactive and social process—not just a cut-and-dried publication system. The scholarly output is not the only or perhaps even the main characteristic of scholarship. The inherent iterative communication process that led to the output that defines the scholarship is equally important to understand (Kling and McKim, 1999). A scientist discovers a problem and forms ideas around discovering insights and solutions to this problem and typically first informally communicates this to colleagues and the relevant scientific community, gaining societal recogni-

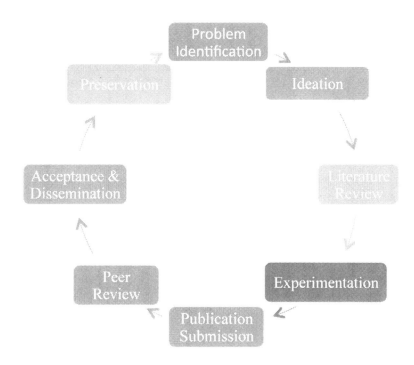

Figure 1.1. Research Cycle

tion for that ownership. The scientific community helps in developing the idea and from that iterative process may emerge experimentation and the final output in a formal publication for dissemination and consumption to a larger group (Garvey and Griffith, 1980). Throughout the process, there is an ongoing series of informal communication between scientists, and the research cycle diagram must incorporate this element, or it is incomplete (figure 1.2).

As far back as 1967, Garvey and Griffith described scientific communication as a social system of interactions among scientists, yet they also explored the orderly manner in which information flows within a discipline (Garvey and Griffith, 1967). This flow characteristic is changing rapidly as web-based communication systems have created a less predictable but much more rapid and dynamic knowledge exchange among scientists and scientific disciplines. Without question, scholarly communication is fully linked and integrated with electronic communication, transforming forever the social process as well as the research cycle process from ideation to formal publication (Kling and Callahan, 2003). Today, electronic scholarly communication has changed every step of the research cycle, including the methods used for collaboration and informal communication, research dissemination, publishing, citation networking, and preservation.

THE SCIENTIFIC, TECHNICAL, AND MEDICAL INDUSTRY

The scientific, technical, and medical (STM) scholarship, communication, and publishing industry is quite distinct from its cousins in the arts, humanities, and social sciences. It is also the largest and fastest-growing sector of scholarly communications and is considered a separate industry. The global

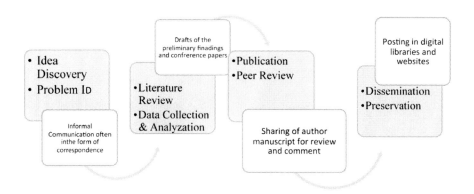

Figure 1.2.   Research Cycle with Informal Communication

scientific and technical revenues grew from $9.480 billion in 2006 to $12,093 billion in 2010, representing a 27.5 percent increase. During the same time period, the medical segment grew $6 billion to almost $8.2 billion, for a 35.6 percent increase (International Association of Scientific, Technical and Medical Publishers, 2013b). Representing revenue growth during a period of economic stress, the numbers may have been even larger had there not been a global recession. In 2011, the growth continued with the scientific and technical segment revenues increasing by 4.3 percent and the medical subsegment by 2.0 percent. The 2011 market for journals, technical information, books, databases, and medical communications was valued at $23.5 billion—$12.8 billion for scientific and technical information and $10.7 million for medical. Revenues from 2011 journals were $9.4 billion and from books and e-books were $3.8 billion (Ware and Mabe, 2012: 19–20).

There is an ongoing shift in the regional share of global revenue. The compound annual growth rate (CAGR) for the United States declined 1.0 percent during the period 2005–2010, while it increased by 7.1 percent in the Asia-Pacific region. The other region experiencing significant growth was South America with an increase of 4.9 percent in CAGR (International Association of Scientific, Technical and Medical Publishers, 2013a). In 2011, the Chinese market grew by 10 percent but still accounts for only less than 5 percent of the global STM market (Ware and Mabe, 2012: 19–20). The low number is somewhat deceptive because China is still strengthening its research infrastructure, and substantial continued growth is projected. Currently, the United States generates approximately 52 percent of global STM revenues for all products. Twelve percent comes from the Asia-Pacific region; 32 percent from the Europe, Middle East, and Africa region; and 4 percent from the Americas, excluding the United States, South Africa, and a few North African countries.

The research and development producers are divided into three primary segments: government, academic, and corporate. Scientists who want to publish their work are the authors or primary producers. There are approximately 1 million authors publishing annually, and about 70 percent of them are academic researchers or scholars. The remaining authors are associated with hospitals, corporations, and government institutions. The corporations heavily investing in research are typically chemical and pharmaceutical companies (Mabe, 2010). In the United States, industry funds approximately two-thirds of research and development, but universities are the main producers of basic research, using a mix of public and private funding. Federal funding covered 59 percent of basic research support, and of that amount, 56 percent was carried out by universities. Since 2006, U.S. federal funding for basic research in science and technology has been declining, while global support is increasing. This is one of the factors driving the shift in global STM revenues. The United States benefits in one way by this shift in that published basic research is accessible to all nations and industries. Contributions to the research and development knowledge base can be measured by the number of patents and the number of publications in peer-reviewed journals.

As of August 2012, there were 28,094 active peer-reviewed journals, consisting of print and electronic editions ("Current Liblicense Archive," 2012). Other database statistics indicate 27,000 journals in the CrossRef database as of March 2012, 8,200 science (10,675 total) journals in the Thomson Reuters' Web of Knowledge, and 18,500 peer-reviewed journals in Scopus. About 95 percent of the 1.7 to 1.8 million articles published annually represent original research (Ware and Mabe, 2012: 22). Most (96 percent) STM journals are available in electronic and print form, indicating a reluctance to abandon historical publishing practices, continued demand from the marketplace in certain areas of the world, and concerns about the readability of digital formats. The medical publishing and scientific and technical publishing segments were almost evenly split in 2011 at approximately 50 percent each. Journal publishing accounted for 42 percent of the scientific and technical segment, but electronic products grew at the fastest rate at 6.4 percent. Leading STM publishers include Reed Elsevier, Springer Science+Business Media, Wolters Kluwer, Pearson, Hearst, and Epocrates (Simba Information, 2012).

SCHOLARLY COMMUNICATION AS AN INDUSTRY

Relationship of Scholarly Communication and STM Industry

Basic and applied research is big business, meaning scholarly research is an industry operating on a specific though transitioning business model. As an industry, scholarly communication has value only if the research is accessible, so scientific information generation processes are intricately tied to access and publication structures. Scientists are producers and receivers at the same time. They author STM materials but need to receive new scientific information quickly and to have access as soon as possible. The relationship of scholarly communication and the STM industry is found at the intersection of supply and demand for academically sound and quality research articles and the commercial market, which is a multi-billion-dollar industry that makes a significant contribution to ongoing scientific research but is ultimately interested in turning a profit. In their purest academic pursuits, apart from issues of tenure and promotion, authors, researchers, and scholars are concerned with scientific content rather than its appeal to a commercial publisher. This fuels the debate concerning the quality of non-peer-reviewed materials added to open access databases. Peer-reviewed publications serve as filters that ensure that content meets rigid quality standards. Publishers or secondary producers have an interest in ensuring that commercial products contain valid and quality information before dissemination and an interest in making a profit. There are two recognized domains in science and technology studies: the sociology of scientific knowledge and the institutional sociology of science. The sociology of scientific knowledge is concerned with searching, collaborating, writing, citing, and publishing. The institutional sociology of science domain is concerned with scholarly communication structures, which include bibliometric evaluation, discipline linking, productivity, innovation, and attitudinal and behavioral norms (Park, 2008). One of the distinguishing features of the scholarly communication industry is the complex relationship between research authors, readers, and publishers, clearly seen in the "invisible college" concept and likely the basis for the tight-knit image the research industry has earned.

The invisible college concept rose out of the question, Do scientists communicate with each other while completing research, or do they just read each other's publications? Crane's research led to the discovery that social networks formed among scientists, leading to scientific change (Crane, 1972). Highly productive researchers can and often do form a central group like a node, and peripheral researchers are linked to the node at the informal and formal levels. The original informal communication system for STM researchers was composed primarily of a community of colleagues or associations established at conferences or lectures. Now informal communication includes electronic invisible colleges. The node-and-spoke model is the same for the citation networks that form in the formal communication process, such as journal articles and their references. A journal or journal article subject field is composed of a collection of articles and papers, and each member of the collection cites an article in the journal or a separately published article at least once. One of the most important characteristics of the invisible college—and the node-and-spoke structures that scientists are influenced by—is that the social structure can cross disciplines. Citations associated with a history journal article on ancient human migration patterns may lead a medical researcher down a new path of gene research, through review of further citations as well as social and informal interactions with historians.

The importance of citation networks and the number of publications a researcher claims has implications for the STM industry. The number of times an author is cited may influence the researcher's market value by raising the author's prestige. There is increasing pressure in the STM industry for scholars to produce new scientific knowledge leading to increased, diversified funding from public and private sources (Mohrman, Ma, and Baker, 2008). Citations are integral to journal sales also. The journal impact factor, a metric reflecting frequency of citations of an average article in a journal in a certain time period, has a direct bearing on the number of paid library subscriptions to a journal. The impact factor is one factor used to judge the importance of individual researchers and their research programs.

The market value of researchers and academics tied to the attention that research publications garner also includes promotions and pay raises, tenure, and job opportunities (Walker, 2002).

The social context can shape the research content, which subsequently shapes the publishing industry. The push to obtain funding has led to funding partnerships between research universities and institutes and private corporations. Private funding then drives the type of research conducted and the publications ultimately produced. In the United States, industry funding for biomedical research flows to pharmaceutical laboratories, non-profit and commercial research institutions, and universities. One study reported that faculty with industry research relationships published significantly more peer-reviewed journal articles than the faculty members without industry funding (Institute of Medicine, 2009).

The social context has also been significantly altered by technology. The emergence of the "ollaborator" or virtual research centers enables scholars to work together without regard to distance, and they are able to share resources (National Research Council, 1993). The ollaborator not only promotes new research approaches but also has propelled interdisciplinary scholarly communication. Scientists join collaborative efforts for their scientific value, but in some cases they also bring individual goals (Sonnenwald, 2007). Ease of collaboration can often make it simpler for junior scientists, for example, to achieve personal goals, such as tenure or a promotion, because of the opportunity to coauthor research publications.

Members of the social network can play different roles. A scholar can produce, read, or review research. Therefore, scholarly communication involves a number of steps in the research and publication process that require scholars to wear different hats. Scholars complete the research; carry out the peer reviews of outputs; purchase research materials; work with editors and publishers to produce final, edited products; and often produce grey literature. In many cases, the research institutions or facilities where the researchers work will purchase the scientific publications that contain articles the institutions funded in the first place (Comba and Bignocchi, 2005).

Along with social networks and media, "grey literature" is mentioned because it is playing an increasing role in the scholarly process. It is defined in different ways, but generally it is produced by government, academics, business, and industries, in both print and electronic forms, and is not controlled by commercial publishing interests. It can be protected by intellectual property rights (Carr, 2014). Once difficult to locate except at special collection libraries and institutional repositories, it is now much more accessible due to the Internet. Grey literature includes government research and reports, prepublication research papers, non-profit reports, preliminary research results, project websites, data archives, filed notes, observations, and so on. It can be mentioned in peer-reviewed journals, giving it integrity and a confirmed source. It does not stand alone, but grey literature does make significant contributions to the STM industry.

Having reviewed the scholarly communication and research process, let's turn our attention to the publishing industry itself in terms of the scope and type of publications and services offered around scholarly communications.

Accessing Publications

As previously described, a central aspect of the STM industry is the communication of research findings. Primary literature, such as journal articles and monographs, form the heart of scientific, technical, and medical research work made available for open and public scrutiny. Though there are informal communication structures, documentation of which is not consistently available, and published grey literature, it is the formal peer-reviewed and published scholarly materials that document claims to new knowledge—our sci-

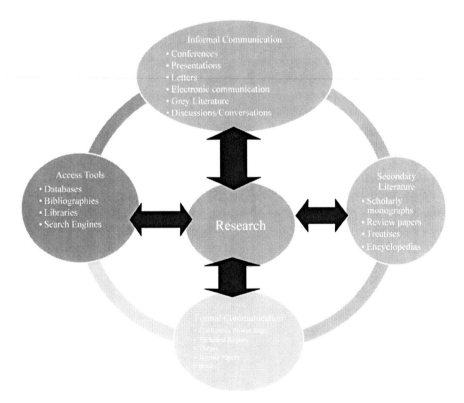

Figure 1.3. Scholarly Communication Research

entific minutes. Knowing the sources of publications is naturally essential to locating the materials.

Articles in scholarly journals are not necessarily peered reviewed, though the terms are often used interchangeably. A scholarly article is an original research article written by experts in a particular discipline. Most scholarly journals publish peer-reviewed articles, but not all. Some scholarly journals may publish a combination of peer-reviewed and non-peer-reviewed articles. In many cases, the scholarly or academic journal will print peer-reviewed articles and scholarly reviews.

There are three main sources of scholarly publications: primary, database providers, and aggregators and distribution search services.

Primary Sources

The primary sources of science, technology, and medicine STM publications are the commercial and scholarly publishers. Journals and peer-reviewed conference papers issued in printed or electronic form by commercial publishers can be divided into two large groups: 1) journals included in indexed databases and 2) journals that are not yet indexed, which are usually recently formed journals. The publishers collect the articles from authors, manage the editing process, package the articles, and disseminate them to end users. The primary users are the same scholars writing the research, and their primary means of access to the published information are the publishers themselves and university and research libraries that purchase access to the journals for secondary access by faculty and students. The top ten publishers accounted for approximately 45 percent of academic journal revenues in 2006, but only three publishers account for approximately 40 percent of all journal articles published for profit—Reed Elsevier, Wiley-Blackwell, and Springer. The remaining for-profit journals and journal articles are published by over 2,000 smaller publishers (Morgan Stanley, 2002; Van Orsdel and Born, 2007). Major professional society publishers include the American Chemical Society, the Institute of Electrical and Electronic Engineers, and the Institute of Physics, to name a few.

An analysis of the Thomson-Reuters Journal Citation database calculated the following breakdown by type of publisher: 64 percent commercial publishers, 30 percent society publishers, 4 percent university publishers, and 2 percent other publishers. The not-for-profit publishers are typically scholarly and professional associations (Ware and Mabe, 2012: 33). University presses, representing still another class of scholarly publishers, are sometimes partially subsidized by research universities and even the authors themselves. Scientific publications are usually in the form of scholarly monographs or journals. The American Association of University Presses has ninety-two U.S. and Canadian members that publish over 11,000 books and 700 learned journals annually (Givler, 2002). The very large presses, such as those at Harvard, Chicago, Oxford, and Cambridge universities and some of the U.S. state-funded universities, achieve profitability by selling a large variety of printed material that includes peer-reviewed monographs, materials of local interest, trade publications, and textbooks. A number of university presses have seen cutbacks in university funding over the past few years for scholarly publishing and are trying to stay in operation by expanding publication of products that are more profitable in print and electronic forms.

Database Providers

Finding the right peer-reviewed articles for research purposes can obviously be a complex process, given the thousands of journals and millions of articles published annually. To simplify the search process, commercial and university publishers have developed bibliographic databases containing both peer-reviewed and non-peer-reviewed journals and journal articles, conference papers, essays, reviews, and other STM materials. A bibliographic database enables users to search for materials based on information, such as author name, number of cited references, subject, whether it is peer-reviewed, and so on. Databases such as Academic Search provided by EBSCO Publishing are commercial and multidisciplinary, while others, such as arXiv at Cornell University, are free and focused on particular disciplines. The Cornell arXiv, for example, includes both peered-reviewed and non-peer-reviewed electronic preprints of scientific research material in physics, mathematics, computer science, quantitative biology, statistics, and nonlinear sciences. The business models for these databases range from a subscription service to free and a combination of free for a certain amount of information or to designated users and a paid service for select data or select users (such as non–society members who may pay a premium if not a member of the sponsoring society publishing the content).

Several of the largest research databases providing access to peer-reviewed materials are Thomson Reuters Web of Science with its Science Citation Index, Ulrich's Periodicals, Elsevier's SCOPUS, JSTOR, and the U.S. National Library of Medicine's MEDLINE/PubMed. Thomson Reuters also publishes the Journal Citation Reports, which uses quantitative data and journal impact and influence metrics to measure journal placement in the body of literature.

Citation analysis has been one of the main factors used by libraries in subscription selection. The first citation index was produced by Eugene Garfield in 1955 and was called the Institute for Scientific Information (ISI), and the acronym is frequently mentioned in research materials. Looking at one of the largest database publishers leads to an understanding of the level of sophistication in web-based scholarly research databases. The ISI is now part of Thomson Reuters Web of Science, which includes a number of database research tools that allow searching of scholarly journals and research evaluation. For example, it is possible to search different databases that include high-impact papers based on citation counts, most-cited journals, or journal publication and citation data.

Despite the ability to do detailed and complex searches, the underlying principles of Garfield's first indexed database have not changed in the databases that rigorously select journals based on high standards of research. High-impact and cited references metrics represent methods of organizing information to make it searchable, and technology has only made it possible to add new search criteria far beyond citations, such as linkages between articles. Bibliographic databases enabling searches by topic and specialty remain the primary methods of researcher information access, ahead of search engines that can possibly take readers directly to an article or abstract on a journal website. Researchers should search across multiple journals using commercial and university databases (Gardner and Inger, 2012).

Aggregators and Gateways

Two terms used frequently, mostly by librarians, are "aggregators" and "gateways," or link resolvers. Aggregators are databases that include full-text versions of journals from multiple publishers. They provide a single point of access to many different journals. The aggregators may be discipline specific or cover multiple disciplines, and they usually impose an embargo on current titles that lasts six months or longer. Any institution, university, business, or individual can buy a bundle or aggregate of journal subscriptions. However, the embargo blocks access to current journal titles for the designated period of time, and access is possible only by paying an additional subscription fee (Cox, 2011).

Gateways, or link resolvers, are another tool for accessing specific journals, articles, and other documents. These services represent agreements between publishers and other organizations to provide access to electronic versions of journals. A gateway is composed of an electronic list of specific electronic journals that allows access by any number of points—topic, discipline, high-impact factor, most cited, and so on. The researcher can choose a specific article, for example, which is sent to the publisher's website or an authorized distributor of the full-text content to retrieve this document. Depending on the rights of the researcher, which can often be determined instantly and at the point of access, the material is provided (or not) to the requesting researcher.

SCHOLARLY PUBLISHING

One of the characteristics of modern scholarly communication is the tension created by the many forces mentioned throughout this discussion: the need to make information widely available to researchers to promote knowledge creation, the need of publishers to maintain a profitable status, the desire of research communities to increase interdisciplinary research access, the globalization of scholarly research, and even the needs of a consumer mass market interested in accessing the scholarly research. The scope of scholarly publications had fairly definitive boundaries before the introduction of the Internet, with the primary one being peer review. Peer reviewing is a self-adjusting process that ensures that scholarly research goes through rigorous testing and questioning.

The scholarly peer-reviewed journal article represents primary research that required a major investment in time and money. It can take as long as three years for a scholarly work to go from initial submission to final publication, with a lot depending on the length of time it takes to complete the peer-review and editing process. In the conventional blind peer-review process, the author does not know who the reviewers are, and in the double-blind peer-review process, the authors and reviewers are anonymous. In either case, the articles are reviewed by scholars outside the publishing house or the organization sponsoring the research. This is the gold standard of scholarly communication. One of the benefits of formally publishing peer-reviewed scholarly communication is that it creates the ability to establish research priority, thus completing the cycle from idea to impact. In the effort to shorten the publishing cycle, the editorial board peer-review process was developed, in which a board of editors, working for the journal, reviews articles.

The scope of scholarly communication extends beyond peer-reviewed journals listed in databases. The conventional scholarly communication market does not have mass access, but technology has created a demand for it. The early efforts to make scientific research more available led to Paul Ginsparg creating a preprint server in 1991 for "publishing" physics papers, which subsequently was taken over by Cornell University and became arXiv. Ginsparg and projects such as the Public Library of Science and BioMed Central challenged the rising subscription costs of science, technology, engineering, and mathematics journals. Eventually, these projects led to the concept of open access, in which scholarly work that meets standards of citation are deposited in electronic repositories to be used however the reader desired (Fitzpatrick, 2012). Following the early efforts of open access supporters, conventional publishers were forced to join the electronic publishing industry to stay competitive and to keep costs as low as possible. Interestingly, most journals are still printed even though 96 percent are available electronically (Ware and Mabe, 2012: 33).

There are many other sources of scholarly publications besides journals. Recalling the definition, to be considered scholarly communication, the scientific material must be reviewed for quality, disseminated, and archived. Peer-reviewed conference papers, articles posted on author websites, essays, and monographs are scholarly communication. Though informal communication before publication produces important research information, it is not formally peer reviewed. Prior to technology, the line between statements intended to be on the record versus informal communication was very clear. Yet technology, such as wikis, Internet whiteboards, scientific forums, and social media exchanges, now documents the informal scholarly communication process, moving the formal-informal boundary and making unpublished material open to review and discussion by the public (Mabe, 2010: 137).

One reason that the conventional printed publication process continues, despite electronic publishing, is that there is still a high demand for printed materials from society members and individuals. The reality is that for-profit publishers would not continue the current business model if they were unable to make profits. There is also an ongoing concern among scholars concerning the ability to fulfill the archival function of the scholarly communication process. Printed material can be safely stored and remain available should a publisher go out of business or take down a website.

ISSUES AND TRENDS

The scope of the scholarly publications industry is slowly changing from one closely held by conventional publishers to one more broadly accessible and affordable by scholars as authors and users. There are a number of issues that remain to be solved as technology advances, libraries are unable to continue paying high subscription prices, and global scholars bypass conventional publishers for electronic self-publishing. One issue concerns how to protect author rights and protect material from being changed by users. Another issue is the need to develop a revised system for assessing scholars who are eligible for promotion and tenure that incorporates publishing in venues such as open access competitive journals.

There is also pressure coming from the U.S. community of scholars to gain free access to all federally funded research and historical databases. Since government research is funded with taxpayer money, researchers believe the material should be made available to the general public. The material includes anything published by the government or federally funded legislation published in a journal sold on a subscription basis.

The issue of credibility in electronic publications must be addressed. If electronic scholarly communication can be published by anyone and accessed by anyone, how can content quality be measured and maintained? Another way to frame the question is, How will users know the content is original and accurate? A corollary to this issue concerns how citation networks can be maintained for indexing purposes if scholarly communication is published online.

Electronic university-based institutional repositories could take on a more important role in the future as scholars look for central locations where all categories of scholarly works can be published, accessed, disseminated, and stored. Clearly, there will be a need for new models for managing scholarly communication in the future.

CONCLUSION

It is almost impossible to discuss scholarly communication and the STM industry and not address technology. Yet technology has not yet changed the foundation principles of scholarly communication. These principles embrace quality, originality, and analysis that represent an addition to the knowledge pool. Peer reviewing verifies all three of these principles in a scholarly product such as a journal article. One of the main reasons that scholars continue to use conventional publishers is due to the protections it affords the scientists. When an article is published in a peer-reviewed journal for public consumption, the reader can have a high assurance level that the article is authentic and of high quality. Peer reviewing that is verified by a journal editorial management process is a method of quality filtering. Online publishing that does not go through a third-party publisher and/or peer review needs an equivalent quality protection system developed and put in place before print journals are abandoned.

The core principles of scholarly communication have not changed with the introduction of electronic publishing. In many ways, technology has strengthened those values by reaffirming the importance of having methods in place for ensuring that the information published is of high quality. Though the conventional methods for producing STM materials may seem more laborious, slower, and less productive compared to online publication, it also keeps the pace of publications at a manageable rate for peer reviewers and users. The production of scholarly communication has developed over centuries and represents the accumulation of methods known to protect the scholar, the information users, and the process itself for the purposes of quality.

REFERENCES

Anderson, Chris. 2009. *Free—The Future of a Radical Price*. New York: Hyperion.

Association of College and Research Libraries, Scholarly Communications Committee. 2003. "Principles and Strategies for the Reform of Scholarly Communication 1." Association of College and Research Libraries. June 24. http://www.ala.org/acrl/publications/whitepapers/principlesstrategies.

Borgman, C. L. 2000. "Digital Libraries and the Continuum of Scholarly Communication." *Journal of Documentation* 58, no. 4 (July): 412–430.

Carr, Dick. 2014. "What Is Gray Literature?" University of New Mexico Health Sciences Library and Informatics Center. Last updated August 11, 2014. http://libguides.health.unm.edu/content.php?pid=200149.

Comba, Valentina, and Marialaura Bignocchi. 2005. "Scholarly Communication and Open Access: Research Communities and Their Publishing Patterns." New Trends in Scholarly Communication: How Do Authors of Different Research Communities Consider OA. Conference paper, August 13, 2005. http://eprints.rclis.org/7276/1/oslo.pdf.

Cox, Christopher. 2011. "Western Libraries Acquisitions Funding Model: A Plan for Change. Developed by the Western Libraries in Consultation with the Senate Library committee." Western Libraries Senate Library Committee. April. http://www.wwu.edu/provost/budget/documents/proposals/LibraryAcquisitionsFundingPlanforChange.pdf.

Crane, D. 1972. *Invisible Colleges: Diffusion of Knowledge in Scientific Communities*. Chicago: University of Chicago Press.

"Current Liblicense Archive—Ulrich's Estimate of Total Number of Active Peer-Reviewed Journals: 28,094 in August 2012." 2012. Center for Research Libraries. August 4. http://listserv.crl.edu/wa.exe?A2=LIBLICENSE-L;17e4abd4.1208.

Fitzpatrick, Kathleen. 2012. "Giving It Away: Sharing and the Future of Scholarly Communication." *Journal of Scholarly Publishing* 43, no. 4: 347–362.

Gardner, Tracy, and Simon Inger. 2012. *How Readers Discover Content in Scholarly Journals: Comparing the Changing User Behaviour between 2005 and 2012 and Its Impact on Publisher Web Site Design and Function. Summary Edition*. Abingdon, UK: Renew Training. http://www.renewtraining.com/How-Readers-Discover-Contentin-Scholarly-Journals-summary-edition.pdf.

Garvey, William, and Belver Griffith. 1967. "Scientific Communication as a Social System." *Science* 157, no. 3792 (September 1): 1011–1016.

Garvey, William, and Belver Griffith. 1980. "Scientific Communications: Its Role in the Conduct of Research and Creation of Knowledge." In *Key Papers in Information Science*, edited by B.C. Griffith, 211–238. White Plains, NY: Knowledge Industry Publications.

Givler, Peter. 2002. "University Press Publishing in the United States." American Association of University Professors. http://www.aaupnet.org/about-aaup/about-university-presses/history-of-university-presses. (Reprint from *Scholarly Publishing: Books, Journals, Publishers and Libraries in the Twentieth Century*, edited by Richard E. Abel and Lyman W. Newman, Wiley, 2002.)

Institute of Medicine, Committee on Conflict of Interest in Medical Research, Education, and Practice. 2009. "4. Conflicts of Interest in Biomedical Research." In *Conflict of Interest in Medical Research, Education, and Practice*, edited by B. Lo and M. J. Field. Washington, DC: National Academies Press. http://www.ncbi.nlm.nih.gov/books/NBK22940.

International Association of Scientific, Technical and Medical Publishers. 2013a. "Shifting Areas of Growth in Global Information Economy." International Association of Scientific, Technical and Medical Publishers. Accessed February 27. http://www.stm-assoc.org/industry-statistics/shifting-areas-of-growth-in-global-information-economy.

International Association of Scientific, Technical and Medical Publishers. 2013b. "STM Market Size and Growth, 2006–2010." International Association of Scientific, Technical and Medical Publishers. Accessed February 27. http://www.stm-assoc.org/industry-statistics/stm-market-size-and-growth-2006-2010.

Kling, Rob, and Ewa Callahan. 2003. "Electronic Journals, the Internet and Scholarly Communication." *Annual Review of Information Science and Technology* 37: 127–177.

Kling, Rob, and Geoffrey McKim. 1999. "Scholarly Communication and the Continuum of Electronic Publishing." *Journal of the American Society for Information Science* 50, no. 10: 890–906.

Mabe, Michael A. 2010. "Scholarly Communication: A Long View." *New Review of Academic Librarianship* 16, no. S1: 132–144.

Mohrman, Kathyrn, Wanhua Ma, and David Baker. 2008. "The Research University in Transition: The Emerging Global Model." *Higher Education Policy* 21: 5–27.

Morgan Stanley. 2002. "Media Industry Overview: Scientific Publishing: Knowledge Is Power." Equity Research Report Europe. September 30. http://www.econ.ucsb.edu/~tedb/Journals/morganstanley.pdf.

National Research Council. 1993. *National Collaboratories. Applying Technology for Scientific Research.* Washington, DC: National Academy Press.

Park, Ji-Hong. 2008. "The Relationship between Scholarly Communication and Science and Technology Studies (STS)." *Journal of Scholarly Publishing* 39, no. 3 (April): 257–273.

Simba Information. 2012. "Combined STM Markets Grew 3.4% in 2011." Press release. January 6. http://www.simbainformation.com/about/release.asp?id=2503.

Sonnenwald, Diane H. 2007. "Scientific Collaboration." *Annual Review of Information Science and Technology* 41, no. 1: 643–681.

Van Orsdel, Lee C., and Kathleen Born. 2007. "Periodical Price Survey 2007: Serial Wars." Library Journal 132, no. 7 (April 15): 43–48.

Walker, T. J. 2002. "Two Societies Show How to Profit by Providing Free Access." *Learned Publishing* 15, no. 4 (October): 279–284.

Ware, Mark, and Michael Mabe. 2012. *The STM Report: An Overview of Scientific and Scholarly Journal Publishing.* 3rd ed. The Hague: International Association of Scientific, Technical and Medical Publishers, November. http://www.stm-assoc.org/2012_12_11_STM_Report_2012.pdf.

Chapter Two

The Scientific Journal

A Historical Perspective to Modern Times

The origins of scholarly publishing date back hundreds of years, and its original purpose has changed very little. It is a forum for scholarly communication that provides authors a means for the dissemination of new theories and research and readers the ability to access new knowledge. The simplest, classical definition of a journal is that it is a peer-reviewed collection of scholarly articles. Though technology has added new considerations and features in terms of access and dissemination, it remains a collection of articles. Over time, the journal has become more delineated by academic disciplines, so there are now journals dedicated to specific disciplines in the science, technology, and medical (STM) industry and in the social sciences and humanities industry. Scientific journals are some of the earliest journals published; in this chapter, the history of the scientific journal is traced from its beginnings to its current state.

The following sections review the history of the journal, the purpose and function of the journal, and the evolution of the journal article and explore some of the journal publishing complexities associated with technology. Though technology is introducing changes in publication methods, knowledge transfer, and journal storage, the modern journal still serves the same purpose and has the same functions it has always claimed—registration, validation, dissemination, and preservation. The characteristics of the journal are the core elements around which technological advances rotate and not the other way around. Understanding the development of the journal and how it reached its current state establishes a basis for evaluating the efficacy and impact of rapid technology open-source-based changes in scholarly communication as well as the development of the genre itself.

WHAT IS A JOURNAL?

The scholarly journal has unique characteristics when compared to other journals. It is not possible to even identify a scholarly journal solely based on its title because sometimes the word "journal" is used in the publication name, but it is sometimes omitted. A journal in its generic sense is a collection of stories, reports, or articles on a particular subject or in a particular discipline. Some newspapers are named journals, such as the *Wall Street Journal*, because the word "journal" indicates a set of informational items. The frequent use of the word "journal" can be confusing when the goal is to access scholarly journals as opposed to magazine or newspaper journals; however, the scholarly journal has a number of distinguishing characteristics.

Definition

A journal is a specialized serial publication appearing regularly throughout the year and from year to year. That is precisely why it is called a "periodical" or "serial" publication. Each journal appearance is an issue, and several issues constitute a volume. A volume number and issue number are assigned, but the volume may or may not coincide with a calendar year. The journal has historically been published four, six, or twelve times a year, and some may be designated by the year, volume, issue, and season or month. Each journal issue contains a number of papers or articles, usually reflecting research in a discipline.

The scholarly journal is unique in several ways. It is peer reviewed or refereed, meaning each article has been reviewed by a panel of experts before publication. The intent of the scholarly journal is to publish original research in a specific discipline or research field. The references cite sources with footnotes, endnotes, and/or bibliographies, and the citations are expected to be high quality and represent a review of existing relevant literature. The scientific paper presents the theory, hypothesis, or findings, accompanied by a review of literature and previous research on which the paper or article information builds on. The literature and research review is usually followed by an in-depth explanation of the research methods used to approach a science-related question, methods of data collection, and data analysis techniques. The scientific article then ends with an interpretation of the data and a discussion of the results achieved. There may also be a description of the implications of the research and suggestions for additional research. The language of the journal articles reflects the specialized language and terminology of the discipline. It usually contains a variety of visual data, such as graphs, charts, data tables, and formulas.

The scientific article does not necessarily present solutions to problems, and it is not meant merely to present summary information concerning previous research efforts. An article that only reports on and summarizes scientific research previously published is called secondary research. Original research publications are called primary research. The literature review in primary research articles provides context for reading the article, placing the new research within a field of study. One of the most important characteristics of the scientific journal is its ability to advance new knowledge and not just confirm what is already known. It presents original research methods and results and serves as a vehicle for formal scholarly communication. A scientific article published in a scientific journal becomes a contribution to the global archive of scientific literature accessed by readers or users. The journal article expands the knowledge base of a particular scientific discipline. As the information in a succeeding section discusses, the growth of scientific disciplines has influenced the journal industry in terms of the number and types of scholarly journals and articles.

Structure and Characteristics

The articles presented in scientific journals are authored by researchers, professors, academics, and scholars, and these are also the same people who are the primary journal readers. Journal papers and articles are typically written by one or more authors who did the research. They may be working in different institutions and different countries. The average author publishes three papers annually with other colleagues. The typical authors of scholarly journals may be working independently, at a research university, at a commercial enterprise engaged in product development, at a government agency, or at a non-profit enterprise doing independent research. Authors are also readers, but there are clearly other researchers and interested parties who read and use the material, such as university students who are not necessarily studying to be scientists, business executives interested in the latest scientific developments, and even interested consumers.

Most peer-reviewed journals are published by commercial publishers, universities, and research organizations, though some are still produced by learned societies. Publishers obtain the journal articles from scholars and researchers, who submit their work in the hopes of being published for numerous reasons, including meeting job requirements. The material in journals includes full-length articles, essays, abstracts, and reviews. Though journals exist in the scientific, social sciences, and humanities research industries, the scientific journal has the specific intent of advancing scientific knowledge through its reporting of unique, peer-reviewed research. The peer-review process is intended to ensure that any material included in the journal meets the highest quality standards in terms of originality, research, content, scientific validity, and reasonableness of conclusions.

Peer review is a process in which articles submitted to publishers are reviewed by other scholars and researchers. The publisher's editor or editorial board will first review the article and decide if the paper should be assessed by peer reviewers. If so, the article or paper is sent to two or more scholars who are qualified to review the research quality. Each reviewer submits a report to the editors that indicates whether the research will be of sufficient interest in the discipline, presents original research, makes a significant knowledge advance, and has apparent significance or value that adds to existing research and research methods. The work must be of interest to the typical journal reader, and it must add to the existing body of knowledge. The editors assess the information submitted by the peer reviewers, looking for conflicting information or differences in quality assessments. Reviewers will note content errors, determine if the interpretations seem reasonable based on the research, assess the paper's organization and readability, and identify other areas where improvement would benefit the final product. Articles are frequently sent back to the author for revisions, thus providing for improvements in research quality before publication (Elsevier, 2013b). The editor will make a recommendation as to whether the article should be published or rejected once the revisions are deemed acceptable. Figure 2.1 shows the journal publication process, from submission by the author through subscription by purchasers.

The types of peer review are single blind, double blind, and open. In a single-blind peer review, the author does not know the name of the reviewer, but the reviewer knows the name of the author. In the double blind, the author and reviewer are anonymous. In an open type of peer review, the author and reviewer know each other's names. The double-blind peer-review process tends not to work well since knowledgeable peer reviewers can determine authorship from context. An estimated 80 percent of scholarly papers require revision (Rowland, 2014). There are ongoing discussions as to whether the peer-review process is flawed because of factors such as reviewer bias, the time the review process adds to the publication time frame, inconsistency of reviews, and abuse of the peer-review process through activities such as purposely blocking a research competitor's article publication (Smith, 2006). It is mentioned at this point in the interest of thoroughness.

In the following section, the history of the journal is reviewed, including the first scientific journals published to the origins of the peer-review process.

HISTORY OF THE JOURNAL

Scholarly communication can be informal or formal. The journal represents the conventional formal communication media for science, technology, and

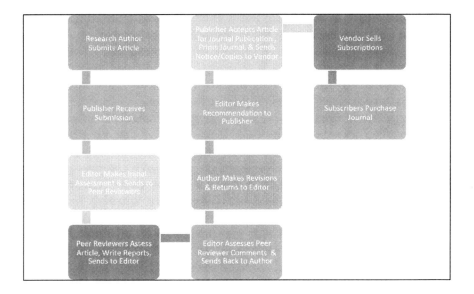

Figure 2.1. Journal Publication Process

medicine. Its roots go back centuries, and there are many facets of journal characteristics that have not changed since the seventeenth century. In this section, the highlights of the evolution of the journal are reviewed, leading up to the origins of the peer-review system and the introduction of electronic publishing.

First Scientific Journals

The history of scientific journals is an interesting story that includes a host of well-recognized names and some intrigue and disagreements as early scientists dealt with the need to protect their claims to research authorship. Leading up to the first journal was a series of events revolving around writings of English statesman and philosopher Francis Bacon. Though he was not a scientist, Bacon is acknowledged as the person who developed the basics of the scientific research method, first described in the 1620 publication *Instauratio Magna*, of which *Novum Organum* is the second part. In the *Novum Organum*, Bacon describes a new scientific investigation method now known as induction. Induction, stated in the simplest terms, is the collection of facts (observations), which are then used to develop new theories. He believed that finding the truth was achieved by finding variances to collected observations, thus eliminating instances and disproving or proving theories, which suggests experimentation. His method of research used empirical and rational starting points and was in direct contrast to Aristotelian deductive reasoning, which used reason as opposed to observations. Bacon supported speculation based on observations, leading to the advancement of knowledge. As previously discussed, modern scientific publications are considered scholarly only if they advance knowledge. In later works, Bacon divided intellectual endeavors, eventually leading to natural history, civil history, and subdivisions of physics, metaphysics, natural magic, and mechanics.

Though Bacon died in 1626, his philosophy of the basic scientific research method continued to spread. Bacon believed that his philosophy, which is now called science, must be carried out by a community of observers and experimenters, now called scientists, who had a common goal. The most well-known early effort by a group to follow Bacon's scientific research method is found in 1648, when a group of scientists formed the "Oxford Experimental Philosophy Club" in London, spearheaded by John Wilkins. The original Oxford club experimented with mechanical devices and scientific instruments and represented the first scholarly society based on Bacon's scientific research philosophy (Purver, 1967).

The club was formalized in 1660 as a chartered society named the Royal Society of London for the Improvement of Natural Knowledge. The London-based Royal Society was chartered in 1662 and was one of the earliest learned societies. The period following 1660 was a time of great interest in advancing scientific areas (Birch, 1968). On January 5, 1665, the first academic journal was published in Paris. The *Journal des sçavans*, established by Denis de Sallo, contained "details of experiments in physics and chemistry, discoveries in arts and in science, such as machines and the useful and curious inventions afforded by mathematics, astronomical and anatomical observations, legal and ecclesiastical judgments from all countries, as well as details of new books and obituaries" (McKie, 1948). Except for one nine-month period, it was published every Monday until 1792, when the French Revolution began and publication ended. However, publication resumed in 1797 under the name *Journal des Savants*, and it is still published in print format, making it the oldest scholarly journal in the world. The journal served as a prototype for more than sixty learned journals in Europe during the seventeenth and eighteenth centuries (Potts, 2011).

Henry Oldenburg was the first secretary of the Royal Society; he was responsible for reading out loud the letters he received from scientists and also reporting back to correspondents on scientific developments in England and Royal Society efforts. The back-and-forth letters by the secretary were the seeds of the first journal. Robert Hooke, a paid assistant to one of the Royal Society's founding members, Robert Boyle, was appointed to the Royal Society as curator of experiments in 1663, and it was his responsibility to oversee the Royal Society's experiments. It was Hooke's idea to print news and research updates on a weekly basis, an idea agreeable to Henry Oldenburg. Oldenburg had hopes as the first editor that publishing a journal would also be a profitable enterprise through subscription sales. The Royal Society of London was one of the groups that had read and discussed the *Journal des sçavans* with great interest and encouraged Oldenburg. The Royal Society was focused on developing new scientific knowledge through research and experimentation, and on March 6, 1665, Oldenburg began editing and binding the letters from scientists, creating the first scientific journal named the *Philosophical Transactions of the Royal Society of London.* The serial journal reported on weekly Royal Society meetings and research, but originally it was a voluntary effort on Oldenburg's part and not an official publication of the Royal Society (Gribbin, 2007).

Philosophical Transactions was designed to distribute new and sometimes controversial scientific postulations and to garner the comments of a broader scientific community. Oldenburg was the gatekeeper for materials, recording the dates of all communications to establish ownership of materials, reviewing submissions, deciding if other English or European scientists should review materials, and deciding which papers would be published in the journal. Oldenburg's efforts formed the early basis for meeting the needs of scientists interested in establishing priority for the latest scientific discoveries, establishing ownership, and gaining peer recognition, which remain the foundations of today's scientific journal. The Royal Society also provided a method for archiving scientific materials (Fjällbrant, 1997). Until this time, scientists jealously guarded their materials out of fear their ideas would be stolen. *Philosophical Transactions* and the Royal Society made it possible for scientists to share materials with peers and obtain their opinions and judgments. *Philosophical Transactions* became the official publication of the Royal Society in 1753.

Priority Disagreements Made Public

The Royal Society developed the custom of having three Royal Society fellows critique submissions. The peer-review process was adopted by some but not all publishers in the following decades, and at times it was the source of tension and even hostility between scientists. Some of those events are notable. For example, mathematician Isaac Newton submitted a report on light and colors that was reviewed by three Royal Society fellows, one of whom was Robert Hooke, a prolific experimenter who delved into projects in optics, meteorology, timekeeping, the physics of gases, microscopy, and more. Hooke wrote a critique that disagreed with Newton's theory, which was not surprising considering Hooke had his own theory of light documented in *Micrographia.* The critique was subsequently read at a Royal Society meeting and sent by Oldenburg to Newton. The critique made Newton very angry, and their disagreement endured for years (Hall and Hall,

1962). Another confrontation between Hooke and Newton ensued in 1684 concerning who could claim priority in the formulation of the inverse square law of gravitation.

There are three reasons for describing these types of acrimonious disagreements. First, *Philosophical Transactions* publications were not designed to promote unity among scientists. They were meant to promote vigorous discussion and document scientific disagreements. Second, the disagreements confirmed the importance of refereeing or peer reviewing scientific works. Third, Robert Boyle, like others of his time, was constantly anxious about "philosophical robbery," so quick publication of registered scientific papers was one strategy employed to minimize accusations of thievery of theories and experimentation. This also encouraged scientists to freely participate in the open exchange of ideas, knowing their work was archived, with authorship, in science (Merton, 1973).

Besides the Boyle-Newton disagreements, another major conflict that developed is now called the Calculus Wars. This "war" was between Isaac Newton and Gottfried Leibniz, both mathematicians, and concerned the question of who could claim the invention of calculus. The disagreement simmered for years over scientific priority, with Newton accusing Leibniz of plagiarism and Leibniz surreptitiously using Newton's notes on mathematical series expansion but taking away nothing on fluxional calculus. This particular disagreement displays the problem of multiple discoveries and convergence of scientific research. The argument ended in 1723 after the death of Leibniz but is one of the first major scientific research priority disputes (Blank, 2009). Priority disputes continue today despite a rigorous journal publication process.

Specialized Journals

Acta eruditroum was one of the first German scientific journals and was published from 1682 to 1782. Though a German publication, it was printed in Latin so that it would appeal to international scientists. Patterned after the *Journal des savants,* topics were science based but included multiple disciplines like physics, mathematics, anatomy, and medicine, making it an early STM journal. This is the journal in which a 1697 Leibniz contribution, claiming the discovery of differential calculus, led to the start of the Calculus Wars. The *Chemisches Journal für die Freunde der Naturlehre, Arzneygelahrtheit, Haushaltungskunst und Manufacturen* by Lorenz Florenz Friedrich von Crell is acknowledged as the first specialized scientific journal. The chemical journal was published from 1778 to 1781, and the specialization reflected the growing number of scientific disciplines and the needs of scientists. Commercially produced journals up to this time contained articles, letters, reports, news, and historical developments from multiple disciplines.

The *Chemisches Journal* was followed by *Neuesten Entdeckungen in der Chemie* (1781–1786), *Chemisches Annalen für die Naturlehre, Arzneyge-lahrtheit, Haushaltungskunst und Manufacturen* (1784–1803), *Beiträge zu den chemischen Annalen* (1785–1799), and *Neueschemisches Archiv* (1784–1791), all of which were intended to be forums for German chemists. The chemical journals became models for discipline-specific journals.

Twenty-five journals were published during the last quarter of the eighteenth century, proving they filled a scientific need. The publishing and dissemination of scientific information encouraged even more research and experimentation activity and scientific discoveries, propelling the growth of scientific disciplines. The specialized journals made it easier for scientists to access research of the most importance to readers. Encouraging the proliferation of journals was the introduction of increasingly efficient printing methods, such as the steam-driven hand press in 1790 and the cylinder steam press, which had the ability to self-ink rollers in 1814 (McGarry, 1981).

In 1886, the *Philosophical Transactions* journal recognized the growth of scientific discovery by dividing its publications into A and B. *Philosophical Transactions A* was dedicated to the physical sciences, including mathematics, physics, and engineering. *Philosophical Transactions B* was dedicated to topics in the life sciences or biological sciences. The publications faced increasing publishing competition from other societies by the nineteenth century.

During the nineteenth century, the journal transitioned from being a method for disseminating correspondence and reports to being a method for collecting, archiving, and disseminating scientific information. As the amount of literature grew, so did the need for a system of classification. Out of that need grew the concept of an abstract and author and subject indexing. The abstract is a brief summary of the journal article's subject matter. It not only provided a means for categorizing articles but also made it possible for readers to decide if it was in their interest to read the full article.

The learned or scholarly societies that formed during the decades after the Royal Society were the primary scholarly publishers until the universities began to play a larger role. The first university presses established in the United States were at Johns Hopkins University (1878), the University of Chicago (1891), the University of California (1893), and Columbia University (1893). At the start of the twentieth century, serious scientific articles and essays were published by societies and universities. Daniel Coit Gilman, Johns Hopkins University founding president, believed strongly that a research university had a noble duty to advance knowledge and diffuse it beyond lecture audiences. He launched the Johns Hopkins University Press in 1878, which soon began publishing the *American Journal of Mathematics*.

The role of universities in publishing scholarly works began much earlier. In fact, Galileo held a University of Pisa position in 1588 and belonged to the

Lyncean Academy, a group of European scientists who regularly met and discussed science and published single works. The university paid Galileo a stipend, enabling him to do research and write. The same was true for Isaac Newton, who held an endowed professorship, the Lucasian Chari of Mathematics, from 1669 to 1702. During his time as a Lucasian Chair, Newton wrote *Principia.* The chair still exists and is currently held by renowned physicist Stephen Hawking.

The university printing presses generated large amounts of research output as a result of its research funding. The large amount of university press output and the inability of learned societies to keep up with the pace of scholarly publications led to the addition of commercial publishers after World War II (Yiotis, 2005).

During World War II, the role of the U.S. government in funding scientific research began to significantly increase, beginning with the creation of the Office of Scientific Research and Development (OSRD), which assimilated the National Defense Research Committee. The agency was established to fund research that would provide immediate benefit to war activities. However, the head of the OSRD, Vannevar Bush, believed the government had a responsibility to fund basic research in areas such as physics, materials sciences, and other scientific disciplines. Government-funded basic research tripled during the war period. When the war ended, Bush continued his advocacy for research funding with a 1945 published essay titled *Science— The Endless Frontier* (Vannevar, 1945). In 1950, the National Science Foundation was established and is now one of the largest U.S. government funding institutions. Research and publishing are entwined. It takes research funding to initiate and support research efforts, and the results need to be published for maximum exposure. Increased research funding leads to increased scholarly communications.

During the first half of the twentieth century, academic journals became the primary method of publication for scholarly communication. The cost of in-house publishing and the inability to keep pace with the rate of research materials that were produced led the universities and societies to commit to support the creation and distribution of scientific research as opposed to just its creation. The learned societies and universities began to form business partnerships with commercial publishers, forever changing the scholarly publication landscape. The commitment to creation and distribution led to a flourishing print publication industry in the 1960s and 1970s. Commercial publishers are interested in making a significant profit, so journal prices began to increase dramatically. The fixed costs driving the cost per subscription include the editorial cost, production cost, marketing cost, and expected number of subscriptions in five years (Baschler, 1998).

The journal publishing process relies on the submission of free scholarly research to the commercial and university publishers. The research agency or business funds the research projects, paying research salaries, benefits, supplies, laboratory, and equipment expenses. The researchers conduct the research and do the peer reviews, still at no charge to the publishing industry. The research agencies and businesses then buy the published research from the publishers—the same research they sent to the publisher at no charge (Dulle and Minishi-Majanja, 2009).

This sets the stage for the first studies on electronic publishing in the 1970s.

Electronic Journal Publishing

In the early 1970s, the concept of the electronic academic journal began to be formed, though the original idea was that journals would be published as archival files in a format that could be read by computers. Sondak and Schwark first conceived of this type of journal in 1973, which was only four years after the introduction of the Internet precursor ARPAnet in 1969. Over the ensuing five years, a host of scholars discussed the various characteristics that an online or virtual journal would assume. However, the first electronic scholarly journal was published in 1979 concerning mental workload within the Electronic Information Exchange System. The journal was refereed and met editorial standards equivalent to printed scholarly journals. Then in 1980, the British Library funded a Loughborough University project to establish an online journal addressing computer human factors. These early electronic journals were one-time experiments that did not become permanent additions because technology was still underdeveloped and researchers failed to see the value of contributing to such articles (Lancaster, 1995). As technology advanced during the 1980s and 1990s and the World Wide Web became more accessible, the number of electronic journals began to expand. The peer-reviewed electronic academic journals founded in 1991 were created in university settings. The Association of Research Libraries (ARL) published its first *Directory of Electronic Journals, Newsletters and Academic Discussion Lists*, which had 636 listings, of which only 1.1 percent were peer-reviewed journals (Weller, 2002). However, the American Association for the Advancement of Science collaborated with the Online Computer Library Center, Inc., to develop the electronic scientific journal *Online Journal of Current Clinical Trials*. As of 1994, there were twenty-five electronic scientific journals developed or being developed (Clement, 1994). By 1997, the ARL listed 9,182 electronic publications, and 1,049, or 11.4 percent, were peer-reviewed journals, indicating significant growth over six years (Weller, 2002).

The electronic journal was not the only scholarly scientific information being adapted to the web. Other inventions included electronic abstracting, indexing, and bibliographic databases (Large, Tedd, and Hartley, 1999). The rapidly increasing cost of print subscriptions made the possibility of gaining access to the same information in electronic form at a lesser cost very appealing to libraries. Electronic publishing also offered other enticements, such as self-archiving or self-publishing, faster dissemination of scholarly work among peers, greater publishing opportunities, greater availability of multidisciplinary research, and increased scientific collaboration. In 1991, the first e-print archive was created by Paul Ginsparg. E-prints are electronic versions of research papers that may or may not be peer reviewed. The Ginsparg e-print server was assumed by Cornell University in July 2001 and is now called arXiv.org. It offers researchers access to preprints of papers in high-energy physics, non-linear sciences, mathematics, and computational linguistics. It is the largest repository of non-peer-reviewed scientific papers in the world (Ramalho Correia and Teixeira, 2005).

There were three events that began to solidify the electronic scientific journal and scholarly communication. In 1999, the Open Archives Initiative emerged. Its stated mission (http://www.openarchives.org/) is to "develop and promote interoperability standards that aim to facilitate the efficient dissemination of content. The Open Archives Initiative has its roots in an effort to enhance access to e-print archives as a means of increasing the availability of scholarly communication." Though e-prints are not journals, the state of electronic journal publishing must be viewed in its entirety. If scholars can e-print and electronically index and archive peer-reviewed scientific articles, essays, and papers, then are journals necessary? The answer to this question and others like it are quite complex and involves the formal and informal communication processes employed by scientists.

The second influential event was the Budapest Open Access Initiative (BOAI), which emerged from a meeting of the Open Society Institute in Budapest in December 2001. The international meeting brought scholars from multiple disciplines together to discuss the many crises impacting scholarly communication—electronic publishing, access to research, lack of access to publicly funded research forcing commercial subscriptions, and so on. The BOAI focused on self-archiving and open access journal articles. Self-archiving refers to publication in free e-print archives. Open access journals are electronic journals made available free of charge. The authors bear all costs for editing, peer review, and submissions, and access. The *Directory of Open Access Journals* (DOAJ) (http://www.doaj.org) is a list of scientific and scholarly subjects, and all content is free. As of March 2013, the DOAJ had 8,826 scientific and scholarly journals listed, and 4,525 journals were searchable at the article level. Not all journals are peer reviewed, but they have gone through editorial review of some kind.

The third event driving online publication was *The Berlin Declaration on Open Access* initiated in October 2003. It defines open access as "immediate, permanent, free online access to the full text of all refereed research journal articles." Authors submitting contributions agree that the material grants users free, irrevocable, worldwide access and the license to "copy, use, distribute, transmit, and display the work publicly and to make and distribute derivative works, in any digital medium for any responsible purpose, subject to attribution of authorship." The Berlin initiative promotes the highest access level to all researchers.

Where does the journal stand today? Most STM journals are now both online and printed. It is estimated that open access journals make up approximately 10 percent of all peer-reviewed journals. There are four types of electronic journals (Mukherjee, 2009: 3):

1. Electronic journals originally distributed in electronic form
2. Electronic journals that have a small print distribution
3. Printed journals that are also distributed electronically
4. Journals initially published in electronic and print forms

Another concept gaining popularity is open peer review. In the open peer-review process, reviewer names are included on the review reports. The author knows the names of the peer reviewers. If the journal article or paper is published, the peer-review reports with names are also published online, along with the prepublication history. The open peer-review process attempts to ensure that the process is as fair as possible to the author and not fraught with bias. It also protects peer reviewers by ensuring that authors do not attempt to pass their responsibilities related to research publication to the reviewers. In another form of the open peer review, scientists can sign up with a journal to serve as a reviewer for articles yet to be published or volunteer to peer review articles needing assessment. The articles and the reviews are posted online.

Open peer review should not be confused with public review. Electronic publishing has opened the discussion as to whether scholars should publish their articles and let the public participate in the review process. With the advent of open access, it is possible to establish a multistage open-peer-review process, followed by publication (figure 2.2).

The interactive peer review and public discussion stage is not a free-for-all. The public peer reviewers must provide citable documentation for any criticisms, objections, notations of scientific flaws, deficiencies noted, or any other negative arguments or discussions concerning the material being reviewed. The peer reviewers simplify the editing and publication process because the first round or more of revisions are already completed (Pöschl, 2012). When the article is submitted to the publisher, it can undergo a conventional and formal peer review if the publisher requires it, though the purpose of the multistage open peer-review process is ultimately to eliminate that step. If the interactive peer-review process becomes fully accepted by

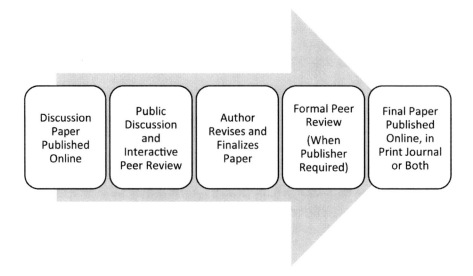

Figure 2.2.   Multistage Open-Peer-Review and Publication Process

scientists at some point, the formal peer-review process will most likely be eliminated in the multistage peer-review process.

The last item to mention concerning the history of the journal is the 2008 U.S. National Institutes of Health (NIH) Public Access Mandate. Per the Consolidated Appropriations Act of 2007, researchers who are funded by the NIH must submit an electronic copy of the final peer-reviewed author's manuscript for public posting. The NIH must follow copyright law, but the electronic copy will be distributed through PubMed Central within twelve months of journal publication. PubMed Central is a government online archive that will provide the research free of charge to the public. The law provoked a contentious discussion between librarians and publishers. Librarians were satisfied that they would no longer have to pay for research that taxpayers had already funded. The Association of American Publishers (AAP) objected to the mandatory submission requirement and claimed the law would harm the STM publishers and the scientific associations that raised funding through publications. The AAP also believes the NIH is taking intellectual property without permission, which involves copyright law (Reid, 2008). An entire discussion paper could be written concerning the rights of authors and publishers, but the NIH mandate is in full force, making it part of the historical time line of the scientific journal.

Most of the discussions about electronic publishing, self-archiving, intellectual rights, authorship, and so on revolve around how the purpose and function of the journal are defined. In the next section, the discussion takes a step back and reviews the reasons the journal was developed and the functions of scholarly communication. The function of the journal drives the discussion as to the appropriateness of open access, open peer review, timeliness of publication, electronic publication, and other related issues.

THE FUNDAMENTALS OF THE JOURNAL

As the previous history indicates, the modern-day journal is a step in an evolutionary process that continues to define its form. The shift from print to electronic media is a process that is far from complete as publishers, libraries, and scholars attempt to balance quality, cost, and accessibility. The electronic journal is no doubt here to stay, but it is important to remember that the characteristics of the modern scientific journal represent features and qualities added to meet scholarly needs as the journal evolved. It is an artifact with form, having the ultimate goal of disseminating scientific knowledge that advances the knowledge pool, with emphasis on "advances."

In this section, the purpose and functions of the journal are isolated— extracted out of the historical context previously discussed. The first section reviews the purposes of the journal followed by the functions of the journal as they are recognized today and includes the roles the journal plays in scholarly communication. The purposes of the journal and the purposes of journal publishing are intertwined. The scientific journal and journal publishing serve the needs of scientists, which has nothing to do with how well modern print publishers are meeting those needs in the current economic environment. That is a whole different discussion better addressed in an analysis of the conventional journal publishing model. The reason this is mentioned is that that are now two basic models of publishing—the traditionally published journal model and the deconstructed journal model developed in response to the availability of new technological tools offering new paths for peer review and publication. The deconstructed journal refers to the taking apart and redistribution of the roles and attributes of the scientific (STM) journal and the process of deconstructing the traditional journal publishing model to move to the new e-print journal model (Smith, 1999).

The traditional journal formation and publication process is the end result of centuries of scholarly communication. It has retained its present form for approximately 250 years for an indisputable reason, that reason being that the journal fulfills the needs of the scientific community. The STM journal developed to serve specific purposes, and it plays various roles that meet those purposes. The roles emerged over time and became more sophisticated as the field of scientific knowledge grew through increased technology and collaboration. Identifying the purposes of the STM journal explains the roles the journal plays.

Reasons for Journal Development

The history of the journal explains the events leading to its creation and subsequent development into its current form. The reasons for journal development are embedded in those events, and the process and structure of the journal satisfy scientific needs. The many discussions concerning electronic publishing are focused not on how to publish online but on how new publishing models can continue to fulfill the needs of the scientists and the STM industry that have been so well defined through the centuries.

The pre-journal scientists faced a number of problems that needed solving if scientific knowledge was to advance. As mentioned, after Bacon died in 1626, a group of natural philosophers at Oxford University formed the experimental science club. The club encouraged innovation, experimentation, and the sharing of ideas. Its first members are considered to be some of the greatest scientific minds of the seventeenth century and included men already mentioned, such as John Wilkins, Robert Boyle, and Robert Hooke, in addition to John Wallis, Seth Ward, Thomas Willis, and Christopher Wren. The uniqueness of this group at the time was due to the fact that the experimental science group had members representing multiple disciplines sharing information and ideas and with great minds. If a small group of philosophers (scientists) could produce remarkable scientific achievements, what could be accomplished if other scientists could share their ideas and add to the group's scientific knowledge? The answer to that question holds the first two reasons for journal development—a need to disseminate scientific inquiries and a method of dissemination. Before the journal, scientists exchanged letters, but the length of time it took to mail letters back and forth slowed scientific progress. There were scientific books published in the seventeenth century, but writing, editing, and publishing a book was slow and expensive, and there was a low readership rate. Printing a book was a financially risky enterprise in the 1600s, much like it is today.

The journal lowered the cost of publishing scientific material and reduced the amount of time it took to publish new material. Ironically, the early journals were less costly to print than books, and weekly issues were affordable and timely, while today's journals are published on a less frequent basis—monthly, quarterly, or semiannually—due to the same reasons of time and cost.

The seventeenth-century scientists developed a clever way to establish priority of discovery in the form of anagrams. The encryption was a single sentence or phrase that had to be unscrambled. The anagram was then given to an official witness or council member for safekeeping. Once safely stored, the scientist could proceed with further research, knowing he could establish priority of discovery. If one scientist laid claim to another scientist's discovery, the person creating the anagram would unscramble it and prove priority.

For example, in 1610, Galileo sent Johannes Kepler, both astronomers, an anagram that read, "smaismrmilmepoetalevmibunenugttaviras." Kepler was unable to unscramble it. It stood for "altissimum planetam tergeminum observari," which meant "I have observed the uppermost planet triple." Galileo was telling Kepler he had observed Saturn's rings for the first time (Meadows, 1974: 50–57). Though the anagram was useful, it was a very flawed process for establishing priority of discovery. The anagram solution could be vague as to its meaning, and the separation of the claim of discovery from the work itself created confusion as to the locus of discovery. Discoveries could overlap, meaning they had to be sorted out. Using anagrams also meant that the review and dissemination of scientific knowledge was suppressed (Kaufer and Carley, 1984).

Over the next decades, scientists continued to discuss, even publicly argue over, ownership of scientific discovers. The Calculus Wars was a good example. The problems with establishing priority of discovery through anagrams and letters led to the use of gatekeepers such as Henry Oldenburg, secretary of the Royal Society, who could register the names of the letter writers and when they were received. Oldenburg's first journal, *Philosophical Transactions*, formalized the registration process in which author names, manuscript submission dates, and descriptions discoveries were recorded before publication in a third-party publication.

Journal development also met the need of scientists for scholarly recognition. With registration procedures in place, scientists could safely share their results with colleagues. The registration process encouraged scientists to share their work instead of hiding the research behind anagrams and secret experimentation. This contributed to the speed at which scientific knowledge advanced in the late seventeenth and eighteenth centuries because the rights of authors were secured (Mabe, 2010).

Bacon's scientific method was so different from the Aristotelian method that there was an anxiousness to get input from other scientists. At the time the journal was developed by Oldenburg, there were myriad formal communication methods that included the letters, anagrams, newspaper articles, books, almanacs, essays, and eventually journal articles. The print journal was able to fulfill the needs of all the stakeholders, including scientists, students, learned societies, libraries, booksellers that sold journals, attorneys dealing with claims of priority of discovery, universities, and readers with a general interest (Fjällbrant, 1997).

The Royal Society was not the first journal publisher, but it is credited with doing the first "peer review." Scientific material was sent to Oldenburg, but the Council of the Royal Society would review the material and recommend items for inclusion in the journal (Royal Society of London, 1665). The review process ensured that quality articles were included in the publications. The Royal Society was certainly not the only society publishing scientific material. Other learned societies included the Deutsche Akademie der Naturforscher Leopoldina (1652), the Académie des Sciences in Paris (1666), and the Royal Swedish Academy of Science (1739), to name a few. The academies or societies increasingly grew interested in quality control, which solidified the importance of peer review. Quality control was critical for scientific, legal, academic, funding, and personal integrity reasons, and peer reviewing offered a process for achieving quality standards that were defensible and applied as uniformly as possible.

The scientific journal also provided stabilization in scientific publishing. With so many methods of communication in use, there was no easy way to archive materials. The journals created such an archive of information, offering a value proposition for research efforts and the advancement of scientific knowledge.

Of course, the number of journals grew because printing was streamlined, the postal system improved, and science became increasingly specialized. As each discipline developed and new societies formed, new journals were published. Scientific disciplines represent the internal differentiation of sciences. Prior to the nineteenth century, scientific knowledge was ordered in general topics for instructional purposes, but there was not a unit of structure or system of communication within each area of interest. The nineteenth century saw the emergence of stabilized, differentiated units of science within the social system, and each had its own communication system and unit divisions of knowledge. Scientists began to specialize, and specialization inevitably led to specialized roles, communication systems, and bodies of knowledge. Scientific disciplines led to the emergence of scientific communities, meaning research was more of a shared experience rather than the result of single scientists (Kuhn, 1970). The journal has mirrored the development of disciplines and then of scientific communities. In the eighteenth century, scientific journals were not specialized and covered general and varied scientific topics. Beginning around 1780, France, Germany, and England saw the publication of specialized journals oriented to a discipline such as physics, geography, medicine, chemistry, and so on. A community of authors focused on publishing research that advanced a scientific specialization, leading to specialized scientific knowledge advancement (Smelser and Baltes, 2001). Communities of scientists now work together on a global basis, producing research with multiple authors, now aided largely by technology. The electronic journal represents a next-evolutionary step as it adapts to how modern scientists work and communicate.

Journal development mirrors scientific development because it is a communication tool. In its earliest days, the journal represented more than a set of articles. It provided the learned societies with a way to bring secretive scientific discussions into the limelight, once priority of discovery was established. The journal continues to fill that role today.

STM Journal Functions

Bacon's scientific method is the seed of the STM journal. He described scientific enterprise as a set of socially organized activities requiring collaboration. The activities make up the many steps required to produce the final journal article, including gathering information, processing data, classifying, and applying written records. Bacon understood that scientific observation and scientific experimentation needs literature to serve as a record that contributes or advances scientific knowledge. Literature should lead to new observations and new experiments and hierarchal progress resulting from inductive inferences. In Bacon's model, literature is a structural component in the organization of knowledge (Frohmann, 2013).

Robert Merton, on the other hand, developed the concept of the sociology of science in 1942, which sees scientific knowledge advancement as being dependent on both structure and a social order with shared values. His focus was on the social order and how it drives scientific effort and direction. In the social order, four norms exist: organized skepticism, disinterestedness, universality, and communalism. The social norms form the "ethos of science," and scientists cultivate the ethos within their disciplines (Merton, 1942). The scientific system has a built-in reward system, with the most important reward being the attachment of the scientist's name to a scientific discovery. Publication is a form of reward in that a scientist's name is forever attached to the article, and the article contains a unit of knowledge (a minute of science is mentioned later in this chapter) (Merton, 1973).

The two theories of scholarly communication and scientific development are mentioned to show that the STM journal article represents the culmination of both scientific structure and the application of social norms. It is now recognized that there are four functions of scholarly communication, and journal publishing fulfills those functions. The four functions were first identified with Oldenburg's journal, and they are so basic and so important to scholarly communication that all journals since then have conformed to the original model (Mabe, 2010). These four functions are registration, verification, dissemination, and preservation. Let's take a more in-depth review of these functions with particular reference to the scholarly journal.

Registration

There has been much discussion about priority of discovery, which is now called registration of discovery. For the early scientists, it was a point of contention before scientific material would be released for public scrutiny. Now, preprint servers can record the date and exact time an electronic document is submitted to a publisher or other website. Many publishers have become a DOI Registration Agency and can assign a Digital Object Identifier (DOI) to record electronic documents. It provides a means for registration of discovery by assigning an actionable, interoperable, and persistent link. DOIs are governed and managed by the International DOI Foundation. Some publishers will allow authors to electronically publish accepted articles that are unedited and unformatted. They are cited using the DOI. This is in response to the pressure from the scientific community to get their research results published sooner.

An ongoing discussion concerns the future of the print journal as a primary registration of discovery document. Even if journals should become primarily electronic, scientists will still need a method for ensuring that priority of discovery and authorship is recorded if those scientists want to ensure that they get credit for their research effort.

Validation (Peer Review)

Peer review is a quality control function. It was first formalized when the Royal Society of London instituted a policy that called for each submitted manuscript to be sent outside the Society for review by experts. This practice was used inconsistently by societies and publishers until the second half of the twentieth century, at which point it became standard practice. In the 1940s, the *Journal of the American Medical Association* and *Science* adopted a policy of peer review, and other journals rapidly followed. Peer reviewers consider a number of factors that include the relevance of the research to the discipline and to the magazine the author is hoping will publish the work, the validity of the research methods, the reasonableness of the interpretations, the clarity of the manuscript presentation, originality, and the literature review and citations.

Peer review performs a secondary function by serving as a filtering process. Each journal receives dozens or hundreds of manuscripts each year. It is impossible to publish everything, but there must be a way to weed out the lower-quality articles or other scientific writings. Peer reviews can identify the highest-quality materials and help editors eliminate those that should not be published.

One of the criticisms of the peer review process is that it adds a significant amount of time to the publication time line. However, the intent of peer review is not to streamline the publishing process. It is to ensure that the articles entering the scientific literature pool are of high quality because, once published, they are forever part of scientific knowledge.

Dissemination

One of the main reasons journals came into existence was due to the need for a method of distributing a growing body of scientific knowledge. Beginning in the mid-sixteenth century, the number of scientists grew rapidly, and exchanging letters by mail was not practical. Scientific information was not reaching a broad enough audience, limiting the ability of science to advance. Binding and copying letters for dissemination was the solution.

The scientific journal continues to fulfill the function of dissemination, though the method of distribution is changing as technology advances. Print and electronic journals serve the dissemination function. There is discussion concerning the continued need for printed journals, but there is never any disagreement about the importance of the dissemination function. Publishing electronic journals—on open access sites, on websites, on preprint servers, and so on—are all methods of dissemination. Ultimately, the goal is to share scientific knowledge in the broadest possible manner so that the appropriate communities of scientists can participate in its use while also ensuring a reliable, consistent, high-quality, and sustainable system of scholarship that ensures that the new knowledge is appropriately being attributed to the discovering author, that the work meets the standards of the scholarly community, and that it is able to be retrieved for all time.

Preservation (Archiving)

The archiving function ensures that the author of the scientific material is forever associated with the scientific material and that the material is always available and unchanged. The methods of archiving have evolved over the centuries. Before computers, printed research materials were stored in libraries and museums, with societies, and at universities and sometimes even with publishers. Today, for electronic journals and related materials, the role of preservation has fallen largely to the producers of scholarly publishers. Large electronic repositories exist at many aggregator sites as well as with publishers and joint programs of publishers in support of preservation efforts. Increasingly, governments, particularly through their national libraries and information science initiatives, are also playing an increasing role in maintaining research data and documents.

One of the concerns expressed about archiving electronic-only journals is the loss of information should the storage entity go out of business or lose large amounts of data. If there is no print copy, the archived records are potentially lost if there is no backup data file. These are the types of issues being addressed as journal publishing moves toward electronic publishing. For example, many information intensive organizations are advocating a "LOCKSS" approach—"Lots Of Copies Keep Stuff Safe"—as they try to address alternatives to direct publisher and aggregators assuming the lead role in preserving scholarly materials.

The Modern Journal's Place in Time

The modern journal plays the same unique role the centuries-old journal played. It provides a method of establishing a public record that has been validated by peers of the author. Once published, it is preserved for current and future research and can lead to new avenues of scientific progress. Unlike the informal communication methods that scientists use, such as oral discussions and e-mails, the peer-reviewed journal article represents a stage in the scientific communication process. Although it may seem like an "ending" at first glance, the published journal article will be cited, evaluated over and over again in reviews, generate new ideas, and perhaps be incorporated into larger works, such as a book of essays. For certain, the peer-reviewed published article becomes part of a set of research efforts. In other words, a journal article has a life larger than its own. The final published article is forever fixed in time in terms of what it says but certainly not in terms of what it can accomplish. The article published in a journal has been called part of the "minutes of science," which is a remarkably accurate metaphor (Mabe, 2006).

THE SCIENTIFIC JOURNAL ARTICLE

Current Format and Access

Peer-reviewed journal articles are different from common magazine articles, and the difference can be visually noticed. The titles and format of the articles are the first clues the article is a scholarly communication. As has been discussed, the journal article has four specific functions, and it is not a report or snapshot of events like other reporting documents, such as newspaper articles. The main contribution of the scientific journal article has not changed since its first stages of development in the seventeenth century. The final published document must advance scientific knowledge. It does not report—it advances. Methods to ensure that each published journal article advances scientific knowledge and gives credit to the author were incorporated over a relatively short period of time given that hundreds of years passed during which the journal article retained its functions and methods of publications. It makes sense that a format also emerged over time so that scientists could consistently approach the article. As a result, journal articles are quite distinctive in their appearance as well as their content. A treatise could be written on each section of the journal article, as presented in figure 2.3.

A conventional, peer-reviewed journal article can have variations in terms of final presentation, but there is little variation in content. The title needs to accurately identify the research focus. There may be numerous authors, but the lead researchers are listed first, prioritized by their contributions and research workloads. The abstract concisely describes the research question and methods and major findings and briefly describes the research significance. The abstract is also used in the literature database so that people looking for particular research can more easily find relevant articles.

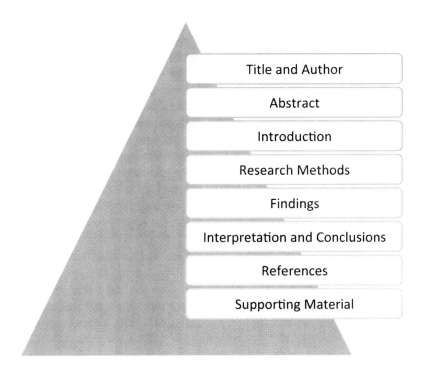

Figure 2.3. Journal Article Format

The research article introduction reviews established scientific knowledge, laying the foundation for the presentation of new knowledge in the article. This harks back to the fact that research articles are meant to expand the existing knowledge base, so the reader needs to understand what the author is building on when forming a hypothesis. The citations are then listed in the references section of the paper.

The research methods section describes the scientific approach and procedures and relevant equipment, measurements, data collection, sources of errors, procedures used to reduce chances of errors or uncertainty, and so on. The extent of the description and the types of details included are determined mostly by the type of research project performed. The scholarly community relies heavily on this section to evaluate the quality of the research approach and to decide if it will accept the results. Once again, research articles are not necessarily intended to solve a problem or arrive at solutions. The publication is examined by scholars, leading to additional knowledge construction as a result of the use and dissemination of the article.

Scholarly communication is composed of both process and structure. Process is the use and dissemination of research through formal and informal channels. The structure of scholarly communication refers to the relationships between people and things involved in the process of scholarly communication, including researchers, authors, reviewers, journals, journal articles, academic institutions, funding agencies, and so on (Park, 2008). The scholarly examination of the journal article is one component of the intellectual structure of the research in that peer reviewers and postpublication scholarly examiners review the materials, methods, and citations, leading to the results. The journal article review by scholars leads to new relationships and serves as a closure mechanism for the research because scientific analysis from different angles eventually leads to the stabilization of the interpretation. Again, a problem is not solved, but a group of scientists will develop additional scientific artefacts resulting from the evaluation of materials and methods and the succeeding sections of results and interpretations. The new artefacts will eventually include re-creations of the experiments, reviews, new topical research, and so on.

The next section of the journal article discusses the results of the research and contains a presentation of the data collected using text, graphs, charts, figures, photographs, and other visual data. The statistical and data analysis methods are presented as well. The results section does not include the author's interpretation so that readers can analyze the data without author influence.

The next-to-last section of the journal article is the discussion and conclusions of the authors. In this section, the authors should present an honest evaluation of the research, including the significance of the research and perhaps a new scientific model. The conclusions should be strictly based on the results and not represent speculation. In this section, the author can bring the research full circle by giving the research context in the body of scientific knowledge.

The last section of the journal article is the list of references. Scientists examine the reference list to determine the depth and breadth of the research. One of the characteristics for which journal article readers are always on alert is bias, which can creep in at any point in the paper—in research methods, data collection, discussion, interpretation, and choice of references.

The structure of the journal article can vary in that some sections may be combined, but all the information must be included. The structure serves a purpose beyond research presentation in that journal articles are archives. Consistency of structure accommodates archiving, one of the functions of the process of scholarly communication.

The Future of the Journal Article

As the journal publishing industry moves toward electronic publishing, the discussion turns to how technology will change the article in the future or if it will change it. The ability to post electronic articles is challenging the traditional journal article as well as journal publishing standards. For example, online articles can be altered a number of times, leading to different versions published online at the same time and without peer review. Online articles often do not have page numbers, so citing them cannot rely on standard conventions. There is no electronic archival standard established yet, and even if one were established, there would be no means of ensuring compliance. Right now, the formal scholarly journal article process and structure is clearly defined, and, once peer reviewed, it is archived as the official and final document.

The "minutes of science" change in this scenario with digital changeability and modification. There is potentially no closure or set of fixed documents that can be referenced to see what was understood in the scientific sense at a moment in time. There is an endless stream of articles, continually evolving and changing.

Currently, recognized electronic scholarly journal articles still go through peer review and are still disseminated by print publishers after editors ensure that the standard formatting is used. Technology has changed the way these tasks are completed and even made them more complicated, unless one is thoroughly familiar with electronic publishing. Librarians who once used typed cards to find archived documents or manage subscriptions must now understand how to use sophisticated software. Electronic submission and printing, online peer review, electronic archiving, and digital subscriptions are just a few changes associated with electronic publishing (Mabe, 2006).

There is a significant ongoing debate among scholars concerning the future of the scholarly journal and journal article. The discussion involves issues much deeper than whether journals will continue to be printed or eventually fully transition to electronic publishing. There is a school of scientists that believe that electronic, open access publishing is the future of publishing, driven by the high cost of subscription rates, changing conventions surrounding academic tenure and promotions tied to publishing, globalization, and a younger generation of scientists who want their research publicly reviewed by the widest audience before the paper is considered final. However, there remain many details to work through concerning the use of accessible primary research, ranging from quality assessments to business models and sustainability.

Previously, it was mentioned that there are now publishers assigning DOIs to preprint journal articles, giving public access to research before it is formalized in a journal. The journal publishers in the future may only manage the validation and preservation or archive functions. If researchers can disseminate their own articles and an electronic service can date stamp the publication, some maintain that the publisher's role is reduced and perhaps will be eventually eliminated in the commercial sector.

Even the method for examining articles is impacted by technology. Publishers are working on new ways to present online articles. The new electronic presentation system moves away from linear article formats, using linked navigation schemes and tabbed movement through article sections. With a hierarchical presentation of figures and text, those who want to read the details can continue to do so, while general readers can read summary sections. The new online formats modularize the article so that researchers can quickly access specific, individual sections of an article, such as data tables, without having to read through entire articles to find relevant research. Other changes include being able to open nonconsecutive pages, adding audio and video, offering basic and extended versions of certain sections (e.g., materials and methods), and creating a graphical abstract and highlight web page (Elsevier, 2013a).

As of now, the stability of the journal publishing system and the scientific quality achieved by the current peer-review system seems to indicate that the formal publication system will continue because there is nothing to replace it. However, technology can increase the sophistication of the informal communication system to a great degree because it makes it possible to converse, correspond, and present online. Verbal chats now take the form of e-mails, leaving a formal record of informal exchanges. Yet the most important function of the scholarly communication process—formal peer review—is still needed to ensure that scientific knowledge advances one unit at a time. The infrastructure of the journal publishing industry is changing and will continue to change, but the scholarly journal, with a structure and functions traceable to Henry Oldenburg, will need to remain intact if we wish to maintain a consistent, verifiable, and reproducible system of scholarly communication that can keep its minutes inviolate.

REFERENCES

Baschler, Edwin F. 1998. "Pricing of Scientific Publications: A Commercial Publisher's Point of View." *Notice of the AMS (American Mathematical Society)*, November 1998, 1333–1343.

Birch, Thomas. 1968. *The History of the Royal Society of London for Improving of Natural Knowledge from Its First Rise: Four Volumes.* New York: Royal Society. (Facsimile of four-volume work published in London, 1757.)

Blank, Brian E. 2009. "Review of *The Calculus Wars: Newton, Leibniz, and the Greatest Mathematical Clash of All Time* by Jason Socrates Bardi." *Notices of the AMS (American Mathematical Society)* 56, no. 5: 602–610. http://www.ams.org/notices/200905/rtx090500602p.pdf.

Clement, Gail. 1994. "Evolution of a Species: Science Journals Published on the Internet." *Database* 17, no. 5: 44–46, 48–52, 54.

Dulle, F. W., and M. K. Minishi-Majanja. 2009. "Researchers' Perspectives on Open Access Scholarly Communication in Tanzanian Public Universities." *South African Journal of Information Management* 11, no. 4 (April 20): 413+.

Elsevier. 2013a. "Elsevier's 'Article of the Future' Is Now Available for All Cell Press Journals." PR Newswire. Accessed March 26. http://www.prnewswire.com/news-releases/elseviers-article-of-the-future-is-now-available-for-all-cell-press-journals-80913137.html.

Elsevier. 2013b. "Understanding the Publishing Process in Scientific Journals." Elsevier.com. Accessed March 24. http://biblioteca.uam.es/sc/documentos/understanding_the_publishling_process.pdf.

Fjällbrant, Nancy. 1997. "Scholarly Communication—Historical Development and New Possibilities." Purdue University. Proceedings of the 1997 IATUL Conference. Paper 5. http://docs.lib.purdue.edu/cgi/viewcontent.cgi?article=1389&context=iatul.

Frohmann, Bernd. 2013. "The Role of the Scientific Paper in Science Information Systems." University of Western Ontario. Accessed March 25. http://instruct.uwo.ca/faculty/Frohmann/ASIS%20Scidoc.PDF.

Gribbin, John. 2007. *The Fellowship: Gilbert, Bacon, Harvey, Wren, Newton, and the Story of a Scientific Revolution*. London: Overlook Hardcover.

Hall, A. Rupert, and Marie Boas Hall. 1962. "Why Blame Oldenburg." *Isis* 53, no. 4 (January): 482–491.

Kaufer, David S., and Kathleen M. Carley. 1984. *Communication at a Distance—The Influence of Print on Sociocultural Organization and Change*. Chicago: University of Chicago Press.

Kuhn, Thomas S. 1970. *The Structure of Scientific Revolutions*. 2nd ed. Chicago: University of Chicago Press.

Lancaster, F. W., ed. 1995. "A Networked Approach to Scholarly Publishing within Universities." *Library Trends—Networked Scholarly Publishing* 43, no. 4 (Spring): 520+.

Large, Andrew, Lucy A. Tedd, and Richard J. Hartley. 1999. *Information Seeking in the Online Age: Principles and Practice*. London: Bowker-Saur.

Mabe, Michael. 2006. "(Electronic) Journal Publishing." *E-Resources Management Handbook*. International Association of Scientific, Technical and Medical Publishing. August 23, 56–66. http://www.stm-assoc.org/2006_08_23_Electronic_Journal_Publishing.pdf.

Mabe, Michael A. 2010. "Scholarly Communication: A Long View." *New Review of Academic Librarianship* 16, no. S1: 132–144.

McGarry, Kevin J. 1981. *The Changing Context of Information: An Introductory Analysis*. London: Bingley.

McKie, Douglas. 1948. "The Scientific Periodical from 1665 to 1798." *Philosophical Magazine* (Commemoration Issue), 122–132.

Meadows, A. J. 1974. *Communication in Science*. London: Butterworths.

Merton, R. K. 1942. "A Note on Science and Democracy." *Journal of Legal and Political Sociology* 1: 115–126.

Merton, Robert K. 1973. *The Sociology of Science*. Chicago: University of Chicago Press.

Mukherjee, Bhaskar. 2009. "Scholarly Communication: A Journey from Print to Web." *Library Philosophy and Practice* (e-journal). http://unllib.unl.edu/LPP/mukherjee.htm.

Park, Ji-Hong. 2008. "The Relationship between Scholarly Communication and Science and Technology Studies (STS)." *Journal of Scholarly Publishing* 39, no. 3 (April): 257–273.

Pöschl, Ulrich. 2012. "Multi-Stage Open Peer Review: Scientific Evaluation Integrating the Strengths of Traditional Peer Review with the Virtues of Transparency and Self-Regulation." *Frontiers in Computational Neuroscience* 6, no. 33 (July 5). doi: 10.3389/fncom.2012.00033.

Potts, Claude H. 2011. "Journal des Savants—From the Republic of Letters to the Cloud Library." *Journal of Scholarly Publishing*, October, 68–75.

Purver, Margery. 1967. *The Royal Society: Concept and Creation*. Cambridge, MA: MIT Press.

Ramalho Correia, Ana Maria, and Jose Carlos Teixeira. 2005. "Reforming Scholarly Publishing and Knowledge Communication: From the Advent of the Scholarly Journal to the Challenges of Open Access." *Information Services & Use* 25: 13–21.

Reid, Calvin. 2008. "Publishers, Librarian Clash over NIH Rule." *Publishers Weekly* 255, no. 1 (January 7): 13.

Rowland, Fytton. 2014. "The Peer Review Process—A Report to the JISC Scholarly Communications Group." Loughborough University. Accessed September 7. http://www.jisc.ac.uk/uploaded_documents/rowland.pdf.

Royal Society of London. 1665. *Order in Council* (March 5).

Smelser, Neil J., and Paul B. Baltes, eds. 2001. *International Encyclopedia of the Social & Behavioral Sciences*. Oxford: Elsevier Science Ltd.

Smith, John W. T. 1999. "The Deconstructed Journal—A New Model for Academic Publishing." *Learned Publishing* 12: 79–91.

Smith, Richard. 2006. "Peer Review: A Flawed Process at the Heart of Science and Journals." *Journal of the Royal Society of Medicine* 99, no. 4 (April): 178–182.

Vannevar, Bush. 1945. "Science—The Endless Frontier." Washington, DC: United States Government Printing Office, July 25. http://www.nsf.gov/od/lpa/nsf50/vbush1945.htm.

Weller, Ann C. 2002. *Editorial Peer Review: Its Strengths and Weaknesses*. Medford, NJ: American Society for Information Science and Technology.

Yiotis, Kristin. 2005. "The Open Access Initiative: A New Paradigm for Scholarly Communications." *Information Technology and Libraries* 24, no. 4: 157–162.

Chapter Three

The Scholarly Book

Its Hard Times and Rise Again

Scholarly research is published in a number of forms. Though the peer-reviewed journal article and journals seem to get most of the attention today, the scholarly book once was on equal footing in terms of quantity and quality of publishing and importance to researchers. As the cost of printing books went up and the cost of printing journal articles went down, largely due to the Internet, books lost some of their popularity. It is yet one more example of how scholarly communication is in a constant state of flux.

In the following sections, the history of scholarly books is reviewed, followed by a discussion on the transition from print to digital books (e-books). The history of books, like journal articles, is intricately tied to the history of academic institutions, so there is also a review of the role of academic and research libraries in influencing book publishing and the impact on scholars and publishers. The discussion concludes with a look at the current status of the scholarly book market and the outlook for this form of scholarly communication in the future.

WHAT IS A SCHOLARLY BOOK?

Definition of the Scholarly Book

There are different types of scholarly books, but the broadest definition is simply that it is a form of formal scholarly communication. The scholarly book (as opposed to a trade publication) contains information that can be critically examined and verified, establishes priority of academic or research work, and establishes authorship. The book may contain text, tables, diagrams, description of methods, results, and any other information the scholar deems appropriate. It is also disseminated to a group of readers (Mukherjee, 2009). One of the main differences between the scholarly book and the scholarly journal is that more inclusive characteristics apply to books than to articles in the scholarly realm. Not all scholarly book chapters are necessarily peer reviewed, for example. They get their authority from the authors, where the authors work, and the publisher's willingness to disseminate their works. In that sense, the University College London definition stating, "Scholarly Communication is the method and route by which academic information is passed from author to reader, via various intermediaries such as libraries and publishers," would consider scholarly books one method of information transmission (University College London, 2010).

Scholarly books do have certain characteristics that define them as scholarly versus popular literature. The purpose of the scholarly book is to discuss original research, provide a review of literature, and advance the body of knowledge of a particular discipline. The work is cited, written by a scholar or researcher, targeted to a scholarly readership, and published by a commercial publisher or university press that specializes in scholarly publishing. Publishers may or may not send materials to peer reviewers before publishing, depending on the type of book, but most scholarly books are heavily edited.

Types of Scholarly Books

Scholarly books represent information that advances academic and research knowledge; therefore, they can include a variety of works, such as monographs, edited volumes or collections, textbooks, reference works, and technical handbooks.

Monographs

The monograph is a one-volume scholarly work that gives extensive treatment of a particular topic. It may be written by one or more scholars, contains a review of relevant literature, and presents original research. The intended audience is other scholars or people who have the same knowledge level. Monographs are particularly suitable for scientific, technical, and medical (STM) publishing because there is a well-defined and established body of knowledge.

The question arises: How are scholarly monographs identified? There are several clues. The author should hold an advanced degree or be recognized as an authority on the subject. Typically, scholars work at universities or research institutions, but they may also work in commercial research organizations. Scholarly monographs are published by university presses, commercial publishers recognized as scholarly works publishers, or scholarly societies.

There are quality citations, meaning there are other scholarly works, such as monographs and peer-reviewed journal articles, supporting the original work.

Edited Volumes or Collections

Edited volumes constitute a collected work that may present original research, summaries of existing research, or reviews of literature. Contributors are carefully selected to ensure that the final product is cohesive. It may be written by one author or by multiple authors from the same research field or a group of related fields. In some forms, each chapter has been written by a different author. The idea is that researchers complement each other's works, adding higher value to the knowledge base. Scholarly edited volumes that review literature should advance scholarship by utilizing and synthesizing the information to present new conceptual information. Authors should have demonstrable authority. Simple reviews of literature do not constitute scholarly works.

Scholarly edited volumes have been heavily edited, and, depending on the collection, often each chapter is peer reviewed to ensure that the material meets the highest quality standards for scholarly research. In a collective work, the authors have generally reviewed each other's material and then used the information to generate original research that advances scholarship (Academy of Science of South Africa, 2009).

Edited volumes are criticized at times for being a means of publishing lower-quality work or research that is significantly outside the mainstream and would likely not be taken up by a scholarly journal. Edited volumes that merely summarize existing research or review literature do not fit the definition of scholarly works unless a new concept is introduced that advances scholarship. The edited volumes do make important contributions to research, but they must be closely scrutinized to ensure that the work meets the definition of scholarly communication. This particular type of scholarly book can vary considerably in quality, depending on the level of review to which it is subjected before publishing.

Textbooks

The typical modern textbook written specifically for classroom use is usually not considered a true scholarly work according to the definition of scholarly communication. It is not peer reviewed and does not present original research. Textbooks are a form of scholarly communication only in the sense that they transmit academic information. However, there are books used in classrooms that were not originally written as textbooks. They may or may not be peer reviewed. They are usually classics written many years ago that presented groundbreaking and seminal research.

Reference Works

Reference works summarize all the known information about a particular subject. The key features of the reference work are that it is comprehensive and heavily edited. These types of works include specialist dictionaries, encyclopedias, and specialty reference manuals. The books can be organized in different ways, including alphabetically or by theme.

Technical Handbooks

STM technical handbooks cover particular techniques, technologies, or procedures. They are intended to be practitioner guides used in the field or as a work reference. They are manuals, clinical references, clinical handbooks, laboratory guides, and so on. Elsevier produced some of the first pocket-sized handbooks, as discussed in succeeding sections.

HISTORY OF THE SCHOLARLY BOOK

Tracing the history of the scholarly book is not easy because scholarly publishing was not formally recognized as such in the 1550s. One of the easiest ways to trace the path of monographs and other scholarly research is to consider some major works plus the history of Elsevier, now one of the largest publishers of scholarly works. This will give a good idea of how scholarly books progressed through the decades.

Until the Gutenberg press was introduced in the middle of the fifteenth century, the nearest thing to a book was the codex, which replaced the scroll. The codex was a set of folded sheets, secured on one edge, with thick front and back covers. This was the main form of book publishing until the Gutenberg revolution, which allowed the mass production of books and other material beginning in 1450 with the first printing press. One of the earliest STM scholars was Robert Recorde, born in 1510 in Wales. He is chosen as a good example of early scholarship because he was one of the first to point out that the mass production of books did not mean that the books advanced medicine. Recorde was accomplished in mathematics and chose to enter medicine as his profession. In his 1548 book *Urinal of Physick*, he asks physicians to "refuse such trifling books, as are set forth in too great a number, and that rather for the advantage of the Printer than for the furtherance of man's health" (Lipscombe, 2012: 383). This foreshadowed issues that would later appear in the modern, technological era, in which content, even scholarly content, can be and perhaps is being more and more commoditized.

Early scholars had an interest in religion, and it was Christians who first adopted the codex for theological writings. Robert Recorde was a typical scholar, publishing books devoted both to religion and to science and math.

Before publishing the *Urinal of Physick*, he published one of the first "arithmetics" to be written in English in 1543 called the *Ground of Artes*. The book is significant because it used a dialogue format and was an early textbook in that it was intended to be a teaching tool (Pycior, 2003). Recorde wrote a trilogy of mathematical books with the *Whetstone of Witte*, published in 1557. Since he was writing in English, he believed it was necessary to develop technical language, something that his publisher allowed him to do. The result was the creation of the equals sign so that the words "is equal to" did not have to be written over and over again. The printers also let him use the plus sign, minus sign, and square-root symbol in the book, written in English (Lipscombe, 2012). The use of symbols showed the power and the innovativeness of the publisher. The forward-thinking publisher of *Whetstone of Witte* was Jhon Kyngstone, who later became a premier Cambridge University printer.

Robert Recorde's other publisher was Reyner Wolfe, who published a trilogy of books and became a master of a guild called the Worshipful Company of Stationers (stationers were booksellers). In 1547, the guild started a register. For four pennies, a guild member could obtain a license to print a named book. In exchange for the payment, the printer obtained exclusive rights to the book, thus creating an early form of the copyright. Fines were assessed if printers published unauthorized books. To prevent books being printed that criticized the Crown, the Worshipful Company of Stationers was given exclusive book printing rights in 1557, giving the guild a publishing monopoly until 1692 (Myers and Harris, 1997). At that point, independent printers began publishing and asked Parliament for protection. The first copyright law is referred to as the 1709 Statute of Anne (long title: An Act for the Encouragement of Learning, by vesting the Copies of Printed Books in the Authors or purchasers of such Copies, during the Times therein mentioned), and it gave fourteen years of protection, with right of renewal for another fourteen years, to authors not yet printed and twenty-one years of protection to published authors instead of publishers (Rose, 1993).

Robert Recorde's books were reprinted several times. Other early STM authors were also publishing monographs. For example, Robert Morison published the first monograph of plant taxon in 1672 titled *Plantarum Umbelliferarum Distributio Nova* and written in Latin. Many consider taxonomy the first "science."

A good way to understand the progression of scholarly book publishing from this point is to consider the history of an academic publishing company such as Elsevier, one of the oldest academic publishing houses. In addition, Cambridge and Oxford universities begin university presses to ensure that scholars could publish "all manner of books" and not just scholarship (Black, 1992).

Origins and Rise of a Publishing Company

Louis Elzevir lived from 1540 to 1617 and is considered one of the greatest early publishers. He was not a scholar. He was a businessman. A Dutch printer and bookseller, he published his first book in the Dutch city of Leiden in 1583 and produced over 150 works by 1617. Sometimes Elzevir would take bold risks, such as publishing Galileo's *Discorsi e dimostrazioni matematiche, intorno a due nuove scienze in 1638* (Lemetti, 2012). The Elzevir family ran the publishing business until 1712, producing between 2,000 and 3,000 titles. The original House of Elzevir went out of business in 1712, leaving a publishing legacy. The original business was started after William the Silent established a Dutch university in 1575, suggesting that the publisher was also an early university press.

One of the distinguishing characteristics of the Elzevir line of scholarly books was the fact they were designed to be practical, sturdy, and affordable, so the books were small in size. As a result, the Elzevir name came to be associated with the "pocket-book," a small book that could be carried in the pocket and was printed with small, compact, and elegant print called the "Elzevir Letter." Books with this format and type of print were subsequently published in the late seventeenth century, and the books quickly became collector items. The earliest printed mention of the Elzevir Letter is found in the 1712 *London Gazette*, which announced, "This day is published, in an Elzevir Letter fit for the Pocket, The second edition of the second Part of Bishop Beveridges private Thoughts upon a Christian Life" (Tooke and Barber, 1712). Pocket-books often had religion as their themes, but by the end of the nineteenth century, the term "pocket-book" was in common usage to describe the diminutive, collectible editions of mainly scientific and theological classics. Some of the original scholarly works published included Desiderius Erasmus's *Opera Omnia* in 1636 and *Textus Receptus*, an edited version of the New Testament, in 1663. The House of Elzevir later also published popular books to subsidize the publishing of classics, a practice many university presses adopted hundreds of years later to survive financial crises.

In 1880, Jacobus Robbers started a Dutch publishing company and named it Elsevier in honor of the House of Elzevir. He wanted to take advantage of the reputation the original publishing house had earned. By then, the small Elzevirs, reprints of the original classics, were even more collectible than they were originally. Robbers was interested mostly in continuing the publishing of classics and other scholarly works. In 1887, the business moved from Rotterdam to Amsterdam, the Netherlands publishing center. A turning point for Elsevier came when it began publishing *Winkler Prins Encyclopedia*. In 1883, having obtained the publishing rights to Brockhaus's encyclopedia illustrations, Elsevier eventually published the *A. J. Prins Illustrated Encyclopedia* (Elsevier, 2013).

Over the next forty years, Elsevier gradually moved to publishing mostly science handbooks, textbooks, and encyclopedias. At the start of the decade beginning in 1930, German was the official scientific language, and Germany was the epicenter of scholarly publishing. When the National Socialist Party came to power in Germany in 1933, the epicenter began shifting as a large exodus of scientists occurred, many finding their way to the United States. With the exodus, European scholarly publishing also shifted to a more international focus, and English became increasingly popular as the language of science (Eliot and Rose, 2007).

Elsevier recognized the need to begin publishing scientific works in English and in 1937 began producing the first English translations of German scientific material. One of the first such works was Paul Karrer's *Organic Chemistry*, which was a translation of *Lehrbuch der Organischen Chemie* (Elsevier, 2013). The internationalization of scientific publishing placed pressure on scholars to begin publishing journals and books rather than just scientific dissertations. The 1937 Elsevier publication and others that followed represented the first multinational scientific publications. Elsevier then opened an office in the United Kingdom in 1939, with plans to open other international offices. However, the Nazi army crossed the Dutch border in 1940 and shut down publishing of all works except those written by authors registered with the Kultuur Kamer, driving off German and Dutch editors and scientists. Many of them fled to the United States. Elsevier, still located in the Netherlands, found itself well placed to serve an international scientific community. The first foothold was in books, followed by scientific journals.

A Transitioning Monograph Publishing Environment

By the 1960s, Elsevier was a leader in scientific book publishing. However, as the number of publishing journals grew, the number of monographs declined. By the end of the 1960s, two major factors further influenced monograph publishing: 1) less demand for scholarly publications as university libraries shifted their resources more and more to journals and 2) rising printing costs. Hundreds of years earlier, Elzevir had close connections to a Dutch university, in effect modeling the company into a university press. However, there were university presses founded for the sole purpose of publishing scholarship in monographic form. While Cambridge University Press (founded 1521) and Oxford University Press (also founded 1521) were formed to publish "all manner of book," more than 300 years later, Johns Hopkins University Press in the United States, established in 1878, was created for the express purpose of publishing scholarship, which would include monographs and textbooks (Givler, 2002). This tied one of the primary functions of the university to publishing, no doubt giving root and impetus to the "publish or perish" requirement for faculty tenure and promotion. The early U.S. university presses wanted to showcase publications produced by faculty, researchers, and students at their own institutions.

The early publishing history of monographs at U.S. universities reflects a struggle to identify the role of the university press and the type of materials the presses should print. For example, at the University of California Press, established in 1893, the first publications for forty years were mostly monograph pamphlets and not books. In the 1915–1916 report on the activities of the press, the professional manger criticized the lack of book publishing, saying that the university press did not service scholars outside the university. In 1929, the rules were changed, and in 1933, the University of California Press became a publisher of scholarly books on a commercial basis. Also of significance was the fact that the press revenues would be used to publish books outside the university, moving the press into a distinctly more commercial activity. However, this move also distanced the press from the faculty and turned the university press into a service and business operation. This is a good example of the turmoil of university presses in general as they transitioned from strictly supporting academic missions through the publication of scholarly books and papers to becoming trade book publishers like many are today (Fitzpatrick, 2009).

University presses began largely because commercial publishers were unwilling to publish research that may not have been profitable, while often university presses subsidized some publications with university funds. In the late 1800s, major university presses were started for this reason. Besides the University of California and Johns Hopkins already mentioned, there was the University of Chicago Press and Columbia University Press, to name just a few others that rose to prominence. The University of California Press became a scholarly publishing house in the Oxford-Cambridge tradition of such presses in 1953 after a years-long, in-house battle over its primary function (Muto, 1993).

Expansion of University Presses and Rise of STM Publishing Conglomerates

University presses continued to form during the early decades of the 1900s. During the 1930s and 1940s, the rate of formation grew, slowed during the 1950s, and then resumed growth until the early 1970s, at which time the number of new U.S. university presses began falling. In the late 1960s, certain situations began developing that would lead to major changes in the scholarly book publishing industry.

During the 1960s, U.S. libraries stopped expanding. Up to that point, there seemed to be an insatiable demand for scholarly publications. However, rising publication costs led to the first budget crisis for libraries, which in many respects continues to this day. As more and more of their budgets were devoted to scholarly journal subscriptions, less money was available for purchasing scholarly books, as library budgets were unable to keep up with either the volume or the cost of scholarly materials. Libraries expanded their interlibrary loan programs, creating even less need to purchase original works. As a result, scientific publishing companies began merging to achieve scale, growth, and margin improvements, creating publishing megacompanies. Elsevier was one of the first when it merged with North Holland in 1970 and then with Excerpta Medica in 1971.

The scholarly book and journal publishing industry entered a transition period in the early 1970s that continued well into the 1990s. Kluwer Publishers merged with Wolters Samson in 1987. In 2003, Kluwer Academic Publishers was sold to private investors, who then merged with Bertelsmann-Springer to form Springer Science+Business Media. In 1989, International Thomson Organization Ltd merged with Thomson Newspapers to form the Thomson Corporation, which then merged with Reuters Group to form Thomson Reuters. Book and encyclopedia publisher Springer Publishing Company began in 1950 and was sold to Mannheim Holdings, LLC, in 2004.

Wiley began in 1807, published as Wiley & Putnam beginning in 1848, and became John Wiley & Son in 1865. Like Elsevier, the company produced technical handbooks. In 1880, the *Field Engineering* handbook was published, and the company expanded into a number of STM fields, including engineering and chemistry. Over the next decades, the publisher established global operations and in 1982 acquired Wilson Learning Corporation. In 1989, Wiley significantly expanded its STM publishing program by acquiring Alan R. Liss, a leading publisher of life sciences books and journals. In 1996, Wiley acquired a 90 percent interest in the STM publisher VCH, followed by the acquisition of Van Nostrand Reinhold. In 1999, Wiley acquired Pearson Education's college textbooks and instructional packages and Jossey-Bass, a publisher of journals and books in management, psychology, business, and education (Wiley, 2013).

This brief historical overview of the ever-changing STM commercial publishers is indicative of an industry that has continually adapted. Adaptability and flexibility became even more important as libraries, their primary market, continued to struggle with flat and, in some years, declining budgets and rising publishing costs as well as the introduction of electronic publishing services. Prior to the introduction of electronic publishing in the 1970s, the scholarly book followed a standard publishing process, and the mergers and acquisitions were geared toward expanding product lines and markets. For example, the merger of Elsevier and North Holland represented a combining of complementary businesses. Once digital scholarly communication became a component of the scholarly publication industry, both university presses and commercial publishers had to make radical changes in processes and product availability.

In 1971, the merger of Elsevier and Excerpta Medica represented Elsevier's early entry into electronic databases. Excerpta Medica was an international medical publishing company in the process of creating an electronic database of all medical literature. Elsevier, North Holland, and Excerpta Medica formed the Associated Scientific Publishers and proceeded to become an internationally recognized medical journal publisher. The enormous success of the venture led to the opening of an office in 1984 in Paris. Currently, the Paris division still publishes the Encyclopédie Médico-Chirurgicale. The introduction of technology in the 1980s was certainly not a panacea for publishing challenges. In fact, little progress was made in the 1980s on practical electronic information delivery systems for primary scholarly communications despite numerous efforts. In the meantime, the scholarly book and journal printing continued as it had for decades but now on an international basis. However, even as the industry tried to expand globally, problems, particularly pricing problems, arose because fluctuating currencies were forcing printing prices up and creating havoc with library budgets. Publishers later began pricing in local currencies and used financial hedging against monetary fluctuations, but it was done a decade later and after much alienation with their core library customers.

In 1991, Elsevier was approached by Pergamon, a British company that published over 400 journal titles and major reference works, including The Encyclopedia of Material Science and Engineering and The International Encyclopedia of Education. The acquisition of Pergamon Publishing was a major step in advancing Elsevier's STM publishing reach and status. The next step was the acquisition of The Lancet, followed by a merger with Reed Publishing—primarily a technical, trade, and business publisher, forming Reed Elsevier.

SHIFT FROM PRINT TO DIGITAL

The history of the scholarly monograph and other books shows that for nearly fifty years, little changed in the publishing world. However, it has been proposed that the decline in monograph publishing actually began as far back as the eighteenth century, with specialization in science and the subsequent growth in the number of scientific disciplines. The specialization eventually led to a corresponding increase in domain-specific and more specialized journals and journal articles. By the time a single monograph could be published, hundreds of journal articles on the same or similar topics were produced. Though the monograph has scientific value, the length of time to prepare a complete publishable work could also be viewed as an impediment to the rapid advance of scientific knowledge.

When the 1960s arrived, the process of book publishing had been largely unchanged for hundreds of years, except for advances in printing technology. Scholars submitted works to a publisher, who then sent it to the printer after editing. The printer then sent the books to a university press, library, or commercial distributor. Books reached the readers as a result of a sale or, in the case of the library, through various circulation systems. In the 1960s, what did change for monograph publishing was the addition of a feedback system to ensure the production of quality content. Up to this point, discipline scholars formally reviewed monographs postpublication. The journal article had a system of peer review in process, and the university presses implemented a similar system of external review of monographs. This professionalized monograph publishing at a time when many institutions of higher education were requiring the publishing of monographs to reach tenure or to be promoted. Up to this point, the application of scholarly standards to monographs had been haphazard. Now there was a move to apply peer review to monographs, and university press editors were largely inexperienced to do so. Therefore, they partnered with commercial publishers (Pochoda, 2013). This created a symbiotic relationship that endured without interruption until electronic publishing entered the picture.

The 1960s saw a huge influx of federal funding into universities, triggering a period of growth. The start of the Vietnam War also prompted significant increases in funding from research agencies, such as the National Science Foundation, to research universities. During this time, libraries would spend a considerable amount of their budgets for university press and commercially published scholarly books as a direct result of these grant programs and funds.

As the Vietnam War dragged on, the early 1970s saw a reduction in federal funding to universities. Libraries subsequently saw large decreases in funding. The 1970s was a difficult period that included a stock market crash, inflation, and a recession. This decade saw the formation of publishing conglomerates as well as increases in small publishing houses, both trying to reduce overhead costs and deal with the new economic realities of scholarly publishing, that is, rising print costs as well as needed investments in automation. Academic libraries would not be able to sustain their purchasing levels with increases in journal subscription prices; the declining university allocations to libraries meant fewer book purchases. The print system for scholarly books was, as it turned out, permanently altered and never returned to the volume of published print materials seen in the 1960s and 1970s.

In the 1980s, the economic viability of continuing to publish monographs was questioned. At that time, the shift to digital scholarly communication

was under way. New publishing software and desktop computers were introduced. Large database management programs also appeared, making it possible to store and transmit large files of scholarly materials and texts. Commercial and academic publishers quickly saw the benefits; however, as seen
with Elsevier, it took a whole decade to make real progress in creating
searchable databases and fully electronic publishing systems for primary
research materials. Up to this point, digital technology supported the existing
print system mainly for computer typesetting but did not lead to major market changes, making it a "sustaining innovation" as opposed to a disruptive
innovation such as it became in the 1990s and beyond (Christensen, 1997).

The 1990s saw a lot of changes in scholarly book publishing. It is nearly
impossible to discuss scholarly books and scholarly journals separately because as journal numbers grew exponentially, scholarly books declined.
Their histories are clearly intertwined. The journal article could be produced
faster and cheaper, and university scholars were given credit for their journal
article publishing when it was time for consideration of promotions, tenure,
and compensation. By the 2000s, a typical monograph would sell approximately 100 to 300 copies at the most, making its publishing economics
difficult if not untenable.

The shift from print to digital may have started slowly in the 1980s, but it
gained speed in the 1990s. Software and computer equipment advances,
including the growing Internet, led to the idea of a totally digital publishing
system—that is, digital from "end to end." A monograph could be electronically created, submitted, edited, reviewed, published, distributed, and
archived as well as preserved.

There was a host of digital monographic-based products developed over
the 1990s and 2000s, accelerating the shift to e-books. For example, search
and discovery tools developed by commercial publishers, university presses,
and libraries made scholarly monograph content readily available. Search
enables the location of specific objects based on its characteristics or properties. Discovery broadened the ability to search for objects based on conceptu-
alized characteristics or properties, thus identifying materials that would not
have fit within specific parameters. As technology advanced, search and
discovery moved beyond identifying materials by traditional bibliographic
data, such as author, title, and subject. Scholars can locate relevant information that includes charts, diagrams, key words in chapter headings, and so on.
The functionalities of the system now take on equal footing in importance
with the content of scholarship. Buyers of these electronic services now
make their purchasing decisions not only on the scope and quality of the
content but also on the system attributes, features, and functionalities.

In 2013, the University of Chicago Press and Oxford University Press
announced the launch of Chicago Scholarship Online on the Oxford University Press Scholarship Online (UPSO) platform. The fully enabled XML

environment provides search and discovery functionality and access to the full text of 300 published monographs that cross disciplines. Past search operations of monographs crossing disciplines required using multiple search engines, creating a barrier to online monograph research. The newest technology allows researchers to access monographs between multiple academic disciplines using a single search engine. In addition to the 300 full-text monographs, the new search and discovery services give scholars access to over 11,000 titles and can do deep searching of chapter titles, bibliographies, and footnotes and is cross-referenced and cross-searchable (Association of Subscription Agents and Intermediaries, 2013).

Coupled with the continued rise of the journal article was the seemingly continuous upgrades in technology. In 1997, Elsevier launched ScienceDirect, a web-accessible full-text database of its full STM journal collection. This may well have signaled a turning point in scholarly publishing, as it offered a huge corpus of primary scholarly materials that was well known in the scientific community and began efforts to find ways to preserve digital information even as technology changed. It was not just journal articles that were first made accessible online; scholarly books were to soon follow. By 2005, Elsevier was producing over 1,800 journals and approximately 3,000 new books annually and making these available over the Internet. Elsevier's journal and book growth was achieved through original publishing and the acquisition of collections. In 2001, Reed Elsevier purchased most of Harcourt General's publications, and much of it was medical works that included imprints by prestigious publishers, such as Mosby, Saunders, and Churchill Livingstone. The Harcourt purchase also brought scientific works published by Academic Press and texts for nurses and allied health practitioners. Elsevier acquired scientific handbooks, medical dictionaries, textbooks, medical reference books, and much more. Elsevier then acquired Hanley & Belfus, Inc., which was a medical textbook publisher.

The impact of a still highly diversified publishing industry but with a few large players meant more opportunities for the publisher producing non–mass market titles, like the university presses, but only if they could afford the significant digital equipment and software expenses connected with electronic publishing. Iowa State University learned early on that it could not afford such equipment and sold its university press to Blackwell Science in 2001. The original target set by the press was that $100,000 per year would be earned on the electronic revenues, which would support future scholarly publications. However, the capital investments required for electronic publishing were significantly greater than originally estimated by Iowa State University Press and other university presses now out of business and caused them to scale back rather than expand their operations (Robertson, 2002).

Commercial publishers have also moved toward including books in their search functions. For example, Thomson Reuters offers the Book Citation Index as part of the Web of Science, making it possible to use a single search engine to search across books, journals, and conference proceedings to identify the citation networks relevant to their research. Currently, 40,000 titles are included, and there are plans to expand the index coverage by 10,000 new titles each year. The Thomson Reuters system includes comprehensive cited reference search, reciprocal links between book records and chapters, times cited for books and book chapters, links from book and book chapters to full text, and full book bibliographies. Titles include books and e-books (Thomson Reuters, 2013). This information is relevant because it provides a comprehensive research review. Since from an early time search and discovery services have focused on journal articles, the wealth of scholarly information in books is often searched using an entirely different process than the one used to search journal articles.

The shift to e-books was also the result of financial pressures. Printed books are expected to be between 100 and 400 pages and to meet certain formatting requirements. Scholars had to be able to fit their materials within the length. Publishers often could not justify the cost of printing the book based on expected sales, and the scholar had to arbitrarily shorten or expand text to fit within the predefined format (Pochoda, 2013). E-books can be any length and made to fit a variety of formats and cost significantly less than print versions. The marginal cost of additional digital printing, unlike physical printing, is negligible—at or very near zero.

E-books also offer an opportunity to expand scholarly communication because they can be quickly and inexpensively published. There is opportunity for increased interactions between authors, readers, and publishers on a pre- and postpublication basis. One challenge that does emerge, however, is the ability to provide proper documentation to the original publication version as well as finding a way to ensure that readers are informed as to the version they are reading. Another challenge is ensuring the integrity of the authors' versions, making sure no changes to this original manuscript were made.

There are other economic reasons why monographs, considered important to scholarship for hundreds of years, began to decline. In the 1980s, the U.S. Congress implemented a tax on publisher inventories. Slow-moving printed works had to be eliminated to reduce the tax bill. Since monographs fit that description, publishing inventories were reduced. Also encouraging the demise of the monograph was the reader's greater interest in books that covered wider topical material as opposed to the more narrow, detailed, and specialized monograph.

One of the impediments to the adoption of e-book versions of monographs is the lack of accreditation by universities as the distinction between formal published and "self-published" arose. Scholars are not given recognition for publishing e-books in the same way that they get credit for print books. There is still an assumption that digital books do not meet strict scholarly standards, such as peer review and extensive editing. Self-publishing is a fairly new concept that is facing resistance from the scholarly and academic communities because of the issue of refereeing and editing.

The Path of Humanities and Social Sciences

The topic of humanities and social sciences (HSS) scholarly books technically goes back to the first known papyrus scrolls dating back to approximately 2400 BC. In 1455, Gutenberg and Fust printed the Bible, which certainly can be considered a humanities book. In 1640, Cambridge Press at Harvard College began publishing Bibles translated into Native American languages and books on law. Before the introduction of the scientific method, there was no distinction made between humanistic studies and science. The Aristotelian view of the physical sciences was entwined with philosophy, theology, ethics, and so on, and his influence lasted until the fourteenth century. During the Renaissance, the term *studia humanitatis* emerged, which referred to the study of poetry, grammar, rhetoric, philosophy, and history. This group of intellectual pursuits is the foundation for the eventual emergence of HSS as a group of disciplines.

The separation of HSS began when Francis Bacon introduced the scientific research method, first published in the 1620 document titled *Instauratio Magna*, in which he introduces the use of inductive reasoning. The importance of this event to HSS is that scholars became increasingly focused on science and the scientific method, perhaps to the detriment of humanistic studies, and that has spurred a centuries-long debate on which has more value—humanities or science, continuing to this day.

The recognition of HSS as separate and distinct from physical sciences (now STM) is traced to the Italian political philosopher Giambattista Vico. He published numerous works on poetry, philosophy, classical authors and antiquities, and much more. He also defended Bacon's scientific philosophy in the 1709 work titled De nostri temporis studiorum ratione. However, as time went on, Vico brooded on the difference between humanities and science and eventually came to a conclusion that impacted scholarly publications from that point forward. He first argued that mathematics was not a discovery; it was a human invention that followed man-made rules. From this followed the belief that science and mathematics were marvelous achievements, but they represented man viewing the world like an audience member watching nature unfold on a stage. These disciplines did not advance the understanding of human activities, thoughts, goals, imagination, feelings, motives, and a host of other intangible emotions. In his opinion, applying the unified rules and laws of physics or other sciences to the human mind, from whence the humanities emanate, was a serious error because it ignored the most important quality of humans, which is the ability to achieve self-awareness (Berlin and University of Illinois at Urbana-Champaign, 1974).

For Vico, the humanities represented an attempt to grasp the "humankind of the past" by analyzing and understanding language, myths, and rites. By "humankind of the past" is meant gaining a greater understanding of what people felt and thought and why they acted as they did, thus gaining insight into present-day feelings, thoughts, and actions. Vico's most influential work was *The New Science*, first published in 1725, which represented the accumulation of his philosophical themes on the humanities, including rhetoric, language, history, philology, causality, truth, and wisdom. The work was revised and published again in 1729 and a third time in 1744. In 1928, the Vico work was edited by Fausto Nicolini, who converted it into the current scholarly book structure of chapters, sections, and numbered paragraphs. Vico believed that the scientific method often forced something to be true, whether or not it was actually true. He distinguishes between "the true" (*il vero*), the object of knowledge addressing the universal and eternal, and "the certain," which concerns human consciousness. This led to the terms "il vero/sienna" and "il cero/coscienza," which are essentially philosophy and philology or history (Costelloe, 2012).

One of the earliest published works on social sciences is the *Encyclopédie ou Dictionnaire Raisonné des Sciences, des Arts et dés Métiers*. It was published during the French Age of Enlightenment over a twenty-six-year period from 1751 to 1777, eventually included twenty-one volumes, and represented the collaboration of more than 140 people through the contribution of articles. The "Philosophes" publishing the *Encyclopédie* believed in using the experimental method to study the natural world and human affairs by studying natural laws that are discoverable through human endeavor rather than supernatural revelations. The Philosophes included Voltaire, Montesquieu, Rousseau, Turgot, and Buffon, to name the most well known. The *Encyclopédie* is the root of the modern encyclopedia and was a major work and quite controversial. Diderot believed that man is a part of nature and that Christianity and the Roman Catholic Church limited man. For centuries prior to the publication of the *Encyclopédie*, religion had played a central cultural role, making this publication a direct attack on the current way of life. In Diderot's philosophy is found the roots of the study of society and its influences and products, from the mercantilist economic policies to government laws, such as the suppression of natural laws of justice. The *Encyclopédie* had three important goals: 1) reach a large audience, 2) encourage research at all production stages, and 3) publish all advanced, developed methods. Ultimately, Diderot and his fellow authors hoped to promote liberal economic views and do away with the mercantilist system that protected certain groups of people (Proust, 1967).

The emergence of HSS took centuries, but it was not until the late nineteenth century that humanities was considered a separate field of study concerned with the expressions of the human mind. It includes linguistics, philology, art history, musicology, and literary theory and all their subsets, such as poetry, logic, theater, and historical disciplines and, in some schools, philosophy and theology. Social sciences is the study of humans in social contexts and includes psychology, sociology, economics, and anthropology and all of the related subsets. A new work proposes that the separation of humanities and science is not important. Rather, the more fundamental question is the extent to which the artifacts representing the expression of the human mind can be called empirical. Manuscripts, monographs, books, paintings, music pieces, literary works, and other products are open to empirical research and thus hypotheses (Zuccala, 2013).

HSS monographs and books have largely been a product of the universities since the mid-1800s. In 1869, Cornell University opened the first university press; its books included one that was a French reader and one on North American ethnology. Johns Hopkins University Press began in 1878 and has continued operating uninterrupted to the present. The university presses started because scholars believed the commercial publishers would exclude too many important scholarly works in the interest of making an excessive profit. By 1937, there were so many university presses in operation that the managers formed the American Association of University Presses.

By 1957, however, there was great interest in the space program. The race to reach the moon prompted a flow of funding into the universities as the NDEA (National Defense Education Act) funded STM research, but it also provided funding for a number of HSS programs and libraries. The money was used for research, publications, and increasing library collections. In 1969, the United States landed on the moon and then turned its attention to the costly Vietnam War. The year 1970 was a turning point in the United States for the publication of HSS monographs—a point of funding decline. As U.S. government funding for higher education fell, the university libraries began to cut back on the purchase of scholarly monographs and primarily in the HSS fields of study. To allocate increasingly scarce resources in acquisition budgets, the libraries shifted money into the purchase of STM scholarly journals. As the journal prices went up and budgets shrank, libraries had to cut serials purchases. Fewer purchases from university presses meant that less cash was available from the sales of scholarly monographs, and that meant less ability to publish new monographs. The university presses relied on funding from groups like the National Endowments of the Humanities, which funded 1,050 scholarly books in the humanities from 1977 to 1995. The Andrew W. Mellon Foundation subsidized humanities book publishing

in the 1970s and 1980s and continues to provide support for university presses. The university presses have been instrumental in publishing HSS books
of regional and community interest, textbooks, and reference books. A good
example is the Yale University Press publication titled *Culture and Civilization of China*, a 75-volume work (Givler, 2002).

The funding issues have created what has often been referred to as an
HSS monograph crisis. The available library and university press funding is
continuing to shrink as budgets get smaller and the price and number of STM
journal titles increase. Lengthy discourses have been written on the equal
importance of the HSS field of study compared to STM scholarly works. Of
importance to this discussion is the move to expand use of electronic monographs (e-monographs) publishing and electronic books (e-books) as a means
of restoring the ability of scholars to publish in nonscientific and technological fields. What has slowed the publishing of HSS e-monographs has been a
proclivity among humanities scholars to use the printed monograph as a
means of registering research, ideas, and thoughts. Tradition and culture have
slowed adoption of the e-monograph, yet there is evidence that younger
scholars are much more willing to adopt e-publications. Since tenure and pay
for faculty scholars continues to be tied to successful publication of scholarly
works, there is increasing pressure on universities and libraries to adopt new
approaches to monograph publishing (Adema and Rutten, 2010). Unlike the
STM industry, most doctoral students in HSS will never see their doctoral
theses published because there has been limited commercial value in these
areas of research (Steele, 2008).

The very issue that Vico addressed concerning an overemphasis on science at the expense of humanities is the same issue of concern today. Yet
there is an undeniable push to restore the importance of publishing HSS
monographs and scholarly books. The structure of academic publishing is
changing, and it may well be that electronic publishing will prove to be the
means for reinvigorating HSS publishing levels. However, it is true that
culture and tradition continue to make printed monographs the preferred HSS
format. Many still do not see the Internet as being an effective means of
dissemination, and thus they still rely on printed books (Steele, 2008). It
remains to be seen if the modern, electronic publishing industry will offer
more opportunity to expand the ability to publish, disseminate, and build a
larger audience in the HSS field of study.

Winners and Losers

Libraries

As libraries shifted their budgets into electronic journals, they lost much of
their power to shape the collection of scholarly book and monograph materi-

als. That scholarly book publishing has declined does not mean libraries would have chosen to reduce book access. It became a matter of offering the largest amount of material to researchers within budgetary constraints. With the introduction of electronic collections, libraries were given access to large and often comprehensive digital libraries of all the material offerings from a publisher in that domain. The so-called bundled journal collections represented marginal price increases for significant content expansion, but some libraries felt that other terms of purchasing these digitally bundled collections were too onerous. As libraries had previously been forced to reduce their print journal holdings, they now saw digital collections both as important and as a way to recover access to some of the journals previously cut from the holdings of the university. However, one of the unintended effects of this increased investment in digital journal collections, when library budgets were flat or declining, was to "squeeze" the purchases of monographs and books.

However, it should also be pointed out that libraries are today increasing access to scholarly books, as e-versions of these materials are becoming more available and in a variety of different access formats. Publishers, through digital production, can once again offer a wider range of books and monographs with specialized topics, while libraries have a variety of business models to choose from in acquiring these types of materials.

Publishers

Publishers have profited financially through the development of large digital content collections for both journals and, more recently, books. These large digital collections have decreased production and customer transaction costs while at the same time meeting a strong library market need to rebuild local collection holdings. The consumption of these large digital collections seems to be most prominent in large academic institutions.

Publishers also have more total control over database content. Often these collections can be customized for individual libraries and thus seem to create opportunities for both university libraries and publishers alike. John Wiley & Sons, a major STM publisher, for example, reported 20 percent e-book growth in the third quarter of 2013, which offset a reduction in print book sales, as print book sales fell 5 percent. Wiley also introduced an alternative online access license based on a calendar year rather than one that is issue specific (Digital Book World, 2013).

It is becoming clear that publishers can create even more value by adding e-books and e-monographs to their publishing platforms. Elsevier, for instance, announced in 2012 that its books division was adding over 1,000 titles to Academic Complete, an online subscription database with over 78,000 e-books (PR Newswire, 2012).

Scholars

Electronic publications are still developing and only beginning to find their way into universities for faculty evaluation purposes. They are also generally overlooked in the review pages of journals. Yet the digital transition has made a wider array of research materials available, as these materials can be accessed without limitation of geography, time, or date of publication. Electronic publishing also opens up new publishing opportunities. Scholars, who would have been overlooked by publishers in the past, have a greater probability of being published when the price of publishing is reduced. In addition, the academic community is beginning to realize the need to overcome biases toward online publishing and establish standards for recognition of published electronic documents.

Finally, the growing desire of scholars to utilize open access forums for publishing and research is increasingly recognized by the universities and publishers. They are slowly responding by changing pricing structures for access to online documents and adding more full-text works, such as monographs—often where the university serves as its own "publisher" itself through its own digital repository program. In 2012, four new digital monograph platforms began competing: Cambridge University Press's University Publishing Online, Oxford University Press's UPSO, Books at JSTOR, and the University Press Content Consortium. Libraries are finding new forms of subscriptions to scholarly monographs and books through these types of resources. Scholars benefit through greater access to research and potentially more developed cross-indexing of books and journal articles.

SCHOLARLY BOOK MARKET

Walt Crawford studied the spending patterns of 661 libraries for the years 2002–2010. The amount spent on serials increased by 51 percent, and the amount spent on books decreased 11 percent. The top quartile of libraries experienced a 41 percent decline in the amount spent on books. The third quartile spent 83 percent of their budgets on subscriptions to e-journals. One view of these trends is that academic libraries are increasingly functioning as article transfer organizations rather than broader scholarly and academic information managers. Researchers needing access to scholarly books, as noted earlier, will find that there has been a decline in the access of these materials (Crawford, 2013).

Sizing the STM book market is not simple because e-book publishing is rapidly changing the picture. A survey of the STM book and e-book market in 2009 involving 170 publishers indicated that 24,000 new titles are published each year. There are over 350,000 scholarly and academic titles already published, including monographs, reference books, handbooks, textbooks, and research reports. In 2009, approximately two-thirds of the publishers were publishing e-books, accounting for 10 percent of total book sales. There are four generic business models used, including subscription, purchase, purchase by book chapter, and rental (Cox and Cox, 2010).

In another survey in 2012, it was estimated that 17 percent of the STM book market was composed of e-books. The e-book market was growing at a faster rate than the total STM market. E-books were growing at 23 percent, while the overall STM market was growing at 4.3 percent. Medical e-books accounted for 35 percent of the e-book market and 44 percent of the print market (Ricci and Ware, 2012). It was believed that commercial publishers had not developed a well-structured distribution of medical e-books, unlike medical e-journals, thus slowing down their acceptance and use. It was also discovered that reference materials were the fastest-growing digital category because they are easy to digitize and are easily adaptable to various multiple uses. Textbooks present greater challenges because they must be adapted to various learning environments (Ware and Mabe, 2012).

Regardless of the type of book material being published, it is clear that e-books are making a significant contribution to the growth of this market. Figure 3.1 illustrates how scholarly book publishing was relatively flat through most of the past decade but grew in volume substantially with the introduction of e-books, as discussed.

University presses continue to be a significant player in the scholarly book publishing market. There are 92 university presses in the United States and Canada that are members of the Association of American University Presses (AAUP). The AAUP reports that its degree-granting U.S. university

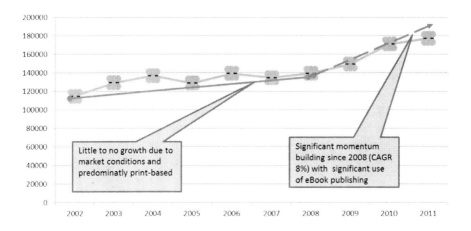

Figure 3.1. Total Scholarly U.S. Book Production by Year, 2002–2011 *Source:* **Bowker annual report on U.S. book publishing, 2011**

members publish approximately 11,000 books per year. Many of the university presses are working on projects, either alone or in collaboration with other universities, to produce e-books and other scholarly communications materials, most notably Johns Hopkins University Press's Project Muse, the Columbia International Affairs Online, MIT Press's Cognet, and a large AAUP project consisting of seven universities working with the American Historical Association and the American Council of Learned Societies (Givler, 2002).

Another segment of the e-book market is shared digital libraries like JSTOR. It is an online library that gets its collection by digitizing content for which it has obtained licenses. The content of JSTOR includes 1,700 academic journals and thousands of monographs and other scholarly material. The material is used by scholars in over 160 countries. Though JSTOR did not originally intend on being a publisher, it has added an initiative to publish scholarly books online. The books collection offers current and backlist books that are cross-searchable with journal articles and other works through citation links and contextualization through book reviews. Currently, there are thirty university presses participating and 15,000 scholarly books available (JSTOR, 2013).

The transition of university presses has led to several printing and publishing initiatives on a large scale. Unlike the small, original versions designed to print only the university's faculty works, the behemoths, such as Cambridge University Press and Oxford University Press, have become global operations. A quick overview of these two university publishers conveys a view of the possible evolution of the small university press into a major, competitive academic publisher. Cambridge University Press has 24,000 authors in 108 countries and publishes through branches in North and South America, Australia, East Asia, Africa, and Iberia. It also has editorial offices located in major global cities. Cambridge University Press publishes print books and e-books for Cambridge University and other universities and learned societies around the world. In the United States, the nonprofit institution has a large group of editors that initiate and manage a wide range of publications. The entire press has over 20,000 titles, which are on display in the UK Press Bookshop (Cambridge University Press, 2013).

Oxford University Press (OUP) publishes more than 6,000 titles annually, including scholarly monographs, journals, higher-education textbooks, dictionaries, and more. An early adopter of computer photocomposition, OUP ended book printing in a print shop in 1989—which had begun in 1478. As the largest university press in the world, OUP now has a presence in over 100 countries. There are online research tools available called Oxford Bibliographies Online. In fact, one of the first online dictionaries was the Oxford English Dictionary, published in 2000.

As the sale of print monographs declined, the large university presses offset these sales by diversifying their publishing programs. Oxford, Cambridge, Johns Hopkins, Yale, Harvard, and Princeton increased publications of reference works, such as encyclopedias and dictionaries. They also publish nonscholarly works, such as trade publications, to subsidize the academic publishing. This led, in many cases, to broad-based publishing efforts made economically viable through the cost-effective use of digital production and distribution technologies and systems.

The Changing Use of Scholarly E-books

ITHAKA is a not-for-profit organization dedicated to helping the academic community make effective use of digital technologies. It offers three services: JSTOR, Portico, and IthakaS+R. ITHAKA conducted the S+R U.S. Faculty Survey in 2012 to identify faculty attitudes, needs, and practices related to research and the discovery, collecting, dissemination, and access of scholarly material. There were a number of interesting results that provided a snapshot of academic researcher attributes and practices as well as insight into the current status of scholarly books and e-books from a researcher perspective. For example, science faculty relied less on scholarly monographs published by academic publishers than faculty in HSS. They relied more on peer-reviewed journals and journal articles and preprint versions of articles destined for publication in peer-reviewed journals (Housewright, Schonfeld, and Wulfson, 2013).

The survey, as expected, found that scholars rely on textbooks for teaching. Science faculty relied more on textbooks but much less on scholarly monographs or monograph chapters than their HSS counterparts. However, the results also indicated that a significant share of respondents assign monograph reading to students. There is also an increasing trend over the past decade or so in which science researchers begin their scholarly research online first rather than at the library. Over half of the scientists surveyed accessed a specific database, and almost 40 percent used a scholarly search engine, such as Google Scholar (Housewright, Schonfeld, and Wulfson, 2013).

The survey also addressed reading patterns involving scholarly monographs. Scholars can now download e-monographs on e-readers, such as the Amazon Kindle, Barnes & Noble Nook, and a variety of Apple products. They can also access e-monographs on Google Books, through library e-book collections, as well as directly from digital libraries of commercial publishers. In the survey, 70 percent of faculty indicated they had used scholarly monographs in the six months before the survey. However, the electronic scholarly monograph was seen as being better suited to some uses, which included searching for a particular topic, exploring references, and skimming the material. Print monographs were seen as better for in-depth reading and reading cover to cover. The key differentiation of e-books that was seen as most important was access to a greater amount of e-monographs, followed by easier navigation; improved ability to download and organize monographs; and improved ability to highlight, annotate, and print scholarly materials. The two most common practices for finding relevant monographs was searching for a freely available online version and using an interlibrary loan system (Housewright, Schonfeld, and Wulfson, 2013).

There are issues concerning scholarly books that must be addressed before e-books can or perhaps should fully replace print versions. Many scholars still want to print out books to use them for markup, monograph comparisons, and convenience. This can get very expensive when using office and home computers, negating any potential cost advantages associated with e-books. Commercial publisher prices for academic e-monographs put them out of reach for many individual researchers and students.

Data security and integrity is another issue that is still evolving in the development of the e-book. Online documents are dynamic, making tracking changes and versioning a challenge. Of course, as in journal publishing, commercial and academic publishers verify the book as primary research, provide a peer-review process, establish a date as the record of publication, and provide a process of preservation and archiving of the final published manuscript through a deposit in the Library of Congress. Without these processes in place, a reader may not know if the document viewed is the published version or if it has been modified in some way.

OUTLOOK FOR SCHOLARLY BOOKS

Overcoming historical scholarly book publishing models appears to be a slow process, but the time line discussed indicates that major changes have occurred in a short period of time. A publishing process that took hundreds of years to develop has been transformed in the past ten to fifteen years. The question now is, What is the outlook for the scholarly book? There are certainly plenty of opinions. Some believe that the narrow focus of the monograph is not a format that fits today's scholarly interdisciplinary research environment. If that is the case, it leads to the conclusion that the scholarly monograph will continue its decline. Yet scientific tradition is strong, and the new improvements and additional functionalities that e-books bring to the market offer a bright future indeed. It is the electronic scholarly book that will likely save the monograph from extinction. The e-book version of the scholarly book is much more affordable than the printed version. Lower production costs and the ability to be included and searched within a larger digital library significantly increase the utility of the e-book. That additional utility is a critical factor as library budgets continue to decline.

Though the future of the e-book seems increasingly bright, the issue of refereeing and editing must be resolved to the satisfaction of the academic community before online publications will be fully accepted as legitimate publishing for purposes of tenure, promotion, and compensation. There are many opportunities to self-publish, and that model is still transitioning. Scholarly books earn "value" based mostly on the publishing house reputation and brand. Recognized, quality academic publishers employ a peer-review process and seek a number of opinions before deciding to publish. The academic community is aware of this process and relies on it as a means of certification, assurance, and verification of quality.

Some analysts theorize that one of the drivers of the continued move to e-books is the fact the younger generation of scholars is more interested in sharing and feedback than in participating in the traditional academic publishing system. These scholars believe that presenting the ideas and concepts and getting critical reviews is more important than a peer-review system following a rigid formula. Right now, nonrefereed monographs would get little attention from academics. Yet there are visions of a digital scholarly publishing system that displaces the hierarchical, structured system that exists today. In the new system, communities of scholars share interests embedded in scholarly book publishing but without restrictions associated with traditional mechanisms for rewarding faculty performance. The communities may be the university at large, a group of scholars from within a discipline, and/or an online community of scholars. The perspective is that community knowledge is greater than individual knowledge, and thus the community can produce higher-quality scholarly works that advance scientific knowledge (Pochoda, 2013). The scholarly monograph may be published online, asking for community feedback. The community can leave feedback, provide peer review, or even add to the product in some cases. A community system of publishing will undoubtedly require community editors to maintain quality.

For such a system to work, the university must be willing to promote the freest and widest system for publishing—one in which the scholars on the web are embraced. In addition, libraries must be capable of redefining some of their core activities, assuming the tasks of locating, sorting, storing, archiving, preserving, and displaying formally reviewed materials and informal scholarly communication. The peer-review process will likely undergo a shift to meet the needs of a less formal publishing environment where open-source publishing becomes a more common practice.

One of the business models that could emerge is the "freemium" model, in which the basic book content is free online but other functions require payment of a fee. Additional services include reformatting, printing, testing, adding class-support tools, updating, and so on. Some universities, such as the Massachusetts Institute of Technology (MIT), are experimenting in adjacent areas with this approach, for example, making course materials freely available online. The MIT Open Courseware project gives access to anyone. They include video lectures, lecture notes, assignments, and exams, and if you want credit for the course, a payment is required. One of the main advantages of online publishing is that the content can be multimedia. This includes audio files, animated graphics, images, videos, software, numeric data files, and so on. These cannot be easily included in print books, requiring a CD or online supplement and thus increasing the cost of the genre even more. The monograph is a comprehensive scholarly inquiry that works out an argument in full and presents all relevant evidence, consequences, and counterarguments (Willinsky, 2009). In the electronic age, these important components can easily be linked to the monographs or other scholarly books. A hundred years ago, it was impossible to add a picture of an atom or DNA to support theories, and now those types of images are integral to scientific discussions. As Clifford Lynch, the executive director of the Coalition for Networked Information, stated, "Just because the existing scholarly publishing system has served the academy fairly well in the past does not mean that it has an intrinsic right to continue to exist in perpetuity. It should not, and must not, become a barrier to our aspirations and our innovations" (Lynch, 2006). Of course, who will drive the new form of publication forward remains an open question for debate and observation. Publishers, commercial and society based, continue to innovate, adding more and more functionality to their content, while universities and other academic institutions experiment with digital repositories for the creation and dissemination of their intellectual properties.

Arguments are made for the belief that the traditional system for inspiring, developing, printing, and disseminating the scholarly book has become a barrier to innovation and limits dissemination. Intellectual output is suppressed in the hundreds-year-old system, whereas the web-based system promotes knowledge creation and dissemination by increasing access. Printed monographs, for example, are easily excluded from the vigorous online discussions that take place. The decline in monograph publishing has been a natural offshoot of university presses losing their alignment with university core administrative structures. Working in isolation, the university presses have become profit centers rather than operations supporting core values of the university (Brown, Griffiths, and Rascoff, 2007).

The future of the scholarly book will depend on a number of factors. Universities must realign the role of their respective university presses so that they support the scholarly values of the academic community. Universities will need to establish formal strategies that incorporate e-books into the scholarly communication system, making them more viable. As both publishers and universities increasingly add electronic publishing options to their services, there will be an eventual change in faculty perceptions. The future of the scholarly book lies in electronic publishing and in giving wider access to what is published. Harvard University recognized this by issuing the Harvard University Declaration in February 2008, which was the first such U.S. policy adopted by faculty and not just administrators. Though first applying only to Harvard's Faculty of Arts and Sciences, it was later taken by the Harvard library to the rest of the institution (Suber, 2008). The declaration makes research available in an open access repository containing books and articles. Following Harvard's lead, a number of universities implemented similar policies. And today, there is the beginning of private-public partnerships to leverage these developments.

In the future, it is highly likely that universities will be challenged to take a leading role in the production, dissemination, archiving, and storage of scholarly books in electronic form. Through a cooperative global network of universities, for example, scholarly e-books could be distributed internationally. University presses will become e-presses if for no other reason than that the high cost of printing will further limit their ability to produce paper documents. As technology advances and e-readers become compatible, scholars will increasingly adopt electronic systems. The academic monograph is reviving, but quality control could shift to the universities as open access services grow. Within the university framework, distribution of scholarly books will ensure that authority is combined with public accessibility (Steele, 2008).

The future of the STM scholarly book is tied to the shifting of science to Asia as well. This will necessitate the adoption of e-book publishing by scholars who do not want to find themselves outside the mainstream of information flow. Before the Internet, the intermediation of publishers was necessary, leading to a scarcity of information due to cost constraints (Hahn, 2008). Commercial publishers may find that their future role is tied more to their ability to develop and support the kind of infrastructure needed to support a global communication system than to their content production and the control of the refereeing and editing system. They may well have the responsibility of maintaining the global indexing and citation databases, tying all the scholarly community together. Citation rates will be one factor exerting quality control in open publishing systems. It is difficult to imagine the traditional system remaining unchanged.

Monographs and other types of scholarly books are likely to see a vigorous revival as the cost of publishing dramatically declines with the increasing use of technology. It is possible that an organized digital scholarly publishing system will emerge from what seems like a somewhat chaotic system in place now. Electronic publishing and dissemination of scholarly works is revitalizing scholarly efforts that were arbitrarily suppressed by an antiquated publishing system. In the meantime, scholars are increasingly turning to the

Internet and electronic publishing as a way to disseminate knowledge—faster and cheaper. Technology gives scholars the ability not only to share research but also to collaborate and copublish. The decline in scholarly printed books will continue, but in its place will be an increase in scholarly e-books with a new robust set of functions and added values, moving the book of the future well beyond a content compendium.

REFERENCES

Academy of Science of South Africa. 2009. "Scholarly Books: Their Production, Use and Evaluation in South Africa Today." Academy of Science of South Africa. August. http://www.assaf.co.za/wp-content/uploads/2009/09/ASSAF-Scholarly-Report-FINAL-Proof.pdf.

Adema, Janneke, and Paul Rutten. 2010. "Digital Monographs in the Humanities and Social Sciences: Report on User Needs." Open Access—Publishing in European Networks. January. http://openreflections.files.wordpress.com/2008/10/d315-user-needs-report.pdf.

Association of Subscription Agents and Intermediaries. 2013. "University of Chicago Press to Make Scholarly Monograph Content Available via OUP's UPSI Platform." Association of Subscription Agents and Intermediaries. Last modified February 26. http://subscription-agents.org/university-chicago-press-make-scholarly-monograph-content-available-oups-upso-platform.

Berlin, Sir Isaiah, and University of Illinois at Urbana-Champaign. 1974. "The Divorce between the Sciences and the Humanities." Tykociner Lecture Committee. University of Illinois. http://berlin.wolf.ox.ac.uk/published_works/ac/divorce.pdf.

Black, Michael H. 1992. *A Short History of Cambridge University Press*. Cambridge: Cambridge University Press.

Brown, Laura, Rebecca Griffiths, and Matthew Rascoff. 2007. "University Publishing in a Digital Age." *Ithaka Report*, July 26, 1–69. http://www.sr.ithaka.org/sites/default/files/reports/4.13.1.pdf.

Cambridge University Press. 2013. "About Us." Cambridge University Press. Accessed June 1. http://www.cambridge.org/us/information/about.htm.

Christensen, Clayton. 1997. *The Innovator's Dilemma: When New Technologies Cause Great Firms to Fail*. Cambridge, MA: Harvard Business School Press.

Costelloe, Timothy. 2012. "Giambattista Vico." The Stanford Encyclopedia of Philosophy. First published June 11, 2003. Substantive revision February 14, 2012. http://plato.stanford.edu/archives/spr2012/entries/vico.

Cox, John, and Laura Cox. 2010. *Scholarly Book Publishing Practice*. Association of Learned & Professional Society Publishers. http://www.alpsp.org/Ebusiness/ProductCatalog/Product.aspx?ID=41.

Crawford, Walt. 2013. *The Big Deal and the Damage Done*. Lulu.com. April 29. http://www.lulu.com/shop/walt-crawford/the-big-deal-and-the-damage-done/ebook/product-20998658.html.

Digital Book World. 2013. "Digital Drives Wiley Revenue Growth in Third-Quarter." *Digital Book Wire*. Digital Book World. March 7. http://www.digitalbookworld.com/2013/digital-drives-wiley-revenue-growth-in-third-quarter.

Eliot, Simon, and Jonathan Rose, eds. 2007. *A Companion to the History of the Book*. Malden, MA: Blackwell Publishing.

Elsevier. 2013. "A Short History of Elsevier." Elsevier. Accessed September 1. http://cdn.elsevier.com/assets/pdf_file/0014/102632/historyofelsevier.pdf.

Fitzpatrick, Kathleen. 2009. *Planned Obsolescence: Publishing, Technology, and the Future of the Academy*. New York: New York University, Media Commons Press.

Givler, Peter. 2002. "University Press Publishing in the United States." American Association of University Professors. http://www.aaupnet.org/about-aaup/about-university-presses/history-of-university-presses. (Reprint from *Scholarly Publishing: Books, Journals, Publishers and Libraries in the Twentieth Century*, edited by Richard E. Abel and Lyman W. Newman, Wiley, 2002.)

Hahn, Karla L. 2008. "Talk about Talking about New Models of Scholarly Communication." *Journal of Electronic Publishing* 11, no. 1 (Winter). http://dx.doi.org/10.3998/3336451.0011.108.

Housewright, Ross, Roger C. Schonfeld, and Kate Wulfson. 2013. "Ithaka S+R US Faculty Survey 2012." April 8, 1–79. http://www.sr.ithaka.org/sites/default/files/reports/Ithaka_SR_US_Faculty_Survey_2012_FINAL.pdf.

JSTOR. 2013. "Content on JSTOR—Books." JSTOR. Accessed June 1. http://about.jstor.org/content/about-books.

Lemetti, Juhana. 2012. *Historical Dictionary of Hobbe's Philosophy*. Plymouth, UK: Scarecrow Press, Inc.

Lipscombe, Trevor. 2012. "First among Equals: Robert Recorde and Innovative Publishing in the Sixteenth Century." *Journal of Scholarly Publishing* 43, no. 4 (July): 381–394.

Lynch, Clifford A. 2006. "Improving Access to Research Results: Six Points." *ARL: A Bimonthly Report*, no. 248 (October): 5–7.

Mukherjee, Bhaskar. 2009. "Scholarly Communication: A Journey from Print to Web." *Library Philosophy and Practice* (e-journal). http://unllib.unl.edu/LPP/mukherjee.htm.

Muto, Albert. 1993. *The University of California Press*. Berkeley: University of California Press.

Myers, Robin, and Michael Harris, eds. 1997. The Stationers' Company and the Book Trade 1550–1990. Winchester: St Paul's Bibliographies.

Pochoda, Phil. 2013. "The Big One: The Epistemic System Break in Scholarly Monograph Publishing." *New Media & Society* 15, no. 3 (April 26): 359–378. http://nms.sagepub.com/content/15/3/359.full.pdf+html.

PR Newswire. 2012. "Elsevier Adds E-books to ebrary's Academic Complete." PR Newswire. August 8. http://www.prnewswire.com/news-releases/elsevier-adds-e-books-to-ebrarys-academic-complete-165404716.html.

Proust, Jacques. 1967. *Diderot et "Encyclopédie"* [Diderot and the Encyclopedia]. Paris: Colin.

Pycior, Helena M. 2003. "Mathematics and Prose Literature." In *Companion Encyclopedia of the History and Philosophy of Mathematics*, vol. 2, edited by Ivor Grattan-Guiness. Baltimore: Johns Hopkins University Press.

Ricci, Laura, and Mark Ware. 2012. *STM E-books: 2012 Market Size, Share, and Forecast*. Outsell.com. http://www.outsellinc.com/store/products/1100-stm-e-books-2012-market-size-share-and-forecast.

Robertson, Kathleen. 2002. "Mergers, Acquisitions, and Access: STM Publishing Today." *Library and Information Services in Astronomy IV (July 2–5, 2002)*, edited by B. Corbin, E. Bryson, and M. Wolf, 95–102. http://www.eso.org/sci/libraries/lisa/lisa4/proceedings/Robertson.pdf.

Rose, M. 1993. *Authors and Owners: The Invention of Copyright*. London: Harvard University Press.

Steele, Colin. 2008. "Scholarly Monograph Publishing in the 21st Century: The Future More Than Ever Should Be an Open Book." *Journal of Electronic Publishing* 11, no. 2 (Spring). http://dx.doi.org/10.3998/3336451.0011.201.

Suber, Peter. 2008. "The Open Access Mandate at Harvard." *SPARC Open Access Newsletter*, no. 119 (March 2). http://legacy.earlham.edu/~peters/fos/newsletter/03-02-08.htm.

Thomson Reuters. 2013. "Completing the Research Picture. The Book Citation Index." Thomson Reuters Web of Science. Accessed May 31. http://wokinfo.com/products_tools/multidisciplinary/bookcitationindex.

Tooke, Benjamin, and John Barber. 1712. *London-Gazette*. Reprint of article printed by Benjamin Tooke at the Temple-gate and John Barber on Lambeth-hill, April 26, 1712. http://www.london-gazette.co.uk/issues/4997/pages/2/page.pdf.

University College London. 2010. "Scholarly Communications." *University College London (UCL) Library Services*. Last modified November 26, 2010. http://www.ucl.ac.uk/Library/scholarly-communication/index.shtml (URL no longer links).

Ware, Mark, and Michael Mabe. 2012. *The STM Report: An Overview of Scientific and Scholarly Journal Publishing*. 3rd ed. The Hague: International Association of Scientific, Technical and Medical Publishers, November. http://www.stm-assoc.org/2012_12_11_STM_Report_2012.pdf.

Wiley. 2013. "Wiley History, Highlights from Wiley's First 200 Years." Wiley. Accessed May 26. http://www.wiley.com/WileyCDA/Section/id-301775.html.

Willinsky, John. 2009. "Toward the Design of an Open Monograph Press." *Journal of Electronic Publishing* 12, no. 1 (February). http://dx.doi.org/10.3998/3336451.0012.103.

Zuccala, Alesia. 2013. "Evaluating the Humanities: Vitalizing 'the Forgotten Sciences.'" *Research Trends*, no. 32 (March). http://www.researchtrends.com/issue-32-march-2013/evaluating-the-humanities-vitalizing-the-forgotten-sciences.

Chapter Four

Secondary Publishing

From Abstracting and Indexing to
Access and Information

In the scientific, technical, and medical (STM) scholarly communication arena, the ultimate goal of research is the "acquisition, accumulation, and integration of scientific information" (Mihhailov, Chernyi, and Gilliarevskii, 1984: 3). The accumulation and integration characteristics are driving forces behind the creation of a body of scientific, technical, and medical knowledge base on which future researchers can build. Continual growth is naturally expected, but 25 years ago no one except a few forward thinkers who were willing to put their reputations on the line predicted the explosive growth information that technology has brought. However, long before the technological explosion, scientists grappled with the problem of how to identify, locate, and retrieve a wealth of information stored in scholarly communication journals, papers, and books. Irretrievable information or information that cannot be efficiently retrieved by a large scientific audience will hinder growth of the STM body of knowledge. Therefore, an entire field previously referred to as documentation—methods of abstracting and indexing (A&I)—emerged, and these methods have changed through the years just as scholarly communication publishing processes have changed.

In the following sections, the definition, history, development, and transformation of A&I is reviewed, taking into consideration the drivers behind their development. The history naturally leads into a discussion of technology and how it has changed the development path. Though technology has always played a role in the scholarly communication industry, it is only recently that the pace of change has increased at an accelerating rate. For example, the introduction of mass printing was followed by a long period of little change until well into the early twentieth century. Compare that to the introduction of computers and computerized databases that revolutionized how STM information is accumulated, stored, indexed, and retrieved. This occurred over a twenty-year period and included several different technological initiatives, such as discovery services, link resolvers, and open access as examples of radical changes in the STM scholarly communication industry.

The focus of the discussion is on scholarly journals; however, keep in mind that much of the discussion also applies to scholarly books and monographs, conference papers and proceedings, and, in some cases, patents, videos, and databases themselves. After reviewing the print and digital transition in A&I services, the discussion turns to the issues facing scholars searching for relevant information among an avalanche of global scientific information and ends with a brief review of changing trends.

DEFINITION OF SECONDARY PUBLISHING

Scientists needed a method for finding specific journal articles and other pieces of information among millions of published research articles and other scholarly documents. The emergence of the secondary services industry was the solution to a problem. These services systematically obtain, review, and select papers or documents that meet established standards for scholarly communication, catalog them in some manner, and then index the literature for convenient access. The secondary services may offer researchers access to abstracts written by professional writers or, as is now usually the case, by the researchers themselves. An abstract is a short summary of the research paper that describes the purpose and scope of the research, the procedures used, important findings, and primary conclusions. Abstracting services, therefore, accumulate abstracts from published articles in journals; sort them into groups based on related characteristics, such as scientific discipline or research area; and provide users with access points so they may read the abstracts to determine the relevance of the journal article to their personal research efforts.

An index is also used to simplify search efforts. An index is an alphabetical list of subjects, names, or other bibliographic elements or a set of reference or locators pointing to where the full information may be found. Indexes are usually located in the back of books or are a collection of descriptors or key words from journal articles, creating an index to journal articles.

A&I services are provided by commercial and non-profit publishers as well as university libraries and government entities. The A&I service indexes content at the article level using abstracts or full texts and/or other bibliographic elements of the journal articles. Other elements include author, title, publisher, publication date, and so on. The entity publishing the A&I service decides what to include in the database. Only a few of them are all-encompassing, meaning that each service indexes a selection of journals, papers, and/or books.

A&I services have two main purposes: to minimize the time and effort it takes to locate specific peer-reviewed scholarly information available in journals and to increase the likelihood of search success by making the search results as precise as possible. The A&I services industry is in transition like the scholarly communication industry, in that technology is making it possible to expand the types of information accessed. For example, the index may now provide shortcuts to particular pieces of information, such as images, charts, and numerical data, in addition to journal articles.

The need for A&I services grew from the proliferation of scientific research and increasing specialization. The index is intended to point the researcher back to original documents, even if stored in surrogate publications, such as books and periodicals. The rapid advancement of online self-publishing and open access repositories may very well be driving indexing back to also covering stand-alone documents published online.

HISTORY OF A&I SERVICES

Both the abstract and the index have a long history that actually goes back thousands of years, though they tend to be thought of as practices that began with the first scholarly journals. However, as far back as the second millennium BC, there is evidence of cuneiform documents encased in clay envelopes with abstracts written on the outside of the envelope. Indexing has roots in the arrangement of chapters and assigned headings that make it easier to search for desired information, one of the main purposes of indexing. Alphabetic indexing, which Western civilization still uses today, appears to have developed when the Hellenistic Greeks of Egypt began creating lists of names in alphabetic order. A fragment of Callimachus's catalog from the Alexandrian Library indicates a listing of authors in alphabetical order and arranged under broad subjects. During Alexandrian times, abstracting began in earnest out of sheer practicality. A single work may encompass over a hundred papyrus rolls, so it made sense to epitomize the larger books. Also abstracted were editions of the great plays written by dramatists. In the sixth century, the first known alphabetic subject index appears in the *Apothegmata*, a listing of Greek sayings actually written in the fifth century. Also in the sixth century is the first introduction of an alphabetic approach to medicinal herbs, *De Materia medica* by Dioscorides Pedanius (Witty, 1973).

The next major alphabetic subject index known to exist is dated in the eighth century and was prepared by John of Damascus in *Sacra Parallela*. The index appeared in the beginning of the text and had a list of headings in alphabetical order; under each heading was an alphabetic list of subjects or theological statements. It was not until the fourteenth century that alphabetic indexing appeared on a more regular basis. Finally, the appearance of universities in the twelfth and later centuries witnessed the rising use of alphabetic indexing. In the fourteenth century, in the work *Sentences of Peter Lombard*, written by Peter Lombard, are found statements of theses with explanations. The index lists the theses by a catchword chosen out of the explanation and then arranges the statements into alphabetic order based on the word. This represented a major step forward in indexing. However, indexing was still not commonly used for another hundred years, and when it was then first used, the organization was simplistic and not always useful (Witty, 1973).

In the sixteenth century, indexes emerged that are considered the true beginnings of what is recognized today. *Gerard's Herbal*, by John Gerard, was published in 1597 and had a number of indexes. In 1652, Peter Heylyn published *Cosmographie in Four Bookes*, which included a series of tables that are alphabetical indexes. The early indexes used only the first letter of an entry as opposed to the letter-by-letter method that is used today and that remained the primary method for the sixteenth century and the early seventeenth century. There were a few indexes that used full alphabetization during this time, but by the eighteenth century it was standard practice (Wellisch, 1991). During the sixteenth and seventeenth centuries, there had been a large increase in the production of books and the introduction of the first scientific publication *Journal des scavans*. The *Journal* was touted as a useful supplement to help book readers who were interested in political events as scientific discoveries. The weekly journal had book abstracts, summaries of letters written by scientists and inventors concerning new discoveries, and other news. An abstract was approximately half a page long, and eventually the *Journal* became an official publication of the Academie francaise. Ten years after the first journal publications, a cumulative index of names and subjects was produced. Though the original abstracts and indexes initially covered books, they soon included articles in scholarly journals. This was important because the number of journals had grown from thirty in the late seventeenth century to over 1,000 by the end of the eighteenth century (Wiegand and Davis, 1994).

The first German A&I journal was published in 1700 and was titled *Monatlicher Auszug aus allerhand neu-herausgegebenen nützlichen und artigen Büchern* and was followed by others, such as the 1712 *Deutsche Acta eruditorum*, which was renamed *Zuverlässige nachrichten von dem gegenwärtigen zustande, veränderung und wachsthum der wissenschaften* in 1740. The *Deutsche Acta eruditorum* was a compilation of scientific reports and book abstracts and reviews. In 1740, the first true journal A&I appeared in that it did not include books and included only journal articles; it was titled *Aufrichtige und unpartheyische Gedancken über die wichtigsten Materien, welche in denen Journalen, Extracten und Monaths-Schrifften vorgetragen warden*. The first A&I journal included forty journals from German-speaking countries and was followed by a bimonthly A&I journal that included content lists from prior years of periodical publications.

In England, the first publication of abstracts and excerpts from journals and books was the 1747 *Universal Magazine of Knowledge and Pleasure*. The 1788 *Analytical Review* published scientific abstracts of foreign works in English and also included other reviews of a non-scientific nature. In France, there were a couple of efforts to publish A&I journals, but the French Revolution curtailed most publishing for a period of time.

The early 1800s was the period during which it became apparent that there was too much information published to abstract or index the entire field of scientific research. There were early attempts by sole authors to compile the first indexes covering the scientific and other fields, but they were short lived. When the author died, the A&I publication ended. However, scientific specialization was developing and disciplines emerging. One of the first A&I publications limited to a discipline was the 1778 *Chemisches Journal* started by L. F. F. von Crell. In 1784, the original publication became the *Chemische Annalen* and the *Neueschemisches Archiv*.

Until about 1823, A&I publications represented early efforts to offer A&I services and were mostly the efforts of one man in each case. Between 1827 and 1837, the first joint effort to produce an A&I medical journal was undertaken. The joint effort included one British, three Germans, one Italian, and staff from the *American Medical Intelligencer*, which was the first American A&I publication.

In 1830, the introduction of the *Pharmaceutisches Centralblatt* set a new standard for A&I services. The A&I journal, founded and edited by Gustave Fechner, became the *Chemischs Zentrablatt* (*CZ*) and gained a reputation for well-written and concise abstracts. First an annual, and then a semiannual, a name and subject index was published so that researchers could easily locate information. In 1897, the *Deutchse Chemische Gesellschaft* took over *CZ*, which led to its demise when German ceased being the scientific language. However, 1830 was a turning point in the history of A&I services in that all major disciplines have been included in A&I services since then. Between 1880 and 1920, the largest A&I services were started by professional societies. In 1884, the *Engineering Index* appeared. In 1897, *Science Abstracts* was started, and in 1920, *Index Medicus* began publication. The twentieth century saw the founding of many A&I services, such as *Chemical Abstracts* in 1907.

The A&I services history continued with the production of the first industry-sponsored publications, followed by U.S. government–sponsored services in 1920. One of the first government A&I services was published in 1920 by the U.S. Public Health Service as *Abstracts from Recent Medical*

and Public Health Papers. During World War II, only the French government's *Bulletin analytique* continued in full operating mode and covered
physics, mathematics, and biology. In 1956, it was renamed *Bulletin signale-
tique* and was also expanded. Once World War II ended, the number of A&I
services grew substantially.

Library Science Abstracts was published from 1950 until 1968, at which
point its publication was continued by *Library & Information Science Abstracts (LISA)*. *LISA* and an index published as *Library Science* were published by the Library Association in the United Kingdom. *Information Abstracts* was published in the United States, and other A&I services were
found in France, Germany, and Russia, but most A&I services were maintained in the United States after World War II.

World War II was a pivotal event in many ways, and one of those ways
was the fact that it convinced President Dwight Eisenhower that science had
won the war and so science was the key to maintaining peace. Founded in
1958, the non-profit National Federation of Advanced Information Services
(NFAIS) was formed after the close of the war, as the United States raced to
compete globally in science and technology. President Eisenhower directed
the National Science Foundation to manage the indexing, abstracting, translation, and other services that would ensure efficient dissemination of scientific information. G. Miles Conrad, director of what was then *Biological
Abstracts*, called a meeting of leading government and non-profit organizations and asked them to join forces to promote A&I as a national priority.
The National Federation of Science Abstracting and Indexing Services was
formed and consisted of fourteen services that included *Chemical Abstracts,
Engineering Index, Current List of Medical Literature*, and others (NFAIS,
2013). By 1972, the group had grown and decided to drop the word "science"
from its title and became NFAIS, open to both profit and non-profit organizations.

In 2007, technology had so changed the research industry that many of
the member organizations of NFAIS had begun developing new systems and
software as they embraced new information services. To support and recognize the importance of the technology, including the web, to distribution
systems, abstracting, research services, and so on, NFAIS changed its name
to the National Federation of Advanced Information Services. Currently,
NFAIS includes a variety of representative organizations, such as private
companies, national and global scholarly associations, government agencies,
public companies, and others. The members are focused on anything to do
with advancing scientific knowledge, and secondary publishing falls within
that arena.

EMERGENCE OF NEW MODELS

The role of the A&I services in promoting and encouraging the advancement of the scientific body of knowledge cannot be overstated. There are three premier indexes that have long histories extending from the late nineteenth and early twentieth centuries and still extant in one form or another. The *Engineering Index*, *Chemical Abstracts*, and *Index Medicus* are good examples of the importance of early A&I services then and now. Also reviewed are the histories of companies and organizations developing new models of information access that emerged, including the Institute for Scientific Information, Reed Elsevier's Scopus, CiteSeer, and the OCLC and RLG partnership. Also briefly discussed is the rise of aggregators, such as the Systems Development Corporation (SDC) and DIALOG Information Services.

Engineering Index and *Compendex*

The *Engineering Index* began in 1884 and published "Index Notes," which appeared in the monthly numbers of the *Journal of the Association of Engineering Societies*. In 1892, the first comprehensive index brought together the annual summaries for the years 1884–1891 in the *Engineering Index*. Volume 1 describes the material as seven annual summaries, "rearranged alphabetically, with numerous cross references, and with a more systematic arrangement of subject matter" (Westin, 1892). It also included materials published before 1884 that were produced by the American Society of Civil Engineers, the American Society of Mechanical Engineers, and the Association of Engineering Societies.

First published by Dr. John Butler, the *Engineering Index* provided engineers with a single source for finding relevant engineering published literature on a global basis. The early editions include descriptions of important engineering feats, such as the Brooklyn Bridge and Daimler's internal combustion engine. In 1969, the *Engineering Index* became the Compendex, an online database maintained by Engineering Village—an Internet service for professional engineers and the first professional information service on the web, created in 1995. The records prior to 1969 are called the Engineering Index Backfile, but even those printed records have been digitized and indexed and are now searchable online. Researchers can access combined databases covering 1884 to the present in addition to Inspec and the NTIS Database. The Inspec database covers literature in areas that include computing, physics, and information technology. The government-produced NTIS database indexes sponsored research from 240 U.S. government agencies, the U.S. Department of Energy, NASA, Germany's Federal Ministry of Technology, Japan's Ministry of International Trade and Industry, and the United

Kingdom's Department of Industry (Elsevier, 2014a). *Engineering Index* is now Elsevier Engineering Information (Ei) and the EiVillage.

Chemical Abstracts

In the late 1800s, there was a general dissatisfaction among American chemists concerning the breadth and depth of coverage given to U.S. chemical literature in the European abstracting journals. As a result of that dissatisfaction, in 1895 the faculty at the Massachusetts Institute of Technology started publishing the *Review of American Chemical Research*. In 1907, the American Chemical Society (ACS) assumed the publication of a more extensive version and renamed the project *Chemical Abstracts* (*CA*). The stated mission of *CA* was to become the most complete abstracting service covering global chemistry literature. As a result, *CA* has included applied and industrial chemistry in one A&I journal. *CA* did not add industrial chemistry until 1919, and the United Kingdom published two separate journals until 1926. One of the important decisions made early in *CA*'s publishing history was that a liberal interpretation would be applied to material as to whether it was chemical or non-chemical in nature (Baker, Horiszny, and Metanomski, 1980).

CA was originally a fairly cursory publication. By 1916, the editor, Evan J. Crane, realized there would have to be a common reference system for compounds so that references in literature were consistent for purposes of research and indexing. He released an early index in 1916, the *CA Decennial Index*, which prompted a search for common chemical nomenclature. Crane was editor for forty-three years, and on his retirement the new editor oversaw the conversion from an ACS supported service to self-supporting Chemical Abstract Services (CAS). There are several important facts that reflect *CA*'s adaptation over the years. It included patent coverage, which became a significant segment of its operation. In 1961, *Chemical Titles* was published and represented the first periodical that was organized, indexed, and composed using a computer, pioneering the Key Word In Context (KWIC) concept. In 1965, CAS used computer algorithms to analyze and store 3D molecular structure descriptions. In 1967, CAS began developing a computer-driven composition system, and by 1970 all *CA* indexes were computerized. Currently, over 95 percent of CAS revenue comes from electronic sources (ACS, 2007). Those electronic sources originally took a leap when CAS introduced an online dictionary of chemical substances in 1980 and went online with *CA* in 1983.

Currently, CAS offers several A&I services. SciFinder enables research on substances, reactions, journal references, and patent information. Users can rely on online tools to search and filter stored information. CAS includes information it considers high quality and coming from a reliable source. STN

(Scientific and Technical Information Network) gives access to CAS content, INPADOC databases, and the Derwent World Patents Index. It is operated jointly by CAS and FIZ Karlsrune on a worldwide basis. Science IP gives customized searching capability of worldwide scientific and technical literature. CAS also maintains Connection Tables, which represent and store chemical structures used in the databases. The CAS Registry Service indexes accepted substances and assigns a Registry number. The level of sophistication achieved is beyond anything that existed before now in A&I. The original *CA* volume contained 15,000 abstracts. Now there are over 1 million abstracts indexed annually. It includes 10,000 journals, fifty national patent offices, electronic journals and preprint services, and technical reports and papers.

Index Medicus

The history of *Index Medicus* is a bit different than *Engineering Index* and CAS in that it exists but now as a subset of PubMed. *Index Medicus* began from a desire of John Shaw Billings to index book volumes and medical journals in the National Medical Library. Billings documented collection materials on cards and ended up with thousands of them. He had a small subset of cards from Aabec to Air printed in a dictionary catalog that combined authors and subjects in one alphabet and then sent the catalog to physicians who then helped Billings lobby for funding to complete an A–Z catalog. After an 1879 launch, the first full *Index-Catalog of the Library of the Surgeon General's Office, United States Army* was completed in 1895 but needed updating almost immediately. In 1879, *Index Medicus* was also developed to serve as a monthly periodical supplement, with book and journal articles arranged by subject. Annually, an author index and alphabetical subject index was published also (Blake, 1980).

In 1927, *Index Medicus* merged with the *Quarterly Cumulative Index* and became the *Quarterly Cumulative Index-Medicus*. Through the years, *Index Medicus* was published under various names, but those in the medical industry knew it as "the list." *Index Medicus* and its companion *Index Catalogue* became the prototypes for the development of MeSH, or Medical Subject Headings, first published in 1954. MeSH was revised in 1960 and 1963 and is still used today to index all subjects in a medical article and not just one subject. The 1963 version deepened the indexing capabilities and increased coverage. MEDLARS (Medical Literature Analysis and Retrieval System) emerged with the capability of allowing a search for a single or multiple headings based on a variety of specific terms related to the main term. MEDLARS became MEDLINE in 1971, the acronym for MEDLARS-on-line. In 1997, after a trial period, PubMed was released, which gave free global access to MEDLINE. PubMed was designed by incorporating the best of

MeSH, such as headings and subheadings and upgrades from other software. Redesigned and upgraded in 2000, PubMed began linking to PubMed full-text articles. In 2001, the Link Out for Libraries program was added, as were a host of new citations. Through the 2000s, a continual host of upgrades led to alternate search interfaces that enhanced interpretations of user queries. Currently, there is access to full-text articles via PubMed Central, a catalog of journals referenced in the National Center for Biotechnology Information (NCBI), the MeSH thesaurus, clinical trials, the ability to link directly from PubMed and the NCBI database to other services including full-text publications and research tools, a single citation matcher, an NCBI batch citation matcher, topic and clinical queries, and more (U.S. National Library of Medicine, 2012). Clearly, *Index Medicus* is unrecognizable from its early days of handwritten cards.

MEAD Data Central

The late 1960s and 1970s can honestly be designated a period of enormous advancement in the search and retrieval of online STM databases. Besides the commercial enterprises mentioned, a host of other companies were busy changing the way researchers accessed information.

In 1972, MEAD Data Central developed the first full-text online search service called LEXIS. LEXIS was developed for legal research. In 1980, MEAD introduced NEXIS, which was developed to provide search and retrieval of news and current events. In 1985, MEAD introduced MEDIS for medicine. These are just a few of the early efforts to computerize databases on a broad discipline basis.

Institute for Scientific Information

Eugene Garfield is considered the father of citation indexing. After earning a degree in chemistry at Columbia University, he became a staff member on the Johns Hopkins University Welch Medical Library's Medical Indexing Project. Eventually, the project led to the National Library of Medicine's development of MeSH. He recognized early on that machines had great potential for handling large data files. While working on the project, he first developed *Contents in Advance*, which became *Current Contents*, which is still published and available online through the Thomson Reuters Web of Knowledge. Originally printed weekly, *Current Contents* began as a set of title page reproductions for journals and included an author index and an early key word subject index. Obtaining a graduate degree (MS in library science) in 1954, Garfield published a groundbreaking paper titled "Citation Indexes for Science: A New Dimension in Documentation through Association of Idea," which proposed a number of new research ideas that included faster processes, the ability to evaluate the work impact, spotting scientific research trends, and tracking scientific thought processes (Yancey, 2013). Garfield was a visionary during those early years. Working with Dr. Joshua Lederberg, he wanted to remove human intervention as much as possible during the research process, expand research access across disciplines, and increase search options beyond searching by subject. One other problem he wanted to solve was the fact that the subject indexes in the late 1950s and early 1960s were usually several months behind, limiting their usefulness to researchers. Since indexes were by subject within a discipline, researchers had to research individual indexes by discipline, learn the discipline "language," and use a lot of judgment when selecting search terms.

Garfield had recognized that journal review articles relied on bibliographic citations to help readers find the original research. He believed that accumulating the citations across disciplines and then developing a method for searching the database would solve most of the problems. The journals with the most number of citations were indexed, leading to the development of the journal impact factor. In 1958, Garfield started a new company that is now called the Institute for Scientific Information (ISI). In 1962, ISI worked with the U.S. National Institutes of Health (NIH) to develop an index for published scholarly works on genetics called the *Genetics Citation Index*. This first single-domain (genetics), multidisciplinary (included non-genetics journal article citations) scientific citation index project first tested various database versions, and the one that included non-genetics-themed journals containing articles related to some area of genetics was found to be the most useful. The broader the citation index, the better the research results. Though the U.S. government chose not to develop a national citation database, Garfield's company published the first *Science Citation Index* (*SCI*) in 1963, which was a five-volume printed set containing 1.4 million citations across 613 multidisciplinary journals (Thomson Reuters, 2013). Obviously, searching such a voluminous set of volumes was tedious and time consuming, but the effort was greatly simplified when the data was converted to magnetic tapes two years later.

The importance of the early *SCI* lies in more than its function as a bibliographic database. It merged technology and an existing citation index system and then expanded the combination to reach across disciplines, making it capable of operating as a highly innovative publishing system. *SCI* led to the creation of new metrics, such as the high-impact factor and source journal publication, factors used to measure scientific research quality (Garfield, Cronin, and Atkins, 2000). The importance of citation analysis is that it recognizes that researchers are creating links between various ideas, concepts, data, and so on in documents. Researchers use recurring patterns of terminology that become standardized (Small, 1978). A high journal impact factor measures the frequency with which a journal article is cited in a predetermined time factor. The factor is found in the *Journal Citation Report* published by Thomson.

SCI was followed by the *Social Sciences Citation Index* in 1973 and the *Arts & Humanities Citation Index* in 1978. Eventually, all were released on CD-ROM. ISI was acquired by Thomson in 1992, with Garfield remaining as chairman emeritus, and it was Thomson that first introduced the Web of Science. ISI and Thomson databases were combined into a huge database called the Web of Science, which remains to this day one of the premier secondary service research tools. The Web of Science was designed for online researchers and eventually included access to current and past bibliographic information, abstracts, and citations, all of which are extracted from science, arts and humanities, and social science journals (Cawkell and Garfield, 2001). The Web of Science includes 12,000 journals, coverage of 148,000 proceedings, journal backfiles to the year 1900, cover-to-cover journal indexing, cited reference and chemical structure searches, analysis capabilities, and much more. Thomson Reuters ISI is in the process of adding tens of thousands of editorially selected books published in 2005 or later. Its current functionality is broad but in many ways still reflects Garfield's original products though in a more technically sophisticated manner. For example, researchers still search multidisciplinary journals across multiple disciplines and still search for high-impact articles. However, everything is now automated and globalized, and searches are significantly more in depth (Thomson Reuters, 2014).

The Thomson Corporation combined with the Reuters Group in 2008 to form Thomson Reuters. The company developed the Web of Knowledge in 2001, which incorporates the Web of Science. The Web of Knowledge brings together a variety of national and international content that includes journal articles, conference papers, web sources, inventions, patents, scholarly books, data studies and data sets, and open access materials. Like the Web of Science, the Web of Knowledge incorporates information from science, arts and humanities, and social science disciplines.

Scopus

A Web of Science competitor emerged in 2004 when Reed Elsevier first introduced Scopus as the "world's largest abstract and indexing database." The competition proved beneficial in that each company continually adds new features and functionality in an effort to attract new customers. Scopus was heavily focused on STM literature, though it also included social sciences on a more limited basis. Until 2004, the Web of Science was the only citation searching product on the market. However, Scopus included citation searching, putting it in direct competition with the Web of Science. Scopus identified a variety of documents that included articles, reviews, letters, notes, editorials, surveys, conference reviews, websites, patents, and books, to name the main ones. One feature that set Scopus apart from the Web of Science was that it covered a much more international territory by including patents from the United States, Europe, and Japanese Patent Offices, and 50 percent of its journal titles were from Europe, the Middle East, and Africa. Unlike Scopus, the Web of Science focused on English language materials, had a United States emphasis, and offered limited coverage of open access journals compared to Scopus. By 2006, Scopus included some preprint servers also, such as arXive and Cogprints (Fingerman, 2006). In 2013, Scopus A&I data included over 5,000 international publishers, over 19,500 peer-reviewed journals, 400 trade publications, 360 book series, and 5.3 million conference papers (Elsevier, 2014b).

CiteSeer

CiteSeer first became public in 1998 and is recognized by some as the first truly automated academic citation indexing system. The public digital library and search engine automatically harvests documents from websites, primarily in the computer and information science disciplines. It was developed by Lee Giles, Kurt Bollacker, and Steve Lawrence, who were researchers at the then NEC Research Institute. It offered citation indexing, citation statistics, reference linking, and citation context. The original intent was to allow querying of web-based documents by citation or document and the ranking of citation impact.

Beginning in 2003, Pennsylvania State University College of Information Sciences and Technology took over the hosting and later development of CiteSeer. This particular original indexing program was quite limited because it accessed only publicly available documents and had architecture design problems. As a result, CiteSeer^X began evolving in 2005, maintaining the same focus on computer and information science documents but adding functionality of interest to scientists. It includes autonomous citation indexing, automatic metadata extraction, citation statistics, reference linking, author disambiguation, citation context, full-text indexing, and more. CiteSeer^X also offers a personal content portal, enabling researchers to maintain personal collections, RSS-like notifications, social networking, and bookmarking (CiteSeer^X, 2014).

Though CiteSeer^X has limitations because the documents included are limited to author submissions and website crawling, it represents cutting-edge open access A&I services. The proof is in its growth. CiteSeer^X was designed largely because the original version had reached 750,000 documents and 1.5 million daily requests, and the architecture could not support that volume easily.

Online Computer Library Center, Inc., and Research Libraries Group

The Online Computer Library Center, Inc. (OCLC), was developed for library cataloging purposes. The Research Libraries Group (RLG) was founded in 1974 through a cooperative effort of Harvard, Columbia, and Yale universities. A non-profit membership organization, RLG moved to Stanford University in 1978 and adopted the Standard University BALLOT processing system, which later became the Research Libraries Information Network (RLIN). RLG developed a shared cataloging database that members could access and named it the RLIN Union Catalog. RLG added databases and services over the years and in 1991 introduced Ariel, a document transmission software for use in interlibrary lending. Until 1992, only libraries could use the system. In 1993, that changed when the search system Eureka was introduced for use by non-librarians. By 1996, anyone in the world with Internet access could use RLG's services.

In 2005, OCLC and RLG published the *Data Dictionary for Preservation Metadata: Final Report of the PREMIS Working Group*. RLG also moved from a mainframe system to an open systems server environment. In 2005, RLG launched ArchiveGrid, which is a state-of-the-art access service for archival and special collections and replaces prior archival programs. In 2006, RLG and OCLC combined organizations, and in 2009, there was further consolidation under the name of OCLC Research and RLG Partnership. In 2011, the OCLC Research Library Partnership replaced the RLG Partnership, completing the integration of OCLC and RLG. OCLC maintains *ArticleFirst*, a journal citations database that includes data from the content pages of 13,000 journals but does not offer full-text data. However, *ArticleFirst* is just one index database among many maintained by OCLC under the brand name of FirstSearch, a collection of reference databases. For example, *WorldCat* is a database that connects millions of books, journals, and databases from libraries around the world. *PapersFirst* is an index of conference papers, while *Proceedings* is an index of conference proceedings. ECO, or *Electronic Collections Online*, is an index of scholarly articles and scholarly journals. These services in the aggregate give researchers access to over 258 million records (OCLC, 2013a).

The reason that this history is important is because it demonstrates the transitioning of the library system as it tries to adapt to advancing technology, the costs of computerization, and the desire of researchers to have wide search and retrieval capabilities of databases.

In the following section, beginning with the rise of aggregators, the digital transition and new models of database search and retrieval are discussed. Up to this point, the discussion has focused on early developments in scientific database developments and access. However, science and technology are so integrated that it has become more and more difficult to separate the two disciplines. That is probably one of the characteristics that most defines STM and its relationship to technology. The web has led researchers down a new path of discovery but also a path of struggle to maintain access to global information at an affordable cost despite the fact researchers can publish at will. Secondary publishing is at the heart of a new model that is not yet finalized.

Rise of the Aggregators

Aggregators are intermediaries between scholarly and academic publishers and institutions such as libraries as well as individual professionals. They create enormous databases of information or links to information that have been produced by a variety of publishers. Full-text aggregators create databases of full-text scholarly works and sell subscriptions for access to everything in the database. There are also gateway model aggregators that create databases comprised of only the links to full-text context. The subscriber buys access to databases of abstracts or relevant metadata from scholarly works but then must go through the publisher to access full texts. A&I services may offer services as an aggregator. Both A&I services and aggregators provide libraries with access to data, and the difference between the two is a matter of the type of information included in the databases.

Early aggregators were SDC and DIALOG. SDC developed the first national online retrieval network (LUCID) in 1964 and continued to expand from that point forward, offering multiple files that included MEDLINE and ERIC, to name two. DIALOG Information Services emerged from work on database development at Lockheed Missiles and Space Corporation in the early 1960s. Eventually, DIALOG offered the ability to search and retrieve data from multiple bibliographic databases (note: DIALOG changed its name to Dialog, so that spelling will be used in later chapters of this book). EBSCO Publishing is yet another full-text aggregator that began in 1984 and provides libraries access to numerous online databases via EBSCO*host*.

TECHNOLOGY AND THE DIGITAL TRANSITION

The rate of change in the scholarly publishing world has been so rapid in just the past ten years that it has been difficult for researchers, librarians, and publishers to manage this volatility. Researchers are dealing with the issue of maintaining methods for identifying quality materials that have passed peer review without stifling creative research efforts. Libraries have had a "serials crisis" in which the cost of maintaining access to scholarly materials has skyrocketed. Publishers had to change their centuries-old publishing model to accommodate the fact that researchers can now post whatever they want in web-based, open access repositories. The one topic that ties everyone together is how to maintain control over quality, with quality including issues that surround peer review and original authorship. However, another topic of interest to everyone in scholarly communication is how to ensure that researchers can locate the information needed among the vast sea of online postings that include digital journals and journal articles, reports, conference papers, and so on. The reality is that posting journals or documents online does not ensure that they are locatable, reliable, or retrievable.

In 1971, the UNISIST (United Nations International Scientific Information System) model presented a new communication model that emphasized channels and levels of information as opposed to simple time lines. The three channels are formal, informal, and tabular (data). The three levels of sources were primary, secondary, and tertiary. The secondary sources include library catalogs and A&I services. UNISIST was developed by the United Nations Educational Scientific and Cultural Organization and the International Council of Scientific Unions. The model is designed to describe the many ways information users and producers interact with libraries and data centers, providing links between the three channels (Søndergaard, Andersen, and Hjørland, 2003).

The UNISIST model was an early attempt to embrace the coming explosion of information flowing back and forth between producers and users. Some of the information is easily recognized formal communication in which the information is peer reviewed and edited, giving it a fixed time stamp. The publishing of a journal article makes it simple to index using abstracts or bibliographic items, and it is fairly simple to locate, search, and retrieve. Informal communication can be posted anywhere by anyone and does not necessarily get the imprimatur of a publisher in terms of peer review and editing. Formal communication represents hundreds of years of customs and disciplinary controls designed to present closure and serve as a basis for the recognition and rewards assigned the author. It has been a tightly controlled process that involves a series of steps that include idea formation, research, document preparation, peer review, editing, document finalizing, publishing, abstracting, and indexing. Now scholars are self-publishing material online and are creating a need for efficient A&I services that accommodate both formal and informal scholarly communication.

The technological revolution that began to take shape in the 1990s has led to important changes in the scholarly communication process affecting archiving and A&I processes as well. In this section, the digital transition and associated developments in A&I services after the 1970s is reviewed. These services include discovery services, link resolvers, and open access.

Discovery Services

Though a lot has changed in twenty years in the area of electronic reference sources, libraries are still responsible for the same basic functions they have served for hundreds of years. Libraries exist to accumulate and preserve information and make it accessible. It used to be that libraries held all materials people could access or had catalogs showing where researchers could find the desired documents not held by the library. When online information became available, the function of the library did not change, but the methods used to carry out the function changed dramatically. Libraries were once filled with rows and rows of books and journal issues and rows of catalog drawers filled with cards that librarians painstakingly prepared to serve as points to information.

A quick glance into most libraries tells the story of online information services. Many of the shelves of books and journals have been removed, and the space is now filled with tables or carrels housing computers or electrical outlets for keeping laptops (and now tablets) charged. However, when researchers sit down at the desks to complete research, they expect to be able to quickly access a wealth of information stored on the local library computers and now increasingly on computers around the world. The web has made it possible to do online research, and researcher expectations are high and getting higher as to how much and what kind of information they want to access. One scholar described the electronic library as "the scholar and his/ her workstation. The purpose of the workstation is to connect the scholar to records of scholarship through local, national and international networks and to provide access not only to bibliographic information but also full-text, numerical databases and visuals" (Borovansky, 1996: 70). That workstation today is as likely to be a home computer enabling remote access to library subscriptions as it is to be a computer at work or even a smartphone.

This lead-in to discovery services is a reminder of why libraries are feeling pressure to provide greater amounts of information that can be accessed simply, quickly, effectively, and accurately. Google Scholar added a new element to the mix. Google Scholar, unlike commercial publishers, enables a simple way to search for scholarly information. As their website explains, "From one place, you can search across many disciplines and sources: articles, theses, books, abstracts, grey literature, court opinions, and holdings come from academic publishers, professional societies, online repositories, universities and other websites. Google Scholar helps you find relevant work across the world of scholarly research" (Google, 2013). The site offers access to abstracts and citations, even if the articles could not be found online by Google. This is going to be less likely as more backfiles are added to the web. Google Scholar also offers access to full-text versions; however, some published research is by subscription only, so those articles can be accessed only through a paid service of some kind.

Discovery services begin with Google Scholar because the single-point entry system to the web is what researchers as well as the general public have indicated is their preference. Therefore, they are demanding that library databases also offer a single point of entry, leading to the development of discovery tools. Discovery tools enable libraries to create a centralized index of multiple databases: libraries, universities, private research laboratories, commercial enterprises, professional societies, and any other entity responsible for providing access to content.

EBSCO and ProQuest are two of the major discovery services used in libraries. Both companies adopted the search-box format and an advanced search feature, similar to Google Scholar, making it easy for novice and experienced researchers to access databases. Naturally, the databases that can be accessed depend on the library subscription service utilized. One of the noticeable characteristics of the current discovery services is that they originally focused on access through one or two search boxes. Now the discovery services focus on helping researchers narrow their searches but without limiting important results while still providing quality search results.

EBSCO Discovery Services (EDS) is a cutting-edge service offering libraries the ability to take full advantage of the transition to digital resources that include Online Public Access Catalogs (OPACs), e-journals, full-text databases, subject indexes, and more. One of advanced features of EDS is that it offers in-depth indexing through broader metadata. While some services index databases based on the information in the table of contents or the article title, EDS metadata includes abstracts, subject headings, full-text articles, key words, journals, author affiliations, and much more. EDS partners with vendors of integrated library systems, which consist of a variety of modules that classify and index materials, manage circulation, track serials holdings, and offer a public interface for users using the OPAC (EBSCO, 2013).

ProQuest developed Summon Discovery Service through Serials Solution, one of its subsidiary businesses. Summon 2.0 describes itself as a "digital front door" to the library's resources. The Summon Discovery Service enables a researcher to narrow the scope of the research to discipline, if desired. The suite of features includes the dynamic display of background information on topics, recommendation of research guides, contextual results that include scholar profiles, and automated query expansion. This last feature will query based on words related to the entered key word (ProQuest, 2014).

Libraries use one other type of A&I service. Union catalogs index holdings of a consortium of libraries to promote interlibrary access and lending. In 2007, the OCLC WorldCat brought discovery tools to the forefront.

WorldCat preceded Summon (2009) and EDS (2010) (Asher, Duke, and Wilson, 2013). WorldCat is a global collection of electronic and digital library materials. To convey a sense of the size of the shared data service, WorldCat recently announced it had reached the 2 trillion holdings mark (OCLC, 2013b).

Link Resolvers

One of the early, vexing problems researchers faced when using electronic and eventually web-based materials was this: how to ensure that the appropriate research document was located after doing a search. A researcher could spend many hours trying to find the right documents when a third-party database was linked to scholarly materials such as journals and journal articles. A question arose as early as 1998 when multiple copies of documents were available. Which copy should come up during a search? Any entity owning multiple licenses to the same resources could lead to inappropriate research results.

The link resolver concept emerged in response to this vexing problem. Ideally, the search result should produce the document that best fits the researcher's needs. Herbert Van de Sompel was in charge of library automation at the University of Ghent in Belgium. He believed the library should develop a link resolver because it is the library that knows what collection licenses it owns and what documents are duplicated across collections. Working with Patrick Hochstenbach, Van de Sompel implemented the SFX link server.

The SFX linking server was a success, and the solution was presented in October 1999 at the Santa Fe Convention, which was organized by Van de Sompel, Paul Ginsparg at Cornell University, and Rick Luce at the Los Alamos National Laboratory.

Ex Libris bought the rights to the software in 2000. Already known for the ALEPH Integrated Library Catalog, Ex Libris did a beta test at several U.S. libraries. In the meantime, an attendee at the Santa Fe Convention who worked at the California Institute of Technology (Caltech) decided the university needed SFX. In 2000, Caltech's manager of the digital library systems wrote the code to link references from the Web of Science databases. Caltech's information about its journal holdings were added, as was information from other holdings. Databases were said to be OpenURL enabled if they were part of the SFX system. In 2001, Caltech decided to release the link resolver to its campus members, allowing linking from the Web of Science to a variety of outside services that included web search engines, full-text articles, OPAC, and so on (McDonald and Van de Velde, 2004).

The OpenURL link resolvers are connected to what is called a "knowledge base," a term first used to reference the universe of resources available.

In OpenURL environments, the providers present citation links that use a standardized structure for an identifier. The OpenURL references the library link resolver, which then interprets the OpenURL and determines the best links to produce useful information. The knowledge base includes data related to electronic sources that may be acquired through individual or bundled subscriptions, giving access to articles and books in electronic form. The knowledge base may be managed by a broad library community, a vendor, or the library.

The current Ex Libris SFX OpenURL link resolver is very sophisticated, with its menu- driven or context-sensitive linking to scholarly articles; a Citation Linker Query form; a list of e-journals; the Knowledge Base, containing e-books, e-journals, and conference proceedings; links to OPAC; and so on. SFX claims 2,400 institutions in fifty countries.

Though Ex Libris SFX was the first link resolver, there are now other vendors that have written link resolver programs, such as EBSCO's Link-Source, Serials Solution's 360 Link and Citation Linker, OCLC WorldCat OpenURL resolution, and others. Today, many content providers are embedding the linking services into secondary services. The link resolver knows if the researcher has rights to view the document and will stop access if not. EBSCO creates the EDS Knowledge Base for a library or other institution. The EDS index record can connect users to full-text articles or other eligible resources that are not in the EDS but are in the client's collections. A user starts by using an OpenURL-enabled system and locates an item of interest. Once clicking on LinkSource, the researcher goes to a menu of links.

CrossRef is another example of a link resolver. However, it is a citation linking service only and does not contain full-text documents. Using the CrossRef Digital Object Identifiers (CrossRef DOI) to create linkages, the DOI tags document metadata provided by publishers. The researcher can click a reference citation, and the DOI takes the user to the cited article. CrossRef is operated by Publishers International Linking Association, Inc., an independent non-profit organization (CrossRef, 2009).

Open Access

This discussion does not delve deeply into open access, but it must be addressed because it is here to stay and presents enormous challenges to A&I services. The 1999 Santa Fe Convention that was the birthplace of link resolvers was also the origin of the Open Archives Initiative movement. This movement aims to develop and promote cross-searchable databases containing scholarly documents and then make these freely available on the web. There are several key issues around open access that have driven its development.

SPARC (Scholarly Publishing and Academic Resources Coalition) was launched in 1997 by the library community to make research papers available as open access. SPARC was designed to build partnerships with scientists and scholarly publishers to bring about change in the electronic scholarly publishing industry. The *Budapest Open Access Initiative* (2002) identified two goals: 1) self-archiving by scholars of refereed journal articles and 2) open access journals that do not charge. The 2003 *Bethesda Statement on Open Access Publishing* promoted discussion on providing access to primary scientific literature to promote research, facilitation of publisher peer-review processes, and distribution of the research to libraries and scientists. The *Budapest Open Access Initiative* defined an open access publication as one in which the author and copyright holders give users free access and the right to copy and distribute the information (Brown, 2003).

The Public Library of Science (PLOS) presented its first case for open access in 2000. It now publishes content under the Creative Commons Attribution License, giving researchers free, immediate, and unrestricted access to materials. PLOS uses Ambra, an open-source platform for publishing open access articles. There is support for multiple journals and for publishing articles with the National Library of Medicine (PLOS, 2013). Another milestone in the open access movement was the *Berlin Declaration on Open Access* issued on October 22, 2003. The statement supports the transition to electronic open access, but it also addresses the need to develop the means and ways to evaluate open access materials and ensure that they meet accepted standards of scientific practice and quality.

There has been a lot of pressure placed on the government to provide free access to publications funded with taxpayer dollars. The NIH issued the NIH Public Access Policy, Division G, Title II, Section 218, of Public Law 110-61 in 2008. The mandate requires that research funded by the NIH must be submitted as an electronic version, if published in 2008 or later, to the National Library of Medicine's PubMed Central. Some commercial publishers offer open access programs for publishing of materials and will also submit the article to PubMed Central. Traditional publishing of articles are sent to the NIH Manuscript Submission System, then to PubMed Central for publishing twelve months after original publication. This presents a good example of how commercial publishers are adapting to open access.

How do A&I services function in open access? As the preceding paragraph on commercial publishers indicates, the largest commercial publishers are offering open access services; articles meeting the definition of scholarly communication can be incorporated into A&I services. The *Directory of Open Access Journals* (DOAJ) lists thousands of searchable scientific and scholarly journals and journal articles. Included journals and articles must be peer reviewed or edited. Articles in the DOAJ are cataloged by journal title level, and if the author sends article metadata, the DOAJ will make it searchable based on the information.

There are three types of submission categories in open access journals. The full open access is called the Gold route, and the peer-reviewed journal is made available immediately after publication. There is a second type of open access in which the publication is not immediately available. It becomes available after a period of time—called an embargo. The third type of open access is the Green route or self-archiving model, in which the publication is immediate or delayed. Green articles have been accepted for publication by a journal, and recommended peer-review changes have been made (Ware and Mabe, 2012).

Though charges have not been discussed, it should be mentioned that open access journals and articles are not free. Most of the open access publishers do charge a fee, but the author pays it. There are also institutional memberships where the institution pays on behalf of its faculty or staff members.

The DOAJ and the new aggregations services represent the next stage of the digital transition. In the next section, some of the issues and trends that arise from these developments are reviewed.

ISSUES AND TRENDS

The secondary publishing industry went through a major transition period as technology became fully embedded. In the initial stage, scholars would sit at a computer workstation or terminal and have access only to whatever the library or aggregator services provided. The materials available were mostly those that had met the strict standards of peer review and editing. The commercial publishers "controlled" the information that made it into the marketplace. The web has rapidly changed those restrictions. In the freewheeling world of the Internet, scholars are asking themselves, Why should access be limited? Gaining access to formal and informal publications would more rapidly expand the scientific knowledge base, and is that not the point of scholarly communication? But what about the quality of that content?

Issues

There are many issues that still must be resolved. Commercial and professional publishers have begun to offer services such as open access, and the A&I services are incorporating the materials into their databases. The result is that researchers may be led to articles and journals by search engines and links that may or may not have abstracts but are not peer reviewed. Now scholars and students must sort through the peer-reviewed journals and articles that are presented. In a sign of the times, most universities have a web page explaining how to find peer-reviewed articles.

Two related issues are access and proliferation of articles. Millions of articles are now self-published online, and informal communication has proliferated. Search engines such as Google Scholar cover a broad spectrum of materials, and researchers must learn how to narrow their searches to quality content. Some believe that the search engines deliver too many unnecessary results, forcing the user to spend considerable time sorting through results and links. It is one reason that traditional publishing and A&I services are still utilized and why libraries and researchers continue to pay for access to their databases. The commercial, library, government, and professional publishers apply consistent quality control standards to their content.

Secondary publishers of A&I content are faced with providing e-content that is compatible with a large variety of integrated library systems that offer the search-box services to researchers. The issue of how the A&I content will be presented in these discovery systems is still of concern. Another A&I service issue is user authentication or limiting access to full-text articles or journals to only those who have permission (Somerville and Conrad, 2013).

The availability of full-text scholarly content online challenges conventional aggregators. Though they have found methods for limiting access through passwords, proxy servers, and other limiters to subscription payers, savvy Internet users can often access full-text journal articles anyway (Research Information Network, 2006). That points out the one issue with the Internet that is difficult to overcome—its accessibility. It is a circular issue because accessibility has prompted a user demand for greater access to scholarly materials.

Quality control has and will likely remain an issue as well. The continuum of publishing on the Internet makes identifying the final version of a document difficult. If an article is self-published with no access limitations put in place, it is difficult to know which documents are the final versions. Authors can post multiple versions of documents at will. That is yet another function of traditional publishing and A&I services that is difficult to replace.

Securing digital archives is yet another issue. If a publisher goes out of business or if appropriate security is not in place, the digital archives are at risk.

Other issues related to A&I services include the following:

- Inadequate digitized journal backfiles
- Multiauthored material where only the first author name is used as metadata
- Limited foreign materials
- Wealth of material that has not yet been digitized
- Inability to access full-text versions even after finding references

Trends

A major issue is managing the large volume of informal scholarly communication found in blogs, social media, e-mails, and so on. The increased accessibility afforded by the Internet has encouraged a school of thought that believes that capturing the informal scholarship is as important as capturing formal scholarly publishing. Traditional A&I services are not prepared to manage the online scientific discussions that can play an important role in advancing the body of scientific knowledge. Before the Internet, conversations between scientists were lost but are now captured in Web 2.0.

Self-publishing on public websites is a trend that is expected to accelerate. The *Herpetological Conservation & Biology* open access, international peer-reviewed journal set out to prove that scholars with and without tenure can and should publish at affordable rates and in a more timely manner. The journal was started in 2006 and filled a void in which traditional journals "shunned manuscripts that were descriptive or natural history oriented." To ensure that authors can publish their research, the online journal charges only a very small fee. Though other open access journals are published today, the *Herpetological Conservation & Biology* journal was a trendsetter and is included in publications such as Thomson Reuters *Journal Citation Report* (Howard, 2011).

A&I services have progressed in their ability to index images and tables so that researchers can directly access information. However, the services will have to continually develop new standards and tools to preserve the minutes of science because the form of the minutes will continue to evolve. Though a radical idea at this point, it is highly likely that the upcoming generation of scholars will embed video and other types of technology in their articles and journals. The A&I services will have to develop the capability of indexing these items as well.

Another trend that is accelerating is that cash-strapped libraries will likely not continue to serve as gatekeepers to scholarly research. Right now, the traditional publishers maintain tight control over the peer-review process. However, as more scholars simply publish their materials online, that control will loosen. The day that the universities begin to consider online self-published materials for purposes of tenure, rewards, and so on, the grip of the commercial publishers will loosen further.

Of course, that leads right back to the issue of quality control. With increasingly sophisticated search engines, it is possible at some point that universities will arrange the peer-review group and authors will self-publish articles. There would not be a need for A&I services as much as there would be a need for search engines to identify peer-reviewed versus non-peer-reviewed documents. When that becomes standard practice, researchers can simply sit at their laptops and access the type of research desired, knowing that quality control has been considered.

CONCLUSION

In 1958, Fairthorne wrote in *Computer Journal* that "indexing is the basic problem as well as the costliest bottleneck of information retrieval" (Fairthorne, 1958: 36–37). Scholarly communication of any kind is not useful if it cannot be accessed. With the introduction of the web, the vast wealth of information made available and the ease of access it provides has forced publishers to rethink traditional methods of indexing. Using abstracts and metadata, greater access has been achieved, but the bottleneck continues to exist.

However, the bottleneck is different things to different people. For libraries, it is the cost of subscription services that limits access to scholarly research. Commercial A&I services index only certain databases, excluding an enormous amount of information that should be accessible to researchers. The bottleneck for supporters of open access is the fact that conventional publishers of scholarly material control who gets to publish and then control who gets to see the published material.

As this discussion explored, indexing has been done for hundreds of years because it serves an important function, whether talking about peer-reviewed journals or open access publishing sites. Indexing makes information more easily available and offers a way for researchers to find information they would not be able to find otherwise. The issues surrounding technology, like quality control and open access, do not change the fact that indexing of abstracts or full-text articles is necessary.

In the recent past, the discussion of the influence of technology on A&I services has been centered on adapting conventional scholarly communication publishing to the web. In the future, the discussion is likely to take a new path. Publishers of A&I services will have to decide how to filter information resources that include both formal and informal communication. It is a difficult challenge to meet because of the sheer volume of materials on the web. How will publishers of A&I services decide what to include and what to exclude? What if libraries or library consortiums refuse to pay subscription fees simply because the budgets do not allow for the expense? How will A&I services manage the interdisciplinary trend? Can conventional A&I services survive open access where authors can self-publish, bypassing the publishing controls? Perhaps the trend will follow the path of the *Herpetological Conservation & Biology* open access international peer-reviewed journal. Online, inexpensive journals will submit themselves to entities responsible for determining, for example, impact factors and to A&I services, creating a blend of old and new.

These are the types of questions the industry is asking itself. Technology seems to be able to manage most challenges as seen by the existence of discovery services, link resolvers, and other sophisticated tools. The increasing refinement of metadata means that discovery services can have very thin information on scholarly material yet offer effective links to full-text materials. Full-text articles can be posted online now, turning restrictive A&I services into a new bottleneck.

Technology does not stand still either. For example, increasing use of mobile technologies enables researchers to access information anywhere and to disseminate it quickly and efficiently. Researchers using this technology will expect software developers to adapt their services to the mobile environment. As A&I services operate now, it would be difficult to use smartphones to do extensive searches, but that is not the story for tablet computers.

The next five to ten years will bring changes to scientific publishing. There are many researchers who believe that conventional peer-reviewed scholarship that is abstracted and indexed cannot be replaced because of the quality control issues. However, technology is forcing new approaches, new business models, and new thinking, and A&I services will not be excluded. Ultimately, it may be that the indexing system that emerges from the current "chaos" will improve publishing and research services.

Right now, there are only a few A&I services, three of which are Google Scholar, Thomson Reuters/ISI, and Elsevier's Scopus, attempting to cover all disciplines and all information forms. As interdisciplinary research becomes the standard, the value of these types of services will increase. If a prediction were to be made, it would be this: A&I services will trend toward the Google Scholar model as current research locked behind the paywall is freed. The NIH was first, and more will follow. The publishing industry must be prepared to operate in a more open environment, where researchers and scholars do not want to be faced with access limitations. It may take five or ten years to reach that point, but there is no way to predict what new technology will be developed in the near future either. The one thing that is certain is that the industry will not be doing "business as usual" much longer.

REFERENCES

American Chemical Society. 2007. "Chemical Abstracts." American Chemical Society. http://acswebcontent.acs.org/landmarks/landmarks/cas/chemabstracts.html.
Asher, Andrew D., Lynda M. Duke, and Suzanne Wilson. 2013. "Paths of Discover: Comparing the Search Effectiveness of EBSCO Discovery Service, Summon, Google Scholar, and Conventional Library Resources." *College & Research Libraries* 74, no. 5 (September): 464–488.

Baker, Dale B., Jean W. Horiszny, and Wladyslaw V. Metanomski. 1980. "History of Abstracting at Chemical Abstracts Services." *Journal of Chemical Information and Computer Science* 20: 193–201.

Blake, John B., ed. 1980. *Centenary of Index Medicus 1879–1979*. Bethesda, MD: U.S. Department of Health and Human Services, National Institutes of Health, National Library of Medicine.

Borovansky, Vladimir T. 1996. "Changing Trends in Scholarly Communication: Issues for Technological University Libraries." *1995 IATUL Proceedings* 5: 68–79. http://docs.lib.purdue.edu/iatul/1995/papers/8.

Brown, Patrick O., et al. 2003. "Bethesda Statement on Open Access Publishing." Earlham College. June 20. http://legacy.earlham.edu/~peters/fos/bethesda.htm.

Cawkell, Terry, and Eugene Garfield. 2001. "Institute for Scientific Information." In *A Century of Science Publishing: A Collection of Essays*, edited by E. H. Fredriksson, 149–160. Lansdale: IOS Press.

CiteSeer[X]. 2014. "About CiteSeer[X]." CiteSeer[X] Pennsylvania State University. Accessed September 12. http://csxstatic.ist.psu.edu/about.

CrossRef. 2009. "The Formation of CrossRef: A Short History." CrossRef.org. http://www.crossref.org/08downloads/CrossRef10Years.pdf.

EBSCO. 2013. "EBSCO Discovery." EBSCO*host*. Accessed May 10. http://www.ebscohost.com/discovery.

Elsevier. 2014a. "Engineering Village." Elsevier.com. Accessed September 12. http://www.elsevier.com/online-tools/engineering-village.

Elsevier. 2014b. "Scopus." Elsevier.com. Accessed September 12. http://www.elsevier.com/online-tools/scopus.

Fairthorne, R. A. 1958. "Automatic Retrieval of Recorded Information." *Computer Journal* 1, no. 1: 36–41.

Fingerman, Susan. 2006. "Electronic Resources Reviews—Web of Science and Scopus: Current Features and Capabilities." *Issues in Science and Technology Librarianship* no. 48 (Fall). doi: 10.5062/F4G44N7B.

Garfield, Eugene, Blaise Cronin, and Helen Barsky Atkins, eds. 2000. *The Web of Knowledge: A Festschrift in Honor of Eugene Garfield*. Medford, NJ: American Society for Information Science.

Google. 2013. "Google Scholar." Google.com. Accessed May 14. http://www.google.com/intl/en/scholar/about.html.

Howard, Jennifer. 2011. "Scholars Create Influential Journal for About a $100 a Year." *The Chronicle of Higher Education*, January 30. http://chronicle.com/article/Hot-Type-Scholars-Create/126090.

McDonald, John, and Eric F. Van de Velde. 2004. "The Lure of Linking. Link Resolvers Are Essential to Getting Optimal Usage of Electronic Content." *Library Journal*, April 1. http://lj.libraryjournal.com/2004/04/ljarchives/the-lure-of-linking.

Mihhailov, A. J., A. I. Chernyi, and R. S. Gilliarevskii. 1984. *Scientific Communication and Informatics*. Arlington, VA: Arlington Information Resources Press.

National Federation of Advanced Information Services. 2013. "Years of Knowledge & Experience." National Federation of Advanced Information Services. Accessed May 14. http://www.nfais.org/history.

OCLC. 2013a. "FirstSearch at a Glance." OCLC. Accessed May 14. http://www.oclc.org/firstsearch/about.en.html.

OCLC. 2013b. "OCLC WorldCat." OCLC. Accessed May 14. http://www.oclc.org/worldcat.en.html.

ProQuest. 2014. "The Summon Service." ProQuest. Accessed September 12. http://www.proquest.com/products-services/The-Summon-Service.html.

Public Library of Science. 2013. "The Case for Open Access." Public Library of Science. Accessed May 13. http://www.plos.org/about/open-access.

Research Information Network. 2006. *Researchers and Discovery Services—Behaviour, Perceptions and Needs*. Research Information Network. November. http://www.rin.ac.uk/our-work/using-and-accessing-information-resources/researchers-and-discovery-services-beha-viour-perc.

Small, Henry G. 1978. "Cited Documents as Concept Symbols." *Social Studies of Science* 8: 327–340.

Somerville, Mary M., and Lettie Y. Conrad. 2013. "Discoverability Challenges and Collabora-tion Opportunities within the Scholarly Communications Ecosystems: A SAGE White Paper Update." *Collaborative Librarianship* 5, no. 1: 29–41. http://collaborativelibrarianship.org/index.php/jocl/article/view/240/181.

Søndergaard, Trine Fjordback, Jack Andersen, and Birger Hjørland. 2003. "Documents and the Communication of Scientific and Scholarly Information—Revising and Updating the UNIS-IST Model." [Electronic version]. *Journal of Documentation* 59, no. 3: 278–320. http://www.emeraldinsight.com/doi/abs/10.1108/00220410310472509.

Thomson Reuters. 2013. "Web of Science. History of Citation Indexing." Thomson Reuters. Accessed September 12. http://wokinfo.com/essays/history-of-citation-indexing.

Thomson Reuters. 2014. "Web of Science." Thomson Reuters. Accessed September 12. http://thomsonreuters.com/products/ip-science/04_062/wos-next-gen-brochure.pdf.

U.S. National Library of Medicine. 2012. "PubMed." U.S. National Library of Medicine. National Institutes of Health. Accessed May 31. http://www.ncbi.nlm.nih.gov/pub-med?cmd_current=Limits&pmfilter_Subsets=History+of+Medicine.

Ware, Mark, and Michael Mabe. 2012. *The STM Report: An Overview of Scientific and Schol-arly Journal Publishing*. 3rd ed. The Hague: International Association of Scientific, Techni-cal and Medical Publishers, November. http://www.stm-assoc.org/2012_12_11_STM_Report_2012.pdf.

Wellisch, Hans H. 1991. *Indexing from A to Z*. 2nd ed. New York, Dublin: H. W. Wilson.

Westin, John. 1982. *Descriptive Index of Current Engineering Literature Volume 1, 1884–1891*. Board of Managers of the Association of Engineering Societies, Washington, DC.

Wiegand, Wayne A., and Donald G. Davis. 1994. *Encyclopedia of Library History*. New York: Taylor & Francis.

Witty, Francis J. 1973. "The Beginnings of Indexing and Abstracting: Some Notes towards a History of Indexing and Abstracting in Antiquity and the Middle Ages." *The Indexer* 16, no. 4 (October): 193–198.

Yancey, Rodney. 2013. "Fifty Years of Citation Indexing and Analysis." Web of Knowledge. September 2005. Accessed June 10. http://wokinfo.com/essays/50-years-citation-indexing (URL now maps to a summary page: http://wokinfo.com/sci-anniversary.html).

Chapter Five

The Rise and Fall of the CD-ROM Technology

The CD-ROM acronym stands for "Compact Disc Read-Only Memory," a technology that was believed, beginning in the 1980s, to be the solution to a host of problems related to information and data storage, search, and retrieval. The expectations for CD-ROM were never met for a variety of reasons. One of those reasons was the fact that other information technologies were advancing at such a fast rate that electronic products rapidly became obsolete as better options were developed. However, as is often the case with technology, the rise and fall of the CD-ROM is the result of a mixture of factors that often present contrasting explanations. For example, libraries embraced the CD-ROM as a practical method for accessing large databases at a fixed price and then quickly moved away from this media to the Internet because the CD-ROM did not provide as much access as the SaaS (Software as a Service) cloud-based systems at an economical price once the price of CD-ROM equipment and staffing was factored in.

The history of scholarly communication is long and varied, and the CD-ROM played a role. Though a popular medium for a relatively short period of time, approximately twelve years, it was one of the first mass-produced electronic products manufactured and was instrumental in leading university libraries and commercial publishers and aggregators permanently into the digital age. The following sections give an overview of the meteoric rise of the CD-ROM and the reasons for its quick popularity, followed by a review of the reasons it just as quickly fell out of popularity. The scholarly community learned many lessons from their experiences with the CD-ROM that were applied to subsequent technologies.

LEADING UP TO THE CD-ROM

The concept of the optical digital recording and playback technology was first introduced in 1965 by an American inventor named James Russell. However, corporations such as Sony and Philips did not really pursue research on optical disc technology until ten years later. In 1976, Sony demonstrated the first twelve-inch optical digital audio disc, and in 1979, Philips launched a new product called a Compact Disc (CD). Made from pressed polycarbonate, it had a spiral track molded into the plastic that is then coated with a thin layer of reflective material, such as aluminum or gold. Data are "burned" into the metallic layer with a laser beam and is accessible via the use of an optical disc drive. After the introduction of this original CD, the technology continued to develop and gain sophistication, resulting in a series of different types of CDs being rapidly introduced.

The first commercial CD was the Compact Disc Digital Audio (CD-DA), which was the original format developed by a collaboration between Philips and Sony in 1980. It was audio only and thus was suitable for adoption by the music industry. Beginning in 1980, CD specifications were introduced, and they are now referred to as *Red Book* audio.

Royal Philips Electronics produced the world's first music CD at its factory in Hanover, Germany, in 1982, which was *The Visitors* by the group ABBA. The CDs and CD players were introduced in Japan first and then in the United States and Europe. In 1982, the first Sony CD was released in the United States—Billy Joel's *52nd Street.* In 1983, music CDs and CD players were mass marketed on a global basis. The popularity of the music CD generated an enormous manufacturing capacity in CD production with facilities around the world from Terre Haute, Indiana, to Kobe, Japan, and in numerous other countries.

FROM INVENTION TO FIRST USE

Until 1984, what began to be known in the industry as the CD-DA was designed for audio only, and people to this day use the acronym CD to indicate a music disc. However, in 1984, technology advanced again when the CD-ROM was introduced. This newest technology enabled the storage and retrieval of data. This was followed by a series of CDs with increasing functionality. The Compact Disc Interactive, the Compact Disc Recordable, and the Video Compact Disc were subsequently developed and introduced to the market at various times between 1985 and 1991.

As mentioned, the CD was primarily a musical storage technology early in its history. The rock band Dire Straits sold the first million music CDs in 1985. However, Philips and Sony had also developed the capability of adding text on a *Red Book*–compliant audio CD. Originally, the CD-Text was designed to add the capability of storing text information concerning the music on the CD, such as the name of the album, the song names, and the name of the music artist. In 1985, the *Yellow Book* standards were developed by Sony and Philips. The *Yellow Book* applied to optical data computer storage data medium or the CD-ROM. The CD-ROM had the same physical format as CDs but was readable by a CD-ROM drive. The CD-ROM drive read the CD-ROM data with a laser technology and digitally transmitted these data to a computer. The CD-ROM technology seemed to be ideal for data storage, as it could store millions of characters and easily search and retrieve these on a disc less than one-eighth of an inch thick that you could hold in the palm of your hand. It promised to change the way people could conduct research.

POPULARITY OF CDS AND CD-ROM TECHNOLOGY

In the mid- to late 1980s, print products and services, such as abstracting and indexing databases, and the printing of scholarly works were faced with adaptation to a rapidly emerging digital environment. In the early stages of technology, the most radical introductions were the personal computer, placing computing power on people's desks, coupled with new media forms for data storage. The 1985 launch of the CD-ROM represented an important breakthrough. Large amounts of data could be stored on the CD-ROM. In fact, the first version could store 550 megabytes, which was more than what the majority of magnetic media could hold and was the equivalent of 650 floppy disks.

CD-ROMs were quickly identified as an ideal method for storing reference books, statistical data, and other textual information. They were not erasable like floppy disks, so they made excellent storage devices for libraries that had to give access to information to large groups of users. The CD-ROM data could be loaded into memory, displayed on a computer, or printed. The high volume of audio CDs produced at manufacturing plants with their increasing excess available capacity began driving production costs down significantly for all forms of compact discs, including the CD-ROM, adding to their appeal.

Sony Digital Audio Disc Corporation built its first CD manufacturing plant in Terre Haute, Indiana, in 1983. Between 1983 and 1992, CD production grew at an astonishing rate at Sony's three plants in Indiana, Japan, and Austria. At the end of 1984, the number of CDs manufactured was only one-tenth the number of vinyl albums. By 1986, CD production was at an astonishing 45 million per year. By 1988, the number had grown to 100 million CDs, and by 1992, production was at 300 million a year. Sony expanded its

CD software production capacity, which also promoted the acceptance of the CD. CD-ROM technology was popular because it offered high-speed random access and direct search capabilities. Though the CD was originally developed for music recording, it quickly found other uses, such as video, games, and text, and factories, such as the one in Terre Haute, could easily keep up with demand through expansion (Sony, 2013).

EARLY ADOPTION OF CD-ROMS BY COMMERCIAL PUBLISHERS AND UNIVERSITIES

Though CD-ROM quickly rose to a high level of popularity with both individuals and institutional customers, the transition was not easy for many of the premier information service providers. Staff at organizations such as the Institute of Scientific Information (ISI), who were early pioneers of digital information services, had to be convinced that the move to CD-ROM was a good one, making strong business sense. An early proponent of electronic files, ISI had been converting files associated with citation indexes, *Current Contents*, and chemical products to magnetic tape. When CD-ROM was developed and then adopted, the data on ISI's magnetic tapes and printed materials had to be converted to the new format—processing that was expensive and time consuming (Baykoucheva, 2010).

The CD-ROM was originally not fully standardized in terms of interfaces and data organization. There was also a general lack of knowledge as to how this electronic media could be effectively used. By 1985, however, the uncertainty was clearing, as some standardization was implemented and people began to understand CD-ROM's storage, search, and retrieval abilities (Akeroyd, 1988).

In the mid- to late 1980s, the adoption of the CD-ROM by commercial academic publishers began. The CD-ROM seemed to be ideal for holding large bibliographic databases. The first commercial adoptions of CD-ROM were converted mainframe databases stored on magnetic storage media. The early conversions included MEDLINE, ERIC, and a host of research literature databases. CD-ROM was seen as providing the means of integrating communication and information technologies by blending audio/visual, print and publishing, and computerization (Hedberg, 1989). The belief that CD-ROM was breakthrough technology representing the future was one of the factors leading to its rapid adoption. It would enable libraries, commercial publishers, societies, archivers, and researchers to use the same multimedia technology.

By 1986, the online library catalog was introduced. After online catalogs came citation databases, providing access to book chapters, journal articles, monographs, and so on. By 1989, there were a growing number of vendors offering libraries public access catalog systems using CD-ROMs for storage. The libraries would supply machine-readable magnetic tapes of their catalogs to CD-ROM vendors. The vendors would index and convert the magnetic tapes to CD-ROMs and send a predetermined number of CD-ROM copies to the libraries for use at computer workstations. As of 1989, most libraries were purchasing online search services for bibliographic and non-bibliographic data. The multidisciplinary services included Dialog, ORBIT, WILSONONLINE, and BRS, to name a few. Libraries were also paying for access to specialized databases addressing a single subject discipline or profession, such as engineering or medicine. These databases included WESTLAW, NEXIS, Chemical Abstracts, Engineering Information, and others. In both types of databases, the same format was used. The commercial producers converted purchased bibliographic and non-bibliographic data to a form readable by their computers and then sold access to subscribers who could perform retrieval operations using vendor-supplied database management software. Researchers could sit at a terminal and initiate searches on the CD-ROMs using local retrieval software (Saffady, 1989). The CD-ROM databases that were available depended on library subscriptions.

A few libraries even chose to maintain their own databases on CD-ROMs. To do so, they had to have custom-developed programs or prewritten software. There were also integrated library systems, such as OCLC, using optical disc technology. In a 1986 newsletter, OCLC indicated its plan to use CD-ROM for bibliographic systems, document delivery, and electronic browsing of monographs and journals. The lower cost of CD-ROM was going to make overseas resource sharing more affordable. In 1987, CD-CAT, a cataloging system on CD-ROM, was introduced, and it was considered more useful than commercial products because it contained more than the Library of Congress MARC (LC-MARC) records. LC-MARC records accounted for only 30 percent of OCLC cataloged monographs so the CD-CAT would be more extensive. The other OCLC project was CD-Reference, consisting of reference materials on CD-ROM that could be accessed using microcomputers. OCLC wanted to create a national and international database that included collections from libraries around the world (Schieber and Lewis, 1986).

The electronic catalogs were precursors to what would develop into more complex databases. The first commercial full-text CD-ROM product to gain general attention was the twenty-one-volume, 9-million-word *Grolier Academic American Encyclopedia*. Published in 1985 as a text-only CD-ROM, the set displayed the storage and retrieval capacity of the new optical media and showcased applicability of the product for personal as well as academic purposes (Foster, 1985). Smaller publishing projects, such as the Grolier encyclopedia, marked the beginning of the commercialization of the CD-ROM by information publishers. When commercial publishers realized that users would be willing to pay for access to text files and bibliographic data, it was just a matter of time before abstracts, books, journals, and conference papers were also added. In the late 1980s and early 1990s, the amount of data available on CD-ROM grew rapidly. Academic publishers such as H. W. Wilson, John Wiley, and Elsevier began offering subscription services to a variety of publications and databases. The CD-ROM technology was particularly suited for reference libraries and the scientific, medical, and technical publishing industry, where large volumes of data needed to be stored and readily accessible.

Some of the larger libraries were able to afford in-house, networked CD-ROM systems. Pennsylvania State University was one of the first U.S. academic libraries to install CD-ROM products. It is a good example of the state of the CD-ROM application in the early 1990s and illustrates many of the issues associated with the adoption of the optical technology. In 1986, the Penn State Pattee Library acquired InfoTrac, a set of full-text databases containing content from academic journals and other sources. Originally, the CD-ROMs were mailed to the university on an agreed-on schedule. The data included a lot of abstracts and some full-length articles. At the end of each article was a pointer directing the reader to the microfilm where the article could be found and accessed by the librarian. Following InfoTrac, Penn State acquired ERIC and Compact Disclosure. Unhappy with InfoTrac equipment performance, it was dropped in 1988, and Penn State purchased eleven other CD-ROM products sold by Wilson, SilverPlatter, University Microfilms, and Disclosure. The library set up a General Reference Section CD-ROM area with ten computer workstations (Faries, 1992).

Penn State set up the new reference area with a separate service desk, which had heavy usage indeed. Though each workstation had instructions on search procedures, users needed a lot of assistance. Each workstation had a time limit on it also, so users had to sign up to use the workstation and then had to complete their research in a short period of time. In the meantime, Penn State Libraries continued adding CD-ROM titles, and after a year, questions arose concerning user practices, requirements, and workloads. Surveys were completed during academic year 1989–1990, and the librarians learned that juniors and seniors were the heaviest CD-ROM users, followed by postgraduate students. Very few faculty or staff were using the technology. Libraries such as Penn State had embraced the technology because it was believed it would put the reference search function into the hands of the users, yet the survey revealed that half the users had to ask for help. Penn State began offering classes on effective CD-ROM searching, but that placed a burden on staff. Most users needed between fifteen and thirty minutes to search, but doctoral students needed at least thirty minutes. In 1991, Penn State added the Colorado Alliance of Research Libraries (CARL) database UnCover, Dialog's Knowledge Index, and Dow Jones News Retrieval and upgraded the online catalog LIAS. Once LIAS was upgraded, the commercial MEDLINE database was added (Faries, 1992).

The same pattern was followed at other academic and research libraries and continued through the 1990s. CD-ROM appeared to be the answer to data storage and reduced telecommunications costs, among other benefits, but proved to be short lived as the Internet grew in size and complexity during the 1990s and early 2000s. Internet-based databases quickly replaced the CD-ROM for many reasons. In the next two sections, the specific reasons for the rise and fall of the CD-ROM in academic and research environments is explored.

RISE OF THE CD-ROM

There were many reasons why the CD-ROM became a popular medium in the academic and research environments. Some of those reasons have been mentioned or alluded to in the previous discussion. For example, the ability to store 550 megabytes on a single disc was important because even large scholarly works could be condensed into a handful of discs. A single disc could hold the equivalent of over 200,000 printed pages. That fact, coupled with the low price per disc, meant libraries could offer access to more research materials than would be possible otherwise.

Another feature of CD-ROM databases that appealed to libraries was the fact that bibliographic databases would usually index some of the in-house journal collections. This could increase use of the expensive journals maintained in libraries as a result of greater in-house access by academics and researchers and increased interlibrary lending. CD-ROM bibliographic databases gave more exposure to collections not covered well by library databases (Nondal, 2013).

When CD-ROM technology appeared, online access to databases was expensive, and it only got more so as time went on. Early aggregation and search services such as Dialog, SDC ORBIT, and BRS grew out of technical environments, giving them access to government funds in many cases. They built large data centers, developed interface software, and purchased licensing rights or gained outright ownership of published materials.

Aggregator services had to pay royalty payments to publishers or other content providers, driving costs up. To recover expenses and make a profit, a transactional payment model for users was developed. In the transactional model, a user pays a fee to the aggregator each time a document is viewed, and the aggregator pays the publisher. The subscription model was different but still expensive. In the subscription model, the aggregator collects subscription fees and pays royalties out of those fees. Dialog was the first aggregator to institute connect-time pricing, which required customers to pay for connection time to the database, charges per record accessed, and charges for the telecommunications network. Each database could have a different fee structure. There were also fees for archiving, special reporting features, and other services. Though the subscription model contracted a set price during the contract period, the contract renewal required paying an additional amount based on the difference between the contracted and actual usage (Plosker, 2004).

CD-ROMs significantly lowered access costs, though there were equipment and staffing expenses, as will be discussed in the next section. In-house CD-ROM systems were accessible without incurring online charges. Informed students and researchers knew how to get a printout of sources, access to abstracts, a printout of full-text products made available by the library, and access to updated information and how to download information, often without needing assistance from librarians. It was a better means than had existed previously for searching scholarly journal collections and other types of databases of interest.

Another set of advantages to using CD-ROMs was related to ease of use. Researchers and academics could use any word or word combination for searching databases. This gave them the option of searching for information even when concepts or thought processes were not fully formed. This made the CD-ROM a potentially powerful research tool. In addition, thousands of pages on a single CD-ROM could be searched while sitting at a workstation. Once CD-ROM systems were networked, searching tens of thousands of records was possible. The CD-ROM jukebox increased search efficiency and breadth of data available.

CD-ROM systems were appealing to libraries because they believed it would largely return the search function to students and not require them to continue the expensive role and function as search intermediary. Before CD-ROM technology, academic researchers relied heavily on library staff for assistance in finding desired information. Using staff services was the only way to access many of the materials as well as control the "taxi meter" transactional pricing of online systems. Mediated library searches were expensive in terms of personnel costs and slowed down research efforts. The CD-ROM search seems slow by today's standards, but over twenty years ago, it appeared to be both speedy and efficient of everyone's time.

The rapid rise in CD-ROM databases was also due to the intensive marketing efforts of the companies producing CDs. Earlier, it was mentioned that the CD-ROM mastering capacity at manufacturing plants exceeded the demand for music CDs. It was simply a good business decision to promote other uses for versions of the CD. The major manufacturing companies, such as Philips and Sony, heavily promoted CD-ROMs for the obvious reasons— they wanted to utilize factory capacity and increase sales.

Perhaps one of the most important implications of CD-ROM was its representation of technology advances. For the first time, CD-ROM blurred the division between internal and external databases for users. For example, researchers could use the same workstations to access Online Public Access Catalogs and library CD-ROMs. The technical difficulty was that CD-ROMs were produced using different classification systems and required users to learn different retrieval procedures (Nondal, 2013).

The rapid rise in the use of CD-ROMs was followed by an equally rapid fall.

FALL OF THE CD-ROM

As more users became familiar with online research, the cost of using aggregator services rose. Individual users had to pay for passwords, to connect to a dial-up network, to view a bibliographic record or abstract, and to print out documents. Libraries paid increasing amounts for subscriptions to CD-ROM updates. A major drawback to CD-ROMs was the fact that they were static information sources. Commercial publishers produced the discs and then had to update them to keep the CD-ROMs current, using information the vendors purchased or data supplied by the libraries. Updates were often on a quarterly time frame. The regular updating increased library expenses, but in between updates, they found themselves paying for an information system in which databases were quickly outdated. References and full-text files had to be regularly updated or new journal issues added to discs on a frequent basis if researchers were to stay current on the most recent information published.

The CD-ROM represented new technology, but it also was a product that showed how fast technology can change. It is safe to say that the introduction of the CD-ROM was seen as a remarkable improvement in the ability to access data, yet it was quickly replaced by the Digital Versatile Disc (DVD). In 1997, the DVD was introduced to the marketplace and offered advantages over the CD. It offered the ability to manage content, giving libraries more control over user experience. It could store even more data than the CD-ROM and provided a multimedia experience. The introduction of the DVD did confuse the computing environment, though, because CD-ROM and DVD-ROM could be accessed only by using a computer, while video DVDs could be viewed only on a DVD player. The DVD-ROM was a computer file, like the CD-ROM, but could more easily manage a broader range of content that included text, images, graphics, numerical data, sound, maps, and much more. The DVD-ROM and CD-ROM performed similar functions, but they used different data-encoding standards and protocols. The DVD was easier and less expensive to maintain because it used a standardized format and ran on standardized networks connected to central servers. The DVD represented a technology transition that gave one of the first indications of how quickly technology would change from this point forward.

The costs of the CD-ROM updates played a key part in its decline, and there were other expenses that became budgetary burdens. Besides the transactional or subscription costs permitting user database access, libraries had to have the appropriate computer equipment able to manage CD-ROM functionality and trained staff capable of systems management and of giving ongoing user assistance. Even something as simple as printing out a text file at the library required the user to fill out a form and the library staff to collect fees, print the article, and distribute the article to the user. CD-ROM systems often required a substantial capital investment. Equipment included workstations, CD-ROM drives, local area networks, a centralized server, printers, file servers, and so on. There was also a likelihood that multiple systems would have to be maintained since commercial vendors supplying the CD-ROMs did not always use the same coding systems.

CD-ROM systems also posed another problem. They required that library staff have specialized training, and in many cases libraries had to pay for a dedicated full-time technical staff to manage CD-ROM products. Besides the periodic updates and conversions that CD-ROM discs required, there was a need for continuous support and conversion services. Material that had been saved on 5¼-inch diskettes was not accessible on CD-ROM drives. That material had to be integrated into newer systems, requiring staff commitments, or staff had to maintain multiple systems, which also required researchers to be familiar with a variety of computer systems (Hovav and Gray, 2001). Supporting different computing platforms and operating platforms was difficult. This also translated into difficulties for vendors selling the products. They had to provide technical support in addition to frequently remastering discs and distributing updates.

By 1999, aggregators and publishers were already moving to Internet-based delivery systems. The Internet streamlined updating of databases, simplified end-user equipment and support requirements, and improved information delivery systems. The Internet offered standardization, making it easier and more cost effective for libraries to access and share resources using standard networks. Databases are stored on a centralized server, and search engines and software linked the server to the web. The databases on the server could be easily updated, while CD-ROM disc updates were complicated and slow. Libraries still had a choice as to whether they maintained their own database server or accessed a vendor's remote server. SilverPlatter and Ovid sold information products that libraries could maintain at their sites. However, one of the most powerful improvements the web-based technology offered was the ability to link databases. For example, citation databases could be linked to full-text databases and then interfaced with the library's online catalog (Breeding, 1999). The CD-ROM systems could not compete with this level of functionality.

There is no end in sight to technological changes either. CD-ROMs are still used, but cloud computing is bringing even more changes. CD-ROMs are currently used for archiving, but the cloud promises to offer unlimited storage space and a system of centralized storage.

LESSONS LEARNED

The rise and fall of the CD-ROM was an early lesson in technology management for libraries, producers and publishers, and aggregators. In the early 1980s, only visionaries really understood how fast technology could change. The first CD-ROMs were introduced in 1984 and the first DVDs in 1996, making twelve short years in which the CD-ROM was considered state-of-the-art technology. After the DVD, the pace of technological change accelerated as the web grew. However, the lessons learned as a result of experiences with the CD-ROM better positioned consumers, publishers, and system integrators and providers to avoid making many of the mistakes associated with the adoption of CD-ROM technology.

Libraries and Other Consumers

Libraries are considered the main consumers of CD-ROMs. Even today, CD-ROM collections are maintained. However, one of the lessons learned has been to assess the effectiveness of database services more thoroughly before purchasing new products. It is better understood that academics and researchers will still need library-mediated services no matter how sophisticated a system gets in terms of simplifying the user experience. In fact, the increasing globalization of databases means system users will need more assistance with accessing online databases external to their libraries.

Libraries also learned that standardization is a critical factor in determining the feasibility of adopting technology. CD-ROMs offered cost savings, but the lack of standardization meant multiple computer systems had to be maintained, significantly increasing equipment and personnel costs. The lack of standards also meant that each vendor could develop a unique code, terminology, and search function. They could develop unique interface systems. This added to user confusion also since knowledge concerning each system was required for efficient use (McCarthy, Krausse, and Little, 1997). The fact is that libraries did not fully understand CD-ROM features before adopting the technology. For example, they did not understand that CD-ROM drives were slow disc readers compared to other options, such as high-performance magnetic disks, and that did not change even when the optical discs were improved.

Another lesson learned concerned the importance of understanding the status of technology developments now and for the future. Emerging technologies can have a significant impact on the ability of libraries to maintain accessible resources over time and to offer users access to resources. It is clear that the power of the web over the decade that CD-ROM discs and drives were becoming more and more popular was not fully understood, as the Internet was in its nascent form. If they had, CD-ROMs would probably have declined at an even faster rate than they did.

Technology is fully embedded in academic and research efforts. Libraries need to make sure they have staff with the appropriate information technology (IT) skills to do service and product assessments. Library IT staff cannot make decisions in a vacuum either. Academic libraries in particular are part of a networked and integrated system of internal and external technologies, and decisions made by teams of professionals that include the library, IT, vendors, and department representatives are without question better informed and less risky.

Publishers and Aggregators

A major lesson publishers and aggregators learned as a result of adopting CD-ROM technology was that long learning curves do not work well with technology. The lack of standardization and interfacing among publishers and aggregators limited the ability of libraries to adopt and manage CD-ROM systems. This naturally slowed and capped sales. They also learned that they need to be more consumer oriented, establish an easily understandable price schedule, and provide better support. Libraries had difficulties continually training a steady flow of new users that needed to learn effective search techniques. Publishers and aggregators learned the power of providing additional training services to librarians who would then train users.

Pricing was a long-term issue with CD-ROMs because the pricing structures were never consistent. Overall, the most important lesson concerned standardization. CD-ROMs were not just a victim of technology improvements. They were also victims of the fact that standardizations of pricing, formats, distribution, and routine updates were never fully established. One of the immediate attractions of the Internet was standardization, simplifying library systems. There was an unpredictability in the CD-ROM era that certainly was not helpful to its development.

CONCLUSION

CD-ROM database products were rapidly adopted by libraries after their introduction in 1986, reflecting a desire to implement user-friendly and expanded resources locally. Though it had a short life span in terms of being the primary database for the search and retrieval of information, the CD-ROM represented the first real effort of academic and research libraries to implement technology that was user friendly. At the time of its adoption, it was hoped that users would have faster and broader access to materials and not be dependent on library staff. Though it did not work out that way, the rise and fall of the CD-ROM taught many important lessons about balancing library services with access to technology, anticipating the rate of technological change, and fully understanding the implications of implementing new technology.

Libraries still manage CD-ROMs today, but they are used primarily as a storage medium. They can contain text, images, data, video, audio, and maps. Text can be PDF files, a database, or HTML documents with links to the web. Data can be raw data, spreadsheets, or databases. CD-ROMs still accompany books as supplemental material. In other words, CD-ROMs may have fallen, but they have not disappeared.

Perhaps of most significance, though CD-ROMs did not survive as media for scholarly communication and distribution, the technology did portend a new business model where digital content would be acquired not using a "taxi meter" transactional model but through more familiar and fixed price subscription models. CD-ROMs also incorporated locally held data and integrated this data with external, proprietary, commercially published content, again signaling a need for local and "open" data resources. Though short lived as a technology, the CD-ROM period transformed the business models and types of scholarly content that are currently in use today.

REFERENCES

Akeroyd, John. 1988. "CD-ROM as an Online Public Access Catalogue." *The Electronic Library* 6, no. 2: 120–124.

Baykoucheva, Svelta. 2010. "From the Institute of Scientific Information (ISI) to the National Federation of Advanced Information Services (NFAIS)." *Chemical Information Bulletin* 62, no. 1 (Spring 2010): 18.

Breeding, Marshall. 1999. "Does the Web Spell Doom for CD and DVD?" *Library Technology Guides, Document Repository. Computers in Libraries* 19, no. 10 (October): 71–75. http://www.librarytechnology.org/ltg-displaytext.pl?RC=6553.

Faries, Cindy. 1992. "Users' Reactions to CD-ROM: The Penn State Experience." *College & Research Libraries* 53, no. 2 (March): 139–149.

Foster, Edward. 1985. "CD-ROM: Megabytes into Minispace." *InfoWorld* 7, no. 38 (September 23): 27–29.

Hedberg, John G. 1989. "CD-ROM: Expanding and Shrinking Resource Base Learning." *Australian Journal of Educational Technology* 5, no. 1: 56–75.

Hovav, Anat, and Paul Gray. 2001. "Managing Academic Electronic Publishing: Six Case Studies." *Global Co-Operation in the New Millennium—9th European Conference on Information Systems*, June 27–29, 751–763. http://csrc.lse.ac.uk/asp/aspecis/20010042.pdf.

McCarthy, Cheryl A., Sylvia C. Krausse, and Arthur A. Little. 1997. "Expectations and Effectiveness Using CD-ROMs: What Do Patrons Want and How Satisfied Are They?" *College and Research Libraries* 58, no. 2 (March): 128–142.

Nondal, Lars. 2013. "Full-Text and Bibliographical Databases on CD-ROM in Research Libraries—Costs, Services and Technology." *International Journal of Special Libraries*, 355–365. Accessed June 6. http://forge.fh-potsdam.de/~IFLA/INSPEL/94-3nola.pdf.

Plosker, George. 2004. "Making Money as an Aggregator." *Information Today* 28, no. 2 (March/April). http://www.infotoday.com/online/mar04/plosker.shtml.

Saffady, William. 1989. "Library Automation: An Overview." *Library Trends* 37, no. 3 (Winter): 276–277.

Schieber, Phil, and Page Lewis. 1986. "SPOTLIGHT OCLC Reaffirms Membership Philosophy." *OCLC Newsletter*, no. 64 (August): 1–20.

Sony. 2013. "Studio Recorders Go Digital." Sony .net. Accessed June 5. http://www.sony.net/SonyInfo/CorporateInfo/History/SonyHistory/2-10.html.

Chapter Six

The Birth of Online

The Internet and the Web Change Scholarly Communication

Using the launch of the online industry as the key milestone, the information age arrived around 1972 and since then has surged forward with relentless progression. The impact of technology on our lives has been and is still debated, and that is as true in the world of scholarly communication as it is for any other discipline. The influence of technology on research and publishing has been profound, shaking traditional practices and activities, such as peer review, research dissemination, and archiving, to their very foundations. The transition from print to digital has been ongoing and difficult because an established system of scholarly communication has worked well for centuries, but one thing is now clear—the Internet and the web have forever changed the scholarly research and publishing processes. Electronic publishing and digital information services have been game changers. It is impossible to know where the scholarly communication system is headed without understanding where it has been.

It could be claimed that electronic publishing has been a process that evolved from the creators of printing press technology always striving to improve the efficiency of information distribution to the masses. One of the earliest goals was to find a way to improve search strategies so researchers could access information with ease. This goal has significant implications for scholarly research because it has made the difference between spending hours in library archives to research a limited set of materials to unlimited access to global records. However, like every innovation, the process is not without its controversies and problems and is yet another reason why it is important to understand how the introduction of online access and the Internet has changed everything. Very little in the information industry has been untouched by computerization, and scholarly communication is no exception.

In the following sections, the progression of electronic publishing and digital information services is reviewed, from its appearance, to the ongoing development leading to a proliferation of databases, to the development of search engines, to the emergence of full-text online publishing, and more. Throughout the review are discussions of the major impact on libraries and scholars as they search for and find data and information and conduct research. The story of the Internet and online scholarly communication is far from over, and in this context, it is helpful to understand how research strategies are generating new processes and forms of dissemination, such as open access and others, which are rapidly changing the scholarly communication landscape.

In the following sections, the chapter discusses the arrival of the information age, how technological advances in print publishing led to the rise of online systems, the introduction of the Internet, and the influence that the Internet and search engines have had on scholarly communication. These changes profoundly influenced the roles of publishers, libraries, and researchers. Whether that is good or bad depends on personal, deep-seated beliefs in the appropriate methods for scholarly communication. However, what is certainly true is that computerization and the Internet will only keep advancing, so scholarly communication needs to continue adapting to its promise of advancing the body of knowledge.

ROOTS OF ELECTRONIC PUBLISHING

Phototypesetting to Computer Composition

Technology is never static. It is always progressive. The first printing press may have seemed to appear suddenly, but it represented ongoing, behind-the-scenes efforts to make it easier to produce and distribute information to as many people as possible. Though there were hundreds of years between the development of printing press technology and electronic publishing, the emergence of information age technology was just as radical and brought about the same type of changes as the printing press. The printing press changed the conditions of information collection, storage, retrieval, review, and discovery, and so did electronic publishing. The printing press also brought unintended consequences, including changes in the roles of publishers, and so has electronic publishing. The impact of the printing press took hundreds of years to be fully appreciated. The impact of electronic publishing is still evolving, but it has been significant already (Dewar, 2013).

Printing technology did not change a lot until the late 1800s when the Mergenthaler Linotype Company's Linofilm and the Harris Intertype Corporation's Fotosetter technology (both brands) emerged in the newspaper industry in the mid-1950s. Before the introduction of this new technology, the original large, noisy equipment pieces were hot-type composition machines that could cast whole lines, called slugs, at the same time. They used hot lead for foundry type letter casting, in which molten lead was injected into molds to cast metal type. Typographic errors required correcting the whole line. The Linotype system set print but could not be used for larger newspaper headlines, so they had to be set separately. The Ludlow system came into use to set headlines for Linotype printing.

The Linotype and Fotosetter propelled a move toward more efficient printing systems. The hot-type composition machines were eventually replaced in general use by cold-composition machines, referring to technology that did not use cast metal type or "hot lead." Combining offset with photocomposition, the type could be set directly onto metal or paper without using the line-casting machines. Originally, a hot-wax chemical process was used that allowed ink from the paper to adhere to treated metal plates that were then applied to a printing cylinder on a press. The new photocomposition machines were computer forerunners able to print about 3,000 words per minute. They could accept key-to-disk and key-to-tape input or could do OCR reading of typewritten input. Composing typewriters could do camera-ready copy, and an early adopter of the technology was academic publishing.

The adoption of photocomposition was slow. In the 1950s, newspapers used it mostly to set display advertising. Journals used it to print advertisements onto film or paper, which were used to make offset plates or photoengraving for letterpress. By the late 1950s, newspapers such as the *South Bend Tribune* began using the new technology to set all of its display advertising. After 1958, adoption of the technology began to increase at a much faster rate. At the same time as photocomposition was developing, teletypesetting appeared. What made teletypesetting so remarkable was that typesetting machines were now operable by remote control. The Linotype teletypesetter represented a major step forward in the printing industry because it used perforated tape to transmit copy to the printer. It required perforator keyboards and high-speed punch machines. However, they increased typesetting speed from around thirty words per minute to 300 words per minute. Headlines had to be set separately (Davies, 2006).

The Chemical Abstracts Service (CAS) was an early adopter of photocomposition technology. In 1966, CAS developed an automated processing system that efficiently produced issues of *Chemical Abstracts* and indexes. It also fed a computer-readable database. CAS continued to adopt technology as it advanced and proceeded to create an online scientific and technical information network (CAS, 2013).

The history of Allen Press is another good example of a publishing company adapting to technology advances. Allen Press was founded in 1935 as a small commercial printer. In 1952, Allen Press added scientific journal publishing beginning with *The Wilson Bulletin* and the *Journal of Mammalogy*. Academic publishing represented 50 percent of the business by 1960, and in the early 1970s, the company moved into academic publishing only. In 1969, the first offset press was purchased. In 1975, Allen Press was using eleven linotype machines, seven letterpresses, and a staff who assembled the journals and used a stapling and gluing machine to add the covers. The company was slow to adopt offset printing and computerized typesetting, but by the late 1970s and into the 1980s, offset printing was producing 300-line-screen black-and-white halftones. The publisher acquired numerous science and medicine journals. During the 1980s, computerized phototypesetting officially replaced the linotypes. The small printer of scholarly journals became a scholarly publisher with the introduction of the Internet and a quality printer for small-run journal issues. Allen Press continues to operate today after competing with ten or more leading journal publishers since the 1970s. The company is still recognized for specialty, high-quality journal publishing and printing (Dolecheck, 2010).

Many of the early leaders in research and scholarly publishing started companies that still exist today or merged with larger publishers. For example, Montague Hyams founded Derwent Information in 1951, a patent documentation publishing company that embraced computer photocomposition and built online databases derived from the electronic print process. In 1974, the company introduced the Derwent World Patents Index database, which became one of the first databases on the Systems Development Corporation (SDC) Online Retrieval of Bibliographic Information Timeshared (ORBIT) search service. The Derwent World Patents Index database is now owned by Thomson Reuters and recently celebrated fifty years of existence.

The use of perforated tapes was an important development though not one that got a lot of headlines outside of the printing industry. The first indications that technology was going to change methods of scholarly research are arguably found at the Massachusetts Institute of Technology (MIT) in 1951, when Bagley developed a computer program to search for encoded abstracts using batch searching (Bourne, 1980). However, the 1960s is the starting point for the true revolution in printing and information retrieval systems. The machine-readable tapes used in automated publishing led to the outgrowth of systems that could do error checking, sorting, and formatting. The tapes eventually led to the ability to provide search services on demand (Lancaster and Warner, 1993).

Libraries play an important role in the development of electronic resources. In 1964, the Council on Library Resources commissioned a study on methods for capturing catalog data in machine-readable form. *The Recording of Library of Congress Bibliographic Data in Machine Form* introduced the concepts to the general audience during presentations at the first Conference on Machine-Readable Catalog Copy, which was held in 1965. The meeting led to a new report titled *A Proposed Format for a Standardized Machine-Readable Catalog Record*. At a second conference, the MARC (machine-readable cataloging) Pilot Project was conceived, and the MARC I format emerged, establishing codes for language, place of publication, and publisher that were usable by specially developed computer software. MARC II improved the system, and by the end of 1972, there were over 300,000 records in the database, leading to new support and search services. At the same time, the Ohio College Library Center (OCLC) developed the first shared library database in 1971. Calling it WorldCat, initially fifty-four libraries could now share bibliographic records (Kamble et al., 2012).

The early systems of the late 1950s and early 1960s used primarily offline batch processing that required serial search methods. Search efforts were matched sequentially against document representations, and a bibliography was produced. The issue with serial search was that the search of the database could be efficiently searched once, and the results represented documents available at the time the database was created. Real-time updates did not exist. To keep the database updated, it had to be periodically matched against new document profiles and the profiles added to the database. The new databases were then mailed or shipped in some manner. It could literally take weeks before search results were available.

The 1960s database search systems represented an enormous improvement in information retrieval. One of the first public batch search services offered was the Medical Literature Analysis and Retrieval System (MEDLARS) of the National Library of Medicine (NLM), created by Davis B. McCarn. That was in 1964. In 1965, there were fewer than twenty databases accessible by the public. By 1977, there were over 300, and fifty were online (Williams, 1977). In the 1960s, retrieval systems were very crude with punched cards containing retrieval queries and databases on tape.

Batch processing had advantages and disadvantages. The advantages included the ability to conduct simultaneous and complex searches; the ability to generate bibliographies based on search results; the capability of producing different outputs, such as printed indexes or specific information; and the ability to duplicate the database as needed (Lancaster and Warner, 1993). The disadvantages included laborious preplanning as to the search terms and strategy to produce the desired results and slow responses. Another disadvantage was the fact there were no browsing capabilities, and professional researchers or librarians familiar with the technology had to do the actual search. The user could not tailor the search as is possible today.

Pioneers and Early Technology

There was an online system before there was an Internet. The earliest online systems are attributed to pioneers such as Carlos Cuadra working at SDC and Roger Summit working at Dialog. Their work in computerization was initially focused on making it easier to access government and scientific information resources. However, there are many other researchers, scientists, and engineers who made significant contributions also. They include Davis B. McCarn, who followed his work at NLM by automating the H. W. Wilson Company, and Charles Bourne, who worked at the Stanford Research Institute and was the director of the Institute of Library Research at the University of California, Berkeley. Between 1977 and 1992, Bourne was vice president of the General Information Division at Dialog Information Services.

In the late 1950s, RAND spun off the division that was eventually responsible for developing the 1963 Air Force Automated radar system called SAGE. SDC was formed in 1957 from that spin-off. SAGE is recognized as one of the original large computer networks that used long-distance telephone services. In 1960, Robert Simons and John Olney with SDC developed the first interactive online system, which was named Protosynthex. A terminal was wired to a computer, and the full text of the *Golden Book Encyclopedia* could be searched for terms and truncated word forms. In 1964, Harold Borko, H. P. Burnaugh, and W. H. Moore developed a system called *Bibliographic Organization for Library Display* (BOLD), which allowed browsing of literature citations on magnetic tapes. That same year, SDC developers E. Franks and P. A. DeSimone demonstrated an online system with interactive capability. In 1965, SDC-Dayton showcased a national online retrieval network that represented work done for the Foreign Technology Division of Wright-Patterson Air Force Base at RECON Central (Wedgeworth, 1993). This effort represented some of the earliest efforts toward developing full-text storage and retrieval.

In 1971, NLM licensed the use of SDC's ORBIT, calling it EHILL after Senator Lister Hill. Carlos Cuadra is recognized as both the originator and the "chief agitator" (his description) of ORBIT. SDC began managing the Abridged Index Medicus (AIM/TWX) online information system for NLM in May 1970. In October 1971, NLM introduced MEDLINE (MEDLARS online) as a free service after expanding AIM/TWX into the database (Bjørner and Ardito, 2003). The pace of technological advances was clearly picking up speed as regular reports of progress emerged.

The SDC Search Service, developed under the inspiration and guidance of Carlos Cuadra, first allowed users to search the data of the Education Resources Information Center (ERIC) from an office or library computer terminal. Cuadra was the manager of the early commercial service, which was established after the Lockheed service. SDC then offered online services to the Pharmaceutical Manufacturers Association (PMA) member companies, and at the time, the database consisted of only MEDLINE. PMA had obtained a copy of MEDLINE, an early example of database sharing, which SDC loaded on its computer, in exchange for providing NLM with indexing and documents. SDC got permission to access the ERIC database and started selling access to the new database to the public in 1972, in addition to its MEDLINE product. SDC charged a monthly search fee of $1,000. SDC then added Chemical Abstracts Condensates as a database in 1973 but experienced great difficulty in making it work. Abstracts of the chemical literature are more complicated than simple text files because of the numerous formulas and diagrams they contain. Additional databases, such as CHEMCON and CAIN, were added and sold. The demands on storage capacity led SDC to allocate the space to different files during certain parts of the day, thus limiting researcher access during certain times (Bourne and Iahn, 2003).

Though NLM had a document-ordering feature in MEDLINE from the beginning, SDC continued to develop new features for the public. In 1974, the first public operation of online document ordering through the SDC Search Service was introduced. Electronic Maildrop could handle requests made to the National Technical Information Service (NTIS) and CIS databases. In 1976, SDC sent a letter out informing users that the service was expanded to include online ordering of more than 5,000 journals included in ISI OATS and dissertations in the University Microfilms International (UMI) system. Full-text copies could be ordered (Bourne and Iahn, 2003). Around the same time, Carlos Cuadra left SDC to start Cuadra Associates, which is still in business. Its flagship product is STAR, introduced in 1978 and designed to provide multiuser search ability. In addition, he began publishing the *Directory of Online Databases* in 1979, which reflected in-depth research of online databases. The first issue was printed in hot type and included 400 databases, but the rapid growth of online services and databases provided the perfect opportunity for STAR to efficiently produce the directories within the mainstream publishing industry.

One of the reasons the online systems that were available by the early 1970s were not widely used is that the cost of long-distance phone lines was prohibitive. Libraries in particular had no room in budgets to assume the considerable expense associated with long-distance charges. Packet switching was an important breakthrough development as a result.

Another pioneer in the rise of online systems is Roger Summit. He is credited with creating the Dialog service in 1962 at the Lockheed Information Sciences Laboratory. In 1964, Summit submitted a proposal to NASA to use Dialog to automate the search and retrieval of over 300,000 bibliographic citations. The first contract was awarded to Lockheed in 1966 but was a dual funding agreement. Lockheed was responsible for an in-house installation and Bunker-Ramo for the dial-up service. NASA's Remote Console Information Retrieval Service (RECON) was installed in the Scientific and Technical Information Facility, and by 1970, Dialog was being used in NASA facilities across the country to search over 700,000 records. NASA RECON and RECON Central, where SDC was doing contract work at the Wright-Patterson Air Force Base, should not be confused because they were different operations. Once becoming proven technology, the Dialog service and language was used in additional installations at the Atomic Energy Commission, the U.S. Office of Education ERIC facility, and others. Lockheed was selling its Dialog Information Retrieval Service commercially by 1972, with the first non-government contract going to General Dynamics to search the Nuclear Science Abstracts.

One of the interesting circumstances of the early years of online systems development is that the technology pioneers interacted and shared information, and each one added something to development. Giering heard about work that SDC was doing in 1967 at Recon Central on full-text files and databases as related to reconnaissance activities. This represented the earliest stages of the development of Management Information Systems (MIS) and Database Management Systems (DBMS). It was determined that specific words could be extracted from big fields of text, and developers used the Department of Defense Form 1498 (project description) as the test bed. Engineers could request information, and an operator would run downstairs and use a console typewriter to search using "AND" and "OR" using SDC software called Data Central. Giering also learned that Wright-Patterson Air Force Base was using SDC's CIRC and CIRCOL (online version), a bibliographic systems in which index terms were manually assigned. He attempted to compare Recon Central's Data Central full-text files to CIRC's index terms. Though the project failed, it created the foundation for doing a search of full-text documents, of monumental importance to scholarly communication systems decades later (Bjørner and Ardito, 2003).

Giering had spent twenty years in the military, and William Gorog of Data Corporation took the opportunity to hire him with a purpose in mind. As a visionary, Gorog wanted to move Data Central into MIS because he believed the future was in full-text capabilities. When Data Corporation's Air Force contract money ended, Giering was charged with turning Data Central into a commercial product. The first task was developing multiple terminal capability because a console typewriter was simply too restrictive. The software was also too restrictive in 1967 because it was still not reiterative. Working with IBM, Giering was running multiple terminals by spring 1968, a remarkable feat in which many people were able to search at the same time. Continuing his work, Giering eventually added a third-level "AND" with an ampersand, "Modify" to reduce the volume of answers, multiple sort keys, proximity searching (searching for words next to or near one another), and Keyword in Color, which represented highlighted search words in the retrieved records. Though color is common today, it was a radical addition in the 1970s and one that people initially did not think would be popular. These "firsts" by Data Central were emulated by Lockheed (Dialog) (Bjørner and Ardito, 2003).

The first commercial full-text system was demonstrated at the 1968 Columbus, Ohio American Society for Information Science (ASIS) conference. Data Corporation was acquired by the Mead Corporation in 1968, and the Information Systems Division was spun off as a subsidiary in 1970 as Mead Data Central under the leadership of Don Wilson and Gerry Rubin. After the ASIS conference and several demonstrations later, the Ohio Bar Automated Research organization was formed by a group of lawyers, and the corporation supplied the keypunched legal content for the development of the search engine LEXIS in 1972. Data Central (eventually Mead Data Central) was different from other companies in that there was a focus on the end user and not just librarians. This was a subtle expansion of the concept of technology as a direct link between the user and available information and data. It is why Mead Data Central developed the Key Word In Context (KWIC) in 1970 in a way that used color terminals and highlighted words and text in different colors, something taken for granted today but now recognized as user friendly.

The perforated tapes gave way to magnetic disks that were used as the primary storage medium in the 1970s. This was the natural next step in the development of online interactive retrieval systems. Online systems relied on full records and inverted indexes. The inverted index contains key data elements from the full record and key links for retrieval purposes. The records and the indexes were stored on magnetic disks, and random access capability was developed. This led to the ability to perform interactive searches as needed. The Lockheed Dialog and SDC ORBIT services databases reflected a switch to computer-assisted photocomposition in the early 1970s, and computer readable magnetic tape could be produced. The ability to produce tapes made it possible to create the central databases essential to online services.

Putting a Price on Information

One of the early issues the online services developers had to deal with was telecommunications. The early companies, such as SDC, Dialog, and Mead Central, negotiated contracts with government agencies for access to communication networks. Contracts were also signed with commercial businesses for file conversions and search access. However, the cost of long-distance telephone services was exorbitant by today's standards. Originally, dial-up modems were used to connect terminals to data service centers. In the 1960s, it cost approximately $50 per hour for calls beyond fifty miles from the initiator. International rates were $180 to $360 per hour for Telex and

TWX services. The telephone rates were in addition to the online search costs of $25 to $35 per hour (Bourne and Iahn, 2003).

Though the 1970s was a progressive decade in terms of technology development, affordable access via telephone lines had to be resolved before there would be widespread adoption of online search services. There was also a need for more reliable data transmission. Out of this need rose the first packet-switched data communications network in 1969 called ARPANET (from the Defense Department's ARPA Multi-Computer Network), resulting from an NLM-commissioned study. As a less expensive alternative, NLM began using the public telecommunication network called Tymnet for cheaper, faster MEDLINE access in 1972. Access prices dropped from a long-distance charge of $25 per hour to $10 per hour. Tymnet was owned by Tymshare. Tymshare sold time-shared computer services on its private data communications network composed of leased lines. The NLM agreement represented the company's first external network node, and the government contract was followed by commercial contracts. This was an important step in the development of the online industry and especially when Dialog quickly became Tymshare's largest customer. The Tymnet system greatly increased transmission speed. Also using Tymnet was the SDC Search Service (Bourne and Iahn, 2003).

Another important development was the launch of the Telenet network in 1975. Dialog became the Telenet Corporation's first customer. The competitive environment this created on the packet-switching telecommunications systems drove access prices down from $10 per hour to $1.60 per hour. The lower communication costs were also due to the fact that the Tenet and Tymnet networks activated only when in use rather than maintaining a permanent long-distance connection.

The online retrieval systems involved the service companies (producer) acquiring documents from the government or business entities and converting them into representations with appropriate citation, index terms, and abstracts. The representations were further converted into machine-readable form and then stored on magnetic tapes. The tapes were used to generate services that included printing indexes, doing offline batch processing of search requests, and loading data onto magnetic disks to create inverted indexes for online searching. Producers either created the databases in-house or leased the tapes to a different company to convert the data to magnetic disks. The company that processed the data for online searching had to provide the correct search software (Lancaster and Warner, 1993). The vendors supplying the online access charged for the software and the search time in a "taxi meter" approach, that is, charging for each based on the time connected or used.

Libraries had a slightly different operating model. In the early years, libraries input records into a centralized database, such as the OCLC World

Cat mentioned earlier. OCLC then provided the appropriate services to the libraries, which included copies of records that corresponded to their collection items. The records were then added by the library, as appropriate, to each existing catalog using MARC. Originally, it was a batch system, but in the 1970s, the databases were offered online so that updates and searches could be done interactively. This system was standardized, unlike the commercial counterparts. The Research Libraries Group (RLG) was founded two years after OCLC in response to certain issues some libraries had with OCLC. RLG was a multilibrary consortium that developed the Eureka interlibrary search engine, among other databases. In a glance ahead, RLG merged with OCLC in 2006, and its records became part of WorldCat.

In the 1970s and 1980s, libraries paid subscription prices to institutional organizations and to commercial publishers. The rates for database access rapidly rose and began to reduce the availability of funds for books and serials. Aggravating the situation was the fact that the database prices were rising at different rates across disciplines. The rates for scientific, technical, and medical (STM) databases saw the steepest increases, setting up a scenario in which the sciences and humanities were in competition for resources. In one case, a university library system approached the problem by first prioritizing for the cost of accessing indexes and databases and then dividing the rest of the money by discipline for the purchase of serials and books (Cox, 2011).

This early online industry was indeed the precursor to the Internet. Until the early 1980s, there was a mixture of systems and processes reflecting changing technology. Journals and books were still printed, but the databases and indexes proliferated. In 1981, as an example, BioSciences Information Service (BIOSIS) was indexing biological materials in two ways while also producing *Biological Abstracts*. First, an indexer would assign "concepts" to a document, and the concepts were standardized subject-heading terms. The title was then enriched with terms from the document itself. All the information was converted to machine-readable form, compiled by a computer, and finally sorted. Two sets of magnetic tapes were produced. One tape went to Dialog to update the BIOSIS Previews database, and the other was used for computer-driven photocomposition of the *Biological Abstracts* page proofs. There were two indexes produced using the subject-heading terms and the KWIC-enriched titles (Cornog, 1983).

The industry that was built out as online services during the 1980s gave rise to secondary services—essentially databases of abstracts and indexing terms describing full-text materials. Two of the earliest aggregators of these expanding secondary services were Dialog and SDC ORBIT. Mead Central Lexis became LexisNexis when it added a news and information service in 1979. The H. W. Wilson Company was another pioneer in the library indexing and abstracting services industry and in the late 1980s was using the electronic format for its publications. The company also served as a gateway to other bibliographic databases.

OCLC expanded its services in 1990 to provide general reference access to its own catalog using the Epic service. Then it became a gateway service to other bibliographic services, such as ERIC. OCLC also offered a prepaid, fixed service amount plan in which libraries bought a certain number of search credits. It was then up to the library to decide whether to charge end users (Wedgeworth, 1993).

The online industry continued to grow. After Mead Data Central began offering full-text access through Lexis, the West Publishing Company developed WESTLAW. Non-scholarly full-text services began appearing, including Dialog's INVESTEXT—a financial services database. In 1983, another aggregator, BRS, worked with the American Chemical Society (ACS) to offer the IRCS MEDICAL SCIENCE database, which had thirty-two full-text medical journals, and the ACS JOURNALS FULLTEXT database with eighteen chemistry journals. In 1984, BRS introduced the COLLEAGUE service, which contained complete texts of journals and reference books in medicine and pharmacology. The Scientific and Technical Information Network (STN) was developed in 1983 through a partnership with FIZ Karlsruhe (Germany) and the ACS as an international scientific and technical information database provider. STN began with CAS databases and physics briefs. STN Express software was developed for desktop searching in 1988 (CAS, 2013).

Each of the leading aggregators and database services focused on a different market segment in the scholarly communication industry, and each continually expanded the number of databases offered and the services provided as technology continued to develop greater opportunities. The early aggregators developed out of technical environments and obtained content from outside publishers by paying up-front license fees followed by royalty fees based on customer usage of the publisher's materials. Early aggregator services used one or more of three models for paying publishers, which then determined the end-user charges. The subscription model was a name that was a bit deceptive because it was not a flat fee. In this model, the aggregator established a royalty pool consisting of the total amount from subscription sales. The aggregator tracked its customer usage and paid the publisher a payment based on the total number of views of the documents in the content that was included in the royalty pool. The problem this created was that subscription rates implied flat fees, yet end-user rates were based on search experiences.

In the transactional model, aggregators charged customers a fee for each document viewed and then turned around and paid the publisher. This became a complicated charging system, also leading to frustrations. The Dialog connect-time pricing was the third model and represented a layered fee system. Customers paid for connect time, record charges, and telecommunications charges. This is another version of the "taxi meter" approach mentioned earlier (Plosker, 2004).

Until 1975, librarians had to serve as search intermediaries. That began to change in 1975 when the Ohio State University Libraries installed computer terminals so that users could do their own searches. The system became one of the first online catalogs searchable by a variety of information fields, such as title, author, call number, and Library of Congress subject headings. The new systems were integrated with acquisitions and circulation systems.

One of the characteristics of pricing arrangements that became obvious was that scholarly communication providers, printers, and then publishers were continually refining and experimenting with business models for the delivery of this information. Printed journal and monograph prices continued to rise, while fees were added to index and abstracting and full-text search services. The fee schedules were complicated, moving from single fees to systems of layered fees, requiring a significant amount of management and making annual budgeting for institutional customers difficult. Pricing models were also driving the level of researcher accessibility to the materials needed, promoting rifts among scholars in different disciplines as they competed for library budgets.

Which is King—Content or Search?

The proliferation of databases and bibliographic utilities continued into the 1980s and 1990s. From 1975 to 1981, the number of databases doubled from 300 to 600. Over the next four years, from 1981 to 1985, the number had grown to 3,000 databases. The number of records grew from 52 million in 1975 to 1.68 billion in 1985. In 1976, there were 2 million online catalog records in the OCLC database, and by 1991, there were 23 million records (Lancaster and Warner, 1993). The rapid increase in the number of databases and other online systems led to the rise of gateway services in the mid-1980s. These services allowed users such as librarians to access multiple databases simultaneously, sometimes creating a new in-house database that could then be searched locally by the end user.

A concern rose among publishers and scholars as the number of databases multiplied. Database and online index developers were focused on making the systems as search friendly as possible while producing citations to the primary literature. The creators also began to produce bibliographic databases that did not point to primary literature. They contained bibliographic information about people and companies and were intended for use primarily by non-scholars. There were also non-bibliographic databases appearing that were designed for online research of full-text documents, such as newspapers, general encyclopedias, reference books, and so on. Also, the aggregators were often the recognizable brand to the customer and not the source publisher.

Content was king for scholars and publishers, and the concept was validated by a peer-review process. Converting content to searchable data and storing it in a repository appeared to be gaining significant momentum and exposure. Any organization, agency, or business could convert documents and submit them to producers. As scholars and researchers learned to use the variety of databases and to identify the ones meeting their purposes, questions were raised about the quality of the search engine, often even prior to the quality of the scholarship. Optimal search ability depended on text content, so it became a question of whether content drove search or whether search drove content. To a large degree, these issues are still being debated today as technologies advance, but without question, search is now seen as a full partner in the delivery of quality research data to those professionals who need this information.

RISE OF THE INTERNET

Early Internet Services

If one system was named as the foundation for the Internet, it would be the appearance of ARPANET in 1969. The first system connected four universities, three in California and one in Utah, and began the process of refining a networked communications system so it was more efficient. By 1970, ARPANET added eight more locations around the country, including Harvard University, the MIT, and the RAND Corporation. In 1972, a new protocol was developed called FTP, the acronym for File Transfer Protocol. FTP was a major technology advance because it allowed file exchanging between computers. Also in 1972, Ray Tomlinson, originator of the "@" symbol for e-mail addresses, showcased the first electronic mail delivery system.

Continuing the march toward the Internet and the ability of scholars to communicate with each other via computers, scientists developed TCP/IP, or Transmission Control Protocol/Internet Protocol in the mid-1970s. Before TCP/IP, computers could transfer files only on the same network. TCP/IP was a major technological advance because it made it possible to transfer data between computer networks. In 1976, the Ethernet was developed by Robert Metcalfe. Ethernet allowed the use of coaxial cables for high-speed data transmission. That was followed by the installation of SATNET, which was a satellite system linking Europe and the United States, establishing a global data delivery system. Until approximately 1980, the crude (by today's standards) data transmission system was used almost exclusively by government and university researchers (Elon University School of Communication, 2013).

In 1980, the National Science Foundation (NSF) developed the Computer Science Research Network, which had over seventy online sites by 1983. Any group using the NSF network paid annual operating fees. More networks emerged, including BITNET and USENET. As early as 1985, the NSFNET was introduced as the first "backbone" connecting computer centers around the United States. This greatly improved transmission quality and expanded connectivity. In 1989, Tim Berners-Lee at CERN, a Geneva particle physics laboratory, wrote a memo suggesting a network that would span the globe. Berners-Lee, a software engineer, had joined CERN in 1984 to develop a system that would enable CERN scientists to exchange computerized data with scientific laboratories and universities around the world.

Berners-Lee effectively made the World Wide Web possible by developing three important technologies in 1990: HyperText Markup Language (HTML), a publishing format; Uniform Resource Identifier, a resource address unique to each item; and Hypertext Transfer Protocol (HTTP), a retrieval system that worked with linked resources. There were also other people and organizations continuing to develop new technologies, so there were overlaps. Archie, written by Alan Emtage in 1990, was the first search engine that simplified resource discovery on a confusing network of files. It could search and index files available on the Internet through FTP, whereas before Archie, the searcher had to identify the correct FTP site and then figure out how to maneuver through the particular file structure to find the correct files. Keeping in mind that the Internet but not the World Wide Web existed at this time, the Archie search engine was an FTP site hosting an index of downloadable directory listings found on public FTP servers and running on small "find and download" lists. This was a very primitive search engine, but it represented the beginning of rapid advances in search capabilities. Berners-Lee wrote the first web page editor and browser for the first server at the end of 1990, and the World Wide Web (now called the web) was born. The Conseil Européen pour la Recherche Nucléaire at CERN began using the system, and it was quickly adopted internationally. In 1991, ARAPANET was decommissioned, the NSFNET became the network backbone, and other people began using the web. Internet service providers (ISPs) also appeared in 1991, offering dial-up services for access to the Internet.

During this time and as a local response to search needs, the client application named Gopher was developed in 1991 at the University of Minnesota. It was designed to provide access to local network files and information and consisted of server software, client software, and a communication protocol. The Gopher client application could be run on a user's own computer, or the researcher would log in to a server using Telnet and then use the Gopher client program on the server. Gopher had menus serving as pointers to text documents, and it had the text documents. The researchers could browse through a hierarchy of files without having to know specific file names and file path names. Gopher was responsible for managing data architectures.

Gopher created a lot of excitement because it was a protocol and set of applications that improved the efficiency of information dissemination on the Internet. It simplified data search because Gopher servers stored information that searchers used and offered a menu of choices to users. It established the first true client-server relationship. By way of contrast in a Telnet session, for example, the user would connect to a host machine and stay connected during the entire session. This made it a heavy resource user. Gopher worked differently. The user connected to a Gopher server and would retrieve an initial menu from the server, and the connection then went idle, freeing up the server and lowering network traffic. When the user requested more information, the connection would be restored. It used a standardized protocol, making it possible to move from server to server through menu selection. A Gopher menu choice took the search to the University of Minnesota's Gopher service, which categorized other Gopher servers in numerous geographic locations. Researchers could then pick a server to access (Buchanan, 1995).

The first web server in the United States was installed at the Stanford Linear Accelerator Center in 1991. Over the next two years, Gopher and the World Wide Web were in competition. There was a Hyptertext'91 Conference to advance the web in 1991 and a GopherCon'92 conference held in 1992 to advance Gopher. A new Gopher version allowed multiple file views of the same document, among other improvements. Late in the year, an enhancement of Gopher was developed by Steven Foster and Fred Barrie at the University of Nevada at Reno and was called Veronica for "Very Easy Rodent-Oriented New-wide Index to Computerized Archives." Veronica had a searchable index of Gopher menus and used a "spider" to crawl around and collect links. In 1993, Rhett Jones at the University of Utah developed Jughead, which stood for "Jonzy's Universal Gopher Hierarchy Excavation and Display." Jughead indexed single sites. Each iteration of Gopher enhanced user friendliness, added functionality such as bookmarking, added graphic user interfaces, and much more.

Of interest to the scholarly community was the development of arXiv in 1991 by Paul Ginsparg, who was working at the Los Alamos National Laboratory. By now, e-mailing of manuscripts between senior researchers was common, raising early concerns that early stage researchers were getting left out of the loop. A physicist friend of Ginsparg was also concerned that e-mailed articles would overrun his disk allocation while he was traveling and suggested the creation of an automated centralized repository for e-mails and an alerting system that would send full texts only on user demand. Ginsparg liked the idea and also believed that such a system would democratize information exchanges, thus bringing more researchers back into the communication process. Subsequently, xxx.lanl.gov was developed as an automated e-mail server. Though originally intended to store submissions for only three months, nothing was ever deleted, and it only grew, quickly attracting the attention of the American Physical Society and the Institute of Physics Publishing. In 1992, a friend of Ginsparg at CERN e-mailed him to discuss the World Wide Web program (a good example of how scholarly communication systems were in a rapid state of change). Ginsparg helped test the first U.S. web server, and after the early web browser Mosaic appeared, the physics e-print archive he had developed became a web server. The xxx.lanl.gov was renamed arXiv in 1998 (Ginsparg, 2011).

By 1993, Gopher was growing rapidly, and libraries and universities were two major adopters. As of April 1994, there were at least 6,958 Gopher servers operating (Treese, 1994). However, Mosaic was introduced in the winter of 1993 by Marc Andreessen and Eric Bina on the National Center for Supercomputing Applications servers at the University of Illinois. It was a graphical browser for the World Wide Web. Mosaic, using a graphical user interface (GUI), is largely credited with making the web appealing to a wider audience than scholars and scientists. The GUI was a major step forward because it allowed users to access information without having to remember software commands, as was necessary with command-line interface browsers. The ease of navigation it offered made it extremely appealing to any web user. In 1994, the World Wide Web and Mosaic were growing at a much faster rate than Gopher. It appeared that by the fall of 1995, the FTP, Gopher, and other non-web protocols were already becoming legacy services (Pitkow and Recker, 1995). Mosaic later became the commercial product for Netscape. In 1994, Tim Berners-Lee had left CERN to found the World Wide Web Consortium at MIT, where he foresaw the growth of web servers and appreciated the implications of the Mosaic browser's ability to support inline graphics.

There were several reasons for Gopher's decline. Gopher pointed to documents through menu files that were separate from the documents. The web used HTTP to access documents in HTML, meaning that document creators could put links into the documents. It is easy to see that HTML is the foundation of the current online scholarly communication system that relies so heavily on linking for indexing, citation tracking, and now full-text retrieval. The web document creators could now place their own pointers in the pages, creating an internal indexing system. Gopher also faded quickly because Mosaic had a richer, better interfacing ability that included GUI, a back button, and the ability to view images in document text. Mosaic could also navigate multiple protocols, including HTTP, FTP, and Gopher (Lee, 2008).

Search Engine Transformations

The transformation of scholarly communication systems was initiated by government and university scientists and engineers who were driven by a desire to advance research efforts and increase the speed of knowledge and information transfers. The 1990s was a decade of one new technology after another, each building on what came before it. Search engines were particularly transformative in the communication sector. The earliest navigation tools required knowing the exact wording of the website and where files were located. Search engines automated repetitive search tasks using "spiders," or software programs that read the pages for indexing purposes and record links. This new technology tool eventually had enormous influence on scholarly communication. For example, links in citations could provide instant access to related full-text materials.

After Archie in 1990, Veronica and Jughead in 1991, and Vlib in 1992 (a virtual library that was set up by Berners-Lee), a string of search engines was created by scholarly communities and commercial enterprises. New versions continued to appear regularly until 2010. In February 1993, six Stanford undergraduates developed Excite, followed in June 1993 by Matthew Gray's World Wide Web Wanderer. Wanderer, developed at MIT, was designed to measure the growth of the web, and it later generated a database called the Wandex. This was the first real "bot," or spider, but it was very inefficient, and the Wanderer lasted only until late 1995. In 1994, four important search engines appeared. January 1994 saw the introduction of Infoseek, which allowed webmasters to submit web pages in real time. That same month, AltaVista entered the market. Developed by Digital Equipment Corporation's Network Systems Laboratory and Western Research Laboratory researchers, it first allowed natural language queries and introduced a much faster crawler than its predecessors.

In April 1994, three more search engines were developed. WebCrawler was created by Brian Pinkerton at the University of Washington. This search engine had the distinction of enabling full-text searches. In June 1995, it was bought by AOL, which subsequently sold it to Excite in 1997. The Yahoo! Directory was developed by Jerry Yang and David Filo, students at Stanford University. It began as a directory of favorite web pages and was not originally a searchable index. Yahoo! grew rapidly, was incorporated in 1995, and eventually became a searchable directory. It was a pioneering search engine because a human editorial description was attached to each Uniform Resource Locator. Lycos followed Yahoo! in July 1994; it originally emerged from a student research project at Carnegie Mellon University. Student Michael Loren Mauldin is credited with developing Lycos, but it took venture capital to form the company, Lycos Inc., founded by Bob Davis. Its groundbreaking features included Ranked Relevance retrieval, prefix matching and word proximity, and the unprecedented ability to identify tens of millions of documents. Lycos could match key words with word proximity and prefixes.

Google was originally the result of the collaboration of Stanford University students Larry Page and Sergey Brin. In 1996, they first developed a search engine called BackRub, which operated on Stanford servers first but grew too large for the university's technology. BackRub used backlinks as its search basis and ranked pages using citation notation. The website authority was based on how many other web pages linked to it. BackRub formed the foundation for a new company called Google. The search engine Google was registered as a domain in 1997, and the company incorporated in 1998. Google developed PageRank technology, which is an algorithm that measures website pages in terms of importance by counting the number and quality of links. The spider was named Googlebot. Though Google is the unquestioned giant of search engine companies today, it had a fairly slow start. In 1999, the company obtained funding for continued technology development and growth, and eventually AOL and Yahoo! chose Google as their search partner. Google launched the Google Toolbar in 2000. After Google, there were more search engines introduced, such as MSN, Overture, AllTheWeb, LiveSearch, Snap, FAST, and finally Bing, a rebuilt and rebranded MSN, which used FAST after Microsoft purchased it.

Technology was giving scholars new ways to access information, but this technology cannot be viewed in a vacuum. At the same time that these new technologies were appearing during the 1990s, there was an increasingly troublesome financial problem growing at research and university libraries. Continually rising publishing costs and declining university library budgets were leading to fewer scholarly books being published as a result of library acquisition budgets being consumed by more expensive journal subscriptions. As the situation worsened into the twenty-first century, it came to be referred to as the "serials crisis." The rise of an electronic means of delivering full-text scientific information contained in journals was increasingly viewed as a possible solution. Bibliographic information was available electronically through OCLC and RLG, and online abstracting and indexing (A& I) databases were now well developed and fully searchable. There were a few full-text databases, but they were behind a paywall and often offered by commercial scholarly publishers that continued to sell print journals.

Even as search engines were giving people greater access to information, the scholarly community was asking important questions that are still debated today. Will electronically distributed journals and books provide libraries financial relief through pricing economies? What licensing and fee arrangements would make sense for the use of copyrighted materials? What demand will exist for different types of electronic materials published at different price levels? What impact will electronic publishing of scholarly information have on peer review? How will plagiarism be controlled and scholarly materials secured? How will the integrity of the original text be guaranteed? How will the archiving function be standardized and institutionalized? How will electronic publications be priced (Ekman and Quandt, 1995)? How could the humanities and social science disciplines be included in the trend toward electronic publishing? There was also a concern that the availability of a wealth of information and materials through networks and networked information could have the unintended consequence of further burdening librarians and researchers who would need to worry about such issues as the currency of information, limited access to a select set of leading journals in a specialty, and personal communication networks where important discussions were taking place (Borovansky, 1996).

From its inception, Google earned a reputation for developing new technology tools, so it is not surprising that it entered the online scholarly community with a unique search engine named Google Scholar. The beta version was launched in 2004 to provide a way for searchers to access scholarly literature databases and full-text files. The service includes peer-reviewed papers, preprints, books, theses, technical reports, abstracts, course reserves, case law, and patents. As Google Scholar development continued, it has added and deleted accessible resources, but it searches science databases, such as the Web of Science, MEDLINE/PubMed, Compendex, Inspec, Journal Citation Reports, and others. It also searches humanities and social science reference materials and blogs. And Google Scholar links directly to the full-text material if and where it is available.

Google Scholar was an important step forward in online search because it was available to everyone, and it sifted out the links that were unlikely to have any academic value. Search engines such as Google and Yahoo! could now recognize the context of words and that the value of search results could be increased on repeated searches that honed the search term precision. The enormous growth in sites and data also made traditional search engines difficult to use in the scholarly environment. Google Scholar narrowed the search results, worked to move specialist academic results higher in page rankings, and focused on making the search user friendly. Until Google Scholar appeared, the search services in existence were limited in scope and often still required professional help from librarians familiar with database structure. For example, OCLC QuestionPoint was designed around the knowledge of reference librarians. Google recognized that even scholars needed help searching databases and understanding how to select the appropriate search results as most likely to be relevant text. Another important characteristic of Google Scholar was that it made actually reaching the desired full-text files a much simpler process, requiring fewer clicks on links (Friend, 2006).

Before Google Scholar, inexperienced (and sometimes experienced) researchers often had to consult with research librarians first to determine the appropriate target database and search process. Online research was already standard practice, but that did not mean researchers were fully comfortable with the process. Google Scholar, therefore, served more than one purpose, as it also empowered researchers to undertake their own searching. However, as library collections declined due to budget restrictions and the move to online publishing and access of research materials increased its pace, even librarians were confronted with a radically different research environment in which maintaining current knowledge about databases and full-text electronic files was challenging. One of the features of the web that had become apparent was its capacity to hold unlimited data. Another feature that was quickly becoming influential in determining expectations was the speed at which the web could produce results.

Like most new introductions to the scholarly world, the first concerns are related to completeness and accuracy of results across disciplines. Originally, Google did not search undisclosed academic publishers, preprint repositories, university collections, and professional societies. However, now it does to some extent. Search results produce links to full-text articles or pay-for-view document delivery. One of the most important implications of Google Scholar had nothing to do with its electronic features. Google Scholar recognized that research is increasingly multidisciplinary. When a searcher entered a key word or search string, Google Scholar would access all available information across the web and not just select databases based on discipline. A search using scientific key words could lead to a humanities database link. This was and remains especially important because Google Scholar recognized a research trend in which interdisciplinary approaches were becoming common. The nuance of this can easily be missed because researchers had been stand-alone within their disciplines and thus used stand-alone journals and stand-alone databases. One reason that Google Scholar continues to be considered "in beta" is because it is continually developing to meet the changing needs of modern scholars.

However, Google Scholar is still not allowed to crawl many of the available society and university publishers and commercial vendor databases, so it should not be considered an end-all search tool. For this reason, Google Scholar is touted as a "first step" in the investigative process that points researchers in new directions. Since its introduction in 2004, the search engine has been in continual transition and continues to offer new features and revamped algorithms. There is an impact on researchers, though, as they continue to attempt to retrieve ideal results by understanding how the search algorithms and indexing systems are changing and functioning, which is not always an easy task due to commercial secrecy and algorithmic complexities.

Google Scholar Citations was introduced in 2011 as yet another tool for scholars. This particular service is used by scholarly authors who want to automatically track and graph citations to their articles. It computes citation metrics, such as the h-index, the i-10 index, and the total number of citations.

It also is used to search for scholar profiles and to create a personal public profile. This service is a reflection of the continued importance of citation analysis in scholarly communications and the important role that online publications have assumed. Google Citation and Google Scholar Metrics are not without their controversies. A paper posted on arXiv.org discussed the potential for data manipulation by unscrupulous authors. The researchers created a fake author profile and assigned six false documents that cited other documents of a research group. As a result, there was an increase of 774 citations in 129 papers. In turn, this increased the journals' and authors' h-index. The project was designed to test the ability to manipulate the online search services and to discuss the temptation that such manipulative ability presents in the way of "citations engineering" (López-Cózar, Robinson-García, and Salinas, 2012).

There are other scholarly search engines that have developed over time. For example, CiteSeer^X was introduced in 1997 at the NEC Research Institute by Steve Lawrence, C. Lee Giles, and Kurt Bollacker and now resides at Pennsylvania State University. It was the first digital library and search engine to use autonomous citation indexing, which locates articles, extracts the citations, identifies citations in different formats, and identifies citation context in the article. CiteSeer^X is the next generation of the search engine, focused on computer and information science and touting itself as providing much more than just access to a digital library. It also provides "resources such as algorithms, data, metadata, services, techniques, and software that can be used to promote other digital libraries" (CiteSeer^X, 2014). It has full-text indexing, automatic article harvesting, citation statistics, context tracking, reference linking, and much more.

The Elsevier Scopus is a subscription search engine and database covering peer-reviewed literature. The abstract and citation database includes research in the fields of science, medicine, technology, social sciences, and arts and humanities. SpringerLink is a search engine that also provides access to scientific journals, books, series, reference works, and protocols primarily for Springer materials.

Even as A&I services made possible by sophisticated search engines were developing, the scholarly publishing industry was consolidating through mergers and acquisitions that started in the 1990s and continued into the 2000s. The net result is an academic publishing industry in which over 42 percent of all journal articles are published by Elsevier, Springer, and Wiley in over 20,000 academic journals (Jha, 2012).

Full-Text Articles

The development of full-text electronic articles was discussed previously in the context of the emerging technology. Experimental electronic journals were posted on the Internet through the Electronic Information Exchange System (EIES) in 1982. EIES was sponsored by the Division of Information Science and Technology of the NSF and represented the first "open access" journals. The first experimental journal forms include a peer-reviewed journal, an interactive journal, a newsletter, and the unreformed journals. Though journals and other scholarly materials continue to be printed, there was an ongoing movement toward publishing online that followed a continuum like this: paper journal to web, paper to web only, electronic format only, fully interactive, or some combination (Murray and Anthony, 1999). When full-text articles began appearing online in the 1980s, visionaries quickly understood that the Internet and then the web offered researchers a tremendous opportunity to expand scholarship in a way not possible before. Printing, copying, faxing, and e-mailing articles as attachments are not nearly as efficient procedures as being able to retrieve and download full-text, peer-reviewed articles.

Mead Data Central, a subsidiary of the Mead Corp, is credited with providing the first full-text articles in electronic form in 1973; the articles were Ohio and New York codes and cases, the U.S. code, and some federal case laws. By 1980, LEXIS offered case law for all fifty states online. In the 1980s, publishers began offering selections of established journals in full-text forms using online database services such as Dialog, SDC, STN, and BRS. The emergence of electronic full-text journal articles was a step-by-step process.

In 1983, the ACS offered eighteen primary journals as full text through the BRS online system. The advantages that the Books and Journals Division of the ACS saw in electronic submissions were a shorter publication time, lower cost of publication, and minimization of proofreading. By 1987, ACS was working on a project leading to electronic processing of technical books. The process started with accepting manuscripts in machine-readable form, entering the manuscript into the ACS computer, completing screen editing, and telecommunicating revised manuscripts to the typesetter. Producing electronic-only journal articles was going slower because of the sheer volume of papers ACS published annually. The first test cases were articles that appeared in *Analytical Chemistry*'s *Fundamental Reviews* and *Environmental Science & Technology* ("Electronic Publishing in Analytical Chemistry," 1987). One factor slowing down more rapid adoption of electronic publishing in the highly technical chemistry discipline was the difficulties in dealing with chemical notations and structures. ACS developed a publishing system for its journals and the journals of other publishers. Also in 1983, Elsevier began using the BRS system to publish biomedical journals in electronic format.

As discussed, Paul Ginsparg at Los Alamos National Laboratory had developed the first preprint archive, arXiv, in August 1991, which was originally dedicated to journal articles in high-energy theoretical physics. This was an important step in the development of electronic full-text articles. Preprints are articles that could be in any stage of the scholarly communication process. The articles may have been through the peer-review process and are ready for journal publishing or are waiting for a decision as to whether they will be published. Preprints can also include articles that have been formally submitted for publication (Tomaiuolo and Packer, 2000).

There was a succession of preprint servers containing full-text articles introduced in the 1990s, and by 2000, there were many opportunities to access files. The CERN document server covered full-text articles from 1994 forward. PubMed Central enabled viewing full text as HTML documents by using their web browser or downloading PDF files. ChemWeb was launched in 1997 as a joint venture between MDL Information Systems, Inc., and the Current Science Group and became a wholly owned subsidiary of Elsevier Science. Membership in the chemistry "club" grew dramatically, and by 1998, ChemWeb had 14 million abstracts in its database and seventy-three journals. Elsevier had purchased MDL Information Systems in 1997. Chem-Web allowed free searching of chemistry journals, but searchers had to pay for full text through subscription or pay-per-article. In 2000, it released a press release that touted itself as the "first commercial web service to combine electronic publishing, databases, journals, and scientific forums, along with informatics technologies for structure-based searching, high-speed text retrieval, and manipulation of 'live' molecular structures" (PR Newswire, 2000). Fourteen years later, ChemWeb is still running and offers access to full-text articles from some of the biggest publishers, including Springer, Wiley, and Elsevier; societies, such as ACS; and other smaller, prestigious publishers, such as Taylor & Francis and Bentham Science. ChemWeb's story is similar to many other commercial enterprises offering full-text journal articles. ChemWeb.com is now owned and operated by ChemIndustry.com. The ChemWeb description shows how quickly events were taking place in the scholarly publishing world.

In 1995, Elsevier's TULIP (acronym for The University Licensing Program) project began. Elsevier partnered with university libraries to investigate the use of academic electronic scientific journals. Elsevier also developed the PEAK project to study the pricing of electronic delivery of full-text articles; this project was also a partnership with libraries. Also in 1995, the Red Sage Project was launched, an experimental digital journal library in health sciences. It was the result of an initial 1992 collaboration between AT&T Bell Laboratories, Springer-Verlag, and the University of California, San Francisco, in which they signed memorandums of agreement with numerous prestigious organizations, such as ACS, the American Medical Association, Blackwell Scientific Publishers, Oxford University Press, John Wiley & Sons, and others, creating an impressive array of professional societies, commercial publishers, and university presses (Butter, 1994).

By 1999, journals such as *Lancet, Journal of Experimental Psychology: Human Perception and Performance, American Journal of Political Science*, and the *Journal of Neuroscience* were accepting preprints for electronic publishing before print publishing. There was a preponderance of scientific journals published electronically, meaning that the humanities and social science disciplines were still largely out of the loop.

By 2003, there were a number of scholarly journals available online, and some were e-journals only and not published in print form. Many of the electronic journals were published by non-traditional scholarly publishers who were testing the new publishing and distribution forum. A discussion on the applicability of open access publishing was beginning as scholars and budding online publishers looked for ways to increase access to journals and enter the commercial, scholarly communications industry, but the discussion was still in the infancy stage.

The market was highly competitive with none of the large publishers able to dominate—Elsevier Science had an 18 percent share; Wolters Kluwer had a 7 percent share; Blackwell, Bertelsmann, and Wiley each had a 4 percent share; Taylor & Francis had a 2 percent share; Sage had a 2 percent share; and Karger had a 1 percent share. The largest and most prestigious university presses, such as Cambridge University Press and Oxford University Press, had only a 1 percent share each of the ISI-rated STM journals (Savenije, 2003).

The development of the rising costs of journals in this period is complex. A study of the journal print market revealed that the factors influencing pricing included inelastic demand, publisher competition based on quality, journals that could be considered their own markets, and relatively few new printed journal entries because of restricted library budgets able to support sales (Savenije, 2003).

The traditional publishing sectors were also consolidating. Some large publishing houses were formed during the period 1990–2000. For example, Bertelsmann bought 80 percent of Springer Verlag and 100 percent of Random House, Reed Elsevier bought Harcourt and Endeavor, Wolters Kluwer bought Ovid Technologies, and so on. The mergers and acquisitions led to a small set of large publishing houses producing unique journals that cannot be substituted because of their topical content. A study by Mark McCabe developed a portfolio model in which a core group of titles were identified so that prices could be tracked as the publishers merged. Before the mergers, the publishers were setting prices for quality, high-demand journals so that they had an apparent lower cost-per-use ratio, thus attracting library purchases. When publishers merged, they did not necessarily take advantage of this high use ratio. The larger firms could take advantage of economies of scale and earn a higher profit, but many more types of information resources were competing for researchers' use (McCabe, 1999, 2001).

Everything is related in the offline and online scholarly publishing environment. Libraries purchased fewer books as a greater percentage of the acquisitions budget was spent on journals. As of 2003, three-fourths of the academic journals were published online, but they were also printed. The "Big Deal" was developed to address this phenomenon. In the Big Deal, publishers offered one subscription price for an online aggregation of journals. The Big Deal was priced so that it only made sense to buy a license for the bundle because breaking it up led to even higher charges. The original Big Deal prices were based on the marginal costs of printing only, so libraries were getting the benefit of the lower cost of online publishing. In return for these marginal prices for both print and online subscriptions, libraries agreed to keep their current level of subscriptions for one year.

There were other pricing and access arrangements offered by publishers to libraries in the early 2000s. Some publishers had developed their own proprietary search and retrieval web-based systems, and their journals were accessed through these systems for a fee. Some journals were available through subscription vendors. There were also journals available on websites. The growing online publishing industry led to the development of platforms such as Project MUSE, an online database established in 1993 as a result of collaboration between Johns Hopkins University Press and the Milton S. Eisenhower Library at Johns Hopkins University. This particular database was dedicated to the humanities and social sciences and has remained a non-profit enterprise for disseminating quality scholarship in the form of full-text journals published by scholarly societies and university presses.

Researchers, now expecting online access to e-journals, often were stymied if their "home" institution did not subscribe to the journal. Interlibrary loan was growing as libraries canceled subscriptions. But the rules for using articles under interlibrary loan were not clear. For example, libraries were not allowed to share electronic journal articles. Doing an interlibrary loan required printing out the journal article and then delivering it in some manner. Researchers outside the library system accessing full-text databases usually had to buy the article from the database provider in an electronic format or request it through interlibrary loan and receive it in print. Finding documents had become easier in terms of access but more challenging in terms of finding desired resources among millions of records. Search engines such as Google Scholar greatly helped end users find library databases and electronic journal collections (Kamble et al., 2012).

In 1991, RLG released the Ariel software as a tool for the rapid delivery of "nonreturnable" (copied) materials in support of interlibrary loans of university libraries. It was specifically designed to solve many of the problems libraries were having with the fax technologies being used by interlibrary loan departments, such as poor image quality, the cost of fax machines and their maintenance, and the amount of preparatory time in sending fax transmission. Ariel was widely accepted in the community, and it is still in commercial use today. In 2003, Infotrieve acquired Ariel from RLG, and it is now used globally in support of document transfer and delivery.

To understand the forward movement to increasing use of the web for publishing, it is necessary to recognize the expansive ongoing effort to eliminate barriers to producing and distributing electronic documents. As mentioned, the late 1990s and the early 2000s was a period of an increasing number of mergers and acquisitions in the commercial publishing industry, of a greater effort by societies and university presses to manage the emerging technologies, and of an increasing competition between the players in academic publishing. Though archiving and journal distribution are now accepted as commercial enterprises, during the early years of the web, the electronic archiving and distribution of journals by societies and commercial publishers represented a move into what had been primarily library functions (Solomon, 2013). The implication is that libraries, university presses, professional societies, and commercial publishers were all struggling to find their roles or "fit" in an electronic scholarly communication world. As early as 1999, the scholars were talking about open access, a discussion initiated by Harold Varmus, the director of the National Institutes of Health, who proposed a freely accessible archive of biomedical research reports. By 2006, an increasing number of journals moved into the open access format, forming a significant new entrant on the publishing landscape (Crow, 2006).

There are scholars who believe that the continued progress toward electronic-only formats is inevitable for two major reasons. First is the prohibitive cost of printing, as discussed. The pricing of serials initiated a change in the relationship between librarians, scholars, and publishers. The introduction of digital distribution only added more impetus for change as traditional roles in peer review, publishing, dissemination, and archiving were reassessed. A second reason is that more scholars are readily converting to a new format. Many have "grown up" with technology, are comfortable with it, and are already exerting pressure on the established scholarly communication system to be more open and accessible on the web. In response to the serials crisis and the expanding online databases, research libraries have been in the process of converting print journal subscriptions to electronic only. By 2006, the Association of Research Libraries had converted approximately 36 percent of its journal subscriptions to electronic-only formats. There was also increasing discussion about the relevancy of open access as a new publishing strategy that could overcome the economics plaguing university systems.

E-Books and Their Relation to Other Media

Journals and journal articles were not the only scholarly materials adapting to electronic publishing. The introduction of the e-book was accompanied by some of the same issues as the e-journal. For example, what was the best delivery model for e-books? In the 1990s, CD-ROMs were used by libraries in storage and retrieval systems. However, the failure of CD-ROM technology was fast and epic as the web developed. It was simply so much easier and more efficient to distribute and retrieve scholarly information over the cloud using the web and personal computers than using cumbersome CD-ROMs. In a 1997 student survey conducted at the University of Rhode Island, researchers reported that CD-ROM student users made a number of suggestions for improvements. One was simply to provide full-text access and full-text databases. CD-ROMs were not designed for accumulating large collections of full-text materials or databases but compared to print were working well for accessing reference index and abstracting databases, such as ERIC, MEDLINE, MLA, NTIS/government documents, and other popular data sets (McCarthy, Krausse, and Little, 1997).

In many ways, monographs and book publishing were the victim of scholarly journals. As discussed, journals were taking a larger and larger share of library budgets beginning in the late 1970s, and it is a trend that continues today. In a cause-and-effect situation, as library budgets declined and serials subscription rates soared, the fewer books were purchased. This was a global issue. In 1976, the Australian National University had a 50:50 ratio of serials to books, but that ratio had drastically changed to 83:17 by 2002 (Steele, 2008). Monograph publishing turned toward a non-academic distribution model where books that were published had more of an international, general appeal in the hopes of increasing sales. University presses came under pressure from university leadership to cut expenses or cut services, and monographs were again the victim. This created a situation, according to J. B. Thompson of Cambridge University, in which academics needed their work published but seemed to lack understanding about the "forces driving presses to act in ways that are sometimes at odds with the aims and priorities of academies" (Thompson, 2005). There was a growing fear among scholars that the decline of monograph printing would hurt scholarly research and intellectual vigor. Digital book publishing was envisioned as a way to reengage the academic community and revive monographs, particularly in the humanities and social sciences. That required technologies that gave scholars not just a means of digital submissions but also a way to research other books, to enable their books to be widely available to readership, and to link citations between books as well as between books and journals, book abstracts, and so on. This could preserve the traditional scholarly communication process.

Project Gutenberg was one of the earliest efforts to create an electronic public library of monographs, and it was hoped that the existence of this online library would revive interest in monograph publishing. Initially, the goal was modest by today's standards because the project planned on adding 10,000 books by the end of 2001. It was conceived and managed by Michael Hart at the University of Illinois. The intent was to democratize book access so that the largest number of people could benefit, and Hart already envisioned e-publishing as the means to that end. In an interesting twist, he was given an operator's account with $100 million in computer time at the university because the university's computer capacity far exceeded its use. He decided that he needed to come up with a new idea that would take advantage of this enormous amount of computer time and decided that the storage, retrieval, and searching of library collections would bring the greatest value. The original e-texts were made available in Plain Vanilla ASCII so that they could meet the needs of 99 percent of the project's audience. The importance of this decision should not be underestimated. Like the original Gutenberg printing press, Project Gutenberg set the tone for using the Internet to reach the masses as opposed to a limited scientific community. However, Project Gutenberg resisted pressures to create "authorized editions" to keep the audience wide but did intend on publishing scholarly-level works. The Project Gutenberg Library is divided into Light Literature, Heavy Literature, and References (Hart, 2010). Project Gutenberg is still operating today, printing free books out of copyright in the United States and copyrighted books that authors have given Project Gutenberg permission to distribute, often on a worldwide basis.

Another early effort to digitize materials other than journals was the Library of Congress's American Memory Project that was piloted between 1990 and 1994 and encompassed a wide variety of materials, including print, sound recordings, photographs, and moving images. The project had to address many new issues associated with technical procedures, intellectual property issues, CD-ROM distribution, and library preservation and access. After 1994, the Internet and the World Wide Web came into more prominent use. The National Digital Library Program was officially launched on October 13, 1994. The American Memory Historical Collections was the first project, and it digitized Library of Congress historical documents and documents from major research archives. By 2000, there were over 5 million items available to researchers, scholars, students, the public, and the global Internet community (Library of Congress, 2013).

JSTOR was founded in 1995 by William Bowen, former president of Princeton University, and was funded by the Andrew W. Mellon Foundation. It, too, was dedicated to creating digital archives. In 1997, the project began with back issues of journals and in 2002 expanded to include creating a digital archive for a variety of scholarly literatures. JSTOR became part of

Ithaka, and the Electronic Archiving Initiative was initiated. In 2005, Portico was launched to balance the needs of publishers and libraries as a third-party digital preservation solution. In 2009, Ithaka and JSTOR merged to become ITHAKA; JSTOR, Portico, and Ithaka are managed by the same organization. In 2012, a "Books" program was launched by JSTOR. "Books" brings scholarly monographs from university and academic publishers to the JSTOR platform and integrates cross-searching of archival journals and monographs through citations, book reviews, and articles. These monographs are preserved in Portico (JSTOR, 2012).

A third important early book digitization effort was the Million Book Project. Started in 2002, the project strived to transfer 1 million books from around the world into digital format. Initiated by Professor Raj Reddy at Carnegie Mellon University, the project worked with international scanning centers to create entries for the Universal Digital Library (UDL). The goal was to create a worldwide, free resource for materials in all languages and disciplines or subjects. Once again, the idea was to give universal access to information rather than limiting information. Optical character recognition software digitized the books into ASCII format and, just as importantly, allowed full-text searching by scholars, researchers, students, global users, and libraries (Linke, 2003).

Oxford Scholarship Online was launched in 2003 with four subject modules: humanities, social science, law, and medicine. It originally offered access to full-text monographs published by Oxford University Press but was expanded to include content from other university presses through University Press Scholarship Online. Libraries can pay an annual subscription fee or negotiate another purchase model. Once purchase is made, there is permanent access to the e-book because it is archived in Portico. Non-subscribers can access abstracts and use key words to search book and chapter levels. As of October 2013, Oxford Scholarship Online had 9,253 digitized monographs with more than 95,000 chapters and over 2 million pages, but the numbers are continually increasing (Oxford University Press, 2013).

All of the original projects are still ongoing and served as the starting point for Google's Larry Page, who was interested in digitally scanning every book that exists in the world. First, he dealt with the technical issues of developing scanning techniques that did not harm the books and managing odd type sizes and features of different languages. In 2004, a Google team visited the Bodleian Library at Oxford University, leading to a formal partnership to digitize Oxford University's library collection of 1 million nineteenth-century public domain books. Google's founders also announced Google Print at the Frankfurt Book Fair in Germany. Joining the project were scholarly publishers such as Blackwell, the University of Chicago Press, Oxford University Press, Blackwell, Springer, Princeton University Press, and others (Google, 2013).

One of the important projects Google has undertaken is the Google Books Library Project, first announced late in 2004. The project was a joint effort between Google and the University of Michigan, Stanford University, the New York Public Library, and Oxford University to digitize 15 million volumes from these collections and make them available online. There was a period of litigation in which copyright issues were debated, and a number of issues were resolved. Google Print was renamed Google Books and employs a robust search engine offering a variety of options to end users. Browsers can search Google Books to find appropriate content based on search terms. If the book is out of copyright, has publisher permission to share, or is in the public domain, the scholar can view a book preview or the entire text. If not, the searcher can find out where to buy or borrow the book or buy the e-book for download. The Google Books Library Project continues to work with libraries to bring collection catalogs online.

Google has been a continuing powerhouse in electronic publishing and archiving of scholarly material. Its efforts were not always welcomed. Sergey Brin published an op-ed in the *New York Times* in 2009, heralding Google Books as a "library to last forever" (Brin, 2009). However, the Google Book Search initiative was a commercial enterprise that intended on monetizing out-of-print books. Libraries found themselves once again worried about the price of institutional subscriptions, but this time it was the subscriptions to Google Books content. Google continued to develop Google Books, adding new features on a regular basis, including a download-a-PDF button to all books out of copyright status; the addition of "About This Book" pages, which use an algorithm to create information pages using rich related book content; navigation ability through books with popular passages; the addition of even more books added by international libraries, such as the Cantonal and University Library of Lausanne, the Ghent University Library, and others; and the addition of "View Plain Text" links to books that are out of copyright. The last enhancement was meant to prepare for anticipated technologies, such as screen readers and Braille (Google, 2013).

For monographs to be published as e-books, technology that is accessible to scholars was required. In 2000, the means of completing peer review of e-publications was far from being a settled issue. Without peer review, online publications did not meet scholarly communication requirements. E-book publishing remained cumbersome through most of the 2000s because e-books had to be read on a computer screen, and mobile technology was underdeveloped or non-existent. The commercial and academic publishers did not embrace e-books as a community, even though there were many projects, such as the ones mentioned, in progress. There were simply not enough e-books being written to justify spending a lot of time and investment to develop the online scholarly monograph publishing system. The conversion of printed books to e-books was a slow and expensive process. The

Andrew W. Mellon Foundation has been a leader in this area and has funded a number of academic societies and university presses over the years to help with the transition to electronic monographs.

For example, the American Council of Learned Societies received $3 million as far back as 1999 to "foster broader acceptance by the scholarly community of electronic monograph-length texts . . . to create the framework for a centralized, non-commercial, electronic publication space . . . develop electronic publishing processes that will streamline production and make the creation and dissemination of electronic texts more cost-effective" (D'Arms and Ekman, 1999). The Andrew W. Mellon Foundation was a major supporter of the Gutenberg Project. Though effort and funding have been put into the transition to e-book publishing, the lack of coordination created a system with significant gaps and shortcomings. The academic monograph has been in decline for decades, but it is making a revival as collaborative publishing projects increase in number and scope. For example, the American Association of University Professors collaborated on the American Council of Learned Societies (ACLS) Humanities E-Book Project to create an online searchable collection of 2,200 humanities books that are reviewed and recommended by scholars. The full-text titles were offered by the ACLS in collaboration with publishers, learned societies, and the librarians at the University of Michigan's Scholarly Publishing Office. STM e-books are coming into maturity also. Springer has over 145,000 STM e-books online that date back to the 1840s. Libraries pay subscription rates, and patrons can access the digital books in PDF or HTML format at the library or from remote locations. Functionality was increased so that students or scholars can download chapters or whole books. Springer and Elsevier are making e-books available on the same digital platforms as journal content. However, commercial publishers are still dealing with the fact that e-book functionality across platforms is still not standardized. But even this is changing, as Elsevier recently acquired Knovel, an online database of technical e-books that uses more standardized formats and data structures for the efficient retrieval of monographic information.

The scholar's perspective on monograph publishing is different from the publisher's perspective. As university libraries and societies moved more toward a sustainable and perhaps even a profit-making model, the debate turns to how the primary market is defined. Three types of publishers have emerged in monograph publishing in the digital age. First are the commercial publishers that still want good manuscripts to resell and that can generate a particular return on investment. The second type of publisher requires the scholar to pay a fee to publish and to present the material in ready-to-publish form. The title is added to a catalog and sold to libraries in a print-on-demand model. The third category of publisher is the research library, which is increasingly reviving monograph publishing and adopting digital processes but to replace, not supplement, university publishing. It has been proposed that this will inevitably have an impact on scholarly communication because it casts university presses as superfluous entities (Lorimer, 2013).

Secondary Publishers

As technology continued to advance, it impacted the secondary publishing industry as well. Aggregation and discovery services developed new technology-based services, and new technologies, such as cloud-based services, are opening up new possibilities for more efficient and reliable services for scholars. As discussed, the path to adoption of new publishing systems had been marked at times by resistance from commercial and academic publishers, pricing issues, and end-user concerns that slowed down changes to the scholarly communication system. However, the secondary publishers have always been on the cusp of technological enhancements and readily adopted enhancements to deliver better search and retrieval services that access more documents. The adoption of technology has not been an issue, but standardization has been.

Like everything else in the scholarly publishing system, discovery tools went through periodic transformations. Print-based catalogs, card catalogs, and bound indexes now seem primitive. Catalogs and reference material were converted for use in integrated library systems, beginning with text-based, menu-driven interface systems that were physically located in the buildings. Web development in the 1990s led to library vendors creating HTTP web-based online catalogs. From that point on, the commercial, society, and academic publishers rapidly developed electronic journals and e-books. The A&I databases and content aggregators developed systems able to access some segment of the web-based materials using CD-ROMs or through menu-driven, text-based networked systems that led to search and retrieval via the web. In the late 2000s, library catalog searches included intuitive functionality and designs that were more like popular information search services, such as Google. Another enhancement was the ability to harvest records from locally hosted library files stored in different formats that were presented in a uniform manner in search results through catalog interfaces. The next generation of catalog tools included faceted navigation, tag clouds, and Web 2.0 social features (Vaughan, 2011).

Secondary publishers, such as Engineering Village, retooled the business model for decades. Engineering Village's story is typical of the transitions the A&I businesses went through over the decades. The company traces its roots to 1884, when Dr. John Butler Johnson at Washington University wrote the first volume of the *Engineering Index* (*Ei*). In 1918, the American Society for Mechanical Engineers acquired *Ei*. In 1967, *Ei* published "Current Information Tape for Engineers," which went by the acronym CITE, which two years later morphed into the COMPENDEX (Computerized Engineering Index), a machine-readable program. It took until 1954, or seventy years, to publish the one-millionth abstract but only twenty-one years to publish the two-millionth. In 1995, Engineering Village launched and made the COMPENDEX available on the web. Elsevier purchased Engineering Index in 1998, and between then and 2007, other services migrated to the Engineering Village platform. They include PaperChem, ENCOMPASS, Inspec, and others. Now Engineering Village is faced with a changing marketplace where individual services have made way for sophisticated discovery services that cross databases and can reach into private and library collections. Engineering Village has evolved, though. It now has a single interface that can link multiple databases and can access journals, government reports, articles in trade publications, reference books, and so on. Quick Search was added to make it easier for engineers to find and manage information by entering key words and selecting databases.

Technology had reached a point where a sophisticated search system could use link resolvers for the selection of content providers, which then led to a publisher's or an aggregator's website. Once at the website, another search could be conducted to find the specific resource. In other words, there was the equivalent of a two-tiered discovery system. The first discovery system could get the user from a library-issued call number and MARC record 856 link to the publisher's website. The second discovery system completed the process by getting the searcher to the book, journal, or journal article, which was the intended end goal. As more records were converted to or published in electronic form, the system became more unwieldy (Vaughan, 2011). Researchers were often unable to locate resources in catalogs, disrupting the discovery process. Being able to eventually get to full-text documents was an improvement but did nothing to resolve the problem of needing multiple interfaces to find the records in the first place.

A&I services regularly expanded their databases, but the next major event was the development of web-scale discovery systems, also called web-scale discovery services. The development of web-scale discovery systems represented a major enhancement because it meant having the capability to search across local and remote web content and provide relevancy-ranked results within an intuitive interface, providing information in a way that people had become familiar with when using the major search engines, such as Google or Yahoo!. It is deep discovery of the web that eliminates information silos. The technology was not new, but the application of the technology to commercial discovery services was very new. It was viewed by libraries in 2011 as a search service that had long been needed. Web-based discovery services harvest content from remotely hosted and local repositories. The harvested content is accumulated in a centralized index in which records consisting of different content types are standardized for more efficient search and retrieval. Using a Google-like query, searchers get Google-like results delivery.

In 2012, five of the leading secondary publishing companies were EBSCO, Summon from ProQuest, Primo from Ex Libris, WorldCat from OCLC, and Google Scholar (already discussed). Web-scale discovery services have the lofty goal of creating an interface similar to a Google search that has a single point of entry into an institution's relevant scholarly data. What is holding up progress to the next stage of development are divergent interests and perspectives between content providers, libraries, and discovery services. There is no common vocabulary or agreement on relevance rankings or the depth and breadth of indexing. To address the issues, two groups—the Open Discovery Initiative and the National Federation of Advanced Information Services—began studying formal standards and best practices. These studies begin to bring full circle the two decades of online and web enhancements in the secondary scholarly publishing industry. Libraries want the discovery services central index to encourage discovery of the library's entire collection, including subscription services. However, libraries have difficulty identifying which index services could provide the widest coverage of the library's subscription services and holdings in terms of information such as journal volumes, abstracts, full text, and so on (Kelley, 2012). Indexes are the sum of what providers submit. A true comprehensive discovery service would not be dependent on provider submissions to the discovery service.

The reality of the A&I industry is that commercial vendors have more to gain by offering unique services and databases. If every service were able to offer search and retrieval from every global database and library collection, there would not be a need for more than a very limited number of businesses. Even Google Scholar, with its broad search ability, has limitations because it does not have access to many scholarly collections or to many proprietary full-text records. For this reason, Google Scholar is often promoted as only a first step in the discovery process.

The impact of technology on the scholarly communication system has been broad by impacting the business models and the relationships between publishers, researchers, libraries, and users. Publishers and aggregation services had to become more service oriented for a couple of key reasons. The first reason is simply due to the fact that clients and end users expected it in the new Internet age. Libraries could not continue committing such a significant amount of their collections budgets to services that failed to meet expectations and placed too many limits on accessibility of information. The end users also had expectations, many of which had been prompted by Google and Google Scholar. The second reason that commercial product providers had to become more service oriented was the fact that more research material was available online at no cost. It is true that the set of free online documents is not nearly as complete as the various scholarly collections maintained by university libraries, commercial publishers, and societies. However, the very accessibility of free, full-text electronic materials is changing the scholarly communication search and retrieval business model, moving it again toward more of an emphasis on what value can be added to the scholarly content.

Institutional repositories are one outcome of the changing technology. They reflect a change in the publisher-library interrelationship as libraries assume more responsibility for the dissemination and archiving of the research materials generated by their own institutions. Institutional repositories began to increase substantially, in total numbers of new records and records maintained, beginning in 2000 and have climbed ever since. Peer-reviewed archives can contain institutional-generated materials and documents from other universities, depending on the arrangements put in place. When archives filled with university press or other publications are coupled with an efficient search engine, the commercial publishers are cut out of the cycle, and libraries have more control over materials accessible by aggregation services. The first decade of the 2000s is best defined as a period in which technology led to a more user article–based consumption behavior, increasing electronic sophistication in navigational tools, and a trend toward more service-oriented scholarly publishing systems (Souto, 2007). These trends have naturally taken scholars down a path toward the integration of scholarly information services into their daily work flow.

The best way to understand how sophisticated aggregation and discovery services have become is to look at some of the most successful and long-running vendors that have worked with libraries and scholars to adapt technology to provide state-of-the-art services. EBSCO Discovery Services is just one example of a commercial vendor offering state-of-the-art aggregation and discovery services. EBSCO*host* offers over 375 full-text and secondary research databases, more than 420,000 e-books, subscription services for over 355,000 e-journals, and access via universities or other educational facilities, libraries, medical and hospital institutions, associations, corporations, and government facilities. Serial Solutions's discovery service, the Summon service, has embraced a vision of a single index and standardized results in its products. Summon service has a single, unified index that enables searching across all of a library's resources and offers users scholarly contextual research assistance. The unified index maps metadata from various resources to a common schema, which is an important step toward standardization. The discovery service produces a single record that accumulates rich metadata and full text from multiple sources to create a record that is more discoverable. Institutional repositories from other institutions can be included with the client's repository, and the library's full catalog can be included in the unified index. Additionally, there is a means for libraries to expand searches to encompass materials in the scope of searches eligible for shared borrowing arrangements.

The Primo discovery service, a product of Ex Libris, is a good example of how searches have been designed to funnel inquiries to a single search box that provides access to library collections and content in the Primo Central Index. Results are presented in a single, ranked listing, a result format that is clearly similar to Google. The Primo information architecture is described by the company as a step forward in the transformation of library infrastructures to "unify back-end management of resources and front-end user services across all resources types." Primo decouples search and discovery functions so that libraries can maintain their systems but add and replace applications as needed. The Primo system can integrate with other vendor applications and a variety of library collections that include the library catalog, knowledge bases, and digital repositories (ExLibris Primo, 2013).

OCLC's WorldCat web-based discovery service functions like a hub in that the searchable database was built through the contributions of hundreds of libraries and other programs and organizations. WorldCat.org gives visibility to the millions of items in library collections on the open web, and WorldCat Local customizes the search application for local use. It is a leader in moving toward linked open data. As a hub, WorldCat partners with numerous other aggregators and content providers.

What does this mean for scholars? Aggregators have a critical responsibility in that they ensure that indexes are compiled using metadata that reflects the language of the disciplines. Discovery services can have reliable search results only if the metadata is carefully constructed. There is also a need for increased cross-sector and cross-discipline aggregation services. However, scholars working with commercial and library aggregation and discovery services are using web-based systems that have greatly reduced the need to log into multiple systems or databases because there is seamless searching.

New technologies are still emerging that will enhance discovery services even more. For example, new products are being developed that collect all sources of information across the web, from current news and videos to published scholarly scientific documents, and produce a standardized report. A scientist could reduce hours of searching time to a single search session.

Aggregation services and discovery services are also turning to cloud computing for data storage and adding a social level to search. Cloud computing is defined by the National Institute of Standards and Technology at the U.S. Department of Commerce as "as a model for enabling ubiquitous, convenient, on-demand network access to a shared pool of configurable computing resources (e.g., networks, servers, storage, applications, and services) that can be rapidly provisioned and released with minimal management effort or service provider interaction" (Mell and Grance, 2011: 2). A&I and other services extract data and content from across the web, libraries, and partnering vendors; aggregate the collected information in the cloud; and then provide search services that retrieve the most relevant content while also providing researchers a social venue for communicating without violating privacy. The next technological enhancement is blending the social and research functions (Hawkins, 2013).

Libraries have been experimenting with cloud computing as a viable alternative to storing and accessing data and information. In fact, there have been predictions that the cloud will eventually replace the integrated library system as a services platform. Library collection management systems could conceivably overlay enormous bibliographic databases established on the web from data gathered from the web. Discovery services were the first forays into the cloud by libraries. OCLC WorldCat was a leader in the effort to aggregate data about collections into common web-based pools. Other cloud-based union catalogs were established by the National Library of Australia, Bibsys in Norway, and the Bayerische Staatsbibliothek in Germany. Now going beyond cataloging are the National Library of Australia, the Hathi Trust, OAIster, and Europeana. Hathi is developing a repository of books and journals digitized for the cloud and collected from U.S. research libraries. OAISTER was first started by the University of Michigan and is now managed by OCLC. Europeana aggregates digitized materials from libraries, galleries, museums, and archives (Goldner, 2010). The cloud gives libraries new opportunities as well as new institutional challenges as they try to navigate the new horizons of shared accessible content across institutions and available directly from source publishers.

Indexing and tagging methods are challenged by the enormous amount of information and publications available on the web and the new sources of that information. Whereas A&I services could once rely on traditional collections for their source of data and information, they are now contending with information sources such as personal repositories and open access databases. End users are also demanding the ability to search across content types, such as pictures, social media, company reports, and so on, and to also access data from "deep indexing." ProQuest has been a leader in developing deep indexing capabilities that create metadata for information hidden in the figures, tables, and representations in journal articles. The goal is to help the scholar find the correct full-text materials, sooner rather than later, by presenting the tables and figures with the text search results. ProQuest searches a variety of databases, including MEDLINE, ERIC, LISA (Library and Information Science Abstracts), and a host of ProQuest databases in health sciences, social sciences, technology, and natural science.

CHANGING ROLES AND CHANGING TRADITIONS

Many of the issues associated with emerging technologies in the scholarly communication system have been reviewed earlier in relationship to the introduction of technology tools. The net effect is that publishers, libraries, and researchers have been assuming new roles as they adapt to the technology and the increasing accessibility to data and information. The technology is far from being fully developed. The economics of this new Internet age are still developing. Communities of scientists and researchers are continuing to experiment with new methods of research, communication, and publishing, using tools such as social media, online peer review, reader ratings, and so forth. In fact, there are new publishing models being developed that include a revival of university presses and the construction of institutional repositories consisting of faculty-generated documents and data. The impact of the growing popularity of e-readers is only beginning to be addressed. These are just some of the changes taking place, and they serve as the foundation for a system in a volatile state.

What continues to serve as the hub of the scholarly communication system are the elements that were established centuries ago—creation, evaluation, dissemination, and preservation. These elements have not changed despite technology. In fact, the Association of College and Research Libraries (ACRL) has adapted the definition of scholarly communication to include those elements but now also recognizes the use of formal and informal means of communications (ACRL, 2003). Following is a review of some additional issues that libraries, scholars and researchers, and publishers are confronting.

Libraries

Discoverability is increasingly cross-sector, meaning that all the constituencies involved in the collaborative scholarly communication process do not have clear demarcation lines where each contributor has specific responsibilities that do not cross into any other contributor's responsibilities. The constituencies include the primary publishers, secondary publishers consisting of A&I services, and academic libraries. Libraries used to have control over the research information that many scholars could access, giving librarians the ability to serve as the initial research starting point for scholars. Now scholars can go directly to the web, use a variety of search engines, access social networks, and buy articles directly from publishers (Gardner and Inger, 2012).

There are no clear answers as to the future role libraries will play and exactly how they will continue to fit into a research system that continues to decentralize. For example, researchers increasingly expect to be able to access information using portable devices and applications. Yet libraries have a lot of capital invested in the creation of fixed assets, such as their physical facilities as well as their computer environment. It is clear that libraries must become more technologically savvy and willing to become partners with primary and secondary publishers. Libraries will have to develop electronic resource management systems and large online public access catalogs and search tools that are web based and collaborative (Somerville and Conrad, 2013). Intricately involved in the changing library role is the question of when, where, and how the library enters points in scholarly work flows.

Institutional repositories are taking on a new life as a means of saving valuable faculty and researcher materials that are being "lost" on the web. The main purpose of the institutional repository is to preserve all of an institution's intellectual output from the university, research laboratories, departments, university presses, and so on. However, the technology has created an environment that promotes the creation of the repositories for other reasons. Faculty, students, and researchers want to be able to assume some control over the archiving process, traditionally the sole function of the libraries. With the Internet, scholars can self-archive into their repository and know that access is available as needed. Of course, for the research materials to be shared with the scholarly community, the repositories must be accessible on the web, abstracted and indexed in a way that search engines and A&I services can access, and regularly maintained. What role libraries will play in technology-based archiving of institutional materials in a local system that blends with the external systems remains unclear.

Publishing models continue to change and emerge. Scholars can easily self-publish online, so a real concern is the capture of materials and the means of access. This does not address the impact that technology has had on the peer-review process. It assumes the materials should be published with some kind of notation as to their evaluation status. That is a discussion best addressed when reviewing the advantages and disadvantages of open access scholarly communication models.

There are some points to keep in mind. Online publication and archiving on the web or in the cloud means that libraries can see a future in which they will not need to maintain huge local reserves containing materials that are seldom used. Second, new pricing models are going to emerge, but it is impossible to say what they will be at this time. Libraries may move to a focus on access rather than local collection development as they upgrade technology in their facilities.

Reference librarians will likely remain mediators, serving as a link between researchers and digitized materials. Increasingly, library professionals are serving as liaisons to faculty in assisting in the transfer to digital repositories and the opportunities open to them in this transition. Currently, librarians also play primary roles in negotiating access licenses, assisting clients with creating and accessing electronic materials, and archiving local resources.

Scholars and Researchers

Scholars are working within a communication system that has radically changed. The life cycle of scholarly works is supported by an extensive, collaborative communication system. Each stage of the scholarly process relied on participants fulfilling long-established and clearly defined roles and a methodical process. Technology has been disruptive at every stage of the scholarly communication process. Scholars can quickly communicate informally with each other using social networks established on the web or through intranets. Discoverability possibilities are increasingly moving to web-based services, where access is provided independent of source content creators or the structure of source content.

Scholars are regularly using informal communication methods, such as blogs and forums, but capturing those discussions as part of the scholarly communication development process remains elusive. A hundred years ago, letters and conference papers could trace the development of ideas. Now much of the discussion is happening on the web or on intranets or social networks, and the preservation of idea development has yet to be solved.

Though scholars and researchers have embraced the online environment, they have also been reluctant until recently to produce and distribute content outside the traditional process. For example, almost all STM journals are available online, but they are also still printed. The reasons for this are wide and varied and include concerns about long-term preservation of materials online, the fact that some researchers prefer print articles, fear that material in an electronic-only journal would be forever lost should the publisher go out of business, and the fact that not everyone (especially in underdeveloped countries) in the global research environment has easy access to needed technology. The concerns about portability are being rapidly eliminated as mobile technology advances, and it would be safe to say that some of the other justifications for maintaining print materials will be eliminated through enhancements such as cloud computing and other technological developments in accessibility (Ware and Mabe, 2012).

There are even more issues that can impact the roles of faculty scholars. Currently, the university systems of tenure, promotion, and compensation are tied to the amount of publishing in scholarly journals. As younger scholars question this relationship, the traditional tenure systems are being reevaluated. If scholars assume the role of self-publishers and self-archivers, the tenure and compensation systems will need revising. Younger scholars are already indicating dissatisfaction with the current tenure systems. As senior faculty members are replaced with fewer tenure-track positions, young academics will find longer intervals between earning the PhD and earning tenure. Many see themselves as alternative academics who want to publish online, hold vigorous conversations using technology, and be rewarded for effort and contributions to the advancement of knowledge no matter what shape the effort takes (Rumsey, 2010).

Of concern particularly to these emerging scholars is the high levels of research that continue to be funneled into traditional publishing venues. It is plausible that one role scholars will need to assume is as participants in a collective voice before the system will be standardized in a way that makes it possible for them to embrace new scholarly models. Tradition often drives the conversation about the appropriate model for scholarly communication. Though the peer-review system has worked in the past, it is highly likely that there are new models that would work just as well when technology is added to the equation.

Publishers

Primary publishers have seen their roles change despite initial efforts to maintain a tightly controlled scholarly publishing system. Elsevier points out in its history narrative published for the company's 125th anniversary that "although electronic publishing like ScienceDirect, Scopus and MD Consult are at the forefront of publishing innovation today, it remains clear to the company that the second Gutenberg Revolution has only just begun: with obsolescence only ever just one new innovation away" (Elsevier, 2013: 10). The biggest challenge for primary publishers has been maintaining currency with technology, providing the kind of services scholars and libraries expect, setting reasonable prices that keep their services affordable, and all the while continuing to create value for their stakeholders.

The traditional functions of commercial and professional society publishers include editing, production, and distribution of the scholarly content. Scholars provide the materials at no cost to the publishers, who then resell the same materials back to the libraries and other institutions or people through subscriptions or per-article arrangements. This system is increasingly becoming antiquated for two reasons. First, increasingly, scholars believe they can find their own editors, publish online, and give as much or as little access as desired to the online community based on where the material is published, tagged, and indexed. Search engine algorithms will continue to rely on the metadata to find relevant information. Word processing and other sophisticated publishing software packages have even equalized the quality of commercially produced products versus self-produced products (Odlyzko, 1999).

One of the most important roles the primary publishers have played is managing the peer-review process by ensuring that only journal articles meeting review standards are published as scholarly research. Though they do not do peer reviewing, they do serve as a funnel for ensuring that the right steps are taken before publication as scholarly material. However, online peer-review systems are emerging outside of the traditional publishing service structure. In other words, primary publishers could conceivably be cut out of the scholarly communication process at some point in the future. Also, as scholarly content becomes more and more available in a variety of formats, it is the new services and expanded access to research databases that may help publishers stay in business. Those services still need to be defined, but adding value to content, whether that is the conversion of non-digitized materials to electronic formats so that researchers can access them via the web or providing predictive analytics to research content, publishers will need to move beyond their traditional roles.

Secondary publishers also find themselves needing to change their traditional approaches in response to the indexing of materials on the web and changes in library discovery services. The challenge they face is finding methods for mapping products for a wide variety of search engines and research platforms. Unless they overcome this challenge, the traditional A&I services will find their services under heavy scrutiny and perhaps even left unused. For example, they will need to provide quick, reliable, and effective conduits of research content and bibliographic data to libraries at the time the products are purchased in order to ensure discoverability (Odlyzko, 1999).

INDUSTRY IN A STATE OF FLUX

The global academic publishing industry is large. The revenues generated by STM publishing alone were estimated to be $26.5 billion in 2012. The STM book market is worth another $4 billion. There were as many as 10,000 journal publishers and 28,100 peer-reviewed journals on the market as of 2012 (Ware and Mabe, 2012). The global content spending by libraries in 2012 was estimated at $24.2 billion, and much of that money was spent on digital content (Outsell, 2013b). Libraries purchase materials, serials, books, e-journal services, and A&I services and fund institutional repositories. The broader information industry as a whole was estimated to have generated $506 billion in 2012, and it is growing (Outsell, 2013a).

The scholarly production process is in the process of being "unbundled" or disaggregated. Authoring, peer review, publishing, and dissemination are no longer following a certain path. Authors can publish and disseminate. Peer review can take place interactively, online, and outside of the traditional publishing process. Publishers disseminate raw data as much as they disseminate full-text articles. Academics are publishing online and bypassing traditional publishers. Libraries are becoming repositories for faculty articles and student theses and dissertations. Monograph publishing is getting attention once again as e-book publishing becomes more affordable, and dissemination to a wider audience is easier due to technology. Journal components are unbundled and rebundled into customizable packages so that end users can access articles instead of journals. Users are demanding and creating more data analytics directly from published scholarly content.

There is no shared reference model among the authors, publishers, and libraries for electronic publishing like there was in the conventional system of scholarship publishing. It is the lack of common understanding that keeps the academic and scholarly publishing business involved in ongoing debate as to how the industry will revamp itself. Also complicating the transition to new models is the fact that the web has widened the industry to include a global community of authors with the same access to the technology as the experienced researchers. In the early years of technological development, access to technology was closely managed in government research centers and libraries. Now, anyone can sit at their home computer, author an article, publish it online, and market it. With the introduction of the cloud, the authors can also archive their scholarly products. That is precisely why some claim that the peer-review element remains so critical to scholarly communication. However, even that element is in transition, as some scholars promote an online peer-review process in which a system of independent referee boards can read preliminary articles, suggest edits, submit questions, and post comments—all online. It has been suggested that the referee boards can work with academic committees evaluating faculty for tenure, promotions, and compensation.

The information industry for scholarly publishing makes the entire system less dependent on conventional publishing by providing options. There are a number of organizations that promote free access to scholarly journals or are publishing their own free journals. They include the Public Library of Science, the Budapest Open Access Initiative, the Scholarly Publishing and Academic Resources Coalition, and others.

Despite the turmoil, the scholarly information industry is clearly moving toward more and more publicly available access to scholarly content—content is being seen as free or ought to be free. A lot of questions and concerns must be addressed before free and open access is fully accepted, but it is a concept that is gaining momentum due to the many forces discussed earlier.

It is appropriate to take heed of the words of a technology pioneer, Paul Ginsparg, the developer of the first preprint archive and a pioneer of open access publishing and archiving. He wrote,

> Fast-forwarding through the first dot-com boom and bust, and the emergent Google-opoly, the effects of the technological transformations of the scholarly communication infrastructure are now ubiquitous in the daily activities of typical researchers, lecturers, and students. We have ready access to an increasing breadth of digital materials difficult to have imagined a decade ago. They include freely available peer-reviewed articles from scholarly publishers, background and pedagogic material provided by its authors, slides used by

authors to present the material, and videos of seminars or colloquia on the material—not to mention related software, online animations illustrating relevant concepts, explanatory discussions on blog sites, often-useful notes posted by third-party lecturers of courses at other institutions, and collective wiki-exegis. (Ginsparg, 2011: 6)

Open access is discussed among scholars as a means of overcoming many of the issues presented throughout this chapter. It is not a new concept by any means. However, there is a whole new set of issues that must be addressed that are associated with open access scholarship. Open access may well be the next stage in the reconfiguring of the scholarly communication system, and it exists only because of one factor—Internet technology. It has changed everything.

REFERENCES

Association of College and Research Libraries, Scholarly Communications Committee. 2003. "Principles and Strategies for the Reform of Scholarly Communication 1." Association of College and Research Libraries. June 24. http://www.ala.org/acrl/publications/whitepapers/principlesstrategies.

Bjørner, Susanne, and Stephanie C. Ardito. 2003. "Online before the Internet, Part 1: Early Pioneers Tell Their Stories." Searcher 11, no. 6 (June). http://www.infotoday.com/searcher/jun03/ardito_bjorner.shtml.

Borovansky, Vladimir T. 1996. "Changing Trends in Scholarly Communication: Issues for Technological University Libraries." *1995 IATUL Conference Proceedings* 5: 68–79. http://docs.lib.purdue.edu/iatul/1995/papers/8.

Bourne, Charles P. 1980. "On-Line Systems: History, Technology, and Economics." *Journal of the American Society for Information Science and Technology* 31, no. 3 (May): 155–160.

Bourne, Charles P., and Trudi Bellardo Iahn. 2003. *A History of Online Information Services, 1963–1976*. Cambridge: Massachusetts Institute of Technology.

Brin, Sergey. 2009. "A Library to Last Forever" (op-ed). *New York Times*, October 8, international edition.

Buchanan, Larry. 1995. "Internet Gopher Basics—Happy Tunneling!" *Multimedia Schools Professional Development Collection* 2, no. 2: 12–31.

Butter, Karen A. 1994. "Red Sage: The Next Step in the Delivery of Electronic Journals." *Medical References Services Quarterly* 13, no. 3 (Fall): 75–81.

Chemical Abstracts Service. 2013. "CAS History." Chemical Abstracts Service—Division of the American Chemical Society. Accessed October 10. https://www.cas.org/about-cas/cas-history.

CiteSeer[X]. 2014. "About CiteSeer[X]." CiteSeer[X]. Pennsylvania State University. Accessed May 29. http://csxstatic.ist.psu.edu/about.

Cornog, Martha. 1983. "A History of Indexing Technology." *The Indexer* 13, no. 3 (April): 152–157.

Cox, Christopher. 2011. "Western Libraries Acquisitions Funding Model: A Plan for Change. Developed by the Western Libraries in Consultation with the Senate Library Committee." Western Libraries Senate Library Committee. April. http://www.wwu.edu/provost/budget/documents/proposals/LibraryAcquisitionsFundingPlanforChange.pdf.

Crow, Raym. 2006. "Publishing Cooperatives: An Alternative for Non-Profit Publishers." *First Monday* 11, no. 9 (September). http://firstmonday.org/ojs/index.php/fm/issue/view/203.

D'Arms, John H., and Richard Ekman. 1999. "ACLS E-Publishing Project for History Monographs." Humanities and Social Sciences Net Online. Announcement ID 123958. July 12. http://www.h-net.org/announce/show.cgi?ID=123958.

Davies, David Randal. 2006. *The Postwar Decline of American Newspapers, 1945–1965, Issue 6.* Westport, CT: Greenwood Publishing.

Dewar, James A. 2013. "The Information Age and the Printing Press: Looking Backward to See Ahead." RAND. Accessed October 3. http://www.rand.org/pubs/papers/P8014.html.

Dolecheck, Melanie. 2010. *Allen Press: A Celebration of 75 Years.* Lawrence, KS: Allen Press.

Ekman, Richard H., and Richard E. Quandt. 1995. "Scholarly Communication, Academic Libraries and Technology." *Change* 27, no. 1 (January–February): 34–44.

"Electronic Publishing in Analytical Chemistry." 1987. *Analytical Chemistry* 59, no. 17 (September): 1021. doi: 10.1021/ac00144a737.

Elon University School of Communication. 2013. "Imagining the Internet's Quick Look at the Early History of the Internet." Elon University School of Communication. Accessed October 5. http://www.elon.edu/e-web/predictions/early90s/internethistory.xhtml.

Elsevier. 2013. "A Short History of Elsevier." Elsevier. Accessed September 1. http://cdn.elsevier.com/assets/pdf_file/0014/102632/historyofelsevier.pdf.

ExLibris. Primo. 2013. "A Solution for Current and Future Library Architecture." ExLibris. Accessed October 8. http://www.exlibrisgroup.com/?catid={CD9897CD-0BD0-435C-A5A0-D9D6BAD2B9AB}.

Friend, Frederick J. 2006. "Google Scholar: Potentially Good for Users of Academic Information." *Journal of Electronic Publishing* 9, no. 1 (Winter). doi: http://dx.doi.org/10.3998/3336451.0009.105.

Gardner, Tracy, and Simon Inger. 2012. *How Readers Discover Content in Scholarly Journals: Comparing the Changing User Behaviour between 2005 and 2012 and Its Impact on Publisher Web Site Design and Function. Summary Edition.* Abingdon, UK: Renew Training. http://www.renewtraining.com/How-Readers-Discover-Contentin-Scholarly-Journals-summary-edition.pdf.

Ginsparg, Paul. 2011. "It Was Twenty Years Ago Today." arXiv.org at Cornell University. September 13. http://arxiv.org/pdf/1108.2700v2.pdf.

Goldner, Matt. 2010. "Winds of Change: Libraries and Cloud Computing." OCLC Online Computer Library Center. http://www.oclc.org/content/dam/oclc/events/2011/files/IFLA-winds-of-change-paper.pdf.

Google. 2013. "Google Books History." Google Books. Accessed October 19. http://www.google.com/googlebooks/about/history.html.

Hart, Michael. 2010. "The History and Philosophy of Project Gutenberg." Project Gutenberg. August 1992. Last modified April 8, 2010. http://www.gutenberg.org/wiki/Gutenberg:The_History_and_Philosophy_of_Project_Gutenberg_by_Michael_Hart.

Hawkins, Donald T. 2013. "Information Discovery and the Future of Abstracting and Indexing Services: An NFAIS Workshop." *Against the Grain*, August 6. http://www.against-the-grain.com/2013/08/information-discovery-and-the-future-of-abstracting-and-indexing-services-an-nfais-workshop.

Jha, Alok. 2012. "Academic Spring: How an Angry Maths Blog Sparked a Scientific Revolution." *The Guardian* (Great Britain), April 9. http://www.theguardian.com/science/2012/apr/09/frustrated-blogpost-boycott-scientific-journals.

JSTOR. 2012. "A New Chapter Begins: Books at JSTOR Launches." JSTOR. November 12. http://about.jstor.org/news/new-chapter-begins-books-jstor-launches.

Kamble, V. T., D. S. Amoji, B. Sangeeta, and Durai Pandy. 2012. "A Brief History of E-Resources." In *National Conference on Knowledge Organization in Academic Libraries (KOAL-2012), September 29*, 103–109. New Delhi: Library Professional Association.

Kelley, Michael. 2012. "Coming into Focus—Web-Scale Discovery Services Face Growing Need for Best Practices." *Library Journal* 137, no. 17 (October 15): 34.

Lancaster, F. Wilfred, and Amy J. Warner. 1993. "The Database Industry." In *Information Retrieval Today*, 21–31. Arlington, VA: Information Resources Press.

Lee, Christopher. 2008. "Where Have All the Gophers Gone? Why the Web Beat Gopher in the Battle for Protocol Mind Share." School of Information and Library Science at University of North Carolina. Original version April 23, 1999; rev. November 4, 2001; April 25, 2008. http://www.ils.unc.edu/callee/gopherpaper.htm.

The Birth of Online 165

Library of Congress. 2013. "American Memory Mission and History." Library of Congress. Accessed October 18. http://memory.loc.gov/ammem/about/index.html.

Linke, Erika C. 2003. "Million Book Project." In *Encyclopedia of Library and Information Science, Second Edition—Volume 3*, edited by Miriam Drake, 1889–1894. Boca Raton, FL: CRC Press. http://books.google.com/books?id=Sqr-_3FBYiYC&pg=PA1889& lpg=PA1889&dq=million+book+project+was+initiated+by&source=bl&ots=X-YNFG-uHA&sig=W9UFCb7GTgQjHNdQJiG9i93rvDo&hl=en&sa=X& ei=NzVkUsz0LIrA8ATuzoCQAQ&ved=0CGsQ6AEwCA#v=onepage& q=million%20book%20project%20was%20initiated%20by&f=false.

López-Cózar, Emilio Degado, Nicolás Robinson-García, and Daniel Torres Salinas. 2012. "Manipulating Google Scholar Citations and Google Scholar Metrics: Simple, Easy and Tempting." *EC3 Working Papers* 6 (May 29): 4–6.

Lorimer, Rowland. 2013. "Libraries, Scholars, and Publishers in Digital Journal and Monograph Publishing." *Scholarly and Research Communication* 4, no. 1 (2013). http://src-online.ca/index.php/src/article/view/43/118.

McCabe, Mark. 1999. "The Impact of Publisher Mergers on Journal Prices: An Update." *ARL* 207 (July 1999). http://mccabe.people.si.umich.edu/Grain.PDF.

McCabe, Mark. 2001. "The Impact of Publisher Mergers on Journal Prices: Theory and Evidence." *The Serials Librarian* 40, no. 1/2: 157–166.

McCarthy, Cheryl A., Sylvia C. Krausse, and Arthur A. Little. 1997. "Expectations and Effectiveness Using CD-ROMs: What Do Patrons Want and How Satisfied Are They?" *College and Research Libraries* 58, no. 2 (March): 128–142.

Mell, Peter, and Timothy Grance. 2011. *The NIST Definition of Cloud Computing* (Special Publication 800-145). Gaithersburg, MD: National Institute of Standards and Technology of the U.S. Department of Commerce, September. http://csrc.nist.gov/publications/nistpubs/800-145/SP800-145.pdf.

Murray, Peter J., and Denis M. Anthony. 1999. "Current and Future Models for Nursing E-Journals: Making the Most of the Web's Potential." *International Journal of Medical Informatics* 53, no. 2/3: 151–161.

Odlyzko, Andrew M. 1999. "Competition and Cooperation: Libraries and Publishers in the Transition to Electronic Scholarly Journals." *Journal of Electronic Publishing* 4, no. 4 (June), in the online collection *The Transition from Paper: Where Are We Going and How Will We Get There?*, edited by R. S. Berry and A. S. Moffatt, American Academy of Arts and Sciences, http://www.amacad.org/publications/trans.htm, and in *Journal of Scholarly Publishing* 30, no. 4 (July 1999).

Outsell. 2013a. "2012 Market Size & Share Rankings Report." *Outsell*, February 28.

Outsell. 2013b. "2013 Library Market Size, Share, Forecast, & Trends." *Outsell*, June 17.

Oxford University Press. 2013. "About Oxford Scholarship Online." Oxford University Online. Accessed October 19. http://www.oxfordscholarship.com/page/85/about.

Pitkow, James E., and Margaret M. Recker. 1995. "Results from the Fourth World-Wide Web User Survey." Georgia Institute of Technology, Graphics, Visualization, and Usability Center. Last modified 1995. http://www.cc.gatech.edu/gvu/user_surveys/survey-10-1995.

Plosker, George. 2004. "Making Money as an Aggregator." *Information Today* 28, no.2 (March/April). http://www.infotoday.com/online/mar04/plosker.shtml.

PR Newswire. 2000. "Chemweb.com to Launch Chemistry Preprint Server." PR Newswire, The Free Library, London. April 3. http://www.thefreelibrary.com/CHEM-WEB.COM+TO+LAUNCH+CHEMISTRY+PREPRINT+SERVER.-a061805864.

Rumsey, Abby Smith. 2010. *Scholarly Communication Institute 8: Emerging Genres in Scholarly Communication*. Scholarly Communication Institute. July.

Savenije, Bas. 2003. "Economic and Strategic Analysis of Scientific Journals: Recent Evolutions." *Liber Quarterly* 13, no. 3/4. http://liber.library.uu.nl/index.php/lq/article/view/URN%3ANBN%3ANL%3AUI%3A10-1-113339/7800.

Solomon, David J. 2013. "Digital Distribution of Academic Journals and Its Impact on Scholarly Communication: Looking Back after 20 Years." *Journal of Academic Librarianship* 39 (April 23): 23–28. doi: 10.1016/j.acalib.2012.10.001.

Somerville, Mary M., and Lettie Y. Conrad. 2013. "Discoverability Challenges and Collaboration Opportunities within the Scholarly Communications Ecosystems: A SAGE White Paper Update." *Collaborative Librarianship* 5, no. 1: 29–41.

Souto, Patricia. 2007. "E-Publishing Development and Changes in the Scholarly Communication System." *Ci. Inf., Brasilia* 36, no. 1 (April): 158–166.

Steele, Colin. 2008. "Scholarly Monograph Publishing in the 21st Century: The Future More Than Ever Should Be an Open Book." *Journal of Electronic Publishing*, 11, no. 2 (Spring). http://dx.doi.org/10.3998/3336451.0011.201.

Thompson, John B. 2005. "Survival Strategies for Academic Publishing." *The Chronicle of Higher Education* 51, no. 41 (June 17): B6–B9. http://chronicle.com/article/Survival-Strategies-for/12735.

Tomaiuolo, Nicholas G., and Joan G. Packer. 2000. "Preprint Servers: Pushing the Envelope of Electronic Scholarly Publishing." *Searcher* 8, no. 9 (October). http://www.infotoday.com/searcher/oct00/tomaiuolo&packer.htm.

Treese, Win. 1994. "The Internet Index," no. 2. Last modified August 2, 1994. http://www.treese.org/intindex/94-08.htm.

Vaughan, Jason. 2011. "Chapter 1: Web Scale Discovery What and Why." *Library Technology Reports of the American Library Association* 47, no. 1 (January): 5–21.

Ware, Mark, and Michael Mabe. 2012. *The STM Report: An Overview of Scientific and Scholarly Journal Publishing.* 3rd ed. The Hague: International Association of Scientific, Technical and Medical Publishers, November. http://www.stm-assoc.org/2012_12_11_STM_Report_2012.pdf.

Wedgeworth, Robert. 1993. *World Encyclopedia of Library and Information Services.* Chicago: American Library Association.

Williams, M. E. 1977. "Data Bases—A History of Developments and Trends from 1966 through 1975." *Journal of the American Society for Information Science and Technology* 28: 71–78. doi: 10.1002/asi.4630280203.

Chapter Seven

Traditional Economics of Academic Publishing

Certainly over the past ten to fifteen years, there has been much discussion about the serials crisis and the enormous pricing pressures associated with journal and monograph pricing and publishing that extended to academic scholars and libraries. Over a period of decades, however, there has been a trend toward higher serials costs and a contention that commercial and society publishers were tightening their control over the publishing process. When the universities shut down their academic printing operations and academic scholars contracted away their rights to publish their material, academic publishing grew into a multi-billion-dollar global industry that is now again in the throes of change, inspired largely by technology.

To understand why and how the industry is changing and perhaps delve into the future of academic publishing, it is important to first understand the traditional economics of publishing for scholarly articles in journals and monographs. This chapter contains a review of the traditional subscription models of journal and book publishing, a general introduction to technology's appearance and influence on a still-changing publishing model, and trends in serials pricing and academic library buying patterns. It should be noted that the commercial publishing pricing trends and the changing publishing environment apply to libraries and academics on a global basis.

TRADITIONAL SUBSCRIPTION MODELS OF JOURNAL AND BOOK PUBLISHING

For almost 200 years, little changed in the academic publishing industry in terms of process. What did change was the growth and influence of commercial and society publishers over published material. Libraries were a key market and in a sense were caught in the middle to a large degree—as scholarly communications grew in number and price, library budgets did not keep up pace in some periods, even with inflationary rates. The process remained constant: the scholarly community published journal articles to disseminate research and advance careers, and to gain access to the published materials, libraries subscribed to the journals on behalf of their constituents. It really is that simple on the surface. The economics of the traditional subscription models are more complex, however. In this section is a review of the two most common subscription models of journal and book publishing: direct subscription (journal by journal) and the "Big Deal."

Direct Subscription—Journal-by-Journal Economics

There are two main publisher classes publishing most of the academic journals. They are the commercial publishers and the learned or professional societies. Assume a journal with limited subscribers, for example, approximately 200 subscribers per year. To gain access, libraries pay an annual subscription amount for a set number of issues. Typically, six to twelve issues per year are published. At $1,000 per subscription for 200 subscriptions, the publisher is collecting $200,000 annually. Out of the subscription revenues, the publisher has to cover the cost of typesetting, marking up in HTML, copy editing, editor expenses, distribution, marketing, advertising, and overhead. Each time a library cancels a subscription, the publisher is faced with the likelihood that it will be unable to sell a new subscription. If six libraries each year decide to cancel their subscription, the publisher loses $6,000 in revenue annually. To recover the lost revenue, the publisher raises the subscription price by 10 percent, so now the publisher is charging $1,100 for 194 subscriptions and earning $213,400 in annual revenue, which is an attempt to cover the increased costs in the categories just mentioned. Notice there are fewer subscribers but more revenue, while the costs to produce the subscriptions are approximately the same. As prices go up, more subscriptions are cancelled, and the price goes even higher (Gasson, 2014). Of course, the problem with this is that it is unlikely that any publisher can sustain 10 percent price increases, and eventually the journal will no longer be viable and will cease publication.

This is not a sustainable publishing-subscription model for small-market and highly specialized journal publications. By 2000, the rate of cancellations exceeded the ability of the publishers to raise prices (this has been referred to as the "serials crisis," as the number of journals and their pricing were causing libraries to cut back many of their subscriptions as library budget increases lagged behind even inflationary increases). At some point, the number of subscriptions will fall below a point where the journal becomes irrelevant because it does not have a wide enough readership. Scholars publish to disseminate research and earn status within their disciplines. When readership falls for journals in which scholars are publishing, goals are left unmet.

The Big Deal

The serials crisis prompted by the cycle of rising prices led to the so-called Big Deal, first introduced in 1996 by Academic Press and shortly thereafter by Elsevier. The cycle of subscription price increases followed by journal cancellations followed by more price increases could not continue indefinitely. In 1993, the Higher Education Funding Council for England (HEFCE) was planning on making budget changes in which portions of the library budgets would be dedicated to particular projects. In response, Academic Press chief executive officer Pieter Bolman and European managing director Jan Velterop developed a new approach to subscriptions. The plan was to ask HEFCE to fund a multiyear license to buy a bundle of journals from Academic Press, and academics would have free access at higher-education facilities. The advantages of bundling journals for the publisher included guaranteed revenues and streamlined administration; the entire portfolio of journals published by Academic Press would be sold as a single subscription. The advantage to academic libraries was that the license fee was predictable for an entire set of journals, and that would relieve some budgetary pressures. The HEFCE approved the first three-year licensing contract in 1996 in the United Kingdom. The idea spread and was adopted by library consortia on a global basis (Poynder, 2011).

The Big Deal, or journal bundling, consisted of a set price for a specified number of years for a specified list of journals. When the bundle included both print and electronic formats, the price was based on the original subscription price for printed copies plus an additional amount for electronic versions. Since there was a contract, price increases were usually capped for the stated number of years. Publishers would typically include a large number of journals, often 100 percent of their titles, giving libraries access to a wider number and variety of journals than they could afford on a journal-by-journal basis. With the advent of technology, researchers could have greater access to research across the bundles. Bundling also gave smaller academic institutions the ability to access new material they would not be able to afford otherwise.

In addition to the single library negotiating a Big Deal, there were library consortia purchasing bundled subscriptions as well. Each consortium would negotiate a contract with the publisher, often as a "site license" for all members of the consortium, and subscriptions were then made available to all members. Interlibrary lending made it possible to share print copies and monographs should there not be enough copies available for every library. Since a consortium represents a group of libraries, it had more bargaining power than a single institution. Another advantage of the consortium Big Deal was that the individual libraries were relieved of the administrative work required for contract development (Stieg, 2011).

Not all librarians liked the Big Deal. A drawback to the Big Deal for some libraries was that individual journal subscriptions could not be canceled at their full retail rate if not wanted or used by the institution's researchers. Another objection was that the Big Deal allowed libraries to cancel paper subscriptions or add additional paper copies, but once the Big Deal was accepted, the library was forced to continue it in order to gain access to the journals it truly wanted or else renegotiate another deal (Frazier, 2001).

The consortia deals had some of the same issues. Once negotiated, the consortia were locked into subscriptions to journals for the term of the agreement. Libraries found that negotiating single journal subscription prices cost more than their share of the consortium Big Deal, so it was often a difficult decision to walk away from these volume agreements. As technology shifted subscriptions from print to more online than print, libraries became licensers instead of owners of the material. Then the questions became how to preserve these online journals and where else the libraries could go to access fifty or sixty years' worth of journal publications owned by commercial academic publishers if those publishers cease doing business.

Also as licensees to this material, there was the question of how to retain access to those materials that were canceled if the library wished to have that access. Publishers responded to this market demand either by charging, at a reduced rate, libraries to access legacy materials or by having a program to download the legacy materials for exclusive use of the library.

These objections were raised in the early years of online services and the Big Deal. The Big Deal does increase access to research material, but it also limits the ability of librarians to manage scholarly communication systems themselves—as they did with their print collections.

Some libraries eventually chose to abandon the Big Deal. One such library was at Duke University. In 2004, the Triangle Research Libraries Network consortium, consisting of four libraries, chose to not renew two Big Deals—one with Elsevier's ScienceDirect and one with Blackwell's Synergy. Access to over 750 journals was lost, but the libraries regained control of their collection development by returning to journal-by-journal pricing (Gibbs, 2005). Big Deals have been most common in the science, technology, and medical (STM) disciplines, and there were criticisms that the Big Deal was hurting humanities and social sciences as greater percentages of the library budgets were dedicated to STM subscriptions. Libraries largely maintained the intact Big Deals until the 2008 recession forced budgetary changes, leading to the facilities reconsidering whether they could provide needed services without the bundled journal contracts.

It often becomes a matter of simple economics. If the library cannot afford the Big Deal, then it finds a way around it. For example, Morris Library at Southern Illinois University chose to eliminate Big Deals because it came down to keeping or cutting other materials that were deemed more valuable than many of the journals in the contract that was held with the publisher. Morris Library cut Big Deals with Elsevier and Wiley, canceling 244 and 597 journals, respectively. Though it could be assumed that research was harmed by the reduction in journal access, the library discovered that electronic downloads are not true indications of research material value. After eliminating the Big Deal at the two publishers, the library received interlibrary loan requests for articles that were found in only 20 percent of the Wiley titles cut and 26 percent of the Elsevier titles. This reflects the long tail principle, which in the library setting means that a small number of journals, articles, or other materials account for most of the material accessed. The University of Oregon had a similar experience (Nabe and Fowler, 2012).

Economics of Monograph Publishing

Monograph publishing became an unprofitable option for commercial publishers and university presses. A typical academic monograph sells 200 to 250 copies. If the price is $150 each and the book is discounted 30 percent to booksellers, it is easy to see that not much profit is left after covering all the direct and indirect costs. Increasing the number of monographs published would increase revenues, but there has to be a market. Unlike journal subscriptions that must be canceled, libraries can simply stop ordering monographs and shift budget monies into journal subscriptions.

The pricing schemes that libraries face for scholarly and nonscholarly electronic publications are complicated. There is the one-title purchase in which the library pays a distributor of e-books who has digital distribution rights. The library can purchase as many copies as it can afford. There are also models in which libraries purchase a license for simultaneous access. A newer model was initiated by HarperCollins, which it is not an academic publisher but may be creating a new access model that will be emulated by the commercial academic publishers in the future. In this model, a subscription to an e-book gives rights to lending or access for a limited number of times. Units are purchased as a group. Other publishers have added variations, such as a time period in conjunction with a finite number of e-book downloads allowed. New funding models include cost-per-checkout and buy-it-now options with the library earning affiliate fees. This implies that access to academic monographs could certainly adapt to the emerging commercial publishing models (Seave, 2013).

Approaches to collection development in libraries is expanding through the use of "patron-driven acquisitions" also known as "demand-driven acquisitions." These approaches are mechanisms that enable students and faculty staff to acquire the books they believe are most appropriate for their research and education needs directly from a library catalog of published titles. Typically, this catalog lists scholarly books that have been published but not yet acquired by the library, and additional titles are added regularly as new titles are published. As these books are used by customers, the library will only then typically purchase the materials and add them to the permanent collection. Under such agreements with publishers, e-books are accessible immediately, while printed book availability is based on its in-stock status from the publisher.

DIMENSIONS OF CHANGING MODELS OF ACADEMIC PUBLISHING

The commercial influences on scholarship have long been a topic of discussion. One of the best ways to understand those influences is to look at the statistics. The partnership between academic or scholarly authors and commercial publishers has grown increasingly strained, and some believe that the complete disintegration of the academic publishing system is possible given technology and market dynamics. It is the profits earned by commercial publishers that have prompted many of the questions concerning charges for publishing, journal subscriptions, and monograph publishing. As technology and digital tools advanced, access and dissemination of scholarly communication changed also, and the main factor was the cost associated with access and dissemination through the large commercial academic publishers and learned societies. The reality is that the traditional scholarly communication system has supported the traditional commercial publications system.

As technology advanced, it became a catalyst for change in the accessing and dissemination of scholarly works. That in turn impacted how libraries carry out their primary functions, which in turn led to changes in library buying patterns. On the commercial publisher side, the publishing models moved from print only to print and digital publishing and now nearly entirely digital. On the library side, the subscription prices reflected the premium added for getting access to print and digital versions—both print and electronic versions are still maintained by many, particularly large, academic libraries. On the dissemination side, open access journals, published by commercial and professional societies, appeared, and many continued to employ a vigorous peer-review process. Also appearing were open access journals that relied on the online scholarly community to review the articles and make public comments, but the traditional peer-review process was not utilized. A fair number of open access journals that simply were shams and would publish almost anything for a fee also cropped up. Technology transitioned from database to web-based searching. For example, the ERIC database developers sought agreements with publishers to allow access to full-text files of published articles. At the same time, Google Scholar was developed as a search engine for accessing links to scholarly articles and other materials, some of which provided full-text results, while others led to links to subscription-based publishers, such as Springer and Elsevier (Beach et al., 2007).

The impact of technology has been profound. Broadly speaking, scholars began to develop new models for publishing and dissemination of research as libraries worked to find ways to continue performing their primary functions of archiving and maintaining the flow of scholarship. Scholars, libraries, and university presses seemed to align themselves on one side of the issue and commercial publishers on the other. Libraries moved toward developing and expanding institutional repositories, while in some instances the once-closed university presses began operating but as digital publishers rather than print ones. The great partnership of libraries and publishers that brought about some of the most stunning and innovative developments in information services seems now to be deeply divided and at times working against each other, and as a result, the whole field of scholarly communications may be constrained by this current division.

Technology also had the interesting impact of creating debate on the democratization of scholarly research. While scholars in developed countries could easily access digitized publications through their respective libraries and professional memberships, scholars in the less developed countries found it more difficult. May advocated that technology could increase access and dissemination of scholarly articles and journals if the publishers would allow web publication of academic works. Publishers did embrace this wider access, and such provisions were incorporated into publisher contracts. For example, the National Reading Conference negotiated a contract with Lawrence Erlbaum Associates (acquired by Taylor & Francis in 2006) that included reduced subscription fees for the *Journal of Literacy Research* charged to Third World countries and the right to publish on the web after two years (Beach et al., 2007).

The complexity of the issues concerning academic publishing led to a variety of new publishing, dissemination, and access models. They represent an effort to find a system that works well for scholars and libraries while protecting the ability of publishers to continue to remain sustainable. Libraries focused on institutional repositories, trying to limit and reduce the amount of money spent on subscriptions at the same time. The institutional repositories allow scholars to self-archive their research. The goal was to facilitate the free exchange of scholarly works, but lack of development led to institutional mandates that required scholars to self-archive. A trend that began in the mid-2000s is library journal publishing. In 2009, a survey of eighty U.S. research libraries indicated that 65 percent were already publishing journals or planned on doing so. In 2007, the Association of Research Libraries (ARL) reported that, of its members already providing publishing services, 88 percent were publishing peer-reviewed journals. The two primary publishing systems used were the Open Journal System (OJS) and Digital Commons, an application developed by Berkeley Electronic Press (Xia, 2009). Of course, this represents a profile similar in form if not volume to what universities were doing in journal publishing in the late nineteenth and early twentieth centuries before the consolidation of these journals into commercial and society publishers.

The Scholarly Publishing and Academic Resources Coalition researched the state of academic library publishing from 2010 to 2011. The report issued indicated that library publishing services were expanding. Approximately three-fourths of the libraries published one to six journals, with most distributed electronically. Half of the libraries published other scholarly materials, including monographs, technical reports, and conference proceedings. Ninety percent chose to start library publishing programs because they wanted to bring about change in the traditional scholarly publishing system. The large majority of libraries were funding their publishing operations through library budget reallocations, grant funding, and temporary institutional funding. The intent was to move toward more self-supporting funding through product revenues, service fees, royalties, and other income generated by programs. OJS and the Berkeley Electronic Press application, Digital Commons, remained the most prevalent publishing platforms (Mullins et al., 2012). The dilemma for libraries is that they need a sustainable financial model through revenue generation, which contrasts with the very reason the libraries chose to get involved in self-publishing—to offer free public access to scholarly research through their website. Academic scholars are attracted to the open access component of the library publishing model. The libraries that are publishing journals are tending to concentrate each journal on one discipline or multiple disciplines that are closely related. Previous research indicated that faculty did not contribute to subject repositories at the hoped-for levels because they preferred to concentrate on their own disciplines rather than contribute to multidiscipline repositories (Beach et al., 2007).

Commercial and society publishers have gone through a series of publishing and access models starting in 2000 and continuing today. They include metered access, toll access, pay-per-view full-text downloads, cost-per-checkout, preprint and postprint research articles, full open access, and hybrid systems. In 2007, the Springer Publishing "open choice" option had authors paying an article processing charge to have the article published as open access. The charge was $3,000 (Xia, 2008). These various models reflect the challenges all parties are having in a changing market that is turning over new business models with regularity. Though the scholarly communications market has gone through a consolidation over the past twenty-five years, it remains highly competitive with a large number of competing publishers, estimated at over 4,000 separate publishing organizations. By 2007, the largest five commercial publishers were controlling less than 25 percent of the peer-reviewed journals market, and the balance were small commercial and not-for-profit publishing organizations (Crow, 2006). The consolidation of the publishers helped them manage the technology costs associated with electronic scholarly publishing. With such scale and better capitalization, libraries and universities realized they could not compete unless they found a new publishing model (Brown, Griffiths, and Rascoff, 2007).

In the movement to electronic publishing, the monograph could not seem to thrive until large commercial distributers such as Amazon appeared and proved that electronic book downloads could be a sustainable business model. Appearing in the scholarly monograph publishing market were publishers such as Oxford Scholarship Online, Springer's SpringerLink, Elsevier's ScienceDirect, and others. Since their introductions, the publishers have continually added e-monographs. The term "journalizing the monograph" came into usage, referring to the inclusion of the monograph in the publishing, dissemination, access, and revenue models in a way that is similar to those used for online journals.

There are significant signs of "cracking" in the current diversified peer-review and publishing system. One of the justifications for maintaining the traditional peer-review system has been that quality control was assured. However, in March 2014, it was revealed that "fake research" had appeared in over 120 papers that were published in peer-reviewed, scientific journals over the preceding few years. These papers were computer generated in the science and math disciplines. Some of the most respected scholarly commercial publishers were involved, but this in no way says they were aware of the deception. This followed a study where it was illustrated that bogus articles were published in numerous open access journals, with seeming little or no review as these articles were entirely fabricated and made to appear clearly bogus. It indicates only that the digital age has created new risks in the scholarly communication process that have not been fully addressed.

In March 2014, a computer scientist, Cyri Labbé of Joseph Fourier University in France, reported that a review of papers published in established scientific journals revealed fraudulent articles. The academic publishers had to take the papers down. Labbé believes that the "publish or perish" system promotes academic publishing at all costs to obtain merit pay and promotions within the academic institutions (Foley, 2014). Looking ahead at the current dilemmas helps with understanding how the system led to the issues concerning academic publishing and library purchases. Technology has forced scholarly communication to adapt, but the falsified research published in scholarly journals suggests that the steps in the printed publishing system cannot be digitalized on a simple one-to-one basis. There will need to be controls to prevent the publication of computer-generated material passed off as scholarly research. This reality applies equally to both traditional journal publishing and open access communications.

TRENDS IN ACADEMIC LIBRARY BUYING PATTERNS PROMPTING CHANGING MODELS

Over the past twenty years, enormous change has taken place in how scholarly communications are bought and sold in economic terms, driven largely by technology. It has forced academic libraries to reevaluate their roles and priorities to ensure that they continue to fill their responsibilities to collect, preserve, manage, and disseminate scholarship. In this section, the trends in budgets and spending are revisited to clearly demonstrate the financial pressures libraries have been under and continue to experience.

The serials crisis has been a double-edged sword because it forced libraries to spend more of their budgets on subscriptions or to cancel subscriptions to lower expenses and forced reallocations of budgets from other categories into subscriptions. Another factor influencing library budgets was the 2008–2010 Great Recession, which led to federal and state reductions in support for academic institutions or caused significant shifting of funds within institutions. A survey of 188 member institutions conducted in November 2009 by the Association of Public and Land-Grant Universities reported that 64 percent of states were reducing funding for higher education. To cope with budget cuts and fund the technology, training, and staffing needed to shift from print to digital, a number of libraries had already eliminated hundreds of journals and were going to rely on interlibrary loans to meet demand. The International Coalition of Library Consortia and the ARL each issued public statements requesting that commercial publishers minimize price increases and calling for the joint development of new pricing models (Henderson and Bosch, 2010).

In 2004, the ARL reported that academic libraries were paying more for subscriptions but for fewer journals. Between 1986 and 2003, the consumer price index increased by 68 percent, and the price of journals increased by 215 percent. The price for monographs was also rising precipitously, increasing by 82 percent during the same time period (Beach et al., 2007). However, with the onset of online journals and the large-scale licensing available through the Big Deal model, the use of this material had never been great or more intense, and numerous studies showed that the cost-per-journal use dropped literally exponentially during the first decade of the twenty-first century. Publishers and libraries enjoy the highest level of cost benefit associated with scholarly communications, perhaps the highest in its glorious history.

Despite the fact that most buyers were buying their subscriptions through some type of volume or bundled purchase, unit pricing of scholarly communications on a journal-by-journal basis has remained contentious in the recent past. Several consumer groups continued to focus on these unit prices; for example, the average 2010 price for scientific disciplines ranged from $1,094 for geography to $3,792 for chemistry. Across the board, the subscription prices increased between 2008 and 2010 by 10 to 50 percent per title. In response to rising subscription prices and budget reductions, universities made significant reductions in journal subscriptions. For example, the University of Minnesota Library canceled 2,250 journal subscriptions costing approximately $1 million (Henderson and Bosch, 2010). Similar statistics are reported in global studies. During the period 2000–2006, median journal prices increased by 42 percent for Oxford journals and by 104 percent for Sage journals, while the median price per page increased 8 percent for Wiley and 75 percent for Taylor & Francis (White and Creaser, 2007).

A study of trends in staffing and collections in U.S. academic libraries indicated that all sizes of libraries have been shifting expenditures into e-serials and e-books. Large libraries had a 699 percent increase in e-serials expenditures compared to 287 percent for small libraries. E-book expenditures grew by 5,429 percent for large libraries and 1,514 percent for small libraries. The large libraries had a 5 percent increase in total operating expenditures, while the small libraries had a 26 percent reduction. Libraries of all sizes saw a decrease in circulation and reference utilizations. The underlying trends for the period 1998–2010 were from print to electronic resources, from labor intensive to capital intensive, and from brick-and-mortar to virtual library space (Regazzi, 2012b). The virtual library space reflects the fact that researchers are using libraries more often as a place where they can access electronic materials and collaborate with colleagues rather than as a place where they must go to gain access to materials through a librarian's assistance. However during this period, large doctoral-granting institutions fared much better than small and medium-size libraries, as the large libraries were able to grow both their staffing and their collections (through e-materials), while small and medium-size libraries had to cut staff and reduce collections. The larger institutions were outpacing their smaller institutional colleagues.

Libraries moving toward greater digitalization of collections are faced with maintaining adequate infrastructures able to meet the increased demand of self-help researchers, digital collections, and digital archiving. There is also a need for library staff trained in providing digital services, which requires very different skills than those needed for the management of print resources. The shift to electronic serials and e-books has been major for the period 1998–2008. In an analysis of survey data collected from 3,700 U.S. degree-granting, postsecondary institutions, expenditures for print serial subscriptions increased by 32.4 percent, while expenditures for electronic serials increased by 506.7 percent. E-book expenditures increased by 260.7 percent. This survey also reported that libraries have seen increases in total expenditures of 11.9 percent above inflation and did not experience the budget reductions that many claimed was the case (Regazzi, 2012b).

The confusion over budgets may be partially due to the shifts in spending, creating an illusion of budget reductions, so to speak. As expenditures on electronic materials increased, spending on computer software and hardware declined for the period 1998–2010. The increased spending on electronic materials was accompanied by declining value in print materials. There is also the visual impression that libraries spend less as print collections on shelving shrink and space is repurposed as meeting and work space (Regazzi, 2012b). In comparing academic libraries to other types of libraries, the increase in expenditures from 1998 to 2008 was 13 percent, which is by far the smallest percentage change. In comparison, public libraries reported a 31 percent increase, K–12 schools reported a 35 percent increase, higher-education auxiliary enterprises reported a 50 percent increase, and other higher-education institutions reported a 45 percent increase. The share of total higher-education spending that academic libraries accounted for during 1998–2010 fell from 3.3 to 2.5 percent (Regazzi, 2012a). All of these factors indicate that, while total expenditures may not have decreased, academic libraries are underperforming other types of libraries in terms of expenditure growth.

CONCLUSION

Academic libraries have been in a period of transition due to the shift of print to digital materials for almost two decades, but 2000 was a turning point in terms of recognizing that scholarly publishing, dissemination, and access were on a path of permanent change due to this underlying technology. The continuing rise in journal subscription prices led to the Big Deal and related business model shifts. Libraries were paying more for journals and getting access to a lot more journals and, in the process, greatly increasing the utilization of these materials. At the same time, researcher expectations changed concerning their ability to self-publish in open access journals and to gain access to electronic materials. Libraries found themselves in a continuing period of deepening change. In a very real sense, libraries are caught in the middle between academic scholars and commercial publishers. As a consequence, libraries are leading the way toward new publishing models, such as library journal publishing and incorporating open access into institutional repositories. One of the problems that will still need to be solved is how to make the institutional repositories economically viable and sustainable. Many believe that the solution to major issues now facing scholars and libraries lies in open access, while others see a rich and robust ecology of scholarly communications around commercial investment and technologies that provide the highest level of access ever seen for these materials.

REFERENCES

Beach, Richard, Amy Carter, Debbie East, et al. 2007. "Resisting Commercial Influences on Accessing Scholarship: What Literacy Researchers Need to Know and Do." Paper presented at the National Reading Conference, Oak Creek, Wisconsin, November 29–December 2, 2006. Published in the *56th Yearbook of the National Reading Conference* (Oak Creek, WI: National Reading Conference, Inc., 2007), 96–110.

Brown, Laura, Rebecca Griffiths, and Matthew Rascoff. 2007. "University Publishing in a Digital Age." *Ithaka Report*, July 26, 1–69. http://www.sr.ithaka.org/sites/default/files/reports/4.13.1.pdf.

Crow, Raym. 2006. "Publishing Cooperatives: An Alternative for Non-Profit Publishers." *First Monday* 11, no. 9 (September). http://firstmonday.org/ojs/index.php/fm/issue/view/203.

Foley, James A. 2014. "Scholarly Journals Accepted 120 Fake Research Papers Generated by Computer Program." *Nature World News*, March 1. http://www.natureworldnews.com/articles/6217/20140301/scholarly-journals-accepted-120-fake-research-papers-generated-by-computer-program.htm.

Frazier, Kenneth. 2001. "The Librarians' Dilemma—Contemplating the Costs of the 'Big Deal.'" *D-Lib Magazine* 7, no. 3 (March). http://www.dlib.org/dlib/march01/frazier/03frazier.html.

Gasson, Christopher. 2014. "The Economics of Academic Publishing." Royal Economic Society. Accessed January 15. http://www.res.org.uk/view/art2Apr04Features2.html.

Gibbs, Nancy J. 2005. "Walking Away from the 'Big Deal': Consequences and Achievements." *Serials* 18, no. 2 (January): 89–94.

Henderson, Kittie S., and Stephen Bosch. 2010. "Periodicals Price Survey 2010: Seeking the New Normal." *Library Journal*, April 15. http://lj.libraryjournal.com/2010/04/budgets-funding/periodicals-price-survey-2010-seeking-the-new-normal/#_.

Mullins, J. L., C. Murray-Rust, J. L. Ogburn, et al. 2012. Library Publishing Services: Strategies for Success: Final Research Report. Washington, DC: Scholarly Publishing and Academic Resources Coalition, 1–18.

Nabe, Jonathan, and David C. Fowler. 2012. "Leaving the Big Deal: Consequences and Next Steps." Southern Illinois University, Carbondale, Morris Libraries. January 1. http://opensiuc.lib.siu.edu/cgi/viewcontent.cgi?article=1070&context=morris_articles.

Poynder, Richard. 2011. "The Big Deal: Not Price but Cost." *Information Today* 28, no. 8 (September). http://www.infotoday.com/it/sep11/The-Big-Deal-Not-Price-But-Cost.shtml.

Regazzi, John J. 2012a. "Comparing Academic Library Spending with Public Libraries. Public K–12 Schools. Higher Education Public Institutions, and Public Hospitals between 1998–2008." *Journal of Academic Librarianship* 38, no. 4 (July): 205–216.

Regazzi, John J. 2012b. "Constrained? An Analysis of U.S. Academic Library Shifts in Spending, Staffing, and Utilization, 1998–2008." *College and Research Libraries* 73, no. 5 (September): 449–468. http://crl.acrl.org/content/73/5/449.full.pdf.

Seave, Ava. 2013. "You'll Need a PhD to Make Sense of the Pricing Schemes Publishers Impose on Libraries." *Media & Education. Forbes*, November 11. http://www.forbes.com/

sites/avaseave/2013/11/19/youll-need-a-phd-to-make-sense-of-the-pricing-schemes-publishers-impose-on-libraries.

Stieg, Kerstin Stieg. 2011. "Traditional Subscriptions, Big Deals or Pay-per-View?—A Comparative Evaluation of Business Models in Austria." Paper presented at the 2011 World Library and Information Congress, 77th IFLA Conference and Assembly, San Juan, Puerto Rico, August 16, 2011. http://www.library.mcgill.ca/ifla-stthomas/papers/stieg_2011.pdf.

White, Sonya, and Claire Creaser. 2007. *Trends in Scholarly Journal Prices 2000–2006*. Loughborough, UK: Loughborough University. http://www.lboro.ac.uk/microsites/infosci/lisu/downloads/op37.pdf.

Xia, Jingfeng. 2008. "A Comparison of Institutional and Subject Repositories in Self-Archiving Practices." *Journal of Academic Librarianship* 34, no. 6 (November): 489–495.

Xia, Jingfeng. 2009. "Library Publishing as a New Model of Scholarly Communication." *Journal of Scholarly Publishing* 40, no. 4 (July): 370–383. Academic Search Premier. EBSCO*host*.

Chapter Eight

Institutional Buyers, Scholars, and Open Access

A Continuing Story

The scholarly communications ecosystem remained mostly unchanged for centuries, with major advances found primarily in the realm of printing press technology. It was the development of the Internet that triggered a series of events that became a perfect storm leading to a serials crisis and new economics in scholarly publishing. The major occurrences wreaking havoc in the scholarly communication environment and leading to a serials crisis include phenomenal growth in research output made possible by technology, development of open access publishing, declining library budgets, and increasing scholarly journal prices. The uniquely identifiable events have two things in common. First, they are connected by principles of economics. Second, they have contributed to an environment in which scholarly researchers, faculty, and students are able to publish without intermediaries and are increasingly demanding that the traditional scholarly communication process adapt to the new publishing environment.

Though referred to as a "serials crisis" because of the critical role that academic libraries play in the scholarly publishing environment as consumers and knowledge managers and their relationship with university publishers, the crisis is better described as a "scholarly communication crisis." One of the defining characteristics of the web is the fact that people can easily go online and do what they want in terms of publishing, and the only restraint is culture and historical practices. Once, scholars could get recognition for published research only by going through a university press or commercial publisher, but now information presented in a blog can get international

attention. Though there are traditional characteristics assigned to publications—such as double-blind peer reviews, journal impact factors, and article
rejection rates, to name a few—that enable readers to identify when publishing scholarly communication versus non-scholarly communication, converg-
ing global trends and a generation of scholars who have grown up with
technology and accept its boundless capabilities are posing questions that the
traditional system is struggling to respond to. Open access publishing is a
good example. Is there any reason that a scholar cannot have a paper peer
reviewed and published in an open access repository maintained in the
cloud? The answer to that question depends on personal perspectives. The
reality is that scholarly communication is really defined by its quality, and
that quality is currently defended by a traditional process of peer review,
verification, and dissemination. If the same objectives can be met in other
ways, is there any reason to ignore the possibilities?

In this discussion is a description of the historical trends and issues that
led to the crises in academic libraries and the scholarly publishing landscape.
In the early 1990s, the introduction of online, peer-reviewed journals was
followed by a series of events that included global initiatives and declarations, foundation funding supporting pursuit of open access publishing, global legislative attempts to manage government-funded research deposited
into open access repositories, and the launch of a series of open access
repositories able to take advantage of new search engines that can access
millions of online documents. Following the history of open access is a
discussion of the sometimes conflicting perspectives of researchers, libraries,
and publishers on the merits of open access. Throughout is included a review
of the technological impacts on the economics of the scholarly communication environment.

EVOLUTION OF OPEN ACCESS

Early Years of the Open Access Movement

The landscape of scholarly communication today looks quite different from
the landscape that existed a mere generation ago. In the 1980s, open access
made its first appearance but was limited mostly to government and non-
profit, professional association journal publishing. At the turn of the decade
in 1990, the Internet was rapidly becoming more ingrained in society, and
personal computers on office desks (and eventually home desks) were contributing to a technological shift from a limited print-based, centralized system to a decentralized, digital system of unlimited publishing ability. By
2000, there were recognized types of open access venues, and it is safe to say
that all scholars, at least in developed nations, had easy computer access. As
self-publishing became a reality, the scalability of the traditional scholarly

communication system has come into question. The slow print and peer-review system did not always fit well in a world that was pursuing global scholarship. There were different levels of technology from country to country, but the need for information sharing was always critical. From 1988 to 2001, the increase in world science and engineering article output by 40 percent was driven mostly by scholars in Western Europe and Japan and in some developing East Asian countries, such as Taiwan, Singapore, South Korea, and China. By 1997, Western European article output was exceeding U.S. output (National Science Board, 2004).

The mission of scholars, publishers, and libraries has not changed over the centuries, but the economics most definitely have changed. Trends in scholarly communication have reached a crisis point that evolved over the past twenty-five years and are still evolving. The discontent of libraries and researchers grew in proportion to the rise in serial subscription prices, prompting publishing innovations, publisher boycotts, and researcher petitions to change the scholarly publishing system. The first catalyst in the shake-up of the scholarly publishing system began with the introduction of the Internet, but the progression toward open access as a result of the many trends in the scholarly environment has kept the change movement active.

Step-by-step, the open access movement inched forward. In 1989, the launch of the first free online journal, *Psycoloquy*, was founded and launched by Hungarian-born Stevan Harnad, a supporter of open access. The journal became a peer-reviewed journal and has been continuously online as an open access serial since 1990, with sponsorship by the American Psychological Association. It should be noted that the peer-reviewed, open access journal elicits non-anonymous commentary on its peer-reviewed articles. In 1990, the journal *Postmodern Culture* served as an experiment in Internet-based scholarly publishing and is still published online as an electronic journal as entirely web based by Johns Hopkins University Press with support from the University of Virginia and the University of California, Irvine. The mutual support arrangement reflects one strategy to maintain journal publishing by university presses within budgetary constraints. There were other experimental online scholarly journals, but they remained experimental for all intents and purposes in the opinions of the general scholarly community.

Paul Ginsparg originally developed the xxx.lanl.gov server in 1991 as a solution to the problem of potential e-mail overruns of disk allocations. By 1991, researchers were e-mailing completed manuscripts to each other. With the new systems, the e-mails were sent to an automated centralized repository, and full texts would be sent only when requested by the user. The first physics e-print archive was the High Energy Physics-Theory archive. The preprint server and e-mail interface system was pursued for more than just storing and sending e-mails. The underlying concept was that information would be more available to a wider group of researchers who were cut out of the private e-mail exchanges. The initial system added a web interface in 1993. The xxx.lanl.gov server was renamed arXiv in 1998 (Ginsparg, 2011).

As new technology emerged, new ideas concerning self-archiving also developed. Stevan Harnad published a self-archiving proposal on the discussion list VPIEJ-L, which was based at Virginia Polytechnic Institute. The list contained hundreds of electronic journals by 1994 but not all of them scholarly. Eventually, the discussion branched out to other lists, including one used by serials librarians. Referred to as the "subversive proposal," Harnad proposed that researchers self-archive, thus removing barriers to access. Publishers would continue to manage the peer-review process but would not do much else. Thus, Harnad publicly challenged the scholarly communication status quo and was addressing the marginal costs of using the Internet versus printing (Okerson and O'Donnell, 1998). He continued to be an advocate for open access long after his first proposal.

Also in 1994, the first print format journal, *Florida Entomologist*, was converted to open access. It was the first journal to put its content in PDF form and post on the Internet and the first life science journal to allow free access to current and back issues on the web. Though still issued in print form today, the journal was breaking new ground in 1994 and proving what was possible. One of the next major events did not occur for several years when the MEDLINE database, originally launched in 1966, became open access.

MEDLINE was the creation of the U.S. National Library of Medicine (NLM) and was one of the earliest online databases. Containing references and journal articles in medicine and the biomedical sciences, it was tedious to use, and access was gained primarily by medical librarians who submitted requests to the NLM. The access was not limited, but practicalities such as search fees, limited computer access, and the technical subject matter were not conducive to general public use. In 1997, free MEDLINE searching on the web was introduced at the same time a new service was developed called PubMed. The search function of PubMed, also a product of NLM, effectively linked MEDLINE users to the websites of publishers so that full text journal articles, where available, were accessible and retrievable. PubMed also added the "see related articles" button, which made discovery of relevant materials much easier (Lindberg, 2000). This function computerized a library service function to some extent. It could conceivably be viewed as one of the early steps toward the librarian function moving more toward archiving rather than primarily assisting users searching for materials.

The Association of Research Libraries (ARL) has been a player in the development of open access since its early years. The Scholarly Publishing and Academic Resources Coalition (SPARC) was established in 1998 specifically to pursue new scholarship communication models, reduce library financial pressures, and develop a more open scholarly communication system. The consortium initially focused on partnering with publishers who developed high-quality alternatives to expensive print publications. SPARC has played a pivotal role in the open access movement by ensuring that the library perspectives and issues were part of the public discussions. One of the main advocates for open access, the coalition sums up the views of open access proponents in its vision statements. SPARC leaves no doubt that their ultimate goal is to have "immediate, barrier-free online availability of scholarly and scientific research articles, coupled with the rights to reuse these articles fully in the digital environment" (ARL, 2013). From 1998 forward, SPARC was (and is) an important voice in the public debate on open access.

In 1998, Vitek Tracz developed the first open access publisher, BioMed Central. Tracz was responding to the disruptive technology of the Internet, the growth of large electronic databases developed by commercial publishers, the ability of researchers to distribute their own research through repositories such as ArXiv, the serials crisis, and the Open Access Movement (Tracz, 2010). What made BioMed Central so unique at its introduction was that it charged authors, instead of readers, an article processing charge.

One of the most comprehensive and fully searchable free repositories of full-text research articles was proposed by the director of the National Institutes of Health (NIH), Harold Varmus, as E-Biomed in May (amended June) 1999. The NIH-managed, web-based repository proposal included preprint and postprint article sections. Preprints are prepublication drafts of research papers before peer review. Postprints are articles or papers after peer review is completed. The physics discipline expressed the earliest interest in adopting preprints after Ginsparg developed the preprint server, and researchers actively shared pre–peer-reviewed papers. However, nothing had changed in terms of the peer-review and journal publication process. Despite a preprint culture, it would take ten years for all physics peer-reviewed articles to become freely accessible alone, thus setting the stage for a continued push for open access (Harnad, 2003).

When E-Biomed was proposed as a national biomedical literature server, it was with the intent of being fully searchable and freely accessible and that it would contain full-text articles as preprints and postprints. The proposal posted on the NIH website in May 1999 was supported by scientists two to one, but by August 1999, PubMed Central was announced as a replacement.

In a startling transformation, E-Biomed was revamped in a way that largely restored barriers to research accessibility. In less than four months, Varmus's broad vision of a true open access repository underwent radical changes. PubMed Central eliminated the inclusion of preprint articles and established a delay between article publication and article archiving. The innovative open access database was reduced to one with embargoed access of past prints only. The PubMed Central design allowed commercial publishers and scientific societies to determine the content and the posting date for articles. The peer-review process was left intact, and copyrights were retained by article publishers and societies. Though reader access was free, the limitations on what was published and when it was published changed the original intent of E-Biomed. It was troubling to the supporters of open access that an open access system, supported by pioneers Harnad and Ginsberg, was converted to a system that essentially prevented self-publishing and preserved peer review (Kling, Spector, and Fortuna, 2004).

When E-Biomed was proposed, library serial subscription and monograph prices had been steadily rising. The open access publishing and archiving system, it was argued, had the potential to significantly lower publishing and subscription costs, a main driver for proponents of open access publishing. Between 1986 and 2002, the serial unit costs and serial expenditures in ARL libraries increased 227 percent. Monograph unit costs rose 75 percent, but monograph expenditures declined 62 percent. The serial unit cost in 1986 was $88.55 and by 2002 had increased to $289.84. The monograph unit cost in 1986 was $28.70 and by 2002 had reached $50.17. The number of monograph purchases fell by 5 percent, and serial purchases increased 9 percent. The New Measures Initiative Projects, the *LibQual+ Project*, indicated that demand for print subscriptions was growing because users did not believe that libraries were able to meet full-text journal article demand via desktop computers (Kyrillidou and Young, 2003).

Harold Varmus continued his efforts to make open access available. In 2000, the Public Library of Science (PLOS) was launched after an online petition initiated by Varmus and colleagues Patrick O. Brown at Stanford University and Michael Eisen at the University of California, Berkeley. The petition called for medical and scientific publishers to make research literature available through online public archives and free to users. PubMed would have been a logical repository, but because of its perceived and real restrictions, many believed that these would limit its open access effectiveness (PLOS, 2013). PLOS is a non-profit organization that was and continues to be a pioneer of open access publishing principles. It launched *PLOS Biology* in October 2003 and *PLOS Medicine* in October 2004. These two online, open access journals eventually began attracting international research articles. PLOS called for free access to articles after a six-month embargo.

The Collection of Open Digital Archives (CODA) was launched by the CalTech Library System in 2000. This initiative was unique in that it created a collection of articles, monographs, and other materials published by faculty. CODA is a collection of archives that have grown in number over the years. Though open access, CODA protects copyrights. It funds itself by charging a publication fee to authors or research sponsors. Also during this same time period, BioMed Central published its first online article. Vitek Tracz strongly encouraged Harold Varmus, promoted PubMed development, and recruited open access supporters. In 2001, most of the PubMed Central titles came from BioMed Central (Guédon, 2001).

The Association of American Universities, the Merrill Advanced Studies Center of the University of Kansas, and the ARL sponsored a group meeting in Tempe, Arizona, on March 2–4, 2000. One of the early documents preceding the declarations to come in later years was issued by this group. The "Tempe Principles for Emerging Systems of Scholarly Publishing" was an effort to build consensus among participants in the scholarly communication process in recognizing that the publishing system was on the cusp of significant change. It clearly addressed the affordability issue when it included the statement that

> the current system of scholarly publishing has become too costly for the academic community to sustain. The increasing volume and costs of scholarly publications, particularly in science, technology, and medicine (STM), are making it impossible for libraries and their institutions to support the collection needs of their current and future faculty and students. Moreover, the pressure on library budgets from STM journal prices has contributed to the difficulty of academic publishers in the humanities and social sciences, primarily scholarly societies and university presses, to publish specialized monograph-length work or to find the funds to invest in the migration to digital publishing systems. (ARL, 2000)

The "Tempe Principles" were attempting to find some consensus because the meeting participants believed that a lack of consensus among relevant parties was allowing the continuing rise in prices.

There were many additions to open access in 2001–2002 that contributed to the Open Access Movement. The Health Internetwork Access to Research Initiative (HINARI) was launched as a result of collaboration between the World Health Organization, the United Nations, and a number of large publishers. The purpose of HINARI is to provide researchers at public institutions in developing countries access to full-text journal articles in biomedical and social sciences. HINARI is a good example of the possibilities that both open access proponents and commercial as well as society publishers saw in cooperative publishing programs to disseminate scholarly materials in the developing world. It was launched to help countries access research information they would not be able to get otherwise and to access it free of charge. The ultimate goals of HINARI were to reduce the unequal distribution of health care by closing the knowledge gap (Katikiredd, 2004).

SHERPA is the acronym for Securing a Hybrid Environment for Research Preservation and Access and was one of the many international open access efforts. It is a consortium of U.K. university libraries and was tasked with establishing e-print archives that are freely available to researchers (SHERPA, 2013). Also in 2002 was the issue of the first set of copyright licenses by Creative Commons. Founded in 2001, Creative Commons is a non-profit organization that enables people to legally publish, share, and use online material in any form. The author can reserve rights and modify copyright terms (Creative Commons, 2013). The Public Knowledge Project (PKP) is a non-profit research initiative formed in 2001 by faculty at Canadian and U.S. universities focused on improving the quality and reach of scholarly research and communication and to promote free access to federally funded research. The PKP released Open Journals Systems in 2001 as open source software for journal publishing (PKP, 2013). The push for the release of research data for public access became an important issue of the Open Access Movement over the next decade. Each of the open access initiatives mentioned are still functioning and continue to develop new open access projects and new repositories.

Types of Open Access

The Open Access Movement consisted of numerous initiatives, projects, consortiums, conferences, presentations, papers, and articles. The effort was global and driven primarily by research libraries and scientists in public and private positions. However, as the pioneers Varmus and Harnad learned, securing the full support of the scholarly community was not easy, as views around improving and maintaining scholarly communications were both diverse and varied. The commercial publishers had an interest in receiving an adequate return on their investments both in the digital innovations undertaken and in overall product quality. The societies had an interest in ensuring that the published research was accurate and high quality and fit their standards for research effort and presentation of scientific and technical information, also requiring significant and ongoing investment. With so many varied efforts and participants in the Open Access Movement, there was a need to begin establishing uniformity in terminology and standards for the benefit of global researchers.

One of the first steps in tightening up the Open Access Movement was to develop copyright conditions for authors interested in archiving their research on the web. SHERPA began the RoMEO Project in 2002–2003 at the University of Loughborough. RoMEO is the acronym for Rights Metadata for Open Archiving. The JISC-funded project was dedicated to investigating the various models for self-archiving (Loughborough University, 2013). As a result of a survey of the U.K. community, the project outcomes produced the first definitions of the types of open access and the SHERPA/RoMEO listing. The listing includes the major publishers of peer-reviewed journals and the rights each publisher assigns to authors. However, the RoMEO project was just one effort. Out of RoMEO emerged one of the first attempts in 2003 to standardize definitions for open access restrictions, rights, and permissions.

Since then, various types of open access developed. They now include Gold Open Access, Green Open Access, and Hybrid Open Access.

Gold Open Access (Gold OA) designates articles in which the author has given immediate open access by publishing in an open access journal or other venue. There are often author fees (article processing fees) paid to the publisher but not always. As open access models have advanced, the Gold OA research article does not always involve a journal, but as long as the peer-review process remains intact, most Gold OA research will remain journal based.

Hybrid Open Access (Hybrid OA) is a subtype of Gold OA in which the research user pays a subscription fee. Once the article processing fee is paid, the reader has open access rights to the material. There are always fees involved in this type of publishing, but the reader access may be embargoed or immediate.

There are two kinds of repositories where Green Open Access (Green OA) materials are deposited. Institutional repositories are maintained by the authors' institutions, such as universities or research facilities. The institution collects all the research output of the faculty and researchers and maintains the material in a central location. The other type of repository is created by community members and is usually hosted and maintained at an appropriate institution. The arXiv repository is a good example (Jeffery, 2006).

Green OA designates self-archived articles and the articles deposited as preprints and postprints in repositories. The author self-archives at the time of publication. Self-archived articles are usually materials that were published in a conventional journal, so Green OA is secondary electronic publishing of articles that normally require payment of an access fee. Green OA can be published as primary and secondary material at the same time, or the electronic version may be published after the primary publication. The types of publications include the traditional peer-reviewed journal, grey literature (non-peer-reviewed), monographs, and conference proceedings. When authors self-deposit materials with traditional publishers in an online repository, there is often an embargo period during which only fee-paying subscribers can access the articles.

Key Conferences and Manifestos Addressing Open Access

As the historical developments concerning open access in scholarly communications unfolded, there was another set of activities greatly influencing progress. They included key conferences producing "manifestos" and "declarations" that addressed the many issues concerning the role of open access in the scholarly communication process, how to blend virtual publishing with traditional publishing, and identifying how open access publishing can best contribute solutions to such trends as the development of the serials crisis experienced by libraries. Like the progression of new repositories, the key conferences and statements occurred over a period of approximately ten years, from 1998 to 2008, and became a worldwide movement.

In March 1998, the "Declaration of San José promoted the construction of a virtual health library. The declaration was prepared by the delegates of the Latin American and Caribbean System on Health Sciences Information at the IV Pan American Congress on Health Sciences Information. The main point made in 1998 is still maintained today, and that point addresses the need to efficiently use technological developments for critical information sharing to benefit human development ("Declaration of San José towards the Virtual Health Library," 1998).

There was significant activity in 1999, beginning with the Universal Pre-print Service meeting held in October, which was called the Santa Fé Convention by the next meeting in early 2000. It was initiated by Paul Ginsparg, Rick Luce, and Herbert Van de Sompel, and the purpose of the meeting was to discuss e-print archives or self-archiving. The meeting led to the launch of the Open Archives Initiative (OAI), dedicated to assisting with scholarly communication transformation by creating a technical and organized framework for accommodating free and commercial publications in e-print archives (Van de Sompel and Lagoze, 2000). Participants in the Santa Fé Convention agreed to implement the OAI framework during 2000, making electronic documents available globally. At the time, the number of established self-archiving repositories was small, with the arXiv still most successful. The intent was that the new e-print archives would be distributed across the Internet and take a variety of forms. Some would be based on particular scholarly disciplines, while others would be institutionally based (OAI, 2001). The OAI is still developing interoperability standards to promote efficient content dissemination and data access. For example, the Open Archives Initiative Protocol for Metadata Harvesting (OAI-PMH) can extract metadata descriptions of archived records. A harvester client application issues OAI-PMH requests. The OAI has now expanded beyond promoting institutional repositories to include projects involved in developing resources for e-science, e-learning, and e-scholarship.

The United Nations Educational, Scientific and Cultural Organization (UNESCO) announced the "Declaration on Science and the Use of Scientific Knowledge" at the World Conference on Science in Budapest, Hungary, held June 26–July 1, 1999. The declaration proposed a new "social contract" in which "the nations and the scientists of the world are called upon to acknowledge the urgency of using knowledge from all fields of science in a responsible manner to address human needs and aspirations without misusing this knowledge," continuing in the preamble to assert that "equal access to science is not only a social and ethical requirement for human development, but also essential for realizing the full potential of scientific communities worldwide and for orienting scientific progress towards meeting the needs of humankind" (UNESCO, 1999). An element of social responsibility, first suggested in the San José declaration, is taken to a higher level.

A critical initiative was launched in February 2002—the Budapest Open Access Initiative (BOAI). It came out of a meeting of the Open Society Institute (OSI), founded by George Soros, and the OSI funded the first three years of BOAI projects for $3 million. Some would argue that it is the official birth of the Open Access Movement because it was an international coalition, and it clearly defined what the initiative authors meant by "open access." The BOAI says,

> By "open access" to this literature, we mean its free availability on the public internet, permitting any users to read, download, copy, distribute, print, search, or link to the full texts of these articles, crawl them for indexing, pass them as data to software, or use them for any other lawful purpose, without financial, legal, or technical barriers other than those inseparable from gaining access to the internet itself. The only constraint on reproduction and distribution, and the only role for copyright in this domain, should be to give authors control over the integrity of their work and the right to be properly acknowledged and cited. (Chain et al., 2002)

The BOAI end goal was open access to peer-reviewed journal articles and called for self-archiving (Green Road) and open access journals that are not bound by market and legislative restrictions (Gold Road). The BOAI assumed there are no embargoes. Since the original declaration was issued, over 5,700 individuals and 673 organizations around the world have added their signatures.

The International Federation of Library Associations (IFLA) issued the "IFLA Internet Manifesto" in 2002, asserting that people should have unhindered access to information on a global basis and that governments should support the unhindered flow of information that is accessible by the Internet and made available by libraries (IFLA, 2002). In 2003, there were two more major declarations concerning open access publishing: the "Bethesda Statement on Open Access Publishing" and the "Berlin Declaration on Open Access to Knowledge in the Sciences and Humanities."

The "Bethesda Statement on Open Access Publishing" arose from a meeting held on April 11, 2003, at the Howard Hughes Medical Institute in Chevy Chase, Maryland. The goal was to develop agreement between interested parties on the development of concrete steps to establish open access to primary scientific literature in the biomedical discipline. In this particular meeting, there were representatives, acting as individuals, who were involved in scholarly publishing at various stages of production, including institutions and funding agencies, research scientists, publishers, librarians, and research readers. The "Bethesda Statement" defined an open access publication as one that meets two conditions. First, the author gives users full rights to use the articles as desired as long as there is proper attribution of authorship. Derivative works are permitted, which was a topic not addressed by the BOAI. Second, a complete version of the articles must be deposited immediately in an appropriate online repository, such as those maintained by universities, scholarly societies, government agencies, and so on ("Bethesda Statement on Open Access Publishing," 2003).

The working groups participating in the "Bethesda Statement" essentially promised to do everything possible to aid the transition to open access publishing, and therein lies the uniqueness of this statement. Libraries agree to develop and maintain mechanisms for the transition and to highlight open access journals in their catalogs. Journal publishers committed to providing open access options for the articles they published and work toward transitioning journals to open access. Publishers also agreed to work on standard electronic formats and develop affordable fee models for researchers in developing countries. The scientists affirmed their support of open access and agreed to take action "by selectively publishing in, reviewing for and editing for open access journals and journals that are effectively making the transition to open access." Importantly, they agreed to advocate for a change in the promotion, tenure, and compensation process for faculty so that it recognizes open access publishing ("Bethesda Statement on Open Access Publishing," 2003).

The European Cultural Heritage Online Project and the Max Planck Society organized a meeting in October 2003 to, for all intents and purposes, ratify the BOAI and the "Bethesda Statement on Open Access Publishing." The Berlin Open Access Conference called for self-archiving without expectation of payment and for article permissions that allow use and reuse of articles. The meeting produced the "Berlin Declaration on Open Access to Knowledge in the Sciences and Humanities." The new document builds on the previous one, mostly by adding humanities and encouraging new activities in support of open access. They include "encouraging the holders of cultural heritage" to provide their resources as open access, advocating that open access "be recognized in promotion and tenure evaluation," and "developing means and ways to evaluate open access contributions and online-journals" to ensure high-quality articles and scientific practice (Open Access, Max-Planck-Gesellschaft, 2013).

On January 30, 2004, the Organization for Economic Cooperation and Development (OECD) supported open access for research data funded by public agencies. The "Declaration on Access to Research Data from Public Funding" was signed by representatives from thirty-four countries. Though the conference members recognized that each country had its own laws concerning scientific research funding and publication, the conference members believed that publicly funded research should bring the greatest value possible to the public paying for the research, and the only way to do that was to make the research publicly accessible. The OECD declaration called for "transparency in regulations and policies" related to international research flows, reduction of information barriers, the establishment of new international frameworks and laws to support "international collaboration in access to digital data," and addressing issues specific to developing countries and transition economies (OECD, 2004). Despite all the discussion on the definition of open access tackled by previous groups, the OECD statement caused some confusion because it began with two statements that used the word "data" rather than "research," sparking debate about whether it included finished research or only the databases. This is but a small example of the difficulties that even well-intentioned activities concerning open access ran up against.

More declarations and initiatives were being issued around the world. The "Valparaiso Declaration for Improved Scientific Communication in the Electronic Medium" was produced at Pontificia Universidad Católica de Valparaíso in Valparaiso, Chile, on January 14–15, 2004. The "Compromisso do Minho: Compromisso Sobre Acesso Livre à Informação Científica em Países em Lusófonos" was issued in Portugal at the Second Open Access Conference in November 2006. There were many others, such as the "IFLA Statement on Open Access to Scholarly Literature and Research Documentation," published February 24, 2004; the "ALPSP Principles of Scholarship-Friendly Journal Publishing Practice," published March 26, 2004; the "Statement on Open Access to Scholarly Information," published by the Australian Group of Eight research universities; and numerous others.

By 2006, there was a plethora of open access projects and research archives in existence around the world. As the discussion so far has shown, various activities would take place in response to specific needs or to simply advocate for open access. There was no comprehensive list of open access repositories for the global community. For this reason, the University of Nottingham in the United Kingdom and Lund University in Sweden developed and launched OpenDOAR in 2006 in order to provide more structure to the open access repository ecosystem. The structure would incorporate repository polices on tagging to indicate peer review or non–peer review, the subject matter, preservation policies, and so on. Maintained by SHERPA Services, the information is accessible by researchers and search engines and includes repositories that may not be OAI-PMH compliant (OpenDOAR, 2011).

The pace of the Open Access Movement continued to accelerate as more open access articles, journals, and repositories appeared on the scene. In August 2007, the final version of the "Kronberg Declaration on the Future of Knowledge Acquisition and Sharing" was issued by UNESCO. A group of experts met in Kronberg, Germany, under the sponsorship of BASF to discuss the future of the information industry over the next twenty-five years. The declaration includes principles of transparency and equity, and it unequivocally supports open access. The "Kronberg Declaration" stresses the need to "promote user-friendly ICT applications to make knowledge acquisition and sharing available to everybody anywhere and anytime; support open access to and free flow of content through the development of open standards, open data structures, and standardized info-structures . . . ; enable the creation of open content by practitioners in the developing world" (UNESCO, 2007).

American President George W. Bush signed the NIH open access policy into law in December 2007. The NIH policy had been voluntary for two years and was the result of the recognition by a 2004 House Appropriations Committee that explored the need for an open access policy. The report recognized the problems plaguing the scholarly community concerning rising scientific journal subscription prices, but its real intent was to address the inefficient public access to NIH-funded research. It is not all that surprising that the health sciences was the focus of an open access policy since so many global declarations had advanced the principle of knowledge sharing as critical to human development. The committee recommended that the NIH develop a policy that would require that any manuscript supporting work funded by the NIH be submitted as an electronic copy to PubMed Central once accepted for publication in a scientific journal recognized in the PubMed directory. The NIH issued a policy report in February 2005 for implementation by May 2, 2005, and recipients of NIH funding were asked to voluntarily submit their articles to PubMed Central. The policy requested submittal of the NIH-funded articles to PubMed Central but also created the twelve-month embargo period. Mandatory article submission became effective December 2007, and the law took effect January 2008.

The opposition to the NIH policy was fierce, and the debate was ongoing between the 2005 policy issue and the 2008 law implementation. The NIH mandate was important because it represented a major adoption of an open access policy that was the end result of a vigorous public debate. The new law also makes public an enormous amount of NIH-funded research because the U.S. NIH is the largest funder of global research. The mandate and implementation of the law also created new expectations among the scholarly communication community that research funded by public funds is justifiably open access (Suber, 2008).

The digitization of books deserves separate mention. There were several alliances formed and projects initiated beginning in the early 2000s. Though not all were concerned with scholarly books, the efforts and subsequent copyright lawsuits do impact the consortiums and book projects devoted to scholarly works. The early alliances also indicated the growing power of major search engines and their joint project efforts with universities and publishers. Google Books launched the Google Print Library Project in December 2004 in partnership with prestigious universities, such as Harvard University, Oxford University, and the University of Michigan, and the New York Public Library. The project name was changed to Google Book Search in 2005 following two lawsuits concerning copyrights and author compensation. The first suit was brought by the Authors Guild, and the second suit was brought by the Association of American Publishers, McGraw-Hill, and several others. The Google Books Library Project was an offshoot of a program in which publishers, libraries, and authors could choose to assign rights for inclusion in the program. From 2006 forward, a series of universities joined the Google Books Library Project, including the University of California System, the University of Virginia, the University of Texas, and many others. The program became international when the Bavarian State Library joined the digitization project in 2007. In 2010, Google announced its intention of scanning all known existing books by the end of the decade, which would naturally include scholarly editions. The Google approach assumed that books they chose would be digitized unless authors explicitly told Google it was not allowed. Google also claimed that digitizing, for the purpose of indexing the book, falls under the "fair use" laws.

The Open Content Alliance (OCA) was formed as an offset group to Google's Book Search, and it also scans and archives books but through the Internet Archive. The OCA was concerned about a commercial enterprise such as Google having ownership of historic works, many of which are also scholarly works. For this reason, the OCA decided that all of its digitized works would come with unrestricted use because it first obtains author permission. The OCA was formed in 2005 by Amazon, Internet Archive, Yahoo!, Microsoft, and others. Microsoft funded the project for several years and withdrew support in 2008, but other major partners joined, including the New York Library Association and the Special Libraries Association.

In 2005, the Authors Guild and its member representatives and the American Society of Media Photographers filed a lawsuit against Google claiming copyright infringement. The long-standing case was dismissed in 2013, the judge ruling that the Google Books project is protected under the U.S. fair use doctrine. Judge Denny noted in his ruling that Google Books was an essential research tool, increased the ability of researchers and readers to efficiently find books, expanded book access, and provided print-disabled researchers a means for accessing materials in a format compatible with useful software (Stempel, 2013). The Authors Guild plans on appealing the ruling.

The implications of the two digitizing projects in 2008 have importance to scholarly authors and libraries. First, libraries were still struggling with their budgets and the Great Recession, and Google raised awareness of the possibilities of digitization for their specific purposes. Second, it also raised awareness that copyright issues concerning digitization of materials for full-text or indexing purposes were far from settled. Third, the projects also added a marketing element in that authors would give permission to scan and index their works in order to increase visibility during search engine–driven Internet browsing (Leetaru, 2008). Finally, the complexities of the Open Access Movement became even more apparent since issues such as these were still being raised and are still far from being settled.

Calling for Boycotts

The library "serials crisis" continued through the Open Access Movement, and as of 2012, the subscriptions prices were still rising at an escalating rate. At the same time, library budgets were continuing to decline. The "2012 EBSCO Library Collections and Budgeting Trends Survey" queried 395 academic libraries and found that 69 percent of the libraries had remained flat, 80 percent planned on decreasing spending for print journals, and 63 percent were going to cut budget amounts allocated to print-plus-online journals. Serials prices continued to climb but more modestly now, with many increasing by 5.5 percent between 2011 and 2012. E-journal prices increased 3 to 6 percent. However, some scholarly disciplines had journal prices that were much higher than others. Consider that chemistry prices per title averaged $4,227, physics was $3,649, technology was $1,746, and agriculture was $1,317. The clear trend among libraries was to decrease print subscription orders and increase e-journal subscriptions (Bosch and Henderson, 2012). In a separate study on the subscription prices for scholarly society journals, it was reported that U.S. journal prices had increased an average of 7.3 percent annually from 1989 to 2011. In 2012, the average annual price increase dropped for the first time since 1989 by almost one full percentage point. However, prices were continuing to increase annually by 6 percent. Also, peer-reviewed journal prices were increasing at a faster rate than non-peer-reviewed titles (Tillery, 2012).

There were many factors influencing the slowdown in serial subscription prices, and quite possibly one of them was a pushback from the scholarly community. In January 2012, a mathematician named Timothy Gowers started the Cost of Knowledge Boycott to protest Elsevier's business practices, including the high prices for subscriptions, bundling practices ("Big Deals"), and the support of measures such as SOPA (Stop Online Piracy Act), the Research Works Act, and PIPA (Protect IP Act) that are designed to restrict the free flow of information. Gowers is a Royal Society research professor in the Department of Pure Mathematics and Mathematical Statistics at Cambridge University. The Cost of Knowledge collected signatures from other academics and researchers who objected to the lack of access to academic research and the high fees charged to access articles the researchers wanted disseminated without a charge. He issued the call for the boycott in a blog. Though Gowers understood the need for making a profit, he made the point that the scholarly community could band together, refuse to publish with or referee for Elsevier, and discover they did not need Elsevier's services (Gowers, 2012). The blog generated a lot of interest among academics, even if all of them did not sign the web-based petition. It also served its purpose of getting the attention of a major publisher, which had so far been slow in responding to the community calls for open access.

The ongoing push for open access scholarly communication saw publishers begin to respond when Elsevier announced in late December 2013 that it was converting seven subscription journals in 2014 to open access. The seven journals would convert to Gold OA on January 1, 2014, and all were in physics and medicine. The change meant that authors would pay an article processing fee and that the journal would no longer be subscription based. This was just one of a series of actions in which open access journals were created, and other publishers were taking the same route (Elsevier, 2013). Elsevier had been offering open access journals since 2005, but the practices Gowers objected to in his boycott call, he believed, were negating many of the advantages in open access publishing.

Gowers was not the only person to boycott major academic publishers, but he got the most attention because he was one of the first to do so publicly. Spurring on the boycotts was the introduction of two U.S. bills that propelled the furor of those who opposed the government interfering with the Internet. (SOPA and PIPA were intended to make it more difficult for websites to sell or distribute material that violates copyrights. Though the intentions were good and the bills were meant primarily to target the music and movie industries, people such as Gowers were unhappy that academic publishers supported the bills because, he viewed, they gave the government the power to, in effect, create an Internet blacklist and to censor—anathema to academics.)

The Role of Foundations

The academics, professional publishers, societies, and university libraries are not the only ones addressing all the issues surrounding open access. The nonprofit foundations also exert enormous influence on the process. There are several that have been particularly active in funding projects in the early stages and continued to do so in the ensuing years. In December 2002, the Howard Hughes Medical Institute, where the "Bethesda Statement" was developed, was the first foundation to make a commitment to cover open access publication fees for its own researchers when they published in a fee-based open access site. The funding was provided as a budget supplement in research budgets. The Gordon and Betty Moore Foundation awarded a $9 million grant to the Public Library of Science in December 2002 to fund open access publishing and the launch of two open access journals. This funding supported the launch of *PLOS Biology* and *PLOS Medicine* using the new business model in which authors are charged modest fees but material is available immediately for access, use, and redistribution once published (Suber, 2002).

The first foundation to make open access a condition of grants funded by a foundation was the Wellcome Trust. In 2001, the Wellcome Trust had commissioned two reports to study the economics and structure of scientific journal publishing. The reports highlighted the increasing subscription prices, the high commercial publishing profits, and the fact that authors were giving their research to publishers for free. The Wellcome Trust adhered to the "Bethesda Statement" issued in 2003, meaning the research it funded needed to be published in an open access publication or in a publication of a journal that led to final disposition in an open access publication. As a result, the Wellcome Trust issued a position statement stating that its funding would have a grant condition that required grantees to publish in open access. All grantees were required to deposit electronic articles in PubMed Central within twelve months (originally six months) after publication in a peer-reviewed journal. The policy took effect with articles published from Wellcome Trust funding awarded after October 1, 2005. In 2004, the Wellcome Trust began working with the National Center for Biotechnology Information to implement the same type of requirement (Terry and Kiley, 2006).

Another foundation that has been supportive of the Open Access Movement is the Andrew W. Mellon Foundation. For example, the foundation supports the activities of the Open Archives Initiative. Foundations around the world have also been involved in the Open Access Movement. The Swiss National Science Foundation has supported the "green path" to open access publishing since 2007. Like the Wellcome Foundation, it requires funded researchers to make their research papers accessible in open access repositories within six months of publication in a peer-reviewed journal. In 2013, the Swiss National Science Foundation announced it would support the "golden path" of publication up to a stated amount as part of a grant budget. Though hybrid journals are not included, this was an important step forward in recognition of open access publishing (ETH-Bibliotheck, 2013).

The Legal Environment and Open Access

Since open access involves copyright issues, there have been several major attempts to legislate open access deposits of government-funded research. These efforts have been particularly notable in the United States, the United Kingdom, and the European Union. As discussed earlier, the U.S. Congress addressed open access for articles funded by NIH grants. Government efforts to require open access for government-funded research was not restricted to the United States. In July 2004, the United Kingdom Science and Technology Select Committee Report recommended that networks of institutional repositories be created and that publicly funded researchers retain some copyright rights and not be allowed to sign all of them over to publishers when the government funded their research (United Kingdom Parliament, 2004). In November 2004, the U.K. government rejected the Select Committee report but also admitted it recognized the potential benefits of institutional repositories and open access publishing.

In June 2012, the *Finch Report* recommended some radical changes to the scholarly publishing system. The Working Group on Expanding Access to Public Research Findings, which was headed by Dame Janet Finch, recommended that the United Kingdom move rapidly toward Gold OA publishing, in which publishers earn revenues from authors rather than reader subscriptions. In this way, the articles would be free and accessible on publication. The report also recommended that publishers move more quickly toward providing reader access to journals in public libraries and university repositories (Finch Group, 2012). The plan was to implement the new recommendations within two years, but not everyone has supported the effort because of the costs. The money to pay for open access fees would have to come from research funds or increased government funding until all scholarly articles were free, which is unlikely to happen for many decades. A parliamentary report issued by the House of Commons's Business, Innovation and Skills Committee was just one group to point out the strain that the move toward open access would cause. By 2013, most funding agencies in the United States and Europe were arguing for Green OA within six to twelve months of publication. If the government paid for Gold OA, the cost would be prohibitive, according to U.K. universities and libraries. Since the U.K. policy was issued, the reality of the marketplace has led to a slowdown of the transition to Gold OA (Van Noorden, 2013).

THREE SIDES OF THE DISCUSSION

For many researchers and institutional buyers, the progress made to date in open access publishing is disappointing. They had hoped that the many private, foundation, and government efforts to promote open access would have led to full acceptance and the embracement of the Open Access Movement because issues such as peer review had been resolved to the scholar community's satisfaction. Instead, there is still significant and tumultuous debate continuing because there are so many factions involved. The commercial publishers stand to lose their main source of revenues without some type of replacement. Researchers advocate for open access, but they also have an interest in having a clear understanding of how open access fits in the traditional faculty promotion, compensation, and tenure system. Libraries are under tremendous pressure to provide research and archiving services but are dealing with the untenable problem of the twin issues of budget cuts and their changing role within the university. Balancing all of these issues and varying perspectives is challenging. To understand the full complexity of the situation, it is necessary to consider the many issues that researchers, libraries, and publishers face concerning open access publishing.

Researchers

Though researchers seem to generally support open access publishing, they also have questions concerning its implementation. For some, shifting the cost of publication to authors means that only those researchers funded by grantors willing to pay the publishing costs will have the primary voice in the marketplace. There are also numerous questions concerning recognition of peer reviewers and the peer-review process, the impact of embargoes, archiving, quality control, and authorship. Concerns about managing preprints and informal communication are part of the ongoing dialogue, too. Many researchers purport that the scholarly discussions leading to the final article are as important as the final product itself because they stimulate intellectual interest and further scholarly pursuits. Yet another issue is the protection of copyrights. If anyone can go online and download research articles, what or who will protect the material copyrights? Right now, the publishing industry tightly controls ownership of materials that flow through their systems. However, many scholars believe that open access is inevitable and the only publishing method that makes sense given the available technology and financial restrictions. Scholars can make the argument that charging authors for publishing limits the scholarly body of knowledge, a paradox given that the end goal is to expand knowledge. A theoretical question is, What vital research has not been published because of author financial limitations? The argument is also made that knowledge should not be treated as if it is a commodity because of its importance to society. Open access offers the democratization of access to research, eliminating barriers created by financial considerations. If only the scholars working for wealthy academic institutions or funded by government can afford to publish, there is obviously knowledge held captive by the system (Saint-André et al., 2013). In 1999, Harold Varmus proposed E-biomed, but the original proposal included peer review, editorial boards, and almost immediate publication of articles that have been reviewed lightly. He wanted readers to have "instantaneous, cost-free access . . . to E-biomed's entire content" so they could pursue personal scholarly interests as efficiently and productively as possible (Varmus, 1999). The goals of open access were presented early and have not since changed significantly.

Libraries

Libraries continue to deal with rising though now more modest subscription prices, even while moving to grow the size and scope of institutional repositories. Traditional publishing companies still publish most of the academic journals, so getting access requires paying subscription fees. The unintended consequence of a publishing industry in flux is that libraries must fund the cost of subscriptions in the traditional publishing industry, the cost of maintaining institutional repositories, and the very real cost of searching for solutions (technology, staff training, time spent in discussions, and so on). The changing role of libraries includes using their expertise to build the infrastructures that support long-term access to scholarly publications.

Institutional repositories of faculty research is one approach libraries have taken to capture and archive faculty publications. In some cases, the repositories also include copies of materials that institutional employees are required to deposit when they publish elsewhere. The system creates a whole new set of questions. Though libraries can archive faculty research, they must still find affordable ways to share that research with readers who are internal and external to the facility. Research has to be disseminated to have full value. How will libraries ensure that the institutional repository materials are included in the worldwide body of knowledge? If the materials are locked away and only local researchers can access them, there is little improvement over the subscription-based model, which limits access through pricing structures. The introduction of the "cloud" offers possibilities for central archiving, but there are so many issues revolving around open access that this fairly new technology is not anywhere near being in a state fully developed enough to convince everyone that it should become central to a primary publishing model. Libraries are still grappling with the question of whether to distribute or centrally archive holdings.

Over the past five years, there has been an increasing number of faculty resolutions at major educational institutions to support open access publishing and depositing of materials in institutional repositories. Harvard University, Stanford University, Trinity University, and Oberlin College are just four of many that have mandates in which the faculty signing the resolutions agree to grant their respective institutions a non-exclusive, irrevocable license or right to disseminate their published articles as they like. The faculty agree to deposit a copy of each published work in the institutional repository. The authors also agree to notify the publisher of this requirement so that there are no copyright issues. The resolutions, such as the one Harvard faculty sign, apply only to scholarly articles in fulfillment of a perceived responsibility to best serve the public interest.

Libraries are increasingly reviving university presses because it makes sense to ensure that faculty output is archived, and the presses have the potential of supporting library operations if profitable. The new university presses are different from the historical presses because they are pursuing leading-edge digital publishing, including in open access journals and books within the institution and with commercial publishers. There are experiments in the works that reflect a belief by some universities that free digital-form-only, peer-reviewed publications in open access archives make up the inevitable future of scholarly publishing. The experimentations will help define the elements of a new economic model. Amherst College Press initiated such an experiment to print scholarly books and novellas out of the belief that libraries have a fundamental obligation to make high-quality information available. In the Amherst funding model, the library funds the positions through endowments and its regular budget but believes the availability of free literature will lead to a reduction in acquisitions spending. The more universities, societies, and commercial presses join and expand the effort, the greater the positive impact will be on library budgets. The library contributes an ever-increasing amount of materials to open access publishing, and eventually the material will reach critical mass. When that happens, library budgets could potentially be freed of many of the expenses associated with providing access to scholarly materials (Amherst College Press, 2013). Amherst is just an example of the bold approaches libraries are taking within their operations and the new roles they are assuming to promote open access.

Publishers

Publishers are often accused of being concerned mostly with lost revenues should scholarly publishing take the route primarily of open access. They also point out that the peer-review process is critical to ensuring research publication quality. Supporters of open access readily claim that articles can be peer reviewed by qualified, voluntary reviewers without going through established major publishers, and some efforts in that direction are already succeeding. One of the functions publishers perform is maintaining a record of publication. How will that record be maintained in a system of open access? There are a couple of reasons that most indexed articles have funneled down to a set of publishers. One is that the commercial publishers establish a reputation for high-quality, centralized article databases. They provide standards for publication, dissemination, and permanent archiving. The open access publication system remains broad, wide, decentralized, and without a uniform set of guidelines.

The fact that commercial publishers continue to experiment with open access publishing, for example, through article process charges assigned to authors or institutions to publish in their digital journals, is a sign that many believe open access publishing will be integrated into the fabric of scholarly communications albeit not the only form of publication. The publishers must also face up to the fact that library budgets are not likely to grow beyond their current amounts and are more likely to shrink unless new sources of public funding are found. With open access available and growing in use and popularity, there is likely to be more pressure on libraries to move away from large serial subscription budgets and move into the world of open access at a higher level. This could be a very slow process, which is a disappointing thought to those who support a singular open access system (Solomon, 2013).

BUDGETS AND SPENDING

Assessing the state of academic library budgets is complex because the 2008 Great Recession led to enormous cuts in state funding to public universities. Between 2008 and 2013, state funding dropped by over $8 billion, and libraries shared in the cuts. An analysis of U.S. academic libraries during the years 1998–2010 indicates that their share of total institutional expenditures expressed in inflation-adjusted dollars declined by 24 percent. Over the same period, total academic library inflation-adjusted expenditures increased by 13 percent compared to 31 percent for public libraries. A telling figure is the 22.7 percent increase in collection expenditures over the ten-year period, with some of the money coming from reductions in staffing and operating expenditures (Regazzi, 2012).

Libraries cannot be treated as a homogeneous group. Large libraries are growing, while small and medium-size libraries continue to decline. It is the large libraries that are driving a shift into electronic materials. For example, between 1998 and 2008, small library expenditures on e-serials grew by 287 percent, while e-serial expenditures for large libraries grew 699 percent. The very small libraries have shown the smallest change in e-serial expenditures at 110 percent. The e-book expenditures increased 2,170 percent for medium libraries and 5,429 percent for large libraries (Regazzi, 2013).

There were 227 academic libraries at the end of fiscal year 2010 that held over 1 million print books, serial backfiles, and other documents. Compare this to those same libraries holding 158.7 million e-books and 1.8 million aggregation services and reference sources. During the fall of 2010, approximately 41 percent of academic libraries provided documents that were digitized by their own staff. Approximately 72 percent of the libraries supported virtual reference services (Phan et al., 2011).

The trends toward materials digitization and archiving and open access, coupled with sophisticated search engines, means researchers can access vast amounts of information without going through or visiting the library. From 1998 to 2008, visits to large libraries were down by 3 percent, circulation was down by 40 percent, and reference utilization was down by 9 percent.

Medium-size libraries had an increase of 6 percent in number of visits but a 31 percent and 21 percent decrease in circulation and reference utilization, respectively. Also, libraries increased the number of non-librarian professional staff (Regazzi, 2013). Looking at the statistics as a whole, it is clear that libraries are in a state of transition as they move toward virtual library space, and virtual space requires heavy investments in technology and specialized training for staff. The need to develop and maintain sophisticated cyberinfrastructures and the special skills required to maintain the system are more easily managed by large libraries, which have greater access to private and public funding. Libraries are also changing their physical space to better accommodate virtual researchers who need computer workstations or areas where they can plug in their personal computers and have access to printers. Search engines are replacing reference desk librarians as the traditional rows of book shelves disappear. The shift to virtual space will require a reanalysis of existing space, budgets, and future funding needed to make the transition possible.

It seems clear that digital scholarly publishing on a large scale is inevitable. There are a number of economic models that could emerge, including authors paying for publishing, researchers and institutions paying for access, organizations paying for publishing with no fee to authors or researchers, or some combination. OpenEdition Freemium is an example of the emerging hybrid economic models. The open access academic publishing site combines open access with paid services that generate income for those producing the materials. The concept was designed to "place libraries at the heart of the development of open access publication" (OpenEdition, 2013). Libraries are likely to be important negotiators in the process because it is their budgets that support journal publishing by commercial publishers. As global efforts to promote open access move ahead, the influence of libraries will grow because options will increase. Though the transition from the traditional commercial publishing model could take additional decades, there is no doubt that it will transition and that academic libraries will be at the center of the effort.

CONCLUSION

Many questions still remain concerning open access academic publishing. Some of the pressure for change is coming from younger faculty members who grew up with technology and the Internet. They do not want their promotional possibilities limited by the "old school" tenure system that depends on "old school" publishing by commercial publishes. Their question is simple: If able to produce a peer-reviewed article, why should it not be published as an open access article? This question is along the same lines of the question academic libraries are asking: If we can publish our faculty output and share it within the academic consortiums, why should we pay exorbitant publisher subscription prices?

The Association of American University Presses issued a report in March 2011 that considers the many factors impacting university publications (Withey et al., 2011). Its key findings made sense and apply to the Open Access Movement. They include sharing lessons learned through digital publishing projects; establishing collaborations between scholarly enterprises, libraries, and university presses; pursuing open access if costs can be managed by those involved parties; and addressing the financial and operational impact of new business models. The Open Access Movement is far from over because the traditional publishing model remains the peer-reviewed model for scholarly publishing.

It is clear that open access is gathering momentum. After a decade, economics and a younger generation of scholars are accelerating change. The Open Society Foundation believes that the Internet has led to the development of a diverse coalition that has the power to bring about advances in the areas of science, health, and medicine. This harks back to the early declarations in which open access was viewed as a means to advance human development and not just a tenure-producing product. In a statement written by Peter Suber, once director of the Harvard Open Access Project, for the tenth anniversary of the BOAI, the point was made that authors do not earn a living from selling their articles. They are writing for impact and not for money (Suber, 2012). The scholarly communication system worked well until two things happened. First, technology changed access and the cost of publishing. Second, the price of publishing rose faster than the consumer price index and library budgets, which only kept pace with the index.

It could also be argued that the generations behind the baby boomers are more technologically savvy and more willing to accept the efficiencies that technology brings. In the world of the scholar, most discussions funnel down to peer-review issues because it is peer review that is meant to ensure research quality. If the proponents of the Open Access Movement can find a means of managing quality and central archiving, two barriers to open access publishing are removed.

REFERENCES

Amherst College Press. 2013. "Home Page." Accessed December 31. https://www.amherst.edu/library/press.

Association of Research Libraries. 2000. "[Tempe] Principles for Emerging Systems of Scholarly Publishing." Association of Research Libraries. Last modified June 6, 2000. http://www.arl.org/storage/documents/publications/tempe-principles-10may10.pdf.

Association of Research Libraries. 2013. "What Does SPARC Do?" Association of Research Libraries. Accessed December 13. http://sparc.arl.org/about.

"Bethesda Statement on Open Access Publishing." 2003. Meeting at Howard Hughes Medical Institute, June 20, 2003. http://legacy.earlham.edu/~peters/fos/bethesda.htm#institutions.

Bosch, Stephen, and Kittie Henderson. 2012. "Coping with the Terrible Twins, Periodicals Price Survey." *Library Journal*, April 30. http://lj.libraryjournal.com/2012/04/funding/coping-with-the-terrible-twins-periodicals-price-survey-2012.

Chain, Leslie, Darius Cuplinkskas, Micahel Eisen, et al. 2002. "Read the Budapest Open Access Initiative." Budapest Open Access Initiative. February 14. http://www.budapestopenaccessinitiative.org/read.

Creative Commons. 2013. "CC History." Creative Commons. Accessed December 14. http://creativecommons.org/about/history.

"Declaration of San José towards the Virtual Health Library." 1998. IV Pan American Congress on Health Sciences Information, March 24–27, 1998.

Elsevier. 2013. "Elsevier to Flip Seven Subscription Journals to Open Access in 2014." Elsevier. December 17. http://www.elsevier.com/about/press-releases/research-and-journals/elsevier-to-flip-seven-subscription-journals-to-open-access-in-2014.

ETH-Bibliotheck. 2013. "Swiss National Science Foundation Funds Publications in Open-Access Journals." ETH-Bibliotheck. http://www.library.ethz.ch/en/ms/Open-Access-an-der-ETH-Zuerich/Aktuell/Schweizer-Nationalfonds-finanziert-Publikationen-in-Open-Access-Zeitschriften.

Finch Group. 2012. "Accessibility, Sustainability, Excellence: How to Expand Access to Research Publications." Research Information Network. June. http://www.researchinfonet.org/wp-content/uploads/2012/06/Finch-Group-report-FINAL-VERSION.pdf.

Ginsparg, Paul. 2011. "It Was Twenty Years Ago Today." arXiv.org at Cornell University. September 13. http://arxiv.org/pdf/1108.2700v2.pdf.

Gowers, Timothy. 2012. "Elsevier—My Part in Its Downfall." *Gowers's Weblog* (blog). January. http://gowers.wordpress.com/2012/01/21/elsevier-my-part-in-its-downfall.

Guédon, Jean-Claude. 2001. "Beyond Core Journals and Licenses: The Paths to Reform Scientific Publishing." *ARL: A Bimonthly Report on Research Library Issues and Actions from ARL, CNI, and SPARC*, no. 218 (October). http://www.arl.org/storage/documents/publications/arl-br-218.pdf.

Harnad, Stevan. 2003. "E-Prints: Electronic Preprints and Postprints." In *Encyclopedia of Library and Information Science*, 2nd ed., vol. 2, edited by Miriam A. Drake, 990–992. New York: Marcel Dekker.

International Federation of Library Associations. 2002. "IFLA Internet Manifesto." International Federation of Library Associations. May 1. http://www.ifla.org/files/assets/faife/publications/policy-documents/internet-manifesto-en.pdf.

Jeffery, Keith G. 2006. "Open Access: An Introduction." *ERCIM News*, no. 64 (January). http://www.ercim.eu/publication/Ercim_News/enw64/jeffery.html.

Katikiredd, Srinivasa Vittal. 2004. "HINARI: Bridging the Global Information Divide." *British Medical Journal* 328, no. 7449 (May 15): 1190.

Kling, Rob, Lisa B. Spector, and Joanna Fortuna. 2004. "The Real Stakes of Virtual Publishing: The Transformation of E-Biomed into PubMed Central." *Journal of the American Society for Information Science and Technology* 55, no. 2 (January): 127–148. doi: 10.1002/asi.10352.

Kyrillidou, Martha, and Mark Young, eds. 2003. "ARL Statistics 2001–02." Association of Research Libraries. http://www.arl.org/storage/documents/publications/arl-statistics-2001-02.pdf.

Leetaru, Kalev. 2008. "Mass Book Digitization: The Deeper Story of Google Books and the Open Content Alliance." *First Monday* 13, no. 10 (October 6). http://firstmonday.org/article/view/2101/2037.

Lindberg, Donald A. B. 2000. "Internet Access to the National Library of Medicine." *Effective Clinical Practices* 4: 256–260.

Loughborough University. 2013. "Project RoMEO." Loughborough University. Accessed December 14. http://www.lboro.ac.uk/microsites/infosci/romeo.

National Science Board. 2004. *Science and Engineering Indicators 2004* (NSB 04-01). Arlington, VA: National Science Board. http://www.nsf.gov/statistics/seind04/c5/c5s3.htm#c5s3ll.

Okerson, Ann Shumelda, and James J. O'Donnell, eds. 1998. "Scholarly Journals at the Crossroads: A Subversive Proposal for Electronic Publishing." Association of Research Libraries. 1995. Last modified April 9, 1998. http://www.arl.org/storage/documents/publications/subversive-proposal-electronic-publishing-jun05.pdf.

Open Access, Max-Planck-Gesellschaft. 2013. "Berlin Declaration on Open Access to Knowledge in the Sciences and Humanities." Open Access, Max-Planck-Gesellschaft. October 22, 2013 (original date). http://openaccess.mpg.de/286432/Berlin-Declaration.

Open Archives Initiative. 2001. "The Santa Fe Convention for the Open Archives Initiative." Open Archives. February 15, 2000. Last modified January 20, 2001. http://www.openarchives.org/sfc/sfc_entry.htm.

OpenDOAR. 2011. "About OpenDOAR." OpenDOAR.org. Last modified February 15. http://www.opendoar.org/about.html.

OpenEdition. 2013. "OpenEdition Freemium." OpenEdition. Accessed December 31. http://www.openedition.org/8873.

Organization for Economic Cooperation and Development. 2004. "Declaration on Access to Research Data from Public Funding." Organization for Economic Cooperation and Development. January 30. http://www.oecd.org/science/sci-tech/sciencetechnologyandinnovationforthe21stcenturymeetingoftheoecdcommitteeforscientificandtechnologicalpolicyatministeriallevel29-30january2004-finalcommunique.htm.

Phan, Tai, Laura Hardesty, Jamie Hug, and Cindy Sheckells. 2011. "Academic Libraries: 2010—First Look." U.S. Department of Education. December. http://nces.ed.gov/pubs2012/2012365.pdf (URL no longer connects).

Public Knowledge Project. 2013. "PKP History." Public Knowledge Project. Accessed December 14. http://pkp.sfu.ca/about/history.

Public Library of Science. 2013. "PLOS Early History." PLOS. Accessed December 6. http://www.plos.org/about/what-is-plos/early-history (URL no longer connects).

Regazzi, John J. 2012. "Comparing Academic Library Spending with Public Libraries, Public K–12 Schools, Higher Education Public Institutions, and Public Hospitals between 1998–2008." *Journal of Academic Librarianship* 38, no. 4 (July): 205–216.

Regazzi, John J. 2013. "U.S. Academic Library Spending, Staffing and Utilization during the Great Recession 2008–2010." *Journal of Academic Librarianship* 39, no. 3 (May): 217–222.

Saint-André, Jean-Paul, Pascal Arnaud, Serge Bauin, et al. 2013. "Qui a Peur de l'Open Access?" *Le Monde*, March 15. http://www.lemonde.fr/sciences/article/2013/03/15/qui-a-peur-de-l-open-acces_1848930_1650684.html.

SHERPA. 2013. "SHERPA: Securing a Hybrid Environment for Research Preservation and Access." Accessed December 14. http://www.sherpa.ac.uk.

Solomon, David J. 2013. "Digital Distribution of Academic Journals and Its Impact on Scholarly Communication: Looking Back after 20 Years." *Journal of Academic Librarianship* 39 (April 23): 23–28. doi: 10.1016/j.acalib.2012.10.001.

Stempel, Jonathan. 2013. "Google Defeats Authors in U.S. Book-Scanning Lawsuit." Reuters. November 14. http://www.reuters.com/article/2013/11/14/us-google-books-idUS-BRE9AD0TT20131114.

Suber, Peter. 2002. "News from Public Library of Science." *Topica* (forum). December 17. http://lists.topica.com/lists/fos-forum/read/message.html?mid=906099880&sort=d&start=518.

Suber, Peter. 2008. "An Open Access Mandate for the National Institutes of Health." *Open Medicine* 2, no. 2. http://www.openmedicine.ca/article/view/213/135.

Suber, Peter. 2012. "Opening Access to Research." Open Society Foundations. September 12. http://www.opensocietyfoundations.org/voices/opening-access-research.

Terry, Robert, and Robert Kiley. 2006. "Chapter 10: Open Access to the Research Literature: A Funders Perspective." Wellcome Trust. http://eprints.rclis.org/7531/1/Chapter_10_final.pdf.

Tillery, Kodi. 2012. "2012 Study of Subscription Prices for Scholarly Society Journals." Allen Press. Last modified August 17. http://allenpress.com/system/files/pdfs/library/2012_AP_JPS.pdf.

Tracz, Vitek. 2012. "The Basement Interviews, Building the Business Model." Interview by Richard Poynder, May 16, 2010. http://ia600201.us.archive.org/13/items/The_Basement_Interviews/Vitek_Tracz_Interview.pdf.

United Kingdom Parliament. 2004. "Appendix 51: Memorandum from Hallward Library. University of Nottingham SHERPA Project (Evidence submitted to the Select Committee on Science and Technology Written Evidence). U.K. Parliament. July 20. http://www.publications.parliament.uk/pa/cm200304/cmselect/cmsctech/399/399we62.htm.

United Nations Educational, Scientific and Cultural Organization. 1999. "Declaration on Science and the Use of Scientific Knowledge." *World Conference on Science for the Twenty-First Century*, June 26–July 1. http://www.unesco.org/science/wcs/eng/declaration_e.htm.

United Nations Educational, Scientific and Cultural Organization. 2007. "Kronberg Declaration on the Future of Knowledge Acquisition and Sharing." United Nations Educational, Scientific and Cultural Organization. June. http://www.unesco.de/fileadmin/medien/Dokumente/Kommunikation/Declaration_fuer_Website.pdf.

Van de Sompel, Herbert, and Carl Lagoze. 2000. "The Santa Fe Convention of the Open Archives Initiative." *D-Lib Magazine* 6, no. 3 (February). http://www.dlib.org/dlib/february00/vandesompel-oai/02vandesompel-oai.html; doi: 10.1045/february2000-vandesompel-oai.

Van Noorden, Richard. 2013. "UK Open-Access Route Too Costly, Report Says." *Nature*, September 10. http://www.nature.com/news/uk-open-access-route-too-costly-report-says-1.13705.

Varmus, Harold. 1999. "E-BIOMED: A Proposal for Electronic Publications in the Biomedical Sciences." Draft May 5, 1999; addendum June 20, 1999. http://www.nih.gov/about/director/pubmedcentral/ebiomedarch.htm.

Withey, Lynne, Steve Cohn, Ellen Faran, et al. 2011. *Sustaining Scholarly Publishing: New Business Models for University Presses*. New York: Association of American University Presses. http://www.uvasci.org/wp-content/uploads/2011/03/aaupbusinessmodels2011.pdf (URL no longer connects).

Chapter Nine

Big Data, Big Science, and Social Academic Networks

With technology came new ways to store, access, and manipulate data, followed by new methods of communicating during the research process. A system of scholarly communication that had been in place for hundreds of years was first disrupted by the introduction of digital storage methods for research materials, such as full-text article databases, and new digital publishing models. The individual databases grew to include text and non-text content, such as charts and images, but they remained largely unconnected, and their size was limited by practical considerations, such as hardware, processing power, and systems interconnectivity. Data were extracted from multiple databases, and the researcher made the connections during the research cycle. The second major disruption in the scholarly research and publication process was the development of Big Data and the creation of wide social academic networks. Big Data, which led to Big Science, was a natural outcome of the massive influx of data coupled with the development of the hardware, processing power, software, and telecommunications capable of capturing, storing, managing, and analyzing it. At the same time, social media was growing in importance, leading to the creation of social academic networks dedicated to enhanced scholarly communication and collaboration.

TOWARD BIG DATA

Before Big Data and Big Science could develop, a robust computing infrastructure was needed. The processors, storage capability, networks, software, algorithms, coding standards, and so on had to be developed. Software was developed to connect applications, but also important in the march toward Big Data was the ability to provide database authenticity, identification, and security. The emergence of library and professional association digital repositories around 2000 laid the foundation for Big Data to come later. The repositories functioned separately and were siloed until the metadata catalogs were created.

Metadata serves three purposes. First, it enables indexing, discovery and the identification of a database entry. Second, it stores the resource's technical details and enables reaching into the resource and extracting specific details. Third, metadata contains the information that scholars particularly rely on to protect their authorship and research authenticity (Knight, 2004). The refinement of metadata coding standards and the increasing sophistication of computer hardware and software led to the interoperability across repositories. Interoperability standards were developed, such as *The Open Archives Initiative Protocol for Metadata Harvesting*, introduced in 2002, an example of an early framework developed for harvesting or moving large amounts of data from multiple digital library collections. It had several important characteristics, including the ability to work with any information format and with any object, including text, sound, and images. Still used, it also requires downloading the software to access the protocols, thus preserving records of access (Breeding, 2007).

Other early digital archives systems, which over time moved across the spectrum of interoperability, included DSpace and Fedora. Once interoperable technical solutions were developed, the academic community, library associations, and foundations, such as the Andrew W. Mellon Foundation, worked together to advance the effort to increase the interoperability of the heterogeneous scholarly repositories to advance ready access and reuse of digital objects in rich value chains. Issues addressed included identifying the necessary protocol-based repository interfaces, the processes for implementation, and the persistence of cross-repository data models over time given the speed of technology advances (Bekaert and Van de Sompel, 2006).

Enormous repositories and global data infrastructures developed. Interlinking of data over the web used Uniform Resource Identifiers (URIs), specific vocabularies, abstractions, and the new open data principles. The URI names resources and has significance because it is a web-naming identifier that uniquely defines character strings so they can be located based on their network location, name, or both. The URI is the superset consisting of the Uniform Resource Locator and the Uniform Resource Name. The development of the URI contributed to the growth of interdisciplinary scholarship because it made crossing databases possible, and its subsets reduced ambiguity.

Big Data

Once it was possible to link library and professional association databases and the computing power was available, the development of Big Data was inevitable. Big Data is a term for data sets that range from terabytes to exabytes in size. It represents a massive database that has collected data from multiple smaller sources and is unmanageable by conventional database systems. The concept of Big Data was imagined as early as the late 1990s, and one of the first times the term was used was in an economics modeling paper presented in 2000 (Diebold, 2000). It took root when, in 2001, the META Group described the "3D" of Big Data as volume, velocity, and variety. The prediction was for an increased use of centralized data warehouses, the development of a common business vocabulary for collaborative purposes, the pursuit of information logistics and data integration, and the coalescence of data, documents, and knowledge through new portal resources and cross–data set indexing strategies. Also addressed was the driving force of e-commerce, which would prove to have long-term impacts on scholarly research and the practical applications in most industries, including manufacturing and health care (Laney, 2001).

For example, in 2011, research indicated that Big Data could help the U.S. health care industry achieve an increase in additional value of $300 billion per year, contributing to a reduction in health care spending by 8 percent. The same report identified numerous ways that Big Data would influence industries by creating transparent and usable information sources for forecasting, experimentation, developing innovative products and services, capturing data value, and so on (Manyika et al., 2011). Big Data sources continue to grow and now include databases, mobile digital data, data from social networks, web server logs, web page content, and other digital sources. A variety of technology feeds Big Data on a global basis.

Big Analytics and Big Science

Big Data has led to Big Science and Big Analytics. The first generation of interoperability functions enabled statistical analysis using clustered samples of observations. Sampling was a necessity because there were still hardware and software limitations associated with accessing Big Data databases. The second generation of interoperability created Big Analytics platforms that are specifically designed to deal with much more voluminous amounts of Big Data, thus improving the ability to access and analyze the data on a larger scale.

Big Analytics and Big Science are integrated concepts. Big Analytics enables the analysis of large samples that include most of a designated population. Big Analytics does not mean only examining large databases. It also means having the ability to examine large databases containing different data types. The Big Data samples are called high dimensional in that the samples contain lots of different information extracted from the huge databases that must be analyzed. Big Analytics enables researchers and scientists to move beyond linear approximation models and make more accurate predictions using sophisticated statistical models. For example, it is possible to manipulate continuous variables into categorical, discrete variables to better determine exact relationships. This ability benefits scientific research and increases the applicability of Big Data to commercial uses, such as predicting production yields, disease trends, or chemical reactions in humans (Nie, 2011).

Big Analytics makes it possible to extract millions of observations and analyze hundreds of thousands of data elements. Small data sets that may disguise correlations are replaced with huge numbers of observations that can potentially increase accurate predicting. The word "potentially" is used because scientists do issue a word of caution about using Big Data and Big Analytics. The sheer size of databases presents challenges that include the need to develop statistical assessment tools specifically designed to minimize the possibility of spurious correlations and/or regression analyses that can arise out of huge samples. The risk of wrong statistical inferences, statistical bias, and false scientific conclusions is increased, and they are aware of the need to address the possibilities during research and experimentation (Siegfried, 2013). Clearly, Big Data and its supporting technologies allow the extraction and analysis of greater amounts of data, reducing the chances for error that naturally are associated with low-incidence populations.

One of the important characteristics of Big Data and the related analytics is that databases could be automatically read by computers. Linked Open Data principles were a critical requirement, making it possible to link and query data from different data sets. The principles were first defined by Tim Berners-Lee as using URIs to denote resources, using Hypertext Transfer Protocol URIs for access, using standards for providing useful information about the resource, and using links to URIs for web publishing and to increase discovery. As these principles appeared, they have collectively been described as the Semantic Web, which refers to linking data based on meaning rather than linking based on the data structures on the web (Berners-Lee, 2014).

Semantic Web

The combining of global digital repositories, library and professional association repositories, open access repositories, and other types of data fueled the creation of Big Data, the use of Linked Open Data, and Semantic Web technologies. The Semantic Web goes beyond the document web and refers to a web of data that permits linking through access to data stores, consistent web vocabularies, and rules for data access. The Semantic Web is a critical item in scientific research in that it contains titles, dates, part numbers, chemical properties, and research data and supports inference, knowledge and not only information systems, and vertical applications so that scientific research and many industries and governments can benefit. The Semantic Web adds reasoning over data for activities such as decision making based on clinical research. It uses SPARQL (SPARQL Protocol and RDF Query Language), RDF (Resource Description Framework), and OWL (Web Ontology Language) as the standard data interchange models on the Web. SPARQL is the Semantic Web query language, RDF is the data modeling language, and OWL is the schema language and allows concepts to be defined based on the structure and components in the language used in context (Gonzalez, 2014).

Adapting to the New Environment

The features of the new research environment are stark compared to the old models of accessing limited research materials and individual databases. The concept of open data was important to advancing scholarly research, but it also went against the grain of the traditional scholarly publishing system in which tight-knit groups of scholars held close control of research and information until publication. Academic scholars were expected to publish new research to achieve professional advancement and increase value and compensation as well as individual reputation and scholarly community recognition. One of the issues concerning open access for traditional research scholars is the sharing of research often before the research project is completed. While some people believe open access and Big Data promotes better scientific experimentation and investigation, others strongly believe there is a need for better standards concerning data set curation and metadata. As a work in progress, scientific use of Big Data and Data Analytics continues to evolve, and the full implications on science are far from being fully understood. However, Big Data and Big Analytics are a fact in the scientific community and are also impacting research in the humanities and social sciences.

The characteristics of the new research environment include the use of high-performance computers to produce large-scale computation results applied to mathematical models, production of scientific visualizations of results, data-intensive research, and enhanced record keeping concerning work flow documentation. And these developments are occurring in all areas of science and industry. Big Data and the related Big Analytics also supported the acceleration of open data reuse and new dissemination methods. One of the terms that emerged to describe the process and results is "digital scholarship." Perhaps one of the best descriptions of digital scholarship is found in a non-scientific journal:

> The contours of this change are large and indistinct: as print and media archives are digitized; as we acquire online access to those archives and databases; as search tools allow us to compile materials from a wide range of sources; as new software for annotation and note-taking aids writing and search; as we learn to capture and digitize work that we wish to study; as digitized material is fluidly cited and repurposed; as we increasingly deploy the link instead of the cite; as social networks, wikis, and other modes of writing and distributing collaborative work evolve; as electronic publishing speeds the process from page to print; as books are digitally distributed. (Friendberg, 2009: 150)

Scholarly research in all forms has changed and continues to change.

ACADEMIC SOCIAL NETWORKS

At the same time that Big Data and Big Analytics were developing, social media was emerging, and social media sites targeting academics appeared. These sites enabled researchers to have ongoing, digital conversations and to share large amounts of materials quickly and easily. The social academic networks are integral to changes in scholarly work flow systems because they change the very nature of communication. In the past, scholars worked within their tight-knit academic communities and quietly produced research that went through extensive commercial-driven editing and peer-review processes. The published item was the end result. Social media changed those previous dynamics of scholarly communication.

Academic social networks are dedicated online communication systems. Researchers construct an academic profile, communicate discovery and dissemination of research findings, and collaborate in a variety of ways through active professional relationships. The dynamics of this kind of process are clearly different than in the traditional scholarly communication process, which follows a much more defined process leading to a research presentation. One of the most stunning impacts of this process is the increased interdisciplinary effect, in which scholars can interact with each other and gain new insights and perspectives not likely when limiting review and comments to academics within the limited circle of influence. Social networking sites are defined by the authors as "web-based services that allow individuals to (1) construct a public or semi-public profile within a bounded system, (2) articulate a list of other users with whom they share a connection, and (3) view and traverse their list of connections and those made by others within the system (Boyd and Ellison, 2007: 211). The ability to communicate and share data along with Big Data increased the potential areas for scholarly applications. Now the sciences, humanities, and social sciences scholars can share data and information.

Like Big Data, the social networks began to appear and proliferate starting in 2000. Social networking offered novel communicative abilities and the ability to link with people interested in the conversation and provided the means of mapping communication. Though general social networking sites appeared in the early part of the decade, popular academic social networking sites, especially those that are science specific, did not appear until the mid-2000s. The first social media sites were dedicated to specific disciplines, and later the more general academic sites were dedicated to scholars. The academic social media sites required the construct of online academic profiles and enabled communication in the form of discovery and dissemination of research findings and questions and answers flowing being researchers and scholars. The sites also meant collaboration was much easier among multiple disciplines and among scholars without regard to location. They could also share insights into the access and use of the data infrastructure. Communication became much broader, and the potential application areas were increased, drawing in the sciences, humanities, and social sciences.

New Dimensions of Research

Academic social networks add two dimensions to the research process. One dimension is that the addition of in-progress communication becomes a new innovative model for research. The second dimension is the culture of sharing outside the traditional research and communication process. Within these two dimensions are a host of scholarly approaches to the use of social media, including social networks specifically established for academics. Like technology, researcher behaviors moved along a continuum from hesitant acceptance of online communication concerning research projects to the full use of academic social networks and publication of papers on open access sites.

The specific uses and strength of belief in the ability of social media to advance scholarly work showed early indications of varying by discipline. In the sciences, researchers have long shared early stage data and ideas, but there was not always immediate acceptance of social networking sites as the best venue in the digital age. In this social network environment, the sharing of ideas and comments as well as the sharing of data one-on-one postpublication have a variety of challenges, as it makes it easier to discuss scientific knowledge more broadly. In 2010, astrophysicists at the University of California, Berkeley, indicated they did not use social networking tools (Web 2.0) for sharing but could envision a day when that would change. One of the perceived events that would increase the use of social networks by scientists was the coming Semantic Web 3.0 (Harley et al., 2010).

On the other hand, in a recent survey, historians were reluctant to share work or put out ideas until it was near completion. The nearly completed works were sent to only a few select, trusted individuals for comments using e-mail. The exceptions were interdisciplinary historians using a social science model with quantitative features. In the humanities discipline, there was no working paper culture for fear that ideas would be taken. The historians surveyed said they did not do a lot of collaborating, but once again the exception was data-based collaboration (Harley et al., 2010). The results of the survey of a variety of scholars in various disciplines noted several times that the age of the scholar, the discipline, and the state of the research influenced their willingness to collaborate online and to adapt to changing scholarly work flows.

As social media becomes more readily accepted as an important tool in the academic culture of sharing, the scholarly communication process is assuming new characteristics. It is difficult to separate the discussion of changing scholarly work flows, emerging social academic communication processes, and the availability of Big Data because the latter two play such an important role in the first. The new characteristics of academic social networks that scholars increasingly were turning to for more open research sharing and collaboration included the fact that the published article or monograph was increasingly no longer viewed as the end result, interdisciplinary work was becoming more common as the boundaries between disciplines shifted, and scholarly crowdsourcing now exists. Social networking was also seen as an important tool by scholars who supported a more open scholarly communication system—one less rigid and more collaborative. Libraries were caught in the middle of the turmoil created by technology involving clashes between the scholars supporting the more rigid, traditional scholarly publishing system and the scholars who wanted to publish works online to the world, gain greater access to the scholarly community as a whole, and have access to tools that enabled easier location, sharing, and reuse of Big Data (Association of College and Research Libraries [ACRL], 2013).

Life Cycle of Information

One of the concepts introduced by the ACRL is the life cycle of information as opposed to a process of discrete publishing. The "life cycle" is the "social life" of information. The traditional scholarly communication process of idea formation, registration, peer review, dissemination, and preservation plus information reuse and impact measurement are now accomplished through a variety of channels, one of which is academic social networks (ACRL, 2013). The increasing move toward online collaboration and use of digital materials spills over into the offline environment also, as witnessed by the trend in libraries to create more shared meeting spaces for collaborative efforts while reducing collection space (Regazzi, 2012b).

The emergence of academic social networking sites is not surprising because scholars were naturally hesitant to use sites developed to serve the general public or specific market segments, such as consumers and business professionals. The reasons go beyond wanting to keep research private and commoditized. Using Big Data for Big Science requires access to the computer hardware and software capable of handling the massive quantities of data available. In this regard, there is a double entendre with the term "Big Science." It can be viewed as "big" in terms of the data and information utilization and "big" in terms of needing large amounts of funding for research projects. For "Little Science" to flourish, it needs funding and support systems as well (Fortin and Currie, 2013). Social networking can enhance research at all levels and also advance academic careers.

Adapting Web 2.0 to the academic research and scholarly communication process was slow because of the desire to keep in-progress research ideas and projects quiet but also because the social networks were not initially integrated with discovery, research, and results interpretation. They were initiated as communication tools and not tools for achieving scientific results. In addition, scientists and other academics already had well-developed communication networks in place. So far, researchers tend not to be interested in blogging because it is time consuming and represents an unneeded form of communication. However, driving the development of academic social networks was Big Data. As an enormous database requiring higher levels of collaboration, social networking becomes one of several tools for supporting community efforts to access and manage the huge amounts of data flooding research efforts. Web 2.0 technologies make it easier to share methods, results, and publications (Crotty, 2010).

Examples of Academic Social Networks

The need for social networking sites for researchers drove the development of academic-based social networking sites, which are technology disrupters in the scholarly communication process. The sites require constructing an online academic profile first and are used to create active research relationships that advance academic efforts. One of the early sites was VIVO (http://www.vivo.cornell.edu), developed by Cornell University and described as a research-focused discovery tool that enables collaboration among researchers across all disciplines. The open source software platform was developed in 2003 to bridge science and networking. It also integrated scientific research and social communication.

The academic social networking sites have proliferated since the first ones appeared. Geared toward scholars, they accommodate the specific needs of scholars. For example, the academic profile can handle the typical numerous links scholars have that lead to books, monographs, research papers, past and upcoming presentations, and so on. The links enable scholars to read research without contacting the author. Scholars can upload published and unpublished research or papers, track research page views (new form of impact measuring), and performs dozens of other tasks. One of the noted benefits of the sites is the ability to distribute past published papers (assuming that author rights are protected) that would languish hidden in the massive databases or locked in remote or inaccessible repositories (Eisen, 2012).

One of the largest academic social networking sites is Academia (http://www.academia.edu), which supports a 2014 community of over 11 million academics and supports sharing papers, book reviews, teaching documents, thesis chapters, talks, and other research efforts; viewing analytics; and following people in the discipline. Network participants can follow a fellow researcher's work and link to professional association memberships. Followers can make comments and ask or answer questions related to the information on the academic's pages.

Another major academic social networking site is Mendeley (http://www.mendeley.com). It is a reference manager and academic social network designed to help with organizing research, increasing collaboration with other academics, and discovering the latest research. It has many advanced features, including the ability to synch information among technologies and share information using mobile and other technology. PDF files can be uploaded into a personalized research library, read, and annotated and annotations shared. The implications for changing scholarly work flows are obvious. Other social bookmarking sites include CiteULike, Zotero, and Quqqa.

A third major academic social networking site is ResearchGate.net. It is an example of a discipline-specific site in that it is for scientists. Developed in 2008, ResearchGate (http://www.researchgate.net) also enables publication sharing, obtaining statistics, connecting and collaborating with fellow scholars, and posting questions and answers. There are discipline-specific social networking sites also, such as BioMedExperts.com (http://www.biomedexperts.com), for life science researchers, academics, and corporations. This networking site supporting biomedical scientists and researchers integrates academia with the corporate environment, reflecting the increasing crossover due to technology. As Big Science and technology advance, the academic social networking sites can benefit the scholarly communications industry, for example, by allowing commercial researchers and health care professionals to gain access to critical research information that was once found only behind a paywall of subscription-only content.

There are major functions associated with academic social networking sites, no matter which site is selected for use. The profiles represent an academic's online presence or digital representation. There is multichannel information integration that includes abilities such as chatting or messaging and creating forums or groups. The sites enable networking with the people who are specifically interested in the discipline and its related research. A social networking site for researchers and academics also enables directing attention to specific research, an important feature in the era of Big Data, Big Analytics, and Big Science. Finally, these sites bridge research and communication.

Limitations and Acceptance

There are limitations to the use of social networks in the scholarly communications process. They are not intended to be original research publishing sites but are more like reprint sites. A formal peer-review process is not included among the functions. The sites requiring membership may end up excluding important contributors to the discussion because not every academic in the discipline will join a single site. This is similar to the issue of accessing repositories that are not linked. Some academics will create profiles on one or more sites but remain inactive. The sites may claim millions of members, giving the impression it has a broad and active community. The question is, How many are actively posting research, joining discussions, and taking advantage of all or most of the other features that come with the sites? For this reason, academics are advised to carefully analyze the various sites and determine those that best meets their needs. This suggestion is also related to the fact that maintaining any social media site requires time and commitment for the member and the site to be successful.

Though studies have reported reluctance among many older academics to join these sites, the younger academic generation is growing up with the technology and is more comfortable with its use. This will undoubtedly drive the development of additional academic social networking sites in the future. It has been suggested that scholarly metrics should begin to include altmetrics arising from engagement activities on the social networking sites, a kind of online impact factor.

Despite the existence of multiple, large academic social networking sites, they are still not fully embedded in the scholarly communication process for the reasons mentioned. They do offer services that reflect an upward trend in the use of open access and the desire to collaborate online. Integrating research and information communication structures seems like an inevitable result with the introduction of Big Data and Big Analytics. Big Data has led to greater use of data in non-scientific disciplines and much larger samples and complex analytics for science-based ones. When social networking is viewed within the larger context of the moves toward open access publishing and online peer-review systems, it becomes a critical support tool that is likely to continue evolving to become fully integrated not only into the scholarly communication process but into industry as well.

CONCLUSION

The next logical step is to discuss academic and professional work flows, but it is important to keep in mind that everything in the technology-enabled research process is integrated. Whereas the traditional system had definitive steps ranging from idea to final publication, the online process scrambles, or "atomizes," the work flow process. For example, publishing may involve iterations of analysis that are opened to the academic community for review and comment using social networking sites. New research and study approaches are data driven as a result of technology, and Big Data and complex computations are made possible by sophisticated hardware and software. Inquiry involves greater exploration of massive data stores that are constantly updated by a host of sources, making traditional work flow much more challenging.

When work flows were discrete, the delivery of peer-reviewed research led to final disposition in one or more repositories. The information available for research was clearly finalized by the author, and the informal conversations played no official role. Academic social networks are adding a new dimension to research that leads to a continual review process. The meta-research collection activities are occurring at every step of the scholarly work flow process and are scooping up artifacts from traditional sources and from second-generation repositories, such as the Semantic Web.

Modern scholarship across disciplines has a foundation on specialized contributions to scholarly debates and conversations. Each contribution represents a fragment of a whole, and once freed of standardized conventions concerning formation, evaluation, annotation, and review, the conversation may have more opportunity to be meaningful and innovative (Ayers, 2013). Those qualities are critical to adapting to a scholarship environment in which Big Data and Big Analytics are present. The conversant web is still trying to find its place in the formal research process and the formal research data infrastructures, but it can fill gaps, keep conversations going that would otherwise end sooner than they should after formal publication, speed up dissemination of research in an environment marked by data volume, and expand the use of research. Big Data, Big Analytics, and Big Science, all possible because of technology, are the provinces of researchers and scholars, but their applications in the public and private sectors are more recognized as technology makes access easier. For example, medical professionals can provide enhanced treatment of patients by accessing the latest research on new drugs or manufacturers, and governments can better minimize negative environmental impacts by analyzing available chemical research and evidence-based scholarly conversations.

In 2004, one of the criticisms of the technology-based scholarly communication system was that it has largely replicated the print system. In 2009, it was predicted that the web would contribute significantly to the scholarly process, integrate scholarly debate with the web-based community debate, and integrate cyberinfrastructures into human work flows (Van de Sompel and Lagoze, 2009). These work flows, driven by technology advances as well as the steady flows of data and online conversations, benefit all professionals, not only the scholarly community. One of those ways is the rapid ability to measure the objective reality and the real-world reality, producing even more information that is assimilated by scholars. The Internet and its related technologies grow and discover new markets that include social networks (Wilbanks, 2009). Thus, Big Data and data-intensive research grows and enables innovation. It is as it should be and extends long-standing scholarly communication traditions and tenets.

REFERENCES

Association of College and Research Libraries. 2013. "Intersections of Scholarly Communication and Information Literacy—Creating Strategic Collaborations for a Changing Academic Environment." Association of College & Research Libraries, 1–26. http://www.ala.org/acrl/sites/ala.org.acrl/files/content/publications/whitepapers/Intersections.pdf.

Ayers, Edward L. 2013. "Does Digital Scholarship Have a Future?" *Educause Review Online* 48, no. 4 (August 5). http://www.educause.edu/ero/article/does-digital-scholarship-have-future.

Bekaert, Jeroen, and Herbert Van de Sompel. 2006. "Augmenting Interoperability across Scholarly Repositories." Meeting notes of meeting of Microsoft, the Andrew W. Mellon Foundation, the Coalition for Networked Information, the Digital Library Foundation, and the Joint Information Systems Committee, April 20–21, 2006, 1–17. http://msc.mellon.org/Meetings/Interop/FinalReport.

Berners-Lee, Tim. 2014. "Design Issues—Architectural and Philosophical Points." W3C. Accessed July 3. http://www.w3.org/DesignIssues.

Boyd, Danah M., and Nicole B. Ellison. 2007. "Social Networks Sites: Definition, History, and Scholarship." *Journal of Computer-Mediated Communication* 13, no. 1 (October): 210–230.

Breeding, Marshall. 2007. "Understanding the Protocol for Metadata Harvesting of the Open Archives Initiative." *Computers in Libraries* 22, no. 8: 24–29.

Crotty, David. 2010. "Science and Web 2.0: Talking about Science vs. Doing Science." *the scholarly kitchen* (blog). February 8. http://scholarlykitchen.sspnet.org/2010/02/08/science-and-web-2-0-talking-about-science-versus-doing-science.

Diebold, Francis X. 2000. "'Big Data' Dynamic Factor Models for Macroeconomic Measurement and Forecasting." Paper presented at the Eighth World Congress of the Econometric Society, November 28, 2000. Seattle, WA.

Eisen, Jonathan. 2012. "Social Networks for Academics Proliferate, despite Some Doubts." *The Chronicle of Higher Education*, April 29. http://chronicle.com/article/Social-Networks-for-Academics/131726.

Fortin, Jean-Michel, and David J. Currie. 2013. "Big Science vs. Little Science: How Scientific Impact Scales with Funding." *PLOS ONE* 8, no. 6 (June 19). doi: 10.1371/journal.pone.0065263.

Friendberg, Anne. 2009. "On Digital Scholarship." *Cinema Journal* 48, no. 2 (Winter): 150–154.

Gonzalez, Rob. 2014. "Introduction to the Semantic Web." Cambridge Semantics. Accessed July 3. http://www.cambridgesemantics.com/semantic-university/introduction-to-the-semantic-web.

Harley, Diane, Sophia Krzys Acord, Sarah Earl-Novell, Shannon Lawrence, and C. Judson King. 2010. *Assessing the Future Landscape of Scholarly Communication.* University of California, Berkeley. January, 1–737. http://escholarship.org/uc/cshe_fsc.

Knight, Gareth. 2004. "An Introduction to Metadata Requirements for an E-Print Repository." SHERPA Project Document. March 8. http://www.sherpa.ac.uk/documents/D2-6_Report_on_Metadata_Issues.pdf.

Laney, Doug. 2001. "3D Data Management: Controlling Data Volume, Velocity, and Variety." *Meta Group. Application Delivery Strategies* (blog). February 6. http://blogs.gartner.com/doug-laney/files/2012/01/ad949-3D-Data-Management-Controlling-Data-Volume-Velocity-and-Variety.pdf.

Manyika, James, Michael Chui, Brad Brown, et al. 2011. *Big Data: The Next Frontier for Innovation, Competition and Productivity.* McKinsey Global Institute. http://www.mckinsey.com/insights/business_technology/big_data_the_next_frontier_for_innovation.

Nie, Norman H. 2011. "The Rise of Big Data Spurs a Revolution in Big Analytics." Revolution Analytics. http://www.revolutionanalytics.com/sites/default/files/the-rise-of-big-data-executive-brief.pdf.

Regazzi, John J. 2012b. "Constrained? An Analysis of U.S. Academic Library Shifts in Spending, Staffing, and Utilization, 1998–2008." *College and Research Libraries* 73, no. 5 (September): 449–468. http://crl.acrl.org/content/73/5/449.full.pdf.

Siegfried, Tom. 2013. "Why Big Data Is Bad for Science." *ScienceNews* (blog). November 26. https://www.sciencenews.org/blog/context/why-big-data-bad-science.

Van de Sompel, Herbert, and Carl Lagoze. 2009. "All Aboard: Toward a Machine-Friendly Scholarly Communication System." In *The Fourth Paradigm*, edited by Tony Hey, Stewart Tansley, and Kristin Tolle, 193–199. Redmond, WA: Microsoft Research. http://research.microsoft.com/en-us/collaboration/fourthparadigm/4th_paradigm_book_complete_lr.pdf.

Wilbanks, John. 2009. "I Have Seen the Paradigm Shift, and It Is Us." In *The Fourth Paradigm*, edited by Tony Hey, Stewart Tansley, and Kristin Tolle, 209–214. Redmond, WA: Microsoft Research. http://research.microsoft.com/en-us/collaboration/fourthparadigm/4th_paradigm_book_complete_lr.pdf.

Chapter Ten

The Rise of Work Flow Systems

One of the most constant characteristics of the scholarly communication system has been the concept of the unit. The unit is represented by a finite library collection, a single scholarly journal, a published article, a specific group of peer reviewers, a definitive dissemination path, and so on. Scholars in science, technology, and medicine (STM) or humanities or social sciences have distinct work flow processes that developed within the disciplines, often with little crossover. As technology advanced, the independent flows of information leading to a unit of publication began to intersect, leading to open access research and publication and continuous feedback loops. The technology-driven sea-change initiatives have changed the nature of scholarly research, which has been in a virtual lockstep system of creation, review, dissemination, and preservation, by adding new forms of discovery, data and information access, publication, and materials storage. As the parts of the scholarly communication system evolved, it was natural for the scholarly work flow system to change as well. That in turn changed the professional work flow processes because researched and reviewed material could be accessed and used by members of the professional communities with more ease in a wide diversity of activities, such as manufacturing, engineering, point-of-care medical systems, climatology, and the publication of textbook materials. The rise of work flow systems is more about sharing scholarly efforts in a collaborative manner while accessing data and information that flows from multiple sources to create adaptable pieces of content rather than units fixed in time at the end of a specific process. The integration of systems and technologies with scholarly information means much more than how packets of information, such as the journal article, are delivered. Delivered scholarship, in this scenario, includes non-textual materials or pieces of content, or the huge amount of data that sits behind published scholarship.

PROFESSIONAL INFORMATION WORK FLOW SPACE

Changing Nature of Scholarly Research

The changing nature of scholarly research is now, without question, fundamentally technology driven. New work flow systems are cross-disciplinary, more collaborative, networked, and data intensive. Over a decade ago, searchers recognized the emergence of knowledge management systems, which became the precursors to the modern work flow systems. The early technology-based systems first dealt with the storage and simple accessing of data, facts, and observations. As new technologies emerged, content and information management became critical. Whole documents were indexed, while discovery services provided the tools for accessing data within documents organized in a meaningful way through linking and automated contexting. Key words and citations are a type of automated contextual process that maps word relationships. Knowledge comes from information or data placed in context and then organized through a system of questioning, communications, or inferences. Knowledge can be explicit or tacit. Explicit knowledge is represented by procedure manuals, documents, articles, journals, and other artifacts. Tacit knowledge embodies the values, beliefs, and conclusions that are developed through experiences (Muthukumar and Hedberg, 2005).

Until technology made it possible, tacit knowledge was difficult to mobilize and convert into a form that was useful by a network of scholars. Researchers relied on the traditional units of research, blocks of data, bundles of journals available through subscriptions, and so on. Modern information-handling technology made is easy to socialize and collaborate on ideas, thoughts, and concepts before they were formalized, converting information into knowledge in a continuous cycle.

Implicit in the changes triggered by technology is a research work flow change. The formal scholarly communication process became intertwined with the scholarly effort itself, largely due to networking and computing technologies enhanced by sophisticated techniques for digital data capture, data mining, collaborative networking, and other enhancements (Van de Sompel et al., 2004). Instead of finite steps and units, the scholarly endeavor began a transformation into a non-stop, value-added process in which steps in the scholarly communication process become ongoing processes. A scholarly article could be posted in open access as textual and non-textual material, made available in open access repositories, reviewed, expanded, reviewed, revised, reviewed, and published over and over again but with each activity adding to its value. In 1999, when the digital age was clearly a rising sun, Robert Darnton envisioned a monograph that would represent a layered pyramid of analysis, documentation, theory, discussion, review, and responses (Darnton, 1999). The pyramiding of scholarly research is simply an ongoing building process that could technically build continually over time.

Implicit again in this process is increased accessibility internally and externally to the scholarly community. Once it was possible to reach into articles, research papers, monographs, and reviews and extract specific information, tables, images, and graphs, two important events naturally happened. The first was a change in the scholarly work flow. The second was the blending of professional and commercial applications with the scholarly communication process, leading to practical, day-to-day use of scholarly information in a variety of industries.

Changing the unit of communication and changing the scholarly work flow system leads to certain issues within the scholarly community as well as with industrial and commercial applications. These issues are a major reason that the scholarly communication process has remained unaltered in terms of definition and process. Despite e-mail systems, digital library sources, open access, new scholarly tools, and sophisticated technology infrastructures, the form of scholarly content remains little changed because formal scholarship follows a careful path toward publication. The publication becomes public and for reuse only once the research and peer-review process is completed. The traditional dissemination through scholarly publishers is often slow, meaning it takes time for the material to be widely read, commented on, and debated among scholarly circles (Ayers, 2013).

However, it is this increased speed from research to publishing online that concerns scholars. Ithaka S+R conducted a survey on digital scholarship with the questions developed in consultation with a committee composed of a scholarly society professional, librarians, and publishers. The survey was sent to a random sample of 5,261 faculty members across eleven colleges and universities to assess their current attitudes toward e-books, technology-based teaching methods, and digital and non-digital factors shaping research efforts. Conducted in 2013, the results indicated that faculty in social sciences, humanities, and sciences were more likely to accept the transition from print to electronic journals but were less comfortable with replacing print subscriptions with electronic access. Digital versions of short monographs were more accepted than long-form reading. The survey found that educational scholars most valued the established scholarly dissemination methods more than the general public or undergraduate instructors. The faculty continued to choose publisher services that followed the traditional peer-review process and offered additional services, such as editing and branding. There was no agreement on the value of newer dissemination methods pursued by libraries to increase access and impact, two of their primary functions (Housewright, Schonfeld, and Wulfson, 2013).

Research Work Flow Change

Blending scholarly communication and the scholarly endeavor opens new avenues of work flows, but the issue of maintaining quality standards is amplified. While preservation and peer-review processes must be standardized to ensure that the final scholarly document is digitally stored and accessible, making scholarly research available for commercial and industry applications also creates the need for standards concerning material licensing, key administrative data, and tracking. There is also the issue of an underdeveloped scholarly infrastructure that limits the ability to make scholarly information universally accessible. The infrastructure for scholarly research and publication must address the development of scalable tools, author inclusiveness (as in the open access system), and enabling connections among the wide variety of unstructured scholarly data files. On the industry side, the infrastructure must have declared administrative metadata for the standardized expression of licensing, peer review, preservation, and tracking (Bilder et al., 2013). The need for improved scholarly infrastructure that connects the research community and professionals is reflected in the development of ORCID (Open Researcher and Contributor ID), a persistent digital identifier for unique identification of a specific scholar's research work flows (http:// orcid.org). ORCID provides automated linkages between a person's works when there are other identifiers used, such as ResearcherID, Scopus, or LinkedIn. This ensures that a scholar's efforts are distinguished from others, and this type of system supports the integration of scholarly and professional works, such as grant submissions, reflecting the increasing connectivity between academia and industry. The ORCID identifier is attached to articles, data sets, citations, patents, experiments, reviews, media stories, and so on. ORCID supports the type of system-to-system communications through the use of Application Programming Interface (API) keys needed before work flows systems can take advantage of the depth and breadth of digital information.

The rise of new work flow systems has emerged slowly over twenty years and is best described as "unbundled." The units of scholarly communication can contribute to scholarly communication without waiting for whole documents to be published in peer-reviewed journals. The relatively slow adoption of digital scholarship is not just due to strong belief in the integrity of the scholarly communication process and its ability to protect quality. It is also due to the need for new technologies that can adequately address the quality and tracking concerns of scholars. Most efforts to date have been to adapt the print scholarship to the digital systems, so focus has been on ensuring that researchers can get access to hundreds of years of research materials. Google Books and JSTOR are two examples of intense efforts to digitize print publications. Digital articles and journals allow scholars, researchers, and professionals to link and access without changing the traditional paper format (Ayers, 2013). Yet the move toward an unbundled digital-only environment continues and could accelerate as new technologies are developed to overcome scholarly concerns.

Size of the Market

Already large, the information industry market is growing as it incorporates new sectors in the scholarly and professional information arenas. There is increasing availability of data, content, software, platforms, and services creating a dynamic marketplace. In 2013, it was estimated that the total information industry value was $753 billion. The industry grew by 4.4 percent in 2013, compared to 3.5 percent in 2012. Search, aggregation, and syndication services were in the segment that grew by more than 10 percent (Alterman and Henry, 2014). It is difficult to definitively size the scholarly information and publishing industry as a separate industry because of the integration of print and digital processes.

WORK FLOW SOLUTIONS

Dynamics of the New Work Flow Solutions

A desire to share research in any form defines the move toward new work flow solutions. Traditionally, scholarly publishing, especially in the STM sector, is a long-tail activity in which a large amount of research is published by a small number of scholars. The Center for Embedded Network Sensing (CENS) is a National Science Foundation Science and Technology Center. A ten-year study of CENS found that researchers were willing to share data if there was certainty the researchers would receive credit and retain publishing rights. In practice, few people outside of the researcher's scholarly network were asking for the privilege (Wallis, Rolando, and Borgman, 2013). What became apparent during the study was that researchers developed personal networks of colleagues, and the individuals in those particular networks were the most likely to share information. In this scenario, there is little incentive to release data to a broader public; this would increase the risk of loss of intellectual property, force the development of systems to manage and protect the data, and potentially lead to policy complications.

Technology has created data-rich environments that make it easier to collect, store, manipulate, disseminate, and reuse research data. If research data is routinely released, it can serve a broader purpose than meeting the needs of networks of cohorts. The data could be used to advance new fields of study; create new products; enhance manufacturing processes; promote knowledge of systems, such as the climate; and advance disciplines, such as medicine and engineering. The true value of data and its conversion to information and then knowledge relies on managed data sharing. One of the primary motivations for sharing data or other units of scholarly communication is giving other researchers the opportunity to reproduce the data to verify research results and conclusions. In fact, replication of research results is one of the standards of the scientific method. While technology has increased access, it has also made research replication more complex because of factors such as interdisciplinary efforts, massive data sets, and the complexity of research projects (Jasny et al., 2011).

There are many efforts to address these issues through the development of postdocument work flow solutions. The realities of how researchers discover, research, describe, publish, respond, and network are changing despite the continuation of the traditional scholarly communication process, especially in the academic environment. The new work flow process is dynamic, enabling constantly regenerating scholarly documents while tagging them, albeit sometimes behind the scenes, each time a document, file, journal, and so on is accessed. New platforms enable aggregating web-based content, embedding and sharing content, creating relationships between content across databases, adding and extracting multimedia components, scraping and annotating metadata, granulating metadata, and editing, analyzing, and citing data (Turkel, 2012). Of critical importance to researchers is the ability to identify and create the relationships across different types of content and to express the relationships in text, video, graphs, and a variety of other media that can be extracted for use in research or professional activities.

ThoughtMesh, developed in 2005, was the product of an early collaborative effort between the University of Maine's Still Water Lab and the University of Southern California's *Vectors* journal. It is still in use as of 2014 and granulates uploaded articles by adding tags that enable the connecting of scholarly works published on different websites. When key words are clicked on the website for research purposes, sections of text related to the same section currently being read and related materials from the current document and across the Internet are displayed. Scalar is another technology platform that pursues scholarly content for using digital multimedia in a variety of contexts (Dietrich and Sayers, 2012).

Scalar was developed by the Alliance for Networking Visual Culture (http://scalar.usc.edu/about) and explores new forms of scholarly publishing that may serve as models for media-rich digital publication. The Alliance has a stated mission of closing the gap between digital visual archives and scholarly publication by creating interpretive pathways through materials, leading to new types of analysis. Integral to achieving the mission is the identification of the most efficient work flows between primary evidence, research, and publication resulting from an alliance between scholars, printing presses, libraries, and archives.

Changing Research

One of the most noticeable characteristics of the new work flow systems, as mentioned earlier, is the integration of the scholarly communication process with the research process. In the traditional scholarly communication system, the researcher goes through definitive steps that lead to the peer-reviewed, published document. In the technology-based system, researchers and scholars are performing activities simultaneously and collaborating across disciplines while publishing open research documents with rich media that encourage peer reviews, comments, and questions for analysis. The documents and/or media may be revised multiple times and reused or republished just as many times. Another critical change in the research process is that researchers now have multiple research starting points, whereas the library was once the first point of research contact. Some scholarly works are produced with minimal or no use of physical libraries.

As the information landscape changes with new technologies, so do the research work flows in response to the prominence and ease of use of search engines, web-based preindexed discovery services, the rise of social networks, globalized interconnectivity of previously isolated or localized scholarly repositories, and the ability to consult multiple online channels at any time. The commercial publisher and peer reviewers have served as scholarly gatekeepers for hundreds of years, but the long-held assumptions are challenged as a result of technology. The traditional actors in the scholarly communication process are still functioning with the same missions and goals: to advance discovery, register and vet research scholarship, improve access, encourage use of scholarly publications, and advance and preserve knowledge creation. Libraries are still collecting, retrieving, preserving, and delivering scholarly works. Publishers are still producing, promoting, and disseminating scholarship. Technology providers are creating platforms that all scholarly actors can use to achieve their missions even if done so in a different work flow process (Somerville and Conrad, 2013).

What is changing is how these functions are managed, and emerging are collaborative relationships or partnerships between technology and the other system participants. If publishers want their products discoverable, they must have technology platforms that make accessibility as broad as possible through a variety of search engines and diverse library platforms. Abstracting and indexing services or secondary publishers must provide the metadata and other information that discovery tools require. Libraries must use technology to ensure that the publisher content purchased through subscription services or bought outright (i.e., e-books, digitized articles, and so on) is searchable and accessible by scholars (Somerville and Conrad, 2013), the point being that multiple work flows underwent revision in the scholarly communication process. Ultimately, the end goal is to improve discoverability by scholars requiring particular research at certain points in their work flow.

Open Access

The availability of open access publications adds a complexity to the scholarly research and communication process. The publications are of growing interest to cross-sector and cross-discipline scholars and professionals. Successful discoverability will include ensuring that these resources are identified and accessible during searches. Whereas the scholar's work flow once required accessing each library collection or paying commercial publishers or professional associations a fee per article or for journal subscriptions, open access articles are available to anyone. There are three main issues here, too. First, open access articles must be discovered in some manner. Second, there may be iterations of publications as draft documents, preprints, revisions, expanded documents, withdrawals, retractions, and so on. Third, open access does not mean the material is in a single location. There are a variety of online locations that include institutional repositories, scholar websites, academic intranets, government archives, commercial publishers, aggregator collections, and others.

Important efforts to create shared and consistent infrastructures for access efficiency include ORCID, which addresses research name ambiguity, and CrossRef (http://www.crossref.org), an association of scholarly publishers addressing citation linking. CrossRef does not hold content. It manages linkages through CrossRef Digital Object Identifiers (CrossRef DOI) and has been doing so since 2000. The database includes over 64 million records for ORCIDs, authors, Digital Object Identifiers (DOIs), titles, International Standard Serial Numbers (ISSNs), FundRefs, and so on. The metadata search covers over 67 million journal articles.

CrossMark (http://www.crossref.org/crossmark) is a CrossRef service that takes online tracking one step further to track publication iterations in multiple locations. A CrossMark logo is attached to PDF, HTML, or ePub documents. Clicking on the logo brings up a pop-up box indicating the status of the document. The status may be current, or there may be updates available. The information also includes where the updates are located and provides the CrossRef link to the publisher's copy. One of the consequences of open access, online publishing is a rise in the number of retractions, and a consequence of that, according to CrossMark, is that retracted articles continue to be cited because the researcher does not realize there has been a retraction. CrossMark is just one example of how technology is changing the work flow process.

The changes to how scholars do research are on several levels, with open access being one. Journals, articles, essays, and other scholarly documents can be published once ready for online posting. That does not assume the material adheres to the editing and peer review-process, but it can if the online publishing site sets those requirements.

PLOS ONE (http://www.plosone.org/static/information), for example, is an international online publication that publishes open access, peer-reviewed, multidisciplinary articles. All works are published under a Creative Commons Attribution License. This means that anyone can download, reuse, modify, reprint, copy, and/or distribute articles as long as the source and author are cited. The authors and sponsors fund the operations. The articles undergo a rigorous peer-review evaluation by a qualified academic editor. Once published, they are indexed in MEDLINE/PubMed, Scopus, Web of Science, AGRICOLA, Chemical Abstract Services, Google Scholar, and other similar secondary services.

The impact of open access publishers adhering to quality standards on scholarly work flows is significant. PLOS ONE published 23,468 articles in 2012 because their publication is, among other reasons, online only and uses a different production model (Hoff, 2013). In 2013, PLOS ONE published 31,500 articles (Graham, 2014). One of the stated goals of PLOS ONE is the acceleration of the publishing schedule.

Open access publishers such as PLOS ONE are using a rolling-volume model that streamlines publishing and scholarly work flows. Some research has indicated that open access and rolling-volume models better fit the focus of scholars on articles rather than journal issues. The journal is no longer the main reference unit for all scholars researching and publishing (Cassella and Calvi, 2010). Publishers such as PLOS One and Hindawi, another open access publisher, are using the rolling-volume model in the belief that the pace of scholarship has accelerated and that getting publications out to the public as quickly as possible without giving up quality is possible and necessary to meet the needs of researchers today. Rather than wait for a collection of articles before publishing as a journal issue, scholarly articles can be published almost as quickly as they are edited, reviewed, and accepted. Of course, commercial and society publishers with well-developed online platforms are moving to this form of production as well to varying degrees.

A study of U.S. open access library information science journals listed in the *Directory of Open Access Journals* as November 2011 was conducted. In addition, only active, scholarly publications were surveyed. It revealed some information concerning work flow perspectives. The most common reason eleven editors out of twenty preferred to publish in discrete journal issues was to make production work flow easier. The next two reasons were more meaningful production deadlines and easier journal publicizing and promotion. The editors that published in rolling volumes indicated the primary reasons were improved production work flow, less reliance on production deadlines, and increased speed and dissemination of information. For rolling volumes, editors commented that technology-enabled open access publishing has sped up the publication cycle for publishers, authors, and readers as well as providing more publishing flexibility in terms of the type of information published (Cirasella and Bowdoin, 2013).

One of the issues associated with publishing in open access is the scholarly community's state of transition. Open access publishing has been only slowly accepted in some academic and research arenas, particularly the tenure and promotion process. Academia still mostly values publishing in traditional peer-reviewed journals for purposes of promotion, tenure, compensation, and reputation. This disposition continues to influence work flows in terms of the time it takes to complete a scholarly communication cycle from idea to publication. The traditional publishing route, though speedier than it was a decade ago, continues often to take up to a year and sometimes more. It takes PLOS ONE and similar publishers typically a couple of months. The slow progression toward full acceptance of open access publishing continues as technology removes barriers associated with tracking and commercial publishers are moving toward print/online and online-only publishing models. However, the editing and peer-review process remains the most time-consuming part of the work flow process.

Scholars can easily access a vast amount of data and information available on a global basis using search engines and indexing and abstracting services and gaining access to library and association repositories. The traditional scholarly communication work flow process had built-in filters, such as publisher management, independent editing, and peer review. When search engines made it possible to access material across the Internet, opening the floodgate of data, information, articles, multimedia, and parts of articles and books rather than whole documents, the filtering process was broken down in some cases and amended in others. The challenge in the new work flow system has been redesigning the filters to ensure that research that claims to be scholarly meets the standards of scholarly communication. Technology has made information accessible to anyone interested in the material, but that does not preclude the need for standards. Thus, all publishers need to continue to be selective in what they publish if the quality of the scholarly research is to remain intact.

Economics and Work Flow Technologies

Economics did play a role in the changing work flow systems, and as one commentator notes, the economics of technology have created opposing impacts. The push to commodify information is driven by the fact that information becomes a more valuable commodity with controlled access. On the other side of the equation, technology makes controlling access more difficult and devalues print materials. Open access represents a means of resisting controlled access and thus information dissemination. This has led to new economic models, such as publishers charging for electronic access to books rather than selling the book, leading to the "renting" of books (Benedict, 2013). The renting of all or part of books increases researcher access to materials that may not be accessible otherwise, primarily due to cost. Deep-Dyve, a commercial service, uses the rental model for access to scientific, technical, and medical articles and gives the option of purchasing and down-loading the articles as a PDF file.

Other work flow changes based on economics take many forms. One of the impacts of technology is the ability to research on a twenty-four-hour basis. Elsevier ScienceDirect has a full-text scientific database of book chapters and journal articles in physical sciences and engineering, agricultural and biological sciences, health sciences, and social sciences and humanities. There are pay-per-view articles with twenty-four-hour access, meaning scholars can work from home or office or use mobile access and are not tied to a single location. In addition, ScienceDirect has an open access section where articles are permanently free and twenty-four-hour accessible. Libraries also adopted online access to digitized collections, subscriptions, and archives, shifting research effort from in-house to remote locations.

Changing research methods involves more than simply accessing digitized records or data. Knovel (http://www.elsevier.com/online-tools/knovel) is a cloud-based application designed specifically for engineers and scientists. Subscribers get access to engineering reference content and the use of a search engine and interactive tools. The search engine accesses a content collection produced by authors, publishers, and societies. This example of a state-of-the-art research service shows how technology has adapted to the needs of researchers and is used to enhance research results. The search function is supplemented with data analysis tools that enable the extraction of data from graphs, tables, and equations. Once extracted, the data can be analyzed and manipulated for further analysis. Specific material and property names can be dragged and dropped into a query builder.

In an interesting approach, Cambridge Journals (http://journals.cambridge.org/action/login) does traditional publishing of peer-reviewed academic journals attractive to research scholars but is also focusing on industry executives. Cambridge Journals accepts registration by individuals, societies, and library subscription holders (organizational users). Since corporations can join many of the participating societies, corporate researchers can access print and online journals, pay-per-view articles, and rented articles. There are also open access articles posted along with the subscription-based journals covering forty-five subject areas. To help fund the many academic-based activities, Cambridge Journals also provides publishing and marketing services to corporate customers, including commercial reprints of single articles and custom collections of related articles for distribution, another path of dissemination. This represents a blending of scholarly publishing and professional work flow.

Wiley provides a host of research and publishing services that include journals, databases, online tools, laboratory protocols, and reference works in the scientific, medical, technical, and scholarly research areas. The content provider has print and online versions of most of its products (Wiley, 2013). The company also has professional development and education divisions. Applying technology to its research services, Wiley launched the Labtiva's ReadCube Web Reader on the Wily Online Library in February 2013. The new tool makes scientific PDFs interactive with the ReadCube Web Reader so that readers get hyperlinked in-line citations, clickable author names, annotations, and direct access to supplemental content. The innovative addition of new functionality to the PDF is designed to integrate document formats with the researcher's communication process (Wiley, 2013).

When the commercial publishers and professional societies began using the early technologies in the scholarly communication process, it was primarily to make it easier for scholars and researchers to find data and information. The sea change is the shift from simply discovering or locating information to extracting the bits of information needed and then manipulating the extractions in other programs as needed. Whereas early versions of research technologies accessed full articles by title, author, or other heading information, the later technologies made it possible for scholars to dip into text and databases based on search terms.

Technology also brought about another change in the scholarly communication process, namely, the integration of the scholarly communication process and various industries that include textbook publishing and educational materials, medical care and drug manufacturing, legal systems, compliance and certification services, and others where accurate data and validated research are critical.

RESEARCH INTEGRATES WITH INDUSTRY

Digital Textbooks

Digital textbooks were developed for technological, educational, and economic reasons. E-textbooks, like other scholarly publications, began as PDF copies of printed pages. Digital educational materials include e-textbooks, interactive teaching and learning programs, and multimedia videos, but the type of materials included in the definition continues to change as technology progresses. A digital textbook is a digitized book, an e-book, but the online textbook is becoming a blend of content delivery that includes scholarly text, videos, assessment tools, images, podcasts, and integrated information from a variety of sources, such as web-based content, which may include open access articles (Jackson, 2014). The new types of digital textbooks may dynamically combine pieces of works and then use the information and content in new e-learning services.

In 2010, digital textbooks accounted for 1 percent of the textbook market in the United States. By 2012, it had grown to 5.5 percent and was projected to grow to 18.8 percent by the end of 2014 (Rivero, 2013). The textbook industry consists of two segments: K–12 and higher education. The higher-education textbook market is led by Wiley, Cengage, McGraw-Hill Education, and Pearson publishers. Similar to the increase in library journal subscription costs, the price of textbooks rose by 82 percent for the period 2002–2012 (U.S. Government Accountability Office, 2012). Also, like other scholarly publications, there is a push to find alternative, less costly ways to publish and deliver textbook materials.

Work flow solutions to rapidly increasing textbook prices, which parallel solutions to scholarly works, are again driven by technological innovations. Solutions include digital textbooks and textbook rental programs. They also include open-source and open access materials. In education, Open Educational Resources (OERs) are teaching, learning, and research resources that include full courses, open textbooks, course materials, videos, software, and anything else that supports gaining access to knowledge. Users of the material are free to retain, reuse, revise, remix, and redistribute because the materials are released under intellectual property license. There are OER publishers, repositories, and OpenCourseWare (OCW). OCW is the digital publication of high-quality, educational materials that are available to any user (SPARC, 2014).

OCW is a broad term. The materials may be established to accommodate traditional classroom sizes, but in the higher-education world, Massive Open Line Courses (MOOCs) are growing in popularity because they allow large-scale student participation. MOOCs extend the ability to instruct or lecture to anyone with Internet access, in effect creating an unlimited class size. There are many examples of MOOCs, including Coursera, edX, and Udacity.com. Coursera is an educational platform that has partnered with prestigious universities, such as Stanford University, Johns Hopkins University, Ludwig-Maximilians-Universität München, and others. All courses are offered online and for free, but students do not earn course credits applicable to a degree. EdX offers interactive online classes and MOOCs and has partnered with the Massachusetts Institute of Technology, Harvard University, the University of California, Berkeley, and other universities. The XSeries of classes lead to an XSeries Certificate, indicating a level of achievement, and some educational institutions may accept the courses for credit.

Many universities are using OERs or MOOCs in the classroom to give educational access to students residing anywhere in the world. Students must pay for the class if they want to earn credits applicable toward a degree, and that further alters the business model. They create an open access educational environment that supports open access scholarship. Some of the advantages of using MOOCs include the ability to use multimedia materials to enhance the learning experience and the ease with which the materials can be updated or revised. The primary issues some scholars and educational institutions have with OERs are similar to the issues concerning open access. Any user can post to the OER, and there is no certainty the information is accurate. MOOCs are not digital scholarship. They make no claim to advance scholarly knowledge or research or disciplinary knowledge. They were created primarily to leverage technology resources to deliver instructional materials to a wider audience. However, there is an interest in adding digital scholarship to MOOCs as an innovative approach to advancing scholarly knowledge (Ayers, 2013).

The technology-based disruption of the traditional textbook industry is ongoing and in many cases could be called radical. Flat World Knowledge enables educators to personalize textbooks, an innovation likely to be expanded on in the future by other commercial publishers. Flat World Knowledge (http://catalog.flatworldknowledge.com) has an inventory of textbooks in business and economics, humanities and social sciences, professionals and applied sciences, mathematics, and sciences. Faculty members can purchase access to the digital textbook, personalize it for their course using an online editor, and rearrange, add, or delete content. Once the textbook is personalized to the satisfaction of the instructor, students are given a unique access link. This represents a radical change in the work flow process.

Another example confirming the trend toward customized textbooks is the OpenStax College (http://openstaxcollege.org) at Rice University. The nonprofit organization offers free, peer-reviewed textbooks, and this initiative is funded by prestigious foundations dedicated to increasing educational access through the use of technology. Professional-quality textbooks cover most disciplines, including physics, sociology, biology, economics, statistics, psychology, chemistry, biology, physiology, and others. Faculty can customize the available textbooks, which meet strict academic publishing standards; StaxDash tracks updates and provides information on errata. Students can also request a low-cost print version of the digital textbooks.

These types of initiatives are growing in number and scope in the digital textbook arena. Commercial publishers are participating in the digital textbook industry but in a different way. Commercial publishers charge a retail price for textbook access, but they also have an editing and review process in place for ensuring quality of content. Thomson Reuters ScholarOne (http://scholarone.com/products/books) offers numerous tools to enhance work flow in book production and enables the management of multiple authors and multiple topics on a worldwide basis. Textbook authors can track the entire publishing process from beginning to end and can create client-specific work flows utilizing ScholarOne's technology.

Technology has led to a host of innovative approaches to textbook development and production. The business models are still in the transformative stage. Commercial publishers may be interested in preserving the traditional model of selling textbooks. Yet they are increasingly adding services that either enable the production of digital textbooks or provide supplemental digital resources to accompany textbooks. For textbook authors, the ability to customize textbooks is just one advantage of digital production. Authors can also combine pieces of other works to dynamically create learning materials, including digital textbooks.

Medical

As much as the textbook industry is being transformed by technology, the medical industry is an industry already benefiting from the work flow process changes discussed so far. Scholarly research and publications have traditionally been available within the closed circle of scholars and were not directly integrated with industry. The research and publications were used by industry research and development professionals but were not directly incorporated into daily operations. In the medical and pharmaceutical industries, technology is making it possible to incorporate medical information into patient systems at the point of care, providing diagnostic and adverse risk management information to health care professionals. The scholarly work flow process is increasingly seamlessly integrated with the delivery of medical services and enhancing medical research.

The integration of medical research and health care practices is called evidence-based health care. It is "the conscientious, explicit, and judicious use of current best evidence in making decisions about the care of individual patients" (Sackett et al., 1996: 71). It refers to a variety of activities that include developing uniform reporting styles for research, conducting statistical meta-analyses of research, promoting randomized clinical trials, and using clinical practice guidelines to make the best decisions for effective patient care (Timmermans and Mauck, 2005). Evidence-based health care represents the intersection of the scholarly communication process in the medical field and the practice of medicine through the application of clinical expertise. Though the concept of evidence-based medicine (EBM) has been used for decades, technology has expanded the ability to integrate through developments such as decision support platforms designed to help medical practitioners diagnose, treat, identify drug interactions, and so forth. The platforms also serve as a forum for the practitioners to share expertise and experiences and fulfill the important purpose of helping medical practitioners narrow their research to selective, patient-driven evidence.

In addition to EBM, there is evidence-based clinical practice and evidence-based health care. Evidence-based health care is more expansive than EBM. It is the conscientious use of current best evidence when making decisions about the medical care of patients or the delivery of health services. It also represents the blending of clinical expertise and up-to-date medical research and addresses identifying the potential for harm from exposure to certain agents, the predictive power of prognostic factors, and the accuracy of diagnostic tests (Cochrane, 1972). Technology has enabled the delivery of evidence-based health care services in a variety of ways, including remote patient monitoring and diagnosis. Evidence-based clinical practice integrates medical practitioner expertise, the best evidence available, and patient preferences to make the optimal decision for the patient (Gray, 1997).

Technology has led to exponential growth in the availability of research applicable to health care and medicine. One of the concerns in EBM is that the gap between available data, information, and knowledge versus the practitioner's ability to access and use the research for decision making is widening. Work flows can be hindered by factors such as time, lack of networked databases, volume of information, and others. There are government sites offering public resources for evidence-based clinical practice guidelines, such as the Agency for Healthcare Research and Quality's National Guideline Clearinghouse (NGC) (http://www.guideline.gov). The initiative represents a joint effort between the U.S. Department of Health, the American Medical Association, and what is now America's Health Insurance Plans. The primary mission of the NGC is to provide the health care industry, from physicians to integrated health delivery systems, with a way to obtain objective and detailed information about clinical practice guidelines. It is a melding of evidence-based health and clinical practice expertise with technology to advance the development, dissemination, implementation, and use of clinical guidelines. Guidelines and information on their development are maintained in a database.

Incorporating medical and drug information into the patient care system is also a risk management strategy. Increasing the awareness of the risks and benefits of evidence, including the use of therapeutics, can lead to optimal patient care when the information is combined with practitioner expertise. The U.S. Centers for Education and Research on Therapeutics (CERTs) (http://certs.hhs.gov) has six research centers and the CERT Scientific Forum, which is a central scientific coordinating center. The research conducted on therapeutics gives health care professionals information on the uses and risk of drugs, drug combinations, and biological products and clinical information to health care providers, pharmacists, health care delivery systems, patients, health maintenance organizations, and others and helps reduce the cost of care by reducing incidences of adverse drug effects. The positive impact on work flows is clear in that groups of experts are providing critical research data, information, and knowledge to the health care industry members who would have to do the research themselves otherwise.

Playing an equally large role in the integration of scientific and medical research with point-of-care health care are commercial companies that have developed platforms dedicated to evidence-based content to assist medical practitioners with work flows. DynaMed (https://dynamed.ebscohost.com) provides evidence-based content as a point-of-care product. The company provides clinical decision support by synthesizing evidence and providing objective or unbiased information. DynaMed monitors over 500 medical journals and evaluates articles on two primary criteria—clinical relevance and scientific validity. The new evidence that passes the editorial process or critical appraisal is integrated into DynaMed's current content, and overall conclusions are revised as necessary.

Epocrates (http://www.epocrates.com) is a subscription-based decision support system for medical practitioners prescribing and monitoring drug therapies. The Epocrates Rx and Epocrates databases include drug pharmacology, dosing, off-label uses, drug interactions, common and adverse reactions, contraindications, disease information, and diagnostic/lab tests. The database was developed by an editorial team of physicians with academic and pharmacy experience. The extensive editorial process assumes a work flow that medical practitioners would have to complete to get the quality of data and information in the Epocrates database. The process includes a review of clinical guidelines, specialty references, Food and Drug Administration indications, pharmacotherapy and medical texts, primary literature, and review articles.

Thomson Reuters (http://thomsonreuters.com), an STM publisher, also offers health care and business solutions. The Clinical Xpert Solution suite of products is designed to provide real-time intelligent information to hospitals and other health care industry practitioners and providers. The sophisticated product deploys a single system that gathers information from across the health care provider's units and creates a database that system participants can use. The system provides patient information, manages procedure codes, reconciles medications, and so on. The Clinical Xpert Navigator also identifies high-risk patients by matching clinical profiles against patient data. Thomson Reuters also offers Micromedex Healthcare Solutions that delivers clinical reference solutions for drugs, diseases, toxicology reference information, evidence-based Order Sets for ambulatory and hospital settings, and more.

Businesses such as DynaMed, Epocrates, and Thomson Reuters offer mobile access to their clinical decision support resources. The convergence of traditional reference data and information with electronic work flow tools is beneficial, however, even without mobility. Add mobile access for work flow content via smartphones, iPads, notebooks, and e-readers, and the deci-

sion support resources become accessible outside traditional medical settings, such as hospitals, as long as some type of Internet access is available.
Work flow content refers to patient-related clinical or operational content and
now converges with mobile content that is referential health care-related
content. The entrance of STM publishers such as Thomson Reuters into the
work flow content and referential content field is natural because it enables
commercial experts in managing databases and reference information to develop new lines of business derived from their repositories of content (Camlek, 2011). The need for high-quality, reviewed evidence will continue, and
using open access resources remains questionable in the health industry for
patient care because of risks of error, both editorial and research based.

Legal Industry

Legal systems are using work flow around case management services, making it possible to spend more time synthesizing casework as opposed to
searching for relevant information. Attorneys do need to research STM information for cases, but their most pressing day-to-day needs are more client-
centric and work flow related. For this reason, LexisNexis (http://
www.lexisnexis.com/en-us/gateway.page), a provider of content-enabled
work flow solutions, has added work flow solutions for the legal profession
and other professional solutions. A pioneer company in providing online
information and now owned by Reed Elsevier, LexisNexis integrated information and technology decades ago.

The LexisNexis workforce solutions do more than discover information.
The company offers a set of products that help legal firms manage the legal
and corporate components of their business. New additions to solutions use a
customer delivery innovation process that caters to various legal segments,
such as solo attorneys or associates, and helps attorneys with different levels
of technology expertise manage their practices (Mulvihill, Brynko, and
Schiller, 2011).

The Electronic Discovery Reference Model is a work flow solution that
funnels the volume of data and information, taking it through automated
review, production, analysis, and presentation steps. The funneling process is
designed to analyze and map data and information so that the end volume is
relevant. Business process management systems are becoming more common in the legal industry because they leverage technology to simplify the
management and movement of large amounts of information by using work
flow tools.

Thomson Reuters Westlaw Next is a legal research system that uses concepts similar to the medical work flow systems discussed earlier. The database includes primary law and exclusive secondary law titles. "A team of
bar-admitted attorneys . . . analyze, categorize, and summarize the law to

help ensure the information is not only accurate but also easy to find and interpret" (Westlaw Next, 2014). The work flow tools search across diverse but uniformly tagged legal content and even unstructured data so that attorney time can be spent more productively on synthesizing casework rather than searching for the cases relevant to the work in progress.

The Business of Science

The convergence of data and information and business is accelerating as new technologies are developed. The need for accessing and pinpointing data is growing, and every industry is using a variety of services able to deliver the data and information on demand. In some of the industries, such as insurance, the data is used to reduce risk and lower costs. In other industries, such as oil and gas, data and information are used to pinpoint natural resources, improve technologies, and minimize risks. Putting data in context is critical for it to be truly useful. Raw data is not adequate. It can lead to false conclusions if misinterpreted, which is why access to data alone is not enough. Analytics need strategies and process so that services such as LexisNexis do not simply provide access to data. They offer teams of experts who analyze the data and information to ensure its integrity and usefulness. The expert analysis leads to new services that ensure that users get the information needed and then offer other services to drill down further, finally offering analytical tools for research outputs.

The insurance industry is a good example of how content is needed in compliance and certification purposes and is being integrated into business services for various reasons. In the insurance industry, data and analytics can be used to improve underwriting practices or rate determinations, reducing the risk of loss. Content can also be used to manage potential fraud by providing the critical information needed to make informed decisions.

LexisNexis has a set of "risk solutions" that address business needs that include identity issues, fraud, compliance, investigation, and collections. The service has designed a data-intensive computer built on a cluster-computing platform, linking technology to convert random data into information and knowledge. The database has over 36 billion public and proprietary records that are refreshed daily with 1 million new search records. The massive amount of data is used for multiple purposes. For example, data and information is used by the insurance industry to analyze weather patterns and losses and identify where business risk levels are highest. The financial services industry uses LexisNexis to assess money-laundering risks and various customer risks associated with behavior patterns or credit.

Knovel has an interactive equations tool that allows mechanical engineers working in the industry to access equations along with worked solutions in mechanics and mechanical engineering, chemistry, chemical engineering, and metals and metallurgy. A toolbox gives access to math functions, programming structures, engineering units, and math symbols. Knovel represents the blending of scholarly endeavors with practical industry applications.

ProQuest provides access to a polymer abstract and index library dedicated to rubbers, plastics, adhesives, and polymeric composites. It is intended for use by both academics and corporate customers. The ProQuest content libraries have an intuitive interface so that searches are increasingly customized to the user. There are work flow tools and customizable content bundles. Another specialty database is intended for academics and corporate researchers in climatology, meteorology, and atmospheric pollution. The database foundation is composed of Meteorological and Geoastrophysical Abstracts produced by the American Meteorological Society. However, the ProQuest Atmospheric Science Collection database is extended by the addition of full-text access and comprehensive discovery made possible by a controlled vocabulary used to structure the abstracts and indexes. The vocabulary is managed by expert editorial teams.

Many more industries are accessing data, data analysis, information, and knowledge, including aerospace, chemicals, financial services, and manufacturing. Academic libraries are also important players in the process of integrating research with business. They have long been in the forefront of adapting to technology, including digitization of primary sources, developing institutional repositories, supporting open access models, and developing consortiums. They continue to invest in collection development while moving steadily toward electronic collections (Regazzi, 2012a). There are now emerging partnerships forming between libraries and corporations for the purpose of advancing research. Research collaborations benefit both sides of the partnership. Corporations need the independent research access, while universities need the data and real-world information that corporations can offer (Williams, 2013).

CONCLUSION

The information industry, of which scholarly communication is a segment, is continually changing as technology advances and researchers and corporations demand access to the highest-quality, reviewed research. The availability of massive amounts of data and the desire to convert that data into information and then knowledge drove the development of enabling new, disruptive technologies. The next phase focused incorporating knowledge into the system. The end result is a sea change in work flow systems and the integration of scholarly research into the corporate world through user accessibility.

Work flows are now cross-disciplinary, collaborative, networked, and data intensive. Biology scholars can coauthor scientific papers with physiology scholars, each working on the other side of the globe while using the same databases and same publication system. The scholarly communication process is entwined with the scholarly endeavor itself. It is this integration that has opened up new avenues of work flows for scholars and for business. Search engines, Big Data and work flow software to manage it, and other technologies made the integration possible; open access was the catalyst for a global discussion on accessibility and availability of research to a broader community than scholars.

The scholar has options today in areas of research and publication and is not locked into the traditional vertical system of journal publication. The ability to publish online has led to a work flow system in which units of the research can be published for comment or review by the wide scholarly community rather than waiting for the slow process of publishing in peer-reviewed journals. After the "document model," a dynamic system has emerged that encourages authors to think outside the traditional journal publication system in terms of finding methods for resolving issues such as peer review of digital and open articles as well as the tracking of articles revised in some manner or withdrawn as new information becomes available. Online scholarly communication is fluid, with billions of bits of new data and articles, essays, monographs, and reviews posted every day. The online system has also converged scholarly research and publication with multimedia, meaning that new forms of data are now available for access and extraction. A scholar can reach into a paper, extract the graph and its data table, and reuse or manipulate the data or information for new research.

New economic models had to accompany the system, and that has influenced work flows as well. Anyone with permission rights can rent many of the online articles and books available today rather than paying much larger sums to purchase them. There are various models, such as pay-per-view, price schedules for electronic or print versions, and free articles in open access. Digital textbooks represent a response to the high cost of textbooks and the availability of online publishing coupled with the new economic models. The digital textbook industry is also becoming increasingly dynamic. Initially, the textbooks were basically digitized versions of print textbooks that could be purchased or rented by students. The more recent advances have led to commercial publishers offering edited and reviewed digital textbooks that can be purchased and then modified by the academic authors. OER and MOOCs are growing in popularity as educational facilities and academics look for ways to deliver instruction to a wider student audience that is mobile, has Internet access, and is looking for a more affordable alternative to expensive print textbooks. Some academics like MOOCs because it gives them more flexibility over course content. Materials can be added, changed, and deleted as often as desired. Not everyone has accepted the OER (and the MOOC in particular), believing it diminishes the learning process by focusing more on entertaining delivery of information and is subject to a decline in quality with specific standards in place. The debate continues on how to best manage the quality issues, and in the meantime, there are academics using OER as supplemental material to the peer-reviewed textbook.

The integration of scholarly research and business is impacting all industries, including health care. The health care industry is already incorporating medical and drug information into point-of-care systems. Point of care originally meant that the care occurred in a hospital or health care system or a clinic, but the development of health care technologies has extended the reach of Internet-based data, information, and knowledge. For example, mobile access and systems make remote delivery of health care possible. Wherever the Internet is accessible means that peer-reviewed information that includes expert knowledge may be used in health care work flow systems. The commercial publishers are developing items such as online drug monographs that contain up-to-date information for diagnosis, treatment, and drug administration. The decision support systems in EBM is another concept that has been practiced for decades but is now being approached in a new way due to the dynamic interaction with databases that technology brings to the arena.

Other industries embracing new work flow processes include legal, manufacturing research and development, engineering, aerospace, financial services, and so on. The ability to access the most current research means that industries such as insurance can reduce risks through enhanced compliance and certification processes that utilize critical data for pricing, risk assessment, certification of real-world projects, and so on.

This is not a perfect world. With the increased flow of data and enhanced ease of access to research come risks. An alternative view of the changing scholarly landscape is that quality is bound to decline when anyone can post articles online and anyone can participate in the information sharing. The question of how to maintain quality and authenticity of research is still not resolved, though publishers, open access systems, and scholars are rapidly developing models for tracking online publications. There are systems in place already for assigning DOIs to online research, along with links that track each iteration. There is little doubt that the technology and software will develop effective tracking systems. Larger issues concern how to identify quality research and how to connect the many online databases and repositories.

The increasing convergence of scholarly research and technology is going to continue. That can be said with definitiveness. The work flow software systems will focus on adapting to the digital scholarly processes and the needs of specific industries. One last prediction is that academic and research libraries, as well as library associations and commercial search and aggregation companies, will assume a larger role in the integration of research and the corporate world. Having access to data does not mean the user knows how to use the data for information purposes or how to add expertise to turn the information into knowledge or how to turn knowledge into a quality shared experience. The expertise of librarians and professional information experts will be greatly needed to help, meaning the scholarly world will see an increasing number of collaborations between libraries and private industry with research and development projects at the private and governmental levels.

REFERENCES

Alterman, Simon, and Harry Henry. 2014. "Information Industry Market Size and Share Rankings: Preliminary 2013 Results." *Outsell*, January 24. http://www.outsellinc.com/store/products/1218.

Ayers, Edward L. 2013. "Does Digital Scholarship Have a Future?" *Educause Review Online* 48, no. 4 (August 5). http://www.educause.edu/ero/article/does-digital-scholarship-have-future.

Benedict, Michael S. 2013. "Copyright, Fair Use, and New Economic Models of Scholarly Publishing." Paper presented at the H-Net affiliate session Scholarly Communication and Copyright at the annual meeting of the American Historical Association, New Orleans, LA, January 5, 2013. https://www.h-net.org/hnetat20/MichaelLesBenedict.pdf.

Bilder, Geoff, Lars Bjornhauge, Johannes Fournier, Camercon Neylon, and Simon Thompson. 2013. "Panel Session, Gold OA Infrastructure." OAI8: Innovations in Scholarly Communication, Geneva, June. http://www.goldoa.org.uk/oai8-innovations-in-scholarly-communication-june-2013-geneva.

Camlek, Victor. 2011. "Healthcare Mobile Information Flow." *Information Services and Use* 31, no. 1–2: 25.

Cassella, Maria, and Licia Calvi. 2010. "New Journal Models and Publishing Perspectives in the Evolving Digital Environment." *IFLA Journal* 36, no. 1 (March): 7–15. http://dx.doi.org/10.1177/0340035209359559.

Cirasella, Jill, and Sally Bowdoin. 2013. "Just Roll with It? Rolling Volumes vs. Discrete Issues in Open Access Library and Information Science Journals." *Journal of Librarianship and Scholarly Communication* 1, no. 4: eP1086. http://dx.doi.org/10.7710/2162-3309.1086.

Cochrane, A. L. 1972. *Effectiveness and Efficiency: Random Reflections on Health Services.* London: Nuffield Provincial Hospitals Trust. (Reprinted in 1989 in association with the BMJ. Reprinted in 1999 for Nuffield Trust by the Royal Society of Medicine Press, London.)

Darnton, Robert. 1999. "The New Age of the Book." *New York Review of Books*, March 18. http://www.nybooks.com/articles/archives/1999/mar/18/the-new-age-of-the-book.

Dietrich, Craig, and Jentery Sayers. 2012. "After the Document Model for Scholarly Communication: Some Considerations for Authoring with Rich Media." *Digital Studies/Le champ numérique* 3, no. 2. http://www.digitalstudies.org/ojs/index.php/digital_studies/article/view/234/301e.

Graham, Kayla. 2014. "Thanking Our Peer Reviewers." *PLOS ONE Community Blog*, January 6. http://blogs.plos.org/everyone/2014/01/06/thanking-peer-reviewers.

Gray, J. A. Muir. 1997. *Evidence-Based Healthcare: How to Make Health Policy and Management Decisions.* London: Churchill Livingstone.

Hoff, Krista. 2013. "PLOS ONE Papers of 2012." *PLOS ONE Community Blog*, January 3. http://blogs.plos.org/everyone/2013/01/03/201.

Housewright, Ross, Roger C. Schonfeld, and Kate Wulfson. 2013. "Ithaka S+R US Faculty Survey 2012." April 8, 1–79. http://www.sr.ithaka.org/sites/default/files/reports/Ithaka_SR_US_Faculty_Survey_2012_FINAL.pdf.

Jackson, Nancy Mann. 2014. "Digital Deliveries." *University Business* 17, no. 1 (January): 445–446.

Jasny, Barbara R., Gilbert Chin, Lisa Chong, and Sacha Vignieri. 2011. "Again, and Again, and Again. . . ." *Science* 334, no. 6060 (December 2): 1225. doi: 10.1126/science.334.6060.1225.

Mulvihill, Amanda, Barbara Brynko, and Kurt Schiller. 2011. "Professional Workflows: The Heart of Content." *Information Today* 28, no. 6 (2011): 1–36.

Muthukumar, and John G. Hedberg. 2005. "A Knowledge Management Technology Architecture for Education Research Organisations: Scaffolding Research Projects and Workflow Processing." *British Journal of Educational Technology* 36, no. 3 (May): 379–395.

Regazzi, John J. 2012a. "Comparing Academic Library Spending with Public Libraries, Public K–12 Schools, Higher Education Public Institutions, and Public Hospitals between 1998–2008." *Journal of Academic Librarianship* 38, no. 4 (July): 205–216.

Rivero, Victor. 2013. "Digital Textbooks: Show Me the Future!" *Internet@Schools* 20, no. 3: 12–13.

Sackett, David L., William M. C. Rosenberg, J. A. Muir Gray, R. Brian Haynes, and W. Scott Richardson. 1996. "Evidence Based Medicine: What It Is and What It Isn't." *British Medical Journal* 312 (January 13): 71–72. http://dx.doi.org/10.1136/bmj.312.7023.71.

Somerville, Mary M., and Lettie Y. Conrad. 2013. "Discoverability Challenges and Collaboration Opportunities within the Scholarly Communications Ecosystems: A SAGE White Paper Update." *Collaborative Librarianship* 5, no. 1: 29–41.

SPARC. 2014. "Open Education." Accessed September 15. http://www.sparc.arl.org/issues/oer.

Timmermans, Stefan, and Aaron Mauck. 2005. "The Promises and Pitfalls of Evidence-Based Medicine." *Health Affairs* 24, no. 1 (January): 18–28. doi: 10.1377/hlthaff.24.1.18.

Turkel, William J. 2012. "A Workflow for Digital Research Using Off-the-Shelf Tools." William J. Turkel (blog). January 1. http://williamjturkel.net/how-to.

U.S. Government Accountability Office. 2013. "College Textbooks—Students Have Greater Access to Textbook Information." U.S. Government Accountability Office, Report to Congressional Committees, GAO-13-368. June. http://www.gao.gov/assets/660/655066.pdf.

Van de Sompel, Herbert, and Sandy Payette, John Erickson, Carl Lagoze, and Simeon Warner. 2004. "Rethinking Scholarly Communication—Building the System That Scholars Deserve." *D-Lib Magazine* 10, no. 9 (September). http://www.dlib.org/dlib/september04/vandesompel/09vandesompel.html.

Wallis, Jillian C., Elizabeth Rolando, and Christine L. Borgman. 2013. "If We Share Data, Will Anyone Use Them? Data Sharing and Reuse in the Long Tail of Science and Technology." *PLOS ONE* 8, no. 7. doi: 10.1371/journal.pone.0067332.

Westlaw Next. 2014. "Know the Difference." Thomson Reuters. Accessed September 15. http://info.legalsolutions.thomsonreuters.com/westlawnext/about/default.aspx.

Wiley. 2013. "Wiley Makes Scientific PDFs Interactive with the ReadCube Web Reader from Labtiva." Press release. Wiley. February 6. http://www.wiley.com/WileyCDA/PressRelease/pressReleaseId-107276.html.

Williams, Kimber. 2013. "Academic-Corporate Research Partnerships Focus of Nov. 12 Talk." *Emory News Center*. November 11.

Bibliography

Academy of Science of South Africa. 2009. "Scholarly Books: Their Production, Use and Evaluation in South Africa Today." Academy of Science of South Africa. August. http://www.assaf.co.za/wp-content/uploads/2009/09/ASSAF-Scholarly-Report-FINAL-Proof.pdf.

Adema, Janneke, and Paul Rutten. 2010. "Digital Monographs in the Humanities and Social Sciences: Report on User Needs." Open Access—Publishing in European Networks. January. http://openreflections.files.wordpress.com/2008/10/d315-user-needs-report.pdf.

Akeroyd, John. 1988. "CD-ROM as an Online Public Access Catalogue." *The Electronic Library* 6, no. 2: 120–124.

Alterman, Simon, and Harry Henry. 2014. "Information Industry Market Size and Share Rankings: Preliminary 2013 Results." *Outsell*, January 24. http://www.outsellinc.com/store/products/1218.

American Chemical Society. 2007. "Chemical Abstracts." American Chemical Society. http://acswebcontent.acs.org/landmarks/landmarks/cas/chemabstracts.html.

Amherst College Press. 2013. "Home Page." Accessed December 31. https://www.amherst.edu/library/press.

Anderson, Chris. 2009. *Free—The Future of a Radical Price*. New York: Hyperion.

Asher, Andrew D., Lynda M. Duke, and Suzanne Wilson. 2013. "Paths of Discover: Comparing the Search Effectiveness of EBSCO Discovery Service, Summon, Google Scholar, and Conventional Library Resources." *College & Research Libraries* 74, no. 5 (September): 464–488.

Association of College and Research Libraries. 2013. "Intersections of Scholarly Communication and Information Literacy—Creating Strategic Collaborations for a Changing Academic Environment." Association of College and Research Libraries, 1–26. http://www.ala.org/acrl/sites/ala.org.acrl/files/content/publications/whitepapers/Intersections.pdf.

Association of College and Research Libraries, Scholarly Communications Committee. 2003. "Principles and Strategies for the Reform of Scholarly Communication 1." Association of College and Research Libraries. June 24. http://www.ala.org/acrl/publications/whitepapers/principlesstrategies.

Association of Research Libraries. 2000. "[Tempe] Principles for Emerging Systems of Scholarly Publishing." Association of Research Libraries. Last modified June 6, 2000. http://www.arl.org/storage/documents/publications/tempe-principles-10may10.pdf.

Association of Research Libraries. 2013. "What Does SPARC Do?" Association of Research Libraries. Accessed December 13. http://sparc.arl.org/about.

Association of Subscription Agents and Intermediaries. 2013. "University of Chicago Press to Make Scholarly Monograph Content Available via OUP's UPSI Platform." Association of Subscription Agents and Intermediaries. Last modified February 26. http://subscription-agents.org/university-chicago-press-make-scholarly-monograph-content-available-oups-upso-platform.

Ayers, Edward L. 2013. "Does Digital Scholarship Have a Future?" *Educause Review Online* 48, no. 4 (August 5). http://www.educause.edu/ero/article/does-digital-scholarship-have-a-future.

Baker, Dale B., Jean W. Horiszny, and Wladyslaw V. Metanomski. 1980. "History of Abstracting at Chemical Abstracts Services." *Journal of Chemical Information and Computer Science* 20: 193–201.

Baschler, Edwin F. 1998. "Pricing of Scientific Publications: A Commercial Publisher's Point of View." *Notice of the AMS (American Mathematical Society)*, November 1998, 1333–1343.

Baykoucheva, Svelta. 2010. "From the Institute of Scientific Information (ISI) to the National Federation of Advanced Information Services (NFAIS)." *Chemical Information Bulletin* 62, no. 1 (Spring 2010): 18.

Beach, Richard, Amy Carter, Debbie East, et al. 2007. "Resisting Commercial Influences on Accessing Scholarship: What Literacy Researchers Need to Know and Do." Paper presented at the National Reading Conference, Oak Creek, Wisconsin, November 29–December 2, 2006. Published in the *56th Yearbook of the National Reading Conference* (Oak Creek, WI: National Reading Conference, Inc., 2007), 96–110.

Bekaert, Jeroen, and Herbert Van de Sompel. 2006. "Augmenting Interoperability across Scholarly Repositories." Meeting notes of meeting of Microsoft, the Andrew W. Mellon Foundation, the Coalition for Networked Information, the Digital Library Foundation, and the Joint Information Systems Committee, April 20–21, 2006, 1–17. http://msc.mellon.org/Meetings/Interop/FinalReport.

Benedict, Michael S. 2013. "Copyright, Fair Use, and New Economic Models of Scholarly Publishing." Paper presented at the H-Net affiliate session Scholarly Communication and Copyright at the annual meeting of the American Historical Association, New Orleans, LA, January 5, 2013. https://www.h-net.org/hnetat20/MichaelLesBenedict.pdf.

Berlin, Sir Isaiah, and University of Illinois at Urbana-Champaign. 1974. "The Divorce between the Sciences and the Humanities." Tykociner Lecture Committee. University of Illinois. http://berlin.wolf.ox.ac.uk/published_works/ac/divorce.pdf.

Berners-Lee, Tim. 2014. "Design Issues—Architectural and Philosophical Points." W3C. Accessed July 3. http://www.w3.org/DesignIssues.

"Bethesda Statement on Open Access Publishing." 2003. Meeting at Howard Hughes Medical Institute, June 20, 2003. http://legacy.earlham.edu/~peters/fos/bethesda.htm#institutions.

Bilder, Geoff, Lars Bjornhauge, Johannes Fournier, Camercon Neylon, and Simon Thompson. 2013. "Panel Session, Gold OA Infrastructure." OAI8: Innovations in Scholarly Communication, Geneva, June. http://www.goldoa.org.uk/oai8-innovations-in-scholarly-communication-june-2013-geneva.

Birch, Thomas. 1968. *The History of the Royal Society of London for Improving of Natural Knowledge from Its First Rise: Four Volumes.* New York: Royal Society. (Facsimile of four-volume work published in London, 1757.)

Bjørner, Susanne, and Stephanie C. Ardito. 2003. "Online before the Internet, Part 1: Early Pioneers Tell Their Stories." *Searcher* 11, no. 6 (June). http://www.infotoday.com/searcher/jun03/ardito_bjorner.shtml.

Black, Michael H. 1992. *A Short History of Cambridge University Press.* Cambridge: Cambridge University Press.

Blake, John B., ed. 1980. *Centenary of Index Medicus 1879–1979.* Bethesda, MD: U.S. Department of Health and Human Services, National Institutes of Health, National Library of Medicine.

Blank, Brian E. 2009. "Review of *The Calculus Wars: Newton, Leibniz, and the Greatest Mathematical Clash of All Time* by Jason Socrates Bardi." *Notices of the AMS* (*American Mathematical Society*) 56, no. 5: 602–610. http://www.ams.org/notices/200905/rtx090500602p.pdf.

Borgman, C. L. 2000. "Digital Libraries and the Continuum of Scholarly Communication." *Journal of Documentation* 58, no. 4 (July): 412–430.

Borovansky, Vladimir T. 1996. "Changing Trends in Scholarly Communication: Issues for Technological University Libraries." *1995 IATUL Proceedings* 5: 68–79. http://docs.lib.purdue.edu/iatul/1995/papers/8.

Bosch, Stephen, and Kittie Henderson. 2012. "Coping with the Terrible Twins, Periodicals Price Survey." *Library Journal*, April 30. http://lj.libraryjournal.com/2012/04/funding/coping-with-the-terrible-twins-periodicals-price-survey-2012.

Bourne, Charles P. 1980. "On-Line Systems: History, Technology, and Economics." *Journal of the American Society for Information Science and Technology* 31, no. 3 (May): 155–160.

Bourne, Charles P., and Trudi Bellardo Iahn. 2003. *A History of Online Information Services, 1963–1976*. Cambridge: Massachusetts Institute of Technology.

Boyd, Danah M., and Nicole B. Ellison. 2007. "Social Networks Sites: Definition, History, and Scholarship." *Journal of Computer-Mediated Communication* 13, no. 1 (October): 210–230.

Breeding, Marshall. 1999. "Does the Web Spell Doom for CD and DVD?" *Library Technology Guides, Document Repository. Computers in Libraries* 19, no. 10 (October): 71–75. http://www.librarytechnology.org/ltg-displaytext.pl?RC=6553.

Breeding, Marshall. 2007. "Understanding the Protocol for Metadata Harvesting of the Open Archives Initiative." *Computers in Libraries* 22, no. 8: 24–29.

Brin, Sergey. 2009. "A Library to Last Forever" (op-ed). *New York Times*, October 8, international edition.

Brown, Laura, Rebecca Griffiths, and Matthew Rascoff. 2007. "University Publishing in a Digital Age." *Ithaka Report*, July 26, 1–69. http://www.sr.ithaka.org/sites/default/files/reports/4.13.1.pdf.

Brown, Patrick O., et al. 2003. "Bethesda Statement on Open Access Publishing." Earlham College. June 20. http://legacy.earlham.edu/~peters/fos/bethesda.htm.

Buchanan, Larry. 1995. "Internet Gopher Basics—Happy Tunneling!" *Multimedia Schools Professional Development Collection* 2, no. 2: 12–31.

Butter, Karen A. 1994. "Red Sage: The Next Step in the Delivery of Electronic Journals." *Medical References Services Quarterly* 13, no. 3 (Fall): 75–81.

Cambridge University Press. 2013. "About Us." Cambridge University Press. Accessed June 1. http://www.cambridge.org/us/information/about.htm.

Camlek, Victor. 2011. "Healthcare Mobile Information Flow." *Information Services and Use* 31, no. 1–2: 25.

Carr, Dick. 2014. "What Is Gray Literature?" University of New Mexico Health Sciences Library and Informatics Center. Last updated August 11, 2014. http://libguides.health.unm.edu/content.php?pid=200149.

Cassella, Maria, and Licia Calvi. 2010. "New Journal Models and Publishing Perspectives in the Evolving Digital Environment." *IFLA Journal* 36, no. 1 (March): 7–15. http://dx.doi.org/10.1177/0340035209359559.

Cawkell, Terry, and Eugene Garfield. 2001. "Institute for Scientific Information." In *A Century of Science Publishing: A Collection of Essays*, edited by E. H. Fredriksson, 149–160. Lansdale: IOS Press.

Chain, Leslie, Darius Cuplinkskas, Micahel Eisen, et al. 2002. "Read the Budapest Open Access Initiative." Budapest Open Access Initiative. February 14. http://www.budapestopenaccessinitiative.org/read.

Chemical Abstracts Service. 2013. "CAS History." Chemical Abstracts Service—Division of the American Chemical Society. Accessed October 10. https://www.cas.org/about-cas/cas-history.

Christensen, Clayton. 1997. *The Innovator's Dilemma: When New Technologies Cause Great Firms to Fail*. Cambridge, MA: Harvard Business School Press.

Cirasella, Jill, and Sally Bowdoin. 2013. "Just Roll with It? Rolling Volumes vs. Discrete Issues in Open Access Library and Information Science Journals." *Journal of Librarianship and Scholarly Communication* 1, no. 4: eP1086. http://dx.doi.org/10.7710/2162-3309.1086.

CiteSeer^X. 2014. "About CiteSeer^X." CiteSeer^X. Pennsylvania State University. Accessed September 12. http://csxstatic.ist.psu.edu/about.

Clement, Gail. 1994. "Evolution of a Species: Science Journals Published on the Internet." *Database* 17, no. 5: 44–46, 48–52, 54.

Cochrane, A. L. 1972. *Effectiveness and Efficiency: Random Reflections on Health Services.* London: Nuffield Provincial Hospitals Trust. (Reprinted in 1989 in association with the BMJ. Reprinted in 1999 for Nuffield Trust by the Royal Society of Medicine Press, London.)

Comba, Valentina, and Marialaura Bignocchi. 2005. "Scholarly Communication and Open Access: Research Communities and Their Publishing Patterns." New Trends in Scholarly Communication: How Do Authors of Different Research Communities Consider OA. Conference paper, August 13, 2005. http://eprints.rclis.org/7276/1/oslo.pdf.

Cornog, Martha. 1983. "A History of Indexing Technology." *The Indexer* 13, no. 3 (April): 152–157.

Costelloe, Timothy. 2012. "Giambattista Vico." The Stanford Encyclopedia of Philosophy. First published June 11, 2003. Substantive revision February 14, 2012. http://plato.stanford.edu/archives/spr2012/entries/vico.

Cox, Christopher. 2011. "Western Libraries Acquisitions Funding Model: A Plan for Change. Developed by the Western Libraries in Consultation with the Senate Library Committee." Western Libraries Senate Library Committee. April. http://www.wwu.edu/provost/budget/documents/proposals/LibraryAcquisitionsFundingPlanforChange.pdf.

Cox, John, and Laura Cox. 2010. *Scholarly Book Publishing Practice.* Association of Learned & Professional Society Publishers. http://www.alpsp.org/Ebusiness/ProductCatalog/Product.aspx?ID=41.

Crane, D. 1972. *Invisible Colleges: Diffusion of Knowledge in Scientific Communities.* Chicago: University of Chicago Press.

Crawford, Walt. 2013. *The Big Deal and the Damage Done.* Lulu.com. April 29. http://www.lulu.com/shop/walt-crawford/the-big-deal-and-the-damage-done/ebook/product-20998658.html.

Creative Commons. 2013. "CC History." Creative Commons. Accessed December 14. http://creativecommons.org/about/history.

CrossRef. 2009. "The Formation of CrossRef: A Short History." CrossRef.org. http://www.crossref.org/08downloads/CrossRef10Years.pdf.

Crotty, David. 2010. "Science and Web 2.0: Talking about Science vs. Doing Science." *the scholarly kitchen* (blog). February 8. http://scholarlykitchen.sspnet.org/2010/02/08/science-and-web-2-0-talking-about-science-versus-doing-science.

Crow, Raym. 2006. "Publishing Cooperatives: An Alternative for Non-Profit Publishers." *First Monday* 11, no. 9 (September). http://firstmonday.org/ojs/index.php/fm/issue/view/203.

"Current Liblicense Archive—Ulrich's Estimate of Total Number of Active Peer-Reviewed Journals: 28,094 in August 2012." 2012. Center for Research Libraries. August 4. http://listserv.crl.edu/wa.exe?A2=LIBLICENSE-L;17e4abd4.1208.

D'Arms, John H., and Richard Ekman. 1999. "ACLS E-Publishing Project for History Monographs." Humanities and Social Sciences Net Online. Announcement ID 123958. July 12. http://www.h-net.org/announce/show.cgi?ID=123958.

Darnton, Robert. 1999. "The New Age of the Book." *New York Review of Books*, March 18. http://www.nybooks.com/articles/archives/1999/mar/18/the-new-age-of-the-book.

Davies, David Randal. 2006. *The Postwar Decline of American Newspapers, 1945–1965, Issue 6.* Westport, CT: Greenwood Publishing.

"Declaration of San José towards the Virtual Health Library." 1998. IV Pan American Congress on Health Sciences Information, March 24–27, 1998.

Dewar, James A. 2013. "The Information Age and the Printing Press: Looking Backward to See Ahead." RAND. Accessed October 3. http://www.rand.org/pubs/papers/P8014.html.

Diebold, Francis X. 2000. "'Big Data' Dynamic Factor Models for Macroeconomic Measurement and Forecasting." Paper presented at the Eighth World Congress of the Econometric Society, November 28, 2000. Seattle, WA.

Dietrich, Craig, and Jentery Sayers. 2012. "After the Document Model for Scholarly Communication: Some Considerations for Authoring with Rich Media." *Digital Studies/Le champ numérique* 3, no. 2. http://www.digitalstudies.org/ojs/index.php/digital_studies/article/view/234/301e.

Digital Book World. 2013. "Digital Drives Wiley Revenue Growth in Third-Quarter." *Digital Book Wire*. Digital Book World. March 7. http://www.digitalbookworld.com/2013/digital-drives-wiley-revenue-growth-in-third-quarter.

Dolecheck, Melanie. 2010. *Allen Press: A Celebration of 75 Years*. Lawrence, KS: Allen Press.

Dulle, F. W., and M. K. Minishi-Majanja. 2009. "Researchers' Perspectives on Open Access Scholarly Communication in Tanzanian Public Universities." *South African Journal of Information Management* 11, no. 4 (April 20): 413+.

EBSCO. 2013. "EBSCO Discovery." EBSCO*host*. Accessed May 10. http://www.ebscohost.com/discovery.

Eisen, Jonathan. 2012. "Social Networks for Academics Proliferate, despite Some Doubts." *The Chronicle of Higher Education*, April 29. http://chronicle.com/article/Social-Networks-for-Academics/131726.

Ekman, Richard H., and Richard E. Quandt. 1995. "Scholarly Communication, Academic Libraries and Technology." *Change* 27, no. 1 (January–February): 34–44.

"Electronic Publishing in Analytical Chemistry." 1987. *Analytical Chemistry* 59, no. 17 (September): 1021. doi: 10.1021/ac00144a737.

Eliot, Simon, and Jonathan Rose, eds. 2007. *A Companion to the History of the Book*. Malden, MA: Blackwell Publishing.

Elon University School of Communication. 2013. "Imagining the Internet's Quick Look at the Early History of the Internet." Elon University School of Communication. Accessed October 5. http://www.elon.edu/e-web/predictions/early90s/internethistory.xhtml.

Elsevier. 2013. "Elsevier to Flip Seven Subscription Journals to Open Access in 2014." Elsevier. December 17. http://www.elsevier.com/about/press-releases/research-and-journals/elsevier-to-flip-seven-subscription-journals-to-open-access-in-2014.

Elsevier. 2013a. "Elsevier's 'Article of the Future' Is Now Available for All Cell Press Journals." PR Newswire. Accessed March 26. http://www.prnewswire.com/news-releases/elseviers-article-of-the-future-is-now-available-for-all-cell-press-journals-80913137.html.

Elsevier. 2013. "A Short History of Elsevier." Elsevier. Accessed September 1. http://cdn.elsevier.com/assets/pdf_file/0014/102632/historyofelsevier.pdf.

Elsevier. 2013b. "Understanding the Publishing Process in Scientific Journals." Elsevier.com. Accessed March 24. http://biblioteca.uam.es/sc/documentos/understanding_the_publishling_process.pdf.

Elsevier. 2014a. "Engineering Village." Elsevier.com. Accessed September 12. http://www.elsevier.com/online-tools/engineering-village.

Elsevier. 2014b. "Scopus." Elsevier.com. Accessed September 12. http://www.elsevier.com/online-tools/scopus.

ETH-Bibliotheck. 2013. "Swiss National Science Foundation Funds Publications in Open-Access Journals." ETH-Bibliotheck. http://www.library.ethz.ch/en/ms/Open-Access-an-der-ETH-Zuerich/Aktuell/Schweizer-Nationalfonds-finanziert-Publikationen-in-Open-Access-Zeitschriften.

ExLibris. Primo. 2013. "A Solution for Current and Future Library Architecture." ExLibris. Accessed October 8. http://www.exlibrisgroup.com/?catid={CD9897CD-0BD0-435C-A5A0-D9D6BAD2B9AB}.

Fairthorne, R. A. 1958. "Automatic Retrieval of Recorded Information." *Computer Journal* 1, no. 1: 36–41.

Faries, Cindy. 1992. "Users' Reactions to CD-ROM: The Penn State Experience." *College & Research Libraries* 53, no. 2 (March): 139–149.

Finch Group. 2012. "Accessibility, Sustainability, Excellence: How to Expand Access to Research Publications." Research Information Network. June. http://www.researchinfonet.org/wp-content/uploads/2012/06/Finch-Group-report-FINAL-VERSION.pdf.

Fingerman, Susan. 2006. "Electronic Resources Reviews—Web of Science and Scopus: Current Features and Capabilities." *Issues in Science and Technology Librarianship*, no. 48 (Fall). doi: 10.5062/F4G44N7B.

Fitzpatrick, Kathleen. 2009. *Planned Obsolescence: Publishing, Technology, and the Future of the Academy*. New York: New York University, Media Commons Press.

Fitzpatrick, Kathleen. 2012. "Giving It Away: Sharing and the Future of Scholarly Communication." *Journal of Scholarly Publishing* 43, no. 4: 347–362.

Fjällbrant, Nancy. 1997. "Scholarly Communication—Historical Development and New Possibilities." Purdue University. Proceedings of the 1997 IATUL Conference. Paper 5. http://docs.lib.purdue.edu/cgi/viewcontent.cgi?article=1389&context=iatul.

Foley, James A. 2014. "Scholarly Journals Accepted 120 Fake Research Papers Generated by Computer Program." *Nature World News*, March 1. http://www.natureworldnews.com/articles/6217/20140301/scholarly-journals-accepted-120-fake-research-papers-generated-by-computer-program.htm.

Fortin, Jean-Michel, and David J. Currie. 2013. "Big Science vs. Little Science: How Scientific Impact Scales with Funding." *PLOS ONE* 8, no. 6 (June 19). doi: 10.1371/journal.pone.0065263.

Foster, Edward. 1985. "CD-ROM: Megabytes into Minispace." *InfoWorld* 7, no. 38 (September 23): 27–29.

Frazier, Kenneth. 2001. "The Librarians' Dilemma—Contemplating the Costs of the 'Big Deal.'" *D-Lib Magazine* 7, no. 3 (March). http://www.dlib.org/dlib/march01/frazier/03frazier.html.

Friend, Frederick J. 2006. "Google Scholar: Potentially Good for Users of Academic Information." *Journal of Electronic Publishing* 9, no. 1 (Winter). http://dx.doi.org/10.3998/3336451.0009.105.

Friendberg, Anne. 2009. "On Digital Scholarship." *Cinema Journal* 48, no. 2 (Winter): 150–154.

Frohmann, Bernd. 2013. "The Role of the Scientific Paper in Science Information Systems." University of Western Ontario. Accessed March 25. http://instruct.uwo.ca/faculty/Frohmann/ASIS%20Scidoc.PDF.

Gardner, Tracy, and Simon Inger. 2012. *How Readers Discover Content in Scholarly Journals: Comparing the Changing User Behaviour between 2005 and 2012 and Its Impact on Publisher Web Site Design and Function. Summary Edition.* Abingdon, UK: Renew Training. http://www.renewtraining.com/How-Readers-Discover-Contentin-Scholarly-Journals-summary-edition.pdf.

Garfield, Eugene, Blaise Cronin, and Helen Barsky Atkins, eds. 2000. *The Web of Knowledge: A Festschrift in Honor of Eugene Garfield.* Medford, NJ: American Society for Information Science.

Garvey, William, and Belver Griffith. 1967. "Scientific Communication as a Social System." *Science* 157, no. 3792 (September 1): 1011–1016.

Garvey, William, and Belver Griffith. 1980. "Scientific Communications: Its Role in the Conduct of Research and Creation of Knowledge." In *Key Papers in Information Science*, edited by B.C. Griffith, 211–238. White Plains, NY: Knowledge Industry Publications.

Gasson, Christopher. 2014. "The Economics of Academic Publishing." Royal Economic Society. Accessed January 15. http://www.res.org.uk/view/art2Apr04Features2.html.

Gibbs, Nancy J. 2005. "Walking Away from the 'Big Deal': Consequences and Achievements." *Serials* 18, no. 2 (January): 89–94.

Ginsparg, Paul. 2011. "It Was Twenty Years Ago Today." arXiv.org at Cornell University. September 13. http://arxiv.org/pdf/1108.2700v2.pdf.

Givler, Peter. 2002. "University Press Publishing in the United States." American Association of University Professors. http://www.aaupnet.org/about-aaup/about-university-presses/history-of-university-presses. (Reprint from *Scholarly Publishing: Books, Journals, Publishers and Libraries in the Twentieth Century*, edited by Richard E. Abel and Lyman W. Newman, Wiley, 2002.)

Goldner, Matt. 2010. "Winds of Change: Libraries and Cloud Computing." OCLC Online Computer Library Center. http://www.oclc.org/content/dam/oclc/events/2011/files/IFLA-winds-of-change-paper.pdf.

Gonzalez, Rob. 2014. "Introduction to the Semantic Web." Cambridge Semantics. Accessed July 3. http://www.cambridgesemantics.com/semantic-university/introduction-to-the-semantic-web.

Google. 2013. "Google Books History." Google Books. Accessed October 19. http://www.google.com/googlebooks/about/history.html.

Google. 2013. "Google Scholar." Google.com. Accessed May 14. http://www.google.com/intl/en/scholar/about.html.

Gowers, Timothy. 2012. "Elsevier—My Part in Its Downfall." *Gowers's Weblog* (blog). January. http://gowers.wordpress.com/2012/01/21/elsevier-my-part-in-its-downfall.

Graham, Kayla. 2014. "Thanking Our Peer Reviewers." *PLOS ONE Community Blog*, January 6. http://blogs.plos.org/everyone/2014/01/06/thanking-peer-reviewers.

Gray, J. A. Muir. 1997. *Evidence-Based Healthcare: How to Make Health Policy and Management Decisions*. London: Churchill Livingstone.

Gribbin. John. 2007. *The Fellowship: Gilbert, Bacon, Harvey, Wren, Newton, and the Story of a Scientific Revolution*. London: Overlook Hardcover.

Guédon, Jean-Claude. 2001. "Beyond Core Journals and Licenses: The Paths to Reform Scientific Publishing." *ARL: A Bimonthly Report on Research Library Issues and Actions from ARL, CNI, and SPARC*, no. 218 (October). http://www.arl.org/storage/documents/publications/arl-br-218.pdf.

Hahn, Karla L. 2008. "Talk about Talking about New Models of Scholarly Communication." *Journal of Electronic Publishing* 11, no. 1 (Winter). http://dx.doi.org/10.3998/3336451.0011.108.

Hall, A. Rupert, and Marie Boas Hall. 1962. "Why Blame Oldenburg." *Isis* 53, no. 4 (January): 482–491.

Harley, Diane, Sophia Krzys Acord, Sarah Earl-Novell, Shannon Lawrence, and C. Judson King. 2010. *Assessing the Future Landscape of Scholarly Communication*. University of California, Berkeley. January, 1–737. http://escholarship.org/uc/cshe_fsc.

Harnad, Stevan. 2003. "E-Prints: Electronic Preprints and Postprints." In *Encyclopedia of Library and Information Science*, 2nd ed., vol. 2, edited by Miriam A. Drake, 990–992. New York: Marcel Dekker.

Hart, Michael. 2010. "The History and Philosophy of Project Gutenberg." Project Gutenberg. August 1992. Last modified April 8, 2010. http://www.gutenberg.org/wiki/Gutenberg:The_History_and_Philosophy_of_Project_Gutenberg_by_Michael_Hart.

Hawkins, Donald T. 2013. "Information Discovery and the Future of Abstracting and Indexing Services: An NFAIS Workshop." *Against the Grain*, August 6. http://www.against-the-grain.com/2013/08/information-discovery-and-the-future-of-abstracting-and-indexing-services-an-nfais-workshop.

Hedberg, John G. 1989. "CD-ROM: Expanding and Shrinking Resource Base Learning." *Australian Journal of Educational Technology* 5, no. 1: 56–75.

Henderson, Kittie S., and Stephen Bosch. 2010. "Periodicals Price Survey 2010: Seeking the New Normal." *Library Journal*, April 15. http://lj.libraryjournal.com/2010/04/budgets-funding/periodicals-price-survey-2010-seeking-the-new-normal/#_.

Hoff, Krista. 2013. "PLOS ONE Papers of 2012." *PLOS ONE Community Blog*, January 3. http://blogs.plos.org/everyone/2013/01/03/201.

Housewright, Ross, Roger C. Schonfeld, and Kate Wulfson. 2013. "Ithaka S+R US Faculty Survey 2012." April 8, 1–79. http://www.sr.ithaka.org/sites/default/files/reports/Ithaka_SR_US_Faculty_Survey_2012_FINAL.pdf.

Hovav, Anat, and Paul Gray. 2001. "Managing Academic Electronic Publishing: Six Case Studies." *Global Co-Operation in the New Millennium—9th European Conference on Information Systems*, June 27–29, 751–763. http://csrc.lse.ac.uk/asp/aspecis/20010042.pdf.

Howard, Jennifer. 2011. "Scholars Create Influential Journal for About a $100 a Year." *The Chronicle of Higher Education*, January 30. http://chronicle.com/article/Hot-Type-Scholars-Create/126090.

Institute of Medicine, Committee on Conflict of Interest in Medical Research, Education, and Practice. 2009. "4. Conflicts of Interest in Biomedical Research." *Conflict of Interest in Medical Research, Education, and Practice*, edited by B. Lo and M. J. Field. Washington, DC: National Academies Press. http://www.ncbi.nlm.nih.gov/books/NBK22940.

International Association of Scientific, Technical and Medical Publishers. 2013a. "Shifting Areas of Growth in Global Information Economy." International Association of Scientific,

Technical and Medical Publishers. Accessed February 27. http://www.stm-assoc.org/industry-statistics/shifting-areas-of-growth-in-global-information-economy.

International Association of Scientific, Technical and Medical Publishers. 2013b. "STM Market Size and Growth, 2006–2010." International Association of Scientific, Technical and Medical Publishers. Accessed February 27. http://www.stm-assoc.org/industry-statistics/stm-market-size-and-growth-2006-2010.

International Federation of Library Associations. 2002. "IFLA Internet Manifesto." International Federation of Library Associations. May 1. http://www.ifla.org/files/assets/faife/publications/policy-documents/internet-manifesto-en.pdf.

Jackson, Nancy Mann. 2014. "Digital Deliveries." *University Business* 17, no. 1 (January): 445–446.

Jasny, Barbara R., Gilbert Chin, Lisa Chong, and Sacha Vignieri. 2011. "Again, and Again, and Again. . . ." *Science* 334, no. 6060 (December 2): 1225. doi: 10.1126/science.334.6060.1225.

Jeffery, Keith G. 2006. "Open Access: An Introduction." *ERCIM News*, no. 64 (January). http://www.ercim.eu/publication/Ercim_News/enw64/jeffery.html.

Jha, Alok. 2012. "Academic Spring: How an Angry Maths Blog Sparked a Scientific Revolution." *The Guardian* (Great Britain), April 9. http://www.theguardian.com/science/2012/apr/09/frustrated-blogpost-boycott-scientific-journals.

JSTOR. 2012. "A New Chapter Begins: Books at JSTOR Launches." JSTOR. November 12. http://about.jstor.org/news/new-chapter-begins-books-jstor-launches.

JSTOR. 2013. "Content on JSTOR—Books." JSTOR. Accessed June 1. http://about.jstor.org/content/about-books.

Kamble, V. T., D. S. Amoji, B. Sangeeta, and Durai Pandy. 2012. "A Brief History of E-Resources." In *National Conference on Knowledge Organization in Academic Libraries (KOAL-2012), September 29*, 103–109. New Delhi: Library Professional Association.

Katikiredd, Srinivasa Vittal. 2004. "HINARI: Bridging the Global Information Divide." *British Medical Journal* 328, no. 7449 (May 15): 1190.

Kaufer, David S., and Kathleen M. Carley. 1984. *Communication at a Distance—The Influence of Print on Sociocultural Organization and Change.* Chicago: University of Chicago Press.

Kelley, Michael. 2012. "Coming into Focus—Web-Scale Discovery Services Face Growing Need for Best Practices." *Library Journal* 137, no. 17 (October 15): 34.

Kling, Rob, and Ewa Callahan. 2003. "Electronic Journals, the Internet and Scholarly Communication." *Annual Review of Information Science and Technology* 37: 127–177.

Kling, Rob, and Geoffrey McKim. 1999. "Scholarly Communication and the Continuum of Electronic Publishing." *Journal of the American Society for Information Science* 50 , no. 10: 890–906.

Kling, Rob, Lisa B. Spector, and Joanna Fortuna. 2004. "The Real Stakes of Virtual Publishing: The Transformation of E-Biomed into PubMed Central." *Journal of the American Society for Information Science and Technology* 55, no. 2 (January): 127–148. doi: 10.1002/asi.10352.

Knight, Gareth. 2004. "An Introduction to Metadata Requirements for an E-Print Repository." SHERPA Project Document. March 8. http://www.sherpa.ac.uk/documents/D2-6_Report_on_Metadata_Issues.pdf.

Kuhn, Thomas S. 1970. *The Structure of Scientific Revolutions.* 2nd ed. Chicago: University of Chicago Press.

Kyrillidou, Martha, and Mark Young, eds. 2003. "ARL Statistics 2001–02." Association of Research Libraries. http://www.arl.org/storage/documents/publications/arl-statistics-2001-02.pdf.

Lancaster, F. W., ed. 1995. "A Networked Approach to Scholarly Publishing within Universities." *Library Trends—Networked Scholarly Publishing* 43, no. 4 (Spring): 520+.

Lancaster, F. Wilfred, and Amy J. Warner. 1993. "The Database Industry." In *Information Retrieval Today*, 21–31. Arlington, VA: Information Resources Press.

Laney, Doug. 2001. "3D Data Management: Controlling Data Volume, Velocity, and Variety." *Meta Group. Application Delivery Strategies* (blog). February 6. http://blogs.gartner.com/

doug-laney/files/2012/01/ad949-3D-Data-Management-Controlling-Data-Volume-Velocity-and-Variety.pdf.

Large, Andrew, Lucy A. Tedd, and Richard J. Hartley. 1999. *Information Seeking in the Online Age: Principles and Practice*. London: Bowker-Saur.

Lee, Christopher. 2008. "Where Have All the Gophers Gone? Why the Web Beat Gopher in the Battle for Protocol Mind Share." School of Information and Library Science at the University of North Carolina. Original version April 23, 1999; rev. November 4, 2001; April 25, 2008. http://www.ils.unc.edu/callee/gopherpaper.htm.

Leetaru, Kalev. 2008. "Mass Book Digitization: The Deeper Story of Google Books and the Open Content Alliance." *First Monday* 13, no. 10 (October 6). http://firstmonday.org/article/view/2101/2037.

Lemetti, Juhana. 2012. *Historical Dictionary of Hobbe's Philosophy*. Plymouth, UK: Scarecrow Press.

Library of Congress. 2013. "American Memory Mission and History." Library of Congress. Accessed October 18. http://memory.loc.gov/ammem/about/index.html.

Lindberg, Donald A. B. 2000. "Internet Access to the National Library of Medicine." *Effective Clinical Practices* 4: 256–260.

Linke, Erika C. 2003. "Million Book Project." In *Encyclopedia of Library and Information Science, Second Edition—Volume 3*, edited by Miriam Drake, 1889–1894. Boca Raton, FL: CRC Press. http://books.google.com/books?id=Sqr-_3FBYiYC&pg=PA1889&lpg=PA1889&dq=million+book+project+was+initiated+by&source=bl&ots=X-YNFG-uHA&sig=W9UFCb7GTgQjHNdQJiG9i93rvDo&hl=en&sa=X&ei=NzVkUsz0LIrA8ATuzoCQAQ&ved=0CGsQ6AEwCA#v=onepage&q=million%20book%20project%20was%20initiated%20by&f=false.

Lipscombe, Trevor. 2012. "First among Equals: Robert Recorde and Innovative Publishing in the Sixteenth Century." *Journal of Scholarly Publishing* 43, no. 4 (July): 381–394.

López-Cózar, Emilio Degado, Nicolás Robinson-García, and Daniel Torres Salinas. 2012. "Manipulating Google Scholar Citations and Google Scholar Metrics: Simple, Easy and Tempting." *EC3 Working Papers* 6 (May 29): 4–6.

Lorimer, Rowland. 2013. "Libraries, Scholars, and Publishers in Digital Journal and Monograph Publishing." *Scholarly and Research Communication* 4, no. 1 (2013). http://src-online.ca/index.php/src/article/view/43/118.

Loughborough University. 2013. "Project RoMEO." Loughborough University. Accessed December 14. http://www.lboro.ac.uk/microsites/infosci/romeo.

Lynch, Clifford A. 2006. "Improving Access to Research Results: Six Points." *ARL: A Bimonthly Report* no. 248 (October): 5–7.

Mabe, Michael. 2006. "(Electronic) Journal Publishing." *E-Resources Management Handbook*. International Association of Scientific, Technical and Medical Publishing. August 23, 56–66. http://www.stm-assoc.org/2006_08_23_Electronic_Journal_Publishing.pdf.

Mabe, Michael A. 2010. "Scholarly Communication: A Long View." *New Review of Academic Librarianship* 16, no. S1: 132–144.

Manyika, James, Michael Chui, Brad Brown, et al. 2011. *Big Data: The Next Frontier for Innovation, Competition and Productivity*. McKinsey Global Institute. http://www.mckinsey.com/insights/business_technology/big_data_the_next_frontier_for_innovation.

McCabe, Mark. 1999. "The Impact of Publisher Mergers on Journal Prices: An Update." *ARL* 207 (July). http://mccabe.people.si.umich.edu/Grain.PDF.

McCabe, Mark. 2001. "The Impact of Publisher Mergers on Journal Prices: Theory and Evidence." *The Serials Librarian* 40, no. 1/2: 157–166.

McCarthy, Cheryl A., Sylvia C. Krausse, and Arthur A. Little. 1997. "Expectations and Effectiveness Using CD-ROMs: What Do Patrons Want and How Satisfied Are They?" *College and Research Libraries* 58, no. 2 (March): 128–142.

McDonald, John, and Eric F. Van de Velde. 2004. "The Lure of Linking: Link Resolvers Are Essential to Getting Optimal Usage of Electronic Content." *Library Journal*, April 1. http://lj.libraryjournal.com/2004/04/ljarchives/the-lure-of-linking.

McGarry, Kevin J. 1981. *The Changing Context of Information: An Introductory Analysis.* London: Bingley.

McKie, Douglas. 1948. "The Scientific Periodical from 1665 to 1798." *Philosophical Magazine* (Commemoration Issue), 122–132.

Meadows, A. J. 1974. *Communication in Science.* London: Butterworths.

Mell, Peter, and Timothy Grance. 2011. *The NIST Definition of Cloud Computing* (Special Publication 800-145). Gaithersburg, MD: National Institute of Standards and Technology of the U.S. Department of Commerce, September. http://csrc.nist.gov/publications/nistpubs/800-145/SP800-145.pdf.

Merton, R. K. 1942. "A Note on Science and Democracy." *Journal of Legal and Political Sociology* 1 : 115–126.

Merton, Robert K. 1973. *The Sociology of Science.* Chicago: University of Chicago Press.

Mihhailov, A. J., A. I. Chernyi, and R. S. Gilliarevskii. 1984. *Scientific Communication and Informatics.* Arlington, VA: Arlington Information Resources Press.

Mohrman, Kathryn, Wanhua Ma, and David Baker. 2008. "The Research University in Transition: The Emerging Global Model." *Higher Education Policy* 21: 5–27.

Morgan Stanley. 2002. "Media Industry Overview: Scientific Publishing: Knowledge Is Power." Equity Research Report Europe. September 30. http://www.econ.ucsb.edu/~tedb/Journals/morganstanley.pdf.

Mukherjee, Bhaskar. 2009. "Scholarly Communication: A Journey from Print to Web." *Library Philosophy and Practice* (e-journal). http://unllib.unl.edu/LPP/mukherjee.htm.

Mullins, J. L., C. Murray-Rust, J. L. Ogburn, et al. 2012. Library Publishing Services: Strategies for Success: Final Research Report. Washington, DC: Scholarly Publishing and Academic Resources Coalition, 1–18.

Mulvihill, Amanda, Barbara Brynko, and Kurt Schiller. 2011. "Professional Workflows: The Heart of Content." *Information Today* 28, no. 6 (2011): 1–36.

Murray, Peter J., and Denis M. Anthony. 1999. "Current and Future Models for Nursing E-Journals: Making the Most of the Web's Potential." *International Journal of Medical Informatics* 53, no. 2/3: 151–161.

Muthukumar, and John G. Hedberg. 2005. "A Knowledge Management Technology Architecture for Education Research Organisations: Scaffolding Research Projects and Workflow Processing." *British Journal of Educational Technology* 36, no. 3 (May): 379–395.

Muto, Albert. 1993. *The University of California Press.* Berkeley: University of California Press.

Myers, Robin, and Michael Harris, eds. 1997. The Stationers' Company and the Book Trade 1550–1990. Winchester: St Paul's Bibliographies.

Nabe, Jonathan, and David C. Fowler. 2012. "Leaving the Big Deal: Consequences and Next Steps." Southern Illinois University, Carbondale, Morris Libraries. January 1. http://opensiuc.lib.siu.edu/cgi/viewcontent.cgi?article=1070&context=morris_articles.

National Federation of Advanced Information Services. 2013. "Years of Knowledge & Experience." National Federation of Advanced Information Services. Accessed May 14. http://www.nfais.org/history.

National Research Council. 1993. *National Collaboratories. Applying Technology for Scientific Research.* Washington, DC: National Academy Press.

National Science Board. 2004. *Science and Engineering Indicators 2004* (NSB 04-01). Arlington, VA: National Science Board. http://www.nsf.gov/statistics/seind04/c5/c5s3.htm#c5s3l1.

Nie, Norman H. 2011. "The Rise of Big Data Spurs a Revolution in Big Analytics." Revolution Analytics. http://www.revolutionanalytics.com/sites/default/files/the-rise-of-big-data-executive-brief.pdf.

Nondal, Lars. 2013. "Full-Text and Bibliographical Databases on CD-ROM in Research Libraries—Costs, Services and Technology." *International Journal of Special Libraries*, 355–365. Accessed June 6. http://forge.fh-potsdam.de/~IFLA/INSPEL/94-3nola.pdf.

OCLC. 2013a. "FirstSearch at a Glance." OCLC. Accessed May 14. http://www.oclc.org/firstsearch/about.en.html.

OCLC. 2013b. "OCLC WorldCat." OCLC. Accessed May 14. http://www.oclc.org/worldcat.en.html.

Odlyzko, Andrew M. 1999. "Competition and Cooperation: Libraries and Publishers in the Transition to Electronic Scholarly Journals." *Journal of Electronic Publishing* 4, no. 4 (June), in the online collection *The Transition from Paper: Where Are We Going and How Will We Get There?*, edited by R. S. Berry and A. S. Moffatt, American Academy of Arts and Sciences, http://www.amacad.org/publications/trans.htm, and in *Journal of Scholarly Publishing* 30, no. 4 (July 1999).

Okerson, Ann Shumelda, and James J. O'Donnell, eds. 1998. "Scholarly Journals at the Crossroads: A Subversive Proposal for Electronic Publishing." Association of Research Libraries. 1995. Last modified April 9, 1998. http://www.arl.org/storage/documents/publications/subversive-proposal-electronic-publishing-jun05.pdf.

Open Access, Max-Planck-Gesellschaft. 2013. "Berlin Declaration on Open Access to Knowledge in the Sciences and Humanities." Open Access, Max-Planck-Gesellschaft. October 22, 2013 (original date). http://openaccess.mpg.de/286432/Berlin-Declaration.

Open Archives Initiative. 2001. "The Santa Fe Convention for the Open Archives Initiative." Open Archives. February 15, 2000. Last modified January 20, 2001. http://www.openarchives.org/sfc/sfc_entry.htm.

OpenDOAR. 2011. "About OpenDOAR." OpenDOAR.org. Last modified February 15. http://www.opendoar.org/about.html.

OpenEdition. 2013. "OpenEdition Freemium." OpenEdition. Accessed December 31. http://www.openedition.org/8873.

Organization for Economic Cooperation and Development. 2004. "Declaration on Access to Research Data from Public Funding." Organization for Economic Cooperation and Development. January 30. http://www.oecd.org/science/sci-tech/sciencetechnologyandinnovationforthe21stcenturymeetingoftheoecdcommitteeforscientificandtechnologicalpolicyatministerialevel29-30january2004-finalcommunique.htm.

Outsell. 2013a. "2012 Market Size & Share Rankings Report." *Outsell*, February 28.

Outsell. 2013b. "2013 Library Market Size, Share, Forecast, & Trends." *Outsell*, June 17.

Oxford University Press. 2013. "About Oxford Scholarship Online." Oxford University Online. Accessed October 19. http://www.oxfordscholarship.com/page/85/about.

Park, Ji-Hong. 2008. "The Relationship between Scholarly Communication and Science and Technology Studies (STS)." *Journal of Scholarly Publishing* 39, no. 3 (April): 257–273.

Phan, Tai, Laura Hardesty, Jamie Hug, and Cindy Sheckells. 2011. "Academic Libraries: 2010—First Look." U.S. Department of Education. December. http://nces.ed.gov/pubs2012/2012365.pdf (URL no longer connects).

Pitkow, James E., and Margaret M. Recker. 1995. "Results from the Fourth World-Wide Web User Survey." Georgia Institute of Technology, Graphics, Visualization, and Usability Center. Last modified 1995. http://www.cc.gatech.edu/gvu/user_surveys/survey-10-1995.

Plosker, George. 2004. "Making Money as an Aggregator." *Information Today* 28, no. 2 (March/April). http://www.infotoday.com/online/mar04/plosker.shtml.

Pochoda, Phil. 2013. "The Big One: The Epistemic System Break in Scholarly Monograph Publishing." *New Media & Society* 15, no. 3 (April 26): 359–378. http://nms.sagepub.com/content/15/3/359.full.pdf+html.

Pöschl, Ulrich. 2012. "Multi-Stage Open Peer Review: Scientific Evaluation Integrating the Strengths of Traditional Peer Review with the Virtues of Transparency and Self-Regulation." *Frontiers in Computational Neuroscience* 6, no. 33 (July 5). doi: 10.3389/fncom.2012.00033.

Potts, Claude H. 2011. "Journal des Savants—From the Republic of Letters to the Cloud Library." *Journal of Scholarly Publishing*, October, 68–75.

Poynder, Richard. 2011. "The Big Deal: Not Price but Cost." *Information Today* 28, no. 8 (September). http://www.infotoday.com/it/sep11/The-Big-Deal-Not-Price-But-Cost.shtml.

PR Newswire. 2000. "Chemweb.com to Launch Chemistry Preprint Server." PR Newswire, The Free Library, London. April 3. http://www.thefreelibrary.com/CHEMWEB.COM+TO+LAUNCH+CHEMISTRY+PREPRINT+SERVER.-a061805864.

PR Newswire. 2012. "Elsevier Adds E-books to ebrary's Academic Complete." PR Newswire. August 8. http://www.prnewswire.com/news-releases/elsevier-adds-e-books-to-ebrarys-academic-complete-165404716.html.

ProQuest. 2014. "The Summon Service." ProQuest. Accessed September 12. http://www.proquest.com/products-services/The-Summon-Service.html.

Proust, Jacques. 1967. *Diderot et "Encyclopédie"* [Diderot and the Encyclopedia]. Paris: Colin.

Public Knowledge Project. 2013. "PKP History." Public Knowledge Project. Accessed December 14. http://pkp.sfu.ca/about/history.

Public Library of Science. 2013. "The Case for Open Access." Public Library of Science. Accessed May 13. http://www.plos.org/about/open-access.

Public Library of Science. 2013. "PLOS Early History." PLOS. Accessed December 6. http://www.plos.org/about/what-is-plos/early-history (URL no longer connects).

Purver, Margery. 1967. *The Royal Society: Concept and Creation*. Cambridge, MA: MIT Press.

Pycior, Helena M. 2003. "Mathematics and Prose Literature." In *Companion Encyclopedia of the History and Philosophy of Mathematics*, vol. 2, edited by Ivor Grattan-Guiness. Baltimore: Johns Hopkins University Press.

Ramalho Correia, Ana Maria, and Jose Carlos Teixeira. 2005. "Reforming Scholarly Publishing and Knowledge Communication: From the Advent of the Scholarly Journal to the Challenges of Open Access." *Information Services & Use* 25: 13–21.

Regazzi, John J. 2012a. "Comparing Academic Library Spending with Public Libraries. Public K–12 Schools. Higher Education Public Institutions, and Public Hospitals between 1998–2008." *Journal of Academic Librarianship* 38, no. 4 (July): 205–216.

Regazzi, John J. 2012b. "Constrained? An Analysis of U.S. Academic Library Shifts in Spending, Staffing, and Utilization, 1998–2008." *College and Research Libraries* 73, no. 5 (September): 449–468. http://crl.acrl.org/content/73/5/449.full.pdf.

Regazzi, John J. 2013. "U.S. Academic Library Spending, Staffing and Utilization during the Great Recession 2008–2010." *Journal of Academic Librarianship* 39, no. 3 (May): 217–222.

Reid, Calvin. 2008. "Publishers, Librarian Clash over NIH Rule." *Publishers Weekly* 255, no. 1 (January 7): 13.

Research Information Network. 2006. *Researchers and Discovery Services—Behaviour, Perceptions and Needs*. Research Information Network. November. http://www.rin.ac.uk/our-work/using-and-accessing-information-resources/researchers-and-discovery-services-behaviour-perc.

Ricci, Laura, and Mark Ware. 2012. *STM E-books: 2012 Market Size, Share, and Forecast*. Outsell.com. http://www.outsellinc.com/store/products/1100-stm-e-books-2012-market-size-share-and-forecast.

Rivero, Victor. 2013. "Digital Textbooks: Show Me the Future!" *Internet@Schools* 20, no. 3: 12–13.

Robertson, Kathleen. 2002. "Mergers, Acquisitions, and Access: STM Publishing Today." *Library and Information Services in Astronomy IV (July 2–5, 2002)*, edited by B. Corbin E. Bryson, and M. Wolf, 95–102. http://www.eso.org/sci/libraries/lisa/lisa4/proceedings/Robertson.pdf.

Rose, M. 1993. *Authors and Owners: The Invention of Copyright*. London: Harvard University Press.

Rowland, Fytton. 2014. "The Peer Review Process—A Report to the JISC Scholarly Communications Group." Loughborough University. Accessed September 7. http://www.jisc.ac.uk/uploaded_documents/rowland.pdf.

Royal Society of London. 1665. *Order in Council* (March 5).

Rumsey, Abby Smith. 2010. *Scholarly Communication Institute 8: Emerging Genres in Scholarly Communication*. Scholarly Communication Institute. July.

Sackett, David L., William M. C. Rosenberg, J. A. Muir Gray, R. Brian Haynes, and W. Scott Richardson. 1996. "Evidence Based Medicine: What It Is and What It Isn't." *British Medical Journal* 312 (January 13): 71–72. http://dx.doi.org/10.1136/bmj.312.7023.71.

Saffady, William. 1989. "Library Automation: An Overview." *Library Trends* 37, no. 3 (Winter): 276–277.

Saint-André, Jean-Paul, Pascal Arnaud, Serge Bauin, et al. 2013. "Qui a Peur de l'Open Access?" *Le Monde*, March 15. http://www.lemonde.fr/sciences/article/2013/03/15/qui-a-peur-de-l-open-acces_1848930_1650684.html.

Savenije, Bas. 2003. "Economic and Strategic Analysis of Scientific Journals: Recent Evolutions." *Liber Quarterly* 13, no. 3/4. http://liber.library.uu.nl/index.php/lq/article/view/URN%3ANBN%3ANL%3AUI%3A10-1-113339/7800.

Schieber, Phil, and Page Lewis. 1986. "SPOTLIGHT OCLC Reaffirms Membership Philosophy." *OCLC Newsletter*, no. 64 (August): 1–20.

Seave, Ava. 2013. "You'll Need a PhD to Make Sense of the Pricing Schemes Publishers Impose on Libraries." *Media & Education. Forbes*, November 11. http://www.forbes.com/sites/avaseave/2013/11/19/youll-need-a-phd-to-make-sense-of-the-pricing-schemes-publishers-impose-on-libraries.

SHERPA. 2013. "SHERPA: Securing a Hybrid Environment for Research Preservation and Access." Accessed December 14. http://www.sherpa.ac.uk.

Siegfried, Tom. 2013. "Why Big Data Is Bad for Science." *ScienceNews* (blog). November 26. https://www.sciencenews.org/blog/context/why-big-data-bad-science.

Simba Information. 2012. "Combined STM Markets Grew 3.4% in 2011." Press release. January 6. http://www.simbainformation.com/about/release.asp?id=2503.

Small, Henry G. 1978. "Cited Documents as Concept Symbols." *Social Studies of Science* 8: 327–340.

Smelser, Neil J., and Paul B. Baltes, eds. 2001. *International Encyclopedia of the Social & Behavioral Sciences*. Oxford: Elsevier Science Ltd.

Smith, John W. T. 1999. "The Deconstructed Journal—A New Model for Academic Publishing." *Learned Publishing* 12: 79–91.

Smith, Richard. 2006. "Peer Review: A Flawed Process at the Heart of Science and Journals." *Journal of the Royal Society of Medicine* 99, no. 4 (April): 178–182.

Solomon, David J. 2013. "Digital Distribution of Academic Journals and Its Impact on Scholarly Communication: Looking Back after 20 Years." *Journal of Academic Librarianship* 39 (April 23): 23–28. doi: 10.1016/j.acalib.2012.10.001.

Somerville, Mary M., and Lettie Y. Conrad. 2013. "Discoverability Challenges and Collaboration Opportunities within the Scholarly Communications Ecosystems: A SAGE White Paper Update." *Collaborative Librarianship* 5, no. 1: 29–41. http://collaborativelibrarianship.org/index.php/jocl/article/view/240/181.

Søndergaard, Trine Fjordback, Jack Andersen, and Birger Hjørland. 2003. "Documents and the Communication of Scientific and Scholarly Information—Revising and Updating the UNISIST Model." [Electronic version]. *Journal of Documentation* 59, no. 3: 278–320. http://www.emeraldinsight.com/doi/abs/10.1108/00220410310472509.

Sonnenwald, Diane H. 2007. "Scientific Collaboration." *Annual Review of Information Science and Technology* 41, no. 1: 643–681.

Sony. 2013. "Studio Recorders Go Digital." Sony.net. Accessed June 5. http://www.sony.net/SonyInfo/CorporateInfo/History/SonyHistory/2-10.html.

Souto, Patricia. 2007. "E-Publishing Development and Changes in the Scholarly Communication System." *Ci. Inf., Brasilia* 36, no. 1 (April): 158–166.

SPARC. 2014. "Open Education." Accessed September 15. http://www.sparc.arl.org/issues/oer.

Steele, Colin. 2008. "Scholarly Monograph Publishing in the 21st Century: The Future More Than Ever Should Be an Open Book." *Journal of Electronic Publishing* 11, no. 2 (Spring). http://dx.doi.org/10.3998/3336451.0011.201.

Stempel, Jonathan. 2013. "Google Defeats Authors in U.S. Book-Scanning Lawsuit." Reuters. November 14. http://www.reuters.com/article/2013/11/14/us-google-books-idUS-BRE9AD0TT20131114.

Stieg, Kerstin Stieg. 2011. "Traditional Subscriptions, Big Deals or Pay-per-View?—A Comparative Evaluation of Business Models in Austria." Paper presented at the 2011 World Library and Information Congress, 77th IFLA Conference and Assembly, San Juan, Puerto Rico, August 16, 2011. http://www.library.mcgill.ca/ifla-stthomas/papers/stieg_2011.pdf.

Suber, Peter. 2002. "News from Public Library of Science." *Topica* (forum). December 17. http://lists.topica.com/lists/fos-forum/read/message.html?mid=906099880&sort=d& start=518.

Suber, Peter. 2008. "The Open Access Mandate at Harvard." *SPARC Open Access Newsletter*, no. 119 (March 2). http://legacy.earlham.edu/~peters/fos/newsletter/03-02-08.htm.

Suber, Peter. 2008. "An Open Access Mandate for the National Institutes of Health." *Open Medicine* 2, no. 2. http://www.openmedicine.ca/article/view/213/135.

Suber, Peter. 2012. "Opening Access to Research." Open Society Foundations. September 12. http://www.opensocietyfoundations.org/voices/opening-access-research.

Terry, Robert, and Robert Kiley. 2006. "Chapter 10: Open Access to the Research Literature: A Funders Perspective." Wellcome Trust. http://eprints.rclis.org/7531/1/Chapter_10_final.pdf.

Thompson, John B. 2005. "Survival Strategies for Academic Publishing." *The Chronicle of Higher Education* 51, no. 41 (June 17): B6–B9. http://chronicle.com/article/Survival-Strategies-for/12735.

Thomson Reuters. 2013. "Completing the Research Picture. The Book Citation Index." Thomson Reuters Web of Science. Accessed May 31. http://wokinfo.com/products_tools/multidisciplinary/bookcitationindex.

Thomson Reuters. 2013. "Web of Science. History of Citation Indexing." Accessed September 12. http://wokinfo.com/essays/history-of-citation-indexing.

Thomson Reuters. 2014. "Web of Science." Thomson Reuters. Accessed September 12. http://thomsonreuters.com/products/ip-science/04_062/wos-next-gen-brochure.pdf.

Tillery, Kodi. 2012. "2012 Study of Subscription Prices for Scholarly Society Journals." Allen Press. Last modified August 17. http://allenpress.com/system/files/pdfs/library/2012_AP_JPS.pdf.

Timmermans, Stefan, and Aaron Mauck. 2005. "The Promises and Pitfalls of Evidence-Based Medicine." *Health Affairs* 24, no. 1 (January): 18–28. doi: 10.1377/hlthaff.24.1.18.

Tomaiuolo, Nicholas G., and Joan G. Packer. 2000. "Preprint Servers: Pushing the Envelope of Electronic Scholarly Publishing." *Searcher* 8, no. 9 (October). http://www.infotoday.com/searcher/oct00/tomaiuolo&packer.htm.

Tooke, Benjamin, and John Barber. 1712. *London-Gazette.* Reprint of article printed by Benjamin Tooke at the Temple-gate and John Barber on Lambeth-hill, April 26, 1712. http://www.london-gazette.co.uk/issues/4997/pages/2/page.pdf.

Tracz, Vitek. 2012. "The Basement Interviews, Building the Business Model." Interview by Richard Poynder, May 16, 2010.http://ia600201.us.archive.org/13/items/The_Basement_Interviews/Vitek_Tracz_Interview.pdf.

Treese, Win. 1994. "The Internet Index," no. 2. Last modified August 2, 1994. http://www.treese.org/intindex/94-08.htm.

Turkel, William J. 2012. "A Workflow for Digital Research Using Off-the-Shelf Tools." William J. Turkel (blog). January 1. http://williamjturkel.net/how-to.

United Kingdom Parliament. 2004. "Appendix 51: Memorandum from Hallward Library. University of Nottingham SHERPA Project (Evidence submitted to the Select Committee on Science and Technology Written Evidence). U.K. Parliament. July 20. http://www.publications.parliament.uk/pa/cm200304/cmselect/cmsctech/399/399we62.htm.

United Nations Educational, Scientific and Cultural Organization. 1999. "Declaration on Science and the Use of Scientific Knowledge." World Conference on Science for the Twenty-First Century, June 26–July 1. http://www.unesco.org/science/wcs/eng/declaration_e.htm.

United Nations Educational, Scientific and Cultural Organization. 2007. "Kronberg Declaration on the Future of Knowledge Acquisition and Sharing." United Nations Educational, Scientific and Cultural Organization. June. http://www.unesco.de/fileadmin/medien/Dokumente/Kommunikation/Declaration_fuer_Website.pdf.

University College London. 2010. "Scholarly Communications." *University College London (UCL) Library Services.* Last modified November 26, 2010. http://www.ucl.ac.uk/Library/scholarly-communication/index.shtml (URL no longer connects).

U.S. Government Accountability Office. 2013. "College Textbooks—Students Have Greater Access to Textbook Information." U.S. Government Accountability Office, Report to Congressional Committees, GAO-13-368. June. http://www.gao.gov/assets/660/655066.pdf.

U.S. National Library of Medicine. 2012. "PubMed." U.S. National Library of Medicine. National Institutes of Health. Accessed May 31. http://www.ncbi.nlm.nih.gov/pubmed?cmd_current=Limits&pmfilter_Subsets=History+of+Medicine.

Van de Sompel, Herbert, and Carl Lagoze. 2000. "The Santa Fe Convention of the Open Archives Initiative." *D-Lib Magazine* 6, no. 3 (February). http://www.dlib.org/dlib/february00/vandesompel-oai/02vandesompel-oai.html; doi: 10.1045/february2000-vandesompeloai.

Van de Sompel, Herbert, and Carl Lagoze. 2009. "All Aboard: Toward a Machine-Friendly Scholarly Communication System." In *The Fourth Paradigm*, edited by Tony Hey, Stewart Tansley, and Kristin Tolle, 193–199. Redmond, WA: Microsoft Research. http://research.microsoft.com/en-us/collaboration/fourthparadigm/4th_paradigm_book_complete_lr.pdf.

Van de Sompel, Herbert, Sandy Payette, John Erickson, Carl Lagoze, and Simeon Warner. 2004. "Rethinking Scholarly Communication—Building the System That Scholars Deserve." *D-Lib Magazine* 10, no. 9 (September). http://www.dlib.org/dlib/september04/vandesompel/09vandesompel.html.

Van Noorden, Richard. 2013. "UK Open-Access Route Too Costly, Report Says." *Nature*, September 10. http://www.nature.com/news/uk-open-access-route-too-costly-report-says-1.13705.

Van Orsdel, Lee C., and Kathleen Born. 2007. "Periodical Price Survey 2007: Serial Wars." Library Journal 132, no. 7 (April 15): 43–48.

Vannevar, Bush. 1945. "Science—The Endless Frontier." Washington, DC: United States Government Printing Office, July 25. http://www.nsf.gov/od/lpa/nsf50/vbush1945.htm.

Varmus, Harold. 1999. "E-BIOMED: A Proposal for Electronic Publications in the Biomedical Sciences." Draft May 5, 1999; addendum June 20, 1999. http://www.nih.gov/about/director/pubmedcentral/ebiomedarch.htm.

Vaughan, Jason. 2011. "Chapter 1: Web Scale Discovery What and Why." *Library Technology Reports of the American Library Association* 47, no. 1 (January): 5–21.

Walker, T.J. 2002. "Two Societies Show How to Profit by Providing Free Access." *Learned Publishing* 15, no. 4 (October): 279–284.

Wallis, Jillian C., Elizabeth Rolando, and Christine L. Borgman. 2013. "If We Share Data, Will Anyone Use Them? Data Sharing and Reuse in the Long Tail of Science and Technology." *PLOS ONE* 8, no. 7. doi: 10.1371/journal.pone.0067332.

Ware, Mark, and Michael Mabe. 2012. *The STM Report: An Overview of Scientific and Scholarly Journal Publishing*. 3rd ed. The Hague: International Association of Scientific, Technical and Medical Publishers, November. http://www.stm-assoc.org/2012_12_11_STM_Report_2012.pdf.

Wedgeworth, Robert. 1993. *World Encyclopedia of Library and Information Services.* Chicago: American Library Association.

Weller, Ann C. 2002. *Editorial Peer Review: Its Strengths and Weaknesses*. Medford, NJ: American Society for Information Science and Technology.

Wellisch, Hans H. 1991. *Indexing from A to Z*. 2nd ed. New York, Dublin: H. W. Wilson.

Westin, John. 1982. *Descriptive Index of Current Engineering Literature Volume 1, 1884–1891*. Board of Managers of the Association of Engineering Societies, Washington, DC.

Westlaw Next. 2014. "Know the Difference." Thomson Reuters. Accessed September 15. http://info.legalsolutions.thomsonreuters.com/westlawnext/about/default.aspx.

White, Sonya, and Claire Creaser. 2007. *Trends in Scholarly Journal Prices 2000–2006*. Loughborough, UK: Loughborough University. http://www.lboro.ac.uk/microsites/infosci/lisu/downloads/op37.pdf.

Wiegand, Wayne A., and Donald G. Davis. 1994. *Encyclopedia of Library History*. New York: Taylor & Francis.

Wilbanks, John. 2009. "I Have Seen the Paradigm Shift, and It Is Us." In *The Fourth Paradigm*, edited by Tony Hey, Stewart Tansley, and Kristin Tolle, 209–214. Redmond, WA: Microsoft Research. http://research.microsoft.com/en-us/collaboration/fourthparadigm/4th_paradigm_book_complete_lr.pdf.

Wiley. 2013. "Wiley History, Highlights from Wiley's First 200 Years." Wiley. Accessed May 26. http://www.wiley.com/WileyCDA/Section/id-301775.html.

Wiley. 2013. "Wiley Makes Scientific PDFs Interactive with the ReadCube Web Reader from Labtiva." Press release. Wiley. February 6. http://www.wiley.com/WileyCDA/PressRelease/pressReleaseId-107276.html.

Williams, Kimber. 2013. "Academic-Corporate Research Partnerships Focus of Nov. 12 Talk." Emory News Center. November 11.

Williams, M. E. 1977. "Data Bases—A History of Developments and Trends from 1966 through 1975." *Journal of the American Society for Information Science and Technology* 28: 71–78. doi: 10.1002/asi.4630280203.

Willinsky, John. 2009. "Toward the Design of an Open Monograph Press." *Journal of Electronic Publishing* 12, no. 1 (February).http://dx.doi.org/10.3998/3336451.0012.103.

Withey, Lynne, Steve Cohn, Ellen Faran, et al. 2011. *Sustaining Scholarly Publishing: New Business Models for University Presses*. New York: Association of American University Presses. http://www.uvasci.org/wp-content/uploads/2011/03/aaupbusinessmodels2011.pdf (URL no longer connects).

Witty, Francis J. 1973. "The Beginnings of Indexing and Abstracting: Some Notes towards a History of Indexing and Abstracting in Antiquity and the Middle Ages." *The Indexer* 16, no. 4 (October): 193–198.

Xia, Jingfeng. 2008. "A Comparison of Institutional and Subject Repositories in Self-Archiving Practices." *Journal of Academic Librarianship* 34, no. 6 (November): 489–495.

Xia, Jingfeng. 2009. "Library Publishing as a New Model of Scholarly Communication." *Journal of Scholarly Publishing* 40, no. 4 (July): 370–383. Academic Search Premier. EBSCO*host*.

Yancey, Rodney. 2013. "Fifty Years of Citation Indexing and Analysis." Web of Knowledge. September 2005. Accessed June 10. http://wokinfo.com/essays/50-years-citation-indexing (URL now maps to a summary page: http://wokinfo.com/sci-anniversary.html).

Yiotis, Kristin. 2005. "The Open Access Initiative: A New Paradigm for Scholarly Communications." *Information Technology and Libraries* 24, no. 4: 157–162.

Zuccala, Alesia. 2013. "Evaluating the Humanities: Vitalizing 'the Forgotten Sciences.'" *Research Trends* no. 32 (March). http://www.researchtrends.com/issue-32-march-2013/evaluating-the-humanities-vitalizing-the-forgotten-sciences.

Index

About the Author

John J. Regazzi has spent over 40 years in the electronic information services and scholarly publishing industries, being called a "pioneer" and "true innovator" of the information industry. He has designed, launched, and managed some of the most innovative and well-known information services in the professional communities, including the Engineering Village, Science Direct, Scopus, and many other electronic information services dating back to the early days of the online and CD-ROM industries.

John spent most of his career with Reed Elsevier and retired as CEO of Elsevier Inc. (NYSE: ENL). Prior to that, he was CEO of Engineering Information Inc., a company that he helped turn around and that was acquired by Reed Elsevier. In 2005, John assumed the role of dean of the College of Information and Computer Science of Long Island University (LIU) and recently stepped down from this post and now lectures and directs the Scholarly Communications and Information Innovation Lab at LIU. He is also part of the U.S. Department of State Expert Speakers Program and has lectured in Germany, Turkey, and Spain.

John presently serves on a variety corporate and industry boards, including the British Standards Institute (BSI) Group (a UK Royal Charter Company) and the American Institute of Physics (AIP) Publishing (a professional publishing organization), and was recently appointed as chairman of the Advisory Board, National Technical Information Service (NTIS), a division of the U.S. Department of Commerce. John currently also serves as chairman of the board of directors of the Law Logix Group, a SaaS company serving law firms and corporations, and as a managing director of Akoya Capital Partners, an executive-led investment bank partnering with leading CEOs around the world.

John lives in Garden City, New York, with his wife, Marie. He is relearning the art of parenting, as he has five (soon to be six) grandchildren.